W9-CBB-084

PAPER TRAILS

PAPER TRAILS

FROM THE BACKWOODS TO THE FRONT PAGE

A LIFE IN STORIES

ROY MacGREGOR

RANDOM HOUSE CANADA

PUBLISHED BY RANDOM HOUSE CANADA

www.penguinrandomhouse.ca

Library and Archives Canada Cataloguing in Publication

Title: Paper trails / Roy MacGregor.
Names: MacGregor, Roy, 1948- author.
Description: Includes index.
Identifiers: Canadiana (print) 20220495734 | Canadiana (ebook) 20220495742 |
    ISBN 9781039000735 (hardcover) | ISBN 9781039000742 (EPUB)
Subjects: LCSH: MacGregor, Roy, 1948- | LCSH: MacGregor, Roy, 1948-—Childhood
    and youth. | LCSH: Journalists—Canada—Biography. | LCGFT: Autobiographies.
Classification: LCC PN4913.M383 A3 2023 | DDC 070.92—dc23

Text design by Andrew Roberts
Jacket design by Andrew Roberts
Image credits: © Mark Reeder; (texture) Here / Shutterstock

Printed in Canada

10 9 8 7 6 5 4 3 2 1

Penguin
Random House
RANDOM HOUSE CANADA

CONTENTS

For the grandchildren: Fisher and Sadie Cation,
Raphaël and Noémie MacGregor Dalle,
Hawkley and Haywood Dzilums

INTRODUCTION

I t was a long walk through the woods to the place I have loved more than any other—our grandparents' log cottage on Lake of Two Rivers in the heart of Ontario's vast Algonquin Park. My mother took me there from the little Red Cross outpost at Whitney when I was all of four days old, so this would have been the first of many, many trails.

Lake of Two Rivers had to be the place, with the Madawaska River entering the lake on the west end and leaving at the east end, that led to a lifelong love of canoeing. Like the hand-carved Indigenous-boy doll in Bill Mason's wonderful 1966 film *Paddle to the Sea,* I could theoretically paddle all the way to the ocean—down the Madawaska, through the Ottawa Valley to the Ottawa River, down the Ottawa to the St. Lawrence River—paddling east until I reached the Atlantic. Theoretically, of course. Not something a four-day-old, let alone a seventy-four-year-old—the age at which I am typing this—would do. But you can dream of the possibility.

Canoe tripping involves a lot of trails, some portages so long and difficult you wonder how the hell you ever came up with such a "vacation" plan. But I have always loved the bush and the Far North. The more off the beaten path the better.

The other trails are all paper, whether newspapers, magazines, scripts or books. Millions upon millions of words, almost exclusively about this amazing country, Canada, and the people who live in it and love it.

I like to say I have written more books than I have read, which is hopefully an exaggeration, but looking back over all those books, all those journalism jobs at various newspapers and magazines, it almost seems possible. The places those trails have taken me to . . . the people I have encountered along the way.

A favourite editor has a term that she claims essentially sums up my career: "MacGregor luck." She says it sarcastically; she says it laughing; she says it often. Sometimes she captures the sentiment in just one word—"horseshoes."

I am forced to admit that there is some merit to what she says. I was lucky enough to spend every summer of a happy childhood in Algonquin Park, where my father, Duncan, worked at his brother-in-law's hardwood lumber mill, where my grandfather, Tom McCormick, served as chief ranger, and where my mother, Helen, was born in a tent on the shores of Brule Lake. Her mother, Bea McCormick, had gone into labour on a steaming-hot early August day, and to keep her cool the nurse at the tiny village in the heart of the park had village loggers set up a tent on the beach, soak blankets in the cool lake water and string the wet blankets on poles set up around the birthing mattress.

Growing up in Huntsville, a pretty, small town in Ontario's cottage country, was another lucky break. Here, I forged lifelong friendships and played competitive hockey, lacrosse and baseball in a sports-mad community. A Huntsville High School English teacher saved me from being booted out of school and started me on the path to journalism. I fell in love with a beautiful young woman in grade eleven and, half a dozen years later, we married. Ellen and I soon had four healthy babies, three girls and a boy, who grew up to be four accomplished adults. Six grandchildren would follow, all healthy, all unique. Horseshoes, indeed.

I should have been fired after publishing my first piece in a national publication. The story that ended up in print had a mistake that was the equivalent to, say, claiming Winnipeg's Guess Who had created the famous rock opera *Tommy*. (Well, that actually *was* the mistake, but more on that later . . .) No matter. Lucky as ever, I wiggled free.

How about the time *Maclean's* magazine dispatched this young, wet-behind-the-ears reporter to Montreal for a cover profile on Mordecai Richler? The famous author's publisher had arranged for us to meet up at the Montreal Press Club, where Richler proceeded to order a fresh round of beer every time I hit the halfway mark of my glass. He suggested we do the formal interview at his apartment, and on our walk he stopped at a dépanneur, where he bought two bottles of Rémy Martin cognac. Next thing I know I'm waking with a thundering headache in my room at the Queen Elizabeth Hotel, still wearing the same clothes I had on when I walked into the press club, the bedcovers untouched . . .

MacGregor luck would save me, once again.

But more on that later.

How things have changed in this business. I wrote my first stories on a portable Viking typewriter my mother bought me at Eaton's as a Christmas present. Eventually, I moved on to electronic IBM typewriters, then, while at the *Toronto Star*, a Radio Shack TRS-80, which we reporters called the "Trash 80." There were other Radio Shack computers—some capable of holding more than one column!—that you hooked up to a pay phone with rubber couplings; you could watch your story go, letter by letter, off to the desk back in Toronto. You waited breathlessly for the signal that your work had arrived safely—otherwise, you did it all again.

Next came laptops, increasingly powerful, and then the internet and cell phones and Bluetooth and even watches that could count your steps, take your blood pressure, catch your incoming e-mails and call 911 if they detected that you'd fallen. When I began at the *Ottawa Citizen*, in 1986, the newsroom was filled with more than a hundred reporters, editors, librarians, secretaries and receptionists. Several dozen print shop workers were in the back typing the stories all over again to create lead-type blocks for the printing process. Other workers carried the heavy blocks over to the plant in another part of the building, where the paper was printed, stacked and taken to the loading ramps for the delivery trucks. The noise throughout the Baxter Road building was numbing: phones constantly ringing, copy editors shouting, doors slamming as a new non-smoking rule went into place and editors ran back and forth between the outdoor smoking area and their blue pencils.

So much change. Who needs a library when you have Google? Who needs receptionists when callers reach a menu that will either stall them or take them to the very person they need to speak to? But who talks anyway when you can send an e-mail or a text? The last time I entered the *Citizen* building there were seven reporters, and it was utterly silent. Today, the building has been transformed into a roller rink, the thinning paper published by a skeleton staff working mostly from home.

Such a journey this has been. *Maclean's* three different times . . . the weekend supplements, *The Canadian* and, later, *Today* . . . *Toronto Star* . . . *Ottawa Citizen* . . . *National Post* . . . then five straight years of five page 2 columns a week at the *Globe and Mail*, followed by another dozen wonderful years at the *Globe* writing sports, features, opinion, the arts. A few years of post-retirement freelancing—the *Globe*, *Cottage Life*, the *New York Times*, *Zoomer* magazine, *Canadian Geographic*—and soon the paper trail ran a full fifty years.

The best times in journalism were elections. I covered Canadian federal and provincial elections for decades. Newspapers had money, I had a company credit card and the assignment was always simple: go wherever you want, "take the pulse of the country," file at the end of each day. There was no better feeling than when the rental car entered a community or a rural area where I knew not a single soul, but I was absolutely confident that by day's end I would file a story about someone, or something, of interest, and the following day it would magically appear in print. Never writer's block; never a missed deadline. Horse-shoes across the country, east to west, south to north.

Somehow, I scraped through without ever losing a lawsuit—even one from a sitting cabinet minister. I survived the death of a magazine and a lost job at a time when Ellen was pregnant with our youngest of four children. There have, over that half-century of journalism, been blown jet engines, threatening weapons at Oka, a snowstorm on James Bay that forced us to take shelter for three days on a barren island, physical threats from unhappy athletes—and more fun than I ever could have imagined. And if the thirteen chapters to come aren't enough, each is followed by one or more "vignettes," pertinent—and sometimes not so pertinent—to the chapter just finished.

My friend the editor has it right. MacGregor luck. There have, of course, been some bad turns—life is not entirely a box of chocolates, I am also here to report. But, by and large, a life in words has been the greatest adventure I could hope for—and more.

1

Brent, Eric and Trouble from Day One

I t was not an auspicious first week of school.

We lived at 15 Lorne Street. Lorne ran southward off the top of Main and made a long climb up the east side of Reservoir Hill. From my bedroom window, I could view the town as if I were sitting on the rim of a large bowl looking down. The sun rose over Lookout Mountain to the east and poured in that bedroom window to launch each day. The sun set behind us, rolling over the upper edges of Reservoir Hill and casting everything below us in shadow. More high ground to the north and south bordered the town, with the Muskoka River running through the bottom of this natural bowl like a snaking crack. Beyond the mountain, Fairy Lake spread like a golden field in the morning sun, turning into a dark blue expanse in the setting sun.

Next door to us, with only an old barn on the vacant lot in between, were the Munroes. Kitty corner to the Munroes were the Rubys— actually, the Rubinovitch family, but the name had been shortened so long ago for their Main Street business, Ruby's Men's & Boys' Wear, that no one, not even the schools, used the longer version of the family name. Three houses, ten kids, three of whom—Brent Munroe, Eric Ruby, me, all born in 1948—would become best friends for life.

They became, for me, the constant, the friendships that would never change no matter how divergent and different our lives. We could pick up as we had last left off, even if that had been years back. They could take the stuffing out of me and put reality back in, for their lives were far more real, and far, far more difficult than the privileged life of a journalist.

It will require some explaining, and some things will need to be omitted for discretion, but life for these three baby boys of 1948 would include triumphs and failures in sports and school and relationships, career paths that would include local radio, policing, cab driving, ski patrol, clothing retail, log-building repair, journalism and even drawing raw timber from the bush by draft horse. One of the three, Brent, had soft, straight brown hair on a square block of a head. Eric then had blond, almost white, hair, with a proboscis so prominent it would earn him the unwanted nickname "Nose" in his teenage years. I had curling, dark hair, almost black, and buckteeth so prominent I would be called "Beaver" in public school. Much sooner than expected, or wanted, we would all go bald.

Two of the three pals would grow so large—Brent was six foot four and 250 pounds, Eric six foot two and 225 pounds—that for a long while I wore size-twelve shoes on my size-ten-and-a-half feet just so I, barely six feet and 180 pounds, would fit in. Time would be spent in jail on two different continents and in a mental health facility in Ontario. Alcohol would all but destroy two of us and then be miraculously overcome. Death would come much too soon to one, be chosen several years later by another.

We will get to all that . . . eventually. But to three young boys in Mrs. Robinson's kindergarten class that fall of 1953, the world was our small and beloved oyster.

The MacGregors had come to Huntsville in 1950 so that Jim, then nearly seven years old, could finally begin school. There were then five of us: parents Duncan and Helen, Jim, five-year-old Ann, and me, two. The youngest, Tom, would be born in the Huntsville hospital in 1954. We had come from Airy, a small and charming settlement along the eastern edge of Ontario's sprawling, 7,600-square-kilometre Algonquin Park. The hamlet was just outside the pretty Madawaska Valley village of Whitney, where I had been born in the little Red Cross clinic. Airy had only six houses, half of them filled with relatives from both sides of the family. There was a barn, a large pigpen, a community well at the bottom of the hill, and a tall water tank alongside the railroad tracks, which headed over a wooden trestle before vanishing into the thick woods of the park.

To get to the little public school in Whitney required walking some two kilometres along the tracks to reach the village. Our mother was reluctant to see her firstborn head down the tracks, with water on one side, thick bush on the other. Oncoming trains you could always step aside for—bears and wolves, not so easily. Her sister, Mary Pigeon, was an elementary school teacher in Huntsville, some 100 kilometres to the west along Highway 60, which ran through the park corridor. Since Duncan worked at the McRae mill, it seemed to make little difference whether he spent his weekends in Huntsville or Whitney, so the decision was made to move.

And so, with a borrowed truck holding all the family possessions, such as they were, we headed for Huntsville. Our new home was a two-storey, red-brick house on the northwest corner of Lorne and Lansdowne Streets. The house was heated by a wood furnace, which meant Helen would have to get up two or three times a night in winter to feed the roaring beast, but the new home had electricity and was on town water. We had our very first flush toilet.

Our mother was delighted with the move, but she also had the realities of town life to contend with all on her own—at least during the weekdays. With three kids to handle and constant traffic on the streets around us, she devised a solution to allow her to do the household chores while the two older children were off at school. She bought a leather harness and a short rope, put me in the harness and tied me outside to a spruce tree.

Three years passed and on the first morning after Labour Day Monday in 1953, Helen walked me to my first day of kindergarten at Huntsville Public School. Mercifully, she did not use the harness.

That same morning, Beryl Munroe walked Brent to his first day of class. Stella Ruby brought Eric. Walking with our mothers, we went two blocks down Lorne Street, turned right on Main Street and continued downhill another block past Olan's Furniture, Trickey's Variety Store and Parker's Bakery. We crossed Main at the Centre Street intersection under the watchful eye of kindly town policeman Sy Payne, who always gave out candy eggs at Easter. You heard that correctly: "Sigh Pain," town cop. It was that sort of place. If you needed deodorant, you could go to the Rexall drugstore, where pharmacist Perc Byers (get it? "Pers Pires") would wait on you.

Brent and Eric and I knew one another from neighbourhood play, so naturally we tried to find seats together for our first day under the tutelage of Mrs. Robinson. Mrs. Robinson, short, stocky, bespectacled, grandmotherly, with grey-white hair curled tight as lamb's wool, had taught kindergarten in the basement of the old red-brick school for years. Our older siblings—Judy Munroe and my sister, Ann—had loved her. It was not Mrs. Robinson that scared us. It was the whole idea of *school*: an entire morning, five days a week, away from our mothers and families and having to get along with thirty or so kids we had never seen before in our lives.

At least we had each other. Eric moved quickly to one desk, Brent grabbed a seat beside him and I took the next seat over.

Mrs. Robinson spoke to us. "I'm very happy to say that this year, finally," she said, "the kindergartners will have their own washroom."

Off to her left side was a separate room—well, not quite a room, but an area cordoned off by freshly painted wood with a door in front. She went to it and opened the door. Inside was a toilet and a small basin with a single tap. She stressed that this washroom was for us and us alone. No other students in the school could use it, and we would not have to climb the stairs and walk along the hall to the main washrooms.

That first week meant getting used to getting ourselves to school on time—our mothers walked us only the first day. There were other playmates from along Lorne Street, Janet Kennedy and Rose Anne Cousins, who began walking with us, along with Donnie Wilston from Dufferin Street higher up Reservoir Hill and Janice Forde from just down Mary Street.

This group of seven walked together to an old school where the walls were graced with copies of art from Tom Thomson and that other Group of Seven. On the main wall hung a portrait of Queen Elizabeth II, looking resplendent in royal dress and crown. On one side of the Queen was a framed portrait of Prime Minister Louis St. Laurent; on the other side a framed portrait of US President Dwight D. Eisenhower. No one ever questioned this; no one ever explained.

Mrs. Robinson had us take turns standing up and telling the class our names and where we lived. We did art, using construction paper and scissors and coloured chalks and glue. We counted from one to ten and back down from ten. We sang a simple song and had a fifteen-minute recess, where for the most part, we stood around and stared at each other as if we were in a zoo for little people. At noon we returned home, sometimes the six or seven of us in a group, but always Eric and Brent and me walking together. We sometimes fought and often ended up running home in tears.

It was not, as I say, an auspicious start. I wet my pants on the first or second day and shuddered to think that the girls sitting opposite me in the circle of desks could see the dark stain on the front of my pants. Eric threw up at his desk, his stomach turning and churning from nerves and the frustration of having to sit still. It would become a lifelong affliction. (Eric would be in his early forties before they would finally diagnose him with ADHD, but there was no such talk then, no Ritalin, and all children were expected to sit still, listen and learn. "'Attention deficit'?" Eric shouted after he'd finally been diagnosed. "They should call it 'attention *surplus*'!")

Perhaps because he noticed that I had already wet my pants, Brent raised his hand and asked to use the new toilet. Mrs. Robinson was only too happy to give him permission. Brent entered the new wooden cubicle and Eric and I giggled because we could hear, or thought we could hear, some splashing. Then the quick sound of a zipper—followed by a *scream!*

Brent was howling and crying beyond the door to the kindergarten toilet. Mrs. Robinson, alarmed, went and stood by the door, wringing her hands. "Brent?" she said from outside the door. "What's wrong?"

"*My weenie's caught in the zipper!*"

Mrs. Robinson swallowed hard and seemed to turn pink. "Are you alright now?" she asked in a calming voice.

"*Noooo!! It hurts!!!*"

Eric and I were sputtering with giggles. The rest of the class seemed in shock. *What was beyond that door? What had happened to poor Brent?* Mrs. Robinson squeaked the door open and peeked in. Brent was sobbing and whimpering at the same time. We could not see what was wrong.

"You stay where you are," she told Brent. "I'll get the janitor."

Mr. Catton was the kindly custodian. He swept the halls with Dustbane, fixed broken chairs, fed coal into the furnace. In winter, he bled the radiators, shovelled the walks and sanded the steps. He also built a wonderful outdoor rink in the schoolyard each winter. The kids adored him.

Mrs. Robinson left and was back quickly with Mr. Catton, who walked into the kindergarten classroom with a pair of pliers in his hand. He knocked on the door before opening it. He slipped in. The whole class sat, intently listening.

We heard some whimpering. We heard a click of metal and one quick screech from Brent, then a zipper being pulled.

"You're okay now," we heard the custodian say.

"It *hurts!*" Brent whined.

"You're fine."

The door opened and Mr. Catton and Brent emerged. The custodian stuffed his pliers in his pocket and left. Mrs. Robinson went over and gave Brent, face wet and red from crying, a hug. He returned to his seat.

It may have been the first—but it would most certainly not be the last—time his weenie would get him in trouble.

Eric and I issued our joint statement on school when we were eleven years old. The Monday evening of Labour Day weekend, the day before the new school year was to start, we rode our bikes down from Reservoir Hill, crossed Main and parked the bicycles behind the school. As dusk fell, we slipped along the side of the building, waited until all was clear, and promptly ran out and deposited two stinking "gifts" on the front steps.

Next morning, the three of us walked to school as if everything was normal, giggling like fools as we came across a crowd of kids pointing and holding their noses while poor Mr. Catton came with a shovel and mop to clear the entrance to Huntsville Public School so the new school year could begin.

Eric hated school and school didn't much care for him. His undiagnosed attention deficit had him spending nearly as much time in the hall and down at the principal's office as sitting at his desk. Brent and I sailed along, often taking our report cards to his grandmother Ware's little apartment closer to the river and happily grabbing the treats she offered for good marks, which we invariably had. The two of us were put into Miss Parker's "accelerated" class that allowed students to do grades three, four and five in two years, thereby "skipping" a year. Eric did not get into that class and so fell a year behind us in school, though it had no effect whatsoever on our friendship.

As a toddler, Eric had severely burned the palm of his right hand when he pulled a hot iron down from his mother's ironing board. The scalding left the skin rough and red, his hand affected during those pivotal months when a child begins to colour and draw and reach for things. It's likely he was left-handed anyway, but one teacher in particular, Mrs. Henry, was determined that Eric should switch from left to right as he learned to print and do arithmetic. She rapped his left hand sharply with the blackboard pointer if she saw he was using it for his work. She made him stand in the wastebasket at the front of the class until he promised to stop holding his pencils with the "wrong" hand. She sent him to stand in the cloakroom until he was ready to write properly. She once taped his left arm to his side for an entire morning, forcing him to try to do his work with his right hand. It was pure cruelty by a woman who simply did not like an overactive child, as the school had any number of left-handed students, my sister Ann among them.

Many years later, when Eric was driving a cab in Huntsville, he happened to notice the then long-retired Mrs. Henry making her way down Main Street. With no care for what it did to traffic, Eric slammed on the brakes, put the taxi in park, got out and in a voice renowned about town for its ability to carry, publicly chewed her out for those decades-old assaults on his pride.

He considered this one of his finest moments.

Like most small-town kids growing up in the late 1950s and early 1960s, we were both good and bad. We all went to Cubs and then Scouts, the girls to Brownies and then Guides. We were polite to our elders, for the most part. Brent and I served communion at All Saints' Anglican Church, down by the first bend in the river past the swing bridge. Eric sang solo in the annual Kiwanis Music Festival. Eric, whose father was Jewish and mother Ukrainian Catholic, even joined us once a year at an Anglican church service. Not because he wanted to convert, but because Ash Wednesday meant the morning off school.

Model citizens . . . for the most part. But we also smoked cigarettes we stole from our parents. Sometimes we even stole smokes from

Trickey's—the store's only line of defence was a sweet-natured woman in a wheelchair who sat by the cash and couldn't possibly put together five-cent grab bags of candy while keeping a sharp eye on the stacks of cheap Chesterfield and Daily Mail cigarette packages. We shouted inappropriately during matinees at the Capitol Theatre. We had BB fights with a "no head shots" rule (though poor aim by me took a tooth out of Ted Harman). We later played golf with .22s in our bags, a three-wood cover conveniently over the barrel in case we came across a grouse on the fifth or sixth holes, which were farthest away from the clubhouse. We sat on the stone wall up from the Baptist church and gave the finger to hoods and greasers cresting the corner of Main and Lorne Streets and letting their straight pipes rumble and roar and back-fire like thunder as they eased up on the gas and drifted down Main, everyone turning to see what the commotion was.

It was the era of *Leave It to Beaver* and the Baby Boom—Canada recorded nearly four children per woman in 1959, births double what they had been three decades earlier. Huntsville was no different. There were kids everywhere, each neighbourhood with its own gang of energetic youngsters. On Reservoir Hill we had Rubys, Munroes, MacGregors, Kennedys, Cousinses, Harmans, Fordes, Wilstons, Millses, Malecs, Cockrams, Guistinis, Hutchesons, Glassfords, Baldwins, Mosbaughs, Adamsons, McIlroys, Gooleys, Eadys. There was also Stewart Wieler, whose older sisters had already left home. There was Tannis Staples (the best baseball player of us all), Jim Gerhart, Tommy St. John, Steve Rayfield, Eric and Franc Mossbaugh, the Huffs, and later on the Hasties and the Fields. Anywhere from a half-dozen to two dozen kids any given year playing sports and biking in the streets, back-yards and, of course, along the paths and secret forts of Reservoir Hill. There were no "play dates" and zero adult supervision. Everyone knew that the tannery whistle would go off at five o'clock and, in winter, that was taken as a signal for winding down, it being increasingly difficult to see under the cone of light spreading down from the one streetlight on

Dufferin. When we played beyond the whistle, each mother had a special call—one mother a sharp two-finger whistle—to bring the child in for supper, "dinner" then being what everyone ate at noon.

The MacGregor boys were active, but Ann was much less so. Around age six she contracted rheumatic fever following a severe strep throat. Doctors believed it all traced back to her falling through the ice at Lake of Two Rivers when the men were using an ice saw to cut large blocks they packed in sawdust and stored in the log ice house each winter for summer use. Our father had pulled her to safety, breaking her arm in the act. The arm healed. The rheumatic fever was a situation for life. She spent more than a year in bed, with me crawling in to play with her and her dolls and the cut-outs she dressed and undressed and dressed again. They took her to a specialist in Ottawa, where our parents were told she should never ride a bike or play strenuous sports.

She never did ride a bike or play team sports, but Ann became a wonderful swimmer, a diver who could slip into the water as smoothly as a letter into an envelope. She also skied and hiked. She would much later, at a pivotal moment in her life, tell me she had loved her childhood, especially the endless summers at Lake of Two Rivers.

There was no real sense of boyfriend-girlfriend until high school, but in an instant everything seemed to change. Huntsville High School had five grade nine classes—9A, 9B, 9C, 9D, 9E—and some instant suspicion that whatever letter you landed with was where the school expected you to score. Brent got into 9B; I was in 9D. On the first introductory day of secondary school, the boys from all five grade nine classes were taken outside by Mr. Bell, the gym teacher, and lined up, tallest to shortest. Brent, of course, was tallest and stood first. I was second shortest, *towering* only over a tiny little guy whose last name was Whitehead. A rather humiliating first day of high school.

Brent was instantly popular, especially with the girls. Tall, well-built, handsome and charming. His voice was a deep purr. While still in high school, he would be hired by the local radio station, CKAR, as a news announcer even though he had not the slightest training. Broadcast would not, however, be his calling. Brent was one of the smartest people I have ever known, but school would fail him as much as he failed it. He flunked out of grade nine and then failed it again. He failed grade ten. After five years of high school, he had his grade ten intermediate certificate—enough to get him into police college and a career in the Ontario Provincial Police, which went well for a while . . .

Brent looked great in his uniform—but then so did Eric. Brent graduated from police college and was posted to the Red Lake district, in northwestern Ontario. One spring Eric went to visit. Eric was fresh from a year working on a ski hill in Leysin, Switzerland, where his long hair, flaming beard and outrageous personality had him nicknamed "Mad Man of the Mountain." Brent had been off shopping and let Eric know they could meet later in a local bar. Eric showed up wearing Brent's uniform, gun belt included. Had the authorities found out, it might have meant the end of Brent's policing career—which would soon enough end on another note, not at all funny.

Brent's popularity with the high-school girls soon had him pestering the older guys about how one might buy a prophylactic in a town where everyone knew everyone else and everyone else's business. The first thing Perc Byers would do if Brent walked into Byers' Rexall pharmacy and asked for a three-pack of Trojan condoms would be to walk the three houses up Mary Street after closing hours and have a concerned word with Mr. and Mrs. Munroe.

The secret to buying safes, it turned out, was the Chinese restaurant. What Brent was advised to do by an older, wiser student was to wrap a one-dollar bill around his forefinger and head for the Huntsville Grill. When all was quiet at the front of the restaurant, he should approach the cash and lay his hand on the counter with the dollar bill wrapped around his finger. Without so much as a word, the older man at the cash would slip off the dollar bill at the same time as he dipped down into the cigarette counter and pulled free a single Sheik condom.

Never one to miss a business opportunity, Brent saw a financial windfall here. From the back of a "men's magazine," he found condoms—some of them novelty—available for mail order. He ordered a gross. He volunteered to pick up the mail for a couple of weeks until, finally, his box of 144 safes arrived and he was able to extricate it from the letters and bills and flyers before reaching home. He was now in business. His locker became the teenage "pharmacy."

Brent gave Eric and me several. We used them for balloons and, most satisfying of all, would attach one to the rear exhaust pipe of one of the town muscle cars if we found one parked near the Capitol Theatre at the top of Main Street. We'd sit on the stone wall by the Baptist church and wait for the guy and his date to emerge from the show and fire up the '57 Chevy with the fender skirts and the ferocious woodpecker decals. Halfway down Main the safe would explode and the greaser would slam on the brakes, jump out and check to see if he'd blown a gasket. You have to make your own fun in a small town.

Sometimes our antics became a bit ridiculous. Naturally, the first thought after turning sixteen was getting a driver's licence. I was no different. I had a job at the Eaton's department store on Main Street—clerking in the hardware and plumbing section in the large store's basement—and hoped to save enough for a used car. I did save enough to purchase, second hand, a little Honda 55 cc motorcycle. It was really a scooter and was perfect for zipping around town and out to the summer dances at Hidden Valley.

It was less successful on long trips—especially with three passengers.

Brent had been talking on the phone to Ken Hastie, whose family had recently left our neighbourhood for the city of North Bay, 125 kilometres up Highway 11 to the north. Brent thought that he and Eric and I should go visit Ken on a Sunday, when none of us would be working. Having no car and not being keen about three teenagers trying to hitchhike together, Brent figured we could all go on the Honda, so long as there was room to fit. He sawed an eight-foot-long, eight-inch-wide plank of pine in half. He then fitted the board under the seat strap so that it extended the "seat" both in front and back. We could all sit on the board.

I was to drive. Brent, being heaviest, was to sit in the middle to act as an anchor for the board, with me basically sitting in his lap like a toddler playing at driving. Eric was to hang over the back end of the bright red scooter as if he was somehow riding the tail of a dragon. Part of him was on the seat, a bit more of him supported entirely by the board. That would be roughly six hundred pounds on a machine meant to carry, at most, a 180-pound driver.

Off we went . . .

We made it past sixty kilometres an hour only on the downslopes. Climbing some of the many long hills was difficult. The back two riders had to dismount and run alongside the scooter, boarding again in full stride as the machine crested the top. We made it to North Bay by noon, ate lunch with the amazed and amused Hastie family and immediately set out for home. We almost made it, too, a tire blowing near Novar, less than half an hour from Huntsville. A man stopped in his pickup to see if he could help; Brent, of course, recognized him, and soon enough the wounded scooter was in the truck's bed and the four of us were crammed into the cab and headed home.

Not all road stories have happy endings in small towns. No one, it seems, gets through a rural or small-town upbringing without losing someone. We were no different. One spectacular crash by the town cemetery cost a handsome young man in Jim's class his life. Eric and Brent and I were friends with a young man from Dwight who, racing about with two rich American cottagers, ended up in a spectacular crash that none of them survived.

My old hockey and lacrosse teammate Donnie Strano and I came close to a crash ourselves the first summer we worked at Eaton's. We were both fifteen. There was a staff get-together at a cottage on Lake Vernon. The men were heavily into the beer, and we slipped away with a car belonging to the head of the shoe department. Racing along Ravenscliffe Road, Donnie lost control on the gravel and we slid and spun down a hill until the old Pontiac flipped up onto its side on a soft shoulder. Using branches as leverage and the luck of gravity, we somehow got the car flipped back upright and went back to the cottage, where the car owner, Bill, reamed us out and charged us five dollars for a new tail light.

Sports kept us out of finding even more trouble. Eric's father, Murray, was our first sports hero. Murray Ruby had once been a champion boxer and was the centre fielder and best hitter for the local fastball team, the Huntsville Merchants. His throws from centre and left field were legendary "ropes" straight into the glove of catcher Gary "Newf" Feltham, who just happened to work at Ruby's Men's & Boys' Wear. Murray's home runs were sometimes lost in the tall grass and brush beyond the far reach of centre field. He once knocked out a charging opponent with a single punch.

We were mad for sports. We spent hours each week at the Huntsville Memorial Arena, whether watching the excellent Huntsville juvenile hockey team—where cousin Don McCormick was a fast-skating forward—or playing our own town league and competitive games against towns such as Parry Sound, Gravenhurst and Bracebridge. We played town-league lacrosse in the outdoor box back of the rink and competitive lacrosse in the arena against top teams from Whitby, Peterborough, St. Catharines and Oshawa.

We played even more games on the streets, mostly Dufferin Street, which was high on Reservoir Hill. Dufferin was short and relatively flat, with little traffic to threaten our snow-chunk goalposts. Mostly we played road hockey, first side to ten goals winning. We played shinny from school's-out to past dark; hockey all day on Saturday and Sunday.

We played hockey under the only streetlight on evenings, when players and their sticks with toothpick blades—worn down by the pavement— would sneak out after supper to cuff a tennis ball around until we were called back in. Brent and Eric and I were among the "little guys," my brother Jim's gang the "big guys." For a few years, one big guy equalled two little guys—but eventually there stopped being any separation at all. After all, Brent and Eric were now bigger than any of the "big guys."

Brother Jim was tall and skinny in his mid-teens. He was heavily into sports, but he also read Henry Miller, Hubert Selby Jr. and William S. Burroughs. Jim had the most up-to-date library in town, Huntsville Public Library included. He was an intellectual who played chess and skipped classes and was a fair hockey player in the town leagues, with a knack for scoring. In road hockey he was smug about his slap shot. He also liked to announce the games as we played. Jim stayed up late hanging over the red Viking radio for every Leafs game and any other NHL match he might pick up from the United States when the reception was good enough. He had the calls down as pat as Foster Hewitt or Danny Gallivan themselves. Nobody else would dare try to call our games, even if there was usually some general annoyance at Jim's self-glorification.

In spring, when the town's interest gradually turned to lacrosse, there would be a month when the road was bare and the snowbanks crystal, and the road-hockey rules would be bent so goaltenders could use lacrosse sticks. They were permitted to pass by throwing, but that was the only stated rule; everything else was understood. Half ice after a goal. No golf shots. No slashing. No cross-checks. No quitting just because it's your ball. Fights were so common, often between siblings, that they would carry on while everyone else continued playing. When the sap was running, Mrs. Wieler would offer up a pail of fresh, clear, sweet sap from the tapped sugar maple near the road. The original Gatorade. And in return we would promise not to chase the ball into her raspberry bushes.

The Wielers put up with us playing endlessly in front of their place because, most often, their son, Stew, would be on the road with us. Stew was brother Jim's age and a superb lacrosse player, one of the town's best. His father, Gord, was a plumber who worked out of his 1949 Fargo truck, the very truck I foolishly stuck my tongue to one winter; Mrs. Wieler had to pour hot water over the side of the cab until I was able to pull free. Still, I left a small chunk of conversation on that frigid steel.

In late spring, until school let out and our family and the Munroes left for cottages, we played lacrosse on Dufferin Street using sponge rubber balls, which were slightly heavier than the tennis balls we used for hockey and not as heavy, or potentially hurtful, as the India-rubber ball of full-equipment lacrosse games at the arena. Often, we would take our sticks and lacrosse balls to the public school and spend hours pounding the balls up against the red-brick walls on a single bounce, then running backward to catch the "pass" from the school.

Jack Bionda was a local lacrosse hero who also played hockey for the Boston Bruins, but he was best known for winning five Mann Cups—symbolic of the best senior lacrosse team in the country—with the Victoria Shamrocks and New Westminster Salmonbellies of British Columbia. Jack was much older than any of us and long gone from town, but he remained a legend in Huntsville for his habit of walking about and playing "catch" with the telephone poles, it being extremely difficult to throw a lacrosse ball onto a round surface and have it rebound directly into the pocket of your stick. He was said to be brilliant at it. We tried to emulate him, invariably chasing more balls than catching them.

Come fall, it was touch football on Dufferin Street—where Jim broke his elbow falling on a rock after catching a pass to the side. We sometimes played full tackle on the sandy grounds of the public school, but would switch back to hockey at first frost, playing for a few weeks on bare pavement but soon sliding on slick roads in a time before road salt. In the era of tire chains and light sanding, it was possible to travel about town by hitching rides on the backs of bumpers as cars paused long enough at stop signs for us to slip out of the dark, crouch down and grab on. Wearing mukluks—deerskin boots with zero tread—we slid along behind the car for blocks without the driver ever being aware that there were extra passengers aboard.

It is difficult now to convey how deeply hockey could penetrate a life back then. We had no television. Jim had a table-top hockey game, the kind where the metal players are controlled by steel rods running beneath. There were no slots in the game surface, however, so the players could not go up and down the ice. All you could do was twist the rod between your thumb and finger so the players could pass and shoot. All four rods that controlled the defence players eventually broke and we realized a shot was faster if we flicked the players manually. And marbles were better than toy pucks. My brother found he could raise the marbles if he slightly bent his player's stick. I suffered my first upper-body hockey injury wearing pajamas in his bedroom.

Maurice Munroe built a large rink each winter in his backyard, which touched ours. He flattened the snow around a massive hemlock tree and watered the ice at night until it was one of the best rinks in town, surely the most unusual with that hemlock handing out checks to anyone failing to lift his head. In 1954, Hurricane Hazel finally took out the big hemlock just as we were starting to get serious about hockey.

Eric wanted to be a goaltender and was fanatical about working on his game. At precisely 8 a.m. on holidays the phone would ring and I knew even before my mother answered that it was Eric, antsy to get out on the road so Brent and I could take shots on him.

Not long after Hurricane Hazel struck, my mother found the two dollars necessary to register me in minor hockey. Saturday mornings now became the long walk to the arena for our town-league games, the three of us carrying our skates, sticks and equipment down Lansdowne Street and across an empty field to the rink tucked in behind the high school.

I had hand-me-down equipment and a stick, and I was off to squirt town-league hockey in the fall of 1955. I started a scrapbook that I still have, the price, fifteen cents, pencilled on the cover. The first page opens on me, eight years old, staring out from a picture that was taken on a day when our little northern Ontario town put on a special display for the three Toronto daily newspapers to show that life goes on in cottage country in the winter as well. I have a black eye. My first but hardly last hockey fight.

Below that treasured photograph is a clipping from the *Huntsville Forester*: "Goals by McGregor Gives Auxiliary Tie with Hay & Co. 2–2" The story begins as follows:

> The Legion Auxiliary's Roy MacGregor turned two spectacular solo rushes into a 2–2 tie with Hay & Co. Saturday morning.
>
> A highlight of a Huntsville Hockey League Squirt playoff game, MacGregor's goals marked the second time Auxiliary had battled from behind a one-goal deficit.
>
> Young defenseman Michael Allemano was especially good for the Hookmen, breaking up many Auxiliary rushes. Both of the Hay & Company goals by Brent Munroe and John Newell, were scored off power plays.

It is important to remember here that this is squirt hockey, for players aged seven and eight, that the full name of the team is the Legion Ladies' Auxiliary, and that the game was played on only one half of the ice, a line of boards being temporarily erected so two games could go on at once. But no matter. This is what small-town hockey is all about. So what if there were no "spectacular solo rushes"? The story was wonderfully imagined, if poorly edited. I remember both goals vividly, one on a scramble, one on a slow shot the length of the ice that the goaltender fanned on. But the local paper knew what it was doing. Creating local heroes. And the day the paper came out there were grown-ups on Main Street who had noticed. Old Winnie Trainor, Tom Thomson's girlfriend, even stopped me, opened her purse, pulled out the clipping, and said I'd soon be in the NHL. Damn right I would.

Today the glue has dried and clippings fall out when the book is opened. "Pee Wee's Cut Down Orillia," "Pee Wee's Batter Burks Falls." The day we won the prestigious Wardell & Company trophy, the story began: "Anglo Canadian's one-two punch of Harry Snowden and Roy MacGregor continued to spark the Hidemen at the Arena on Tuesday night." It was glorious. The teams had nicknames—the Hidemen meant you were sponsored by the local tannery, the Hookmen meant the local lumberyard—and the goal scorers were transformed magically in the local paper from goofy kids who had barely stopped wetting the bed into *somebodies*.

Looking back all those years, I cannot help but wonder what was lost when so many small- and medium-sized communities lost their weekly newspapers. The *Huntsville Forester* had a section called "Personals," which listed everything from who was visiting whom over the weekend to the skunk that had taken up residence under the steps to the United Church. But missed most of all are the sports reports, the photographs of the little ballerinas, the winners of the music festivals. When I saw my name in the newspaper, I wanted it there as often as possible. Only back then I thought I'd be the story, not the one telling it.

I see on one page of the scrapbook where I have practised writing my autograph for when I would be an NHLer with my own Upper Deck hockey cards. I smile at the small-town myth for the harmless, happy days it gave me and God knows how many tens of thousands of others. Hockey, for most of us, was the first time—and so often the only time— we felt we mattered.

In 1960, the year I turned twelve, the family stopped spending two straight months at Lake of Two Rivers with our grandparents. Jim had a summer job bagging groceries at the A&P and Ann got work at Bell Telephone as an operator. It was my one glorious year in sports, when I made the town all-star teams in hockey, lacrosse and baseball.

Eric and I made the town "rep" team that summer, he as a left-handed pitcher, I as catcher. We played teams around the area—Port Sydney, Kearney, Burk's Falls—and one tournament in Sudbury, where the Rubys had relatives. Eddie Shack, known as the Toronto Maple Leafs' great "Entertainer" of the 1960s, was one of the several Sudbury cousins. He and Eric looked uncannily alike, especially in later years.

The tournament went badly. In the warm-up I caught an Eric fastball and threw it quickly to first base, only to realize that Terry Stinson, our first baseman, wasn't looking my direction. The ball caught him flat on the left eye, causing such instant swelling that he was lost for the game. At the end of the match, Eric's parents presumed Eric had returned to Huntsville with a few teammates in the coach's car. We in the coach's car presumed he had gone off with his parents and cousins. Everyone drove off, leaving Eric sound asleep on a large, flat rock back of the ball diamond. His parents got all the way home to Huntsville, three hours away, before a phone call from the relatives alerted them that they'd have to go right back.

Huntsville sports were changing. A pure hockey town, with a smattering of baseball and lacrosse, it had a new sports director in Jim Bishop, a slim, handsome man with dark, tipping eyebrows and such a passion for the sport that he would one day be declared "Mr. Lacrosse" by the Ontario Lacrosse Association. Single-handedly, he turned Huntsville into a lacrosse powerhouse. In the 1960s, his Oshawa Green Gaels would win seven consecutive Minto Cup junior Canadian championships, in no small part led by players from Huntsville.

The original Green Gaels were from Huntsville, however. Brent, Eric and I played not only on the same dominant town-league team that won the local championship, but also for Bish and the Huntsville Green Gaels all-star team. Bish ran us hard. I recall kids throwing up in our early practices. But we lost not a single game the entire season and went on to win the Ontario peewee A championship in a tournament played in Peterborough. Three members of our team—Jim Higgs, Don Stinson and Ivan Thompson—would eventually join Bish in the Canadian Lacrosse Hall of Fame.

Hockey, however, was the game I loved most. I was a good skater and had a fair shot, but I was negligent when it came to checking and by second year peewee I was wearing thick, ugly horn-rimmed glasses. To this day, I do not know if I gave up going into corners because I was afraid of opponents or more afraid of my mother if I returned home with yet another broken lug or snapped frame or shattered lens. I played only town league in my final year of bantam. The town's full-time coach, Mye Sedore, came to one game and tried to talk me into giving rep hockey another chance, but I wasn't interested.

Brent and Eric and I are remembered—entirely by ourselves—for one spectacular moment in Huntsville minor hockey, but unfortunately it had nothing to do with anything that happened on the ice. We were still in bantam and attending the annual awards ceremony at the Legion hall. Mayor Frank Hubbell was speaking. I was nervous but still fairly confident I would win the bantam-level most valuable player trophy that my older brother and an older cousin already had their names on. The mayor was speaking and one of us—we don't need to know who— passed wind. It was such a wicked slap shot of a fart that it stopped His Worship in mid-sentence. Eric started giggling. Brent started giggling. I started giggling. In a moment we were all three of us underneath the table, hiding behind the white tablecloths and sputtering like tight balloons.

There was not a sound from the three hundred players and coaches and managers and executives and honoured guests. Finally Mrs. Kelly from the Ladies' Auxiliary came out from the kitchen and stuck her head down under the tablecloths.

"If you boys can't behave yourselves," she said in a loud, no-nonsense voice, "you will have to leave."

The evening got worse. I didn't win the trophy. Brent did. And Eric won for top goaltender. The three of us walked home up Lansdowne Street, Brent holding his Robin Hood Oats trophy, Eric holding his, and I holding back my tears, grateful for the poor street lighting about which our parents so often complained.

I made a new friend that season. A fairly new kid, Ralph Cox, who had moved to town from Toronto when his father opened a Chrysler dealership. I thought him a dirty player and hated playing against him. Every time our teams met, we got into a fight and got kicked out of the game.

One night, with my team leading, he upended me from behind and I went crashing into the boards. I leapt up, swinging, and soon we were being hauled back by the linesmen and the referee was signalling that we were out of the game. He was sending us to the dressing room.

Only thing was, there was only one dressing room available. We both had to go in. We sat as far away from each other as possible.

"What did you do that for?" I finally asked.

Ralph grinned. "Coach told me to."

Ralph's coach, Joe Pollard, had but one instruction for Ralph every time we played. His assignment was to take me out of the game, which he did nearly effortlessly time and time again.

With nothing else to do—we couldn't even watch the game—we started talking. Turned out we both collected coins. We decided to meet after school and see what each of us had. More than sixty years later, Ralph is my brother-in-law. He married Ellen's sister, Jackie, and they moved to Ottawa a few years ago after several successful years in business in North Bay. During the Covid restrictions of 2020 and 2021 we walked my dog, Piper, together several times a week. Not once did Ralph try to take me out.

By sheer circumstance of date of birth and location, location, location, I have been able to tell stunned colleagues at work and at the after-hockey beer table that "Oh, yeah, I played for years against Bobby Orr . . ."

It's true, but more impressive without the details. Bobby Orr was born in 1948; I was born in 1948. He learned to skate on the frozen bay by Parry Sound; I learned to skate on the Munroes' frozen backyard. At squirt level (ages eight to nine) Orr made the Parry Sound all-star team; I made Huntsville's all-star team. We played rep hockey through squirt, peewee and bantam, at which point Bobby headed off to Oshawa to play for the Oshawa Generals junior team; I headed off to the town optometrist to pick up my latest pair of Coke bottle–thick glasses.

Right from the very first drop of the puck, I could tell—even as a seven-year-old—that Bobby Orr was different. One of our squirt goal-tenders, Guy Lassetter—son of the man who delivered by horse and wagon the wood we heated with—was so short that he needed another head to reach the crossbar of the net he was asked to guard against Parry Sound. Orr, even then, was so strong he could "roof" a shot, the puck sailing over Guy's head like a tiny flying saucer.

By peewee hockey, ages ten to twelve, our coach, Mye Sedore, was beside himself searching for a plan that could stop this little kid from Parry Sound with the near-white brush cut. Mye, a heavy man with a red face and black, slicked-back hair, had once starred for the Sundridge Beavers, a senior team that had quite a reputation in northern Ontario. He still wore his now somewhat ragged team jacket. He was on the payroll of the local lumber company but never, ever did any work for them. The man who owned the lumber company also happened to be the mayor and had a son excelling in hockey. He wanted his town to have a good minor hockey program. Mye's job with the lumber company was to serve as full-time coach of the all-star teams and part-time skate sharpener for the Huntsville Memorial Arena.

Our team was sponsored by the few local physicians in town, one of whom had a son, Peter Salmon, on the team. We were formally known as the Huntsville Doctors but invariably referred to in the local paper and on the town's new radio station, CKAR, as the "Pill Rollers," a moniker never again to be seen in the sports world. Parry Sound's team was the "Shamrocks" and featured Bobby Orr and the Bloomfields, Roddy and Roger. Our best player was Tim Kelly, who was often compared to Orr early in his career. Tim, unfortunately, suffered a bad knee injury in junior hockey and, instead, came back to Huntsville to have a long and rewarding career with Bell Telephone.

The Shamrocks were coached by Bucko McDonald, who had once played in the National Hockey League—winning Stanley Cups with the Detroit Red Wings and the Toronto Maple Leafs—and who always, always wore a fedora. It was Mye's great ambition to one day beat one of Bucko's teams.

To that end, Mye not only trained us hard on the ice but also began to use psychological tricks to fire us up. Before every game at the "little NHL" level, as it was then known, all the players had to sign a game sheet, and the signatures were then checked against league sheets to ensure that no team was using an over-age ringer. We were the home team at the Huntsville rink, so Parry Sound signed first.

Mye came in through the dressing-room doors snickering to himself and shaking the game sheet that the Shamrocks had signed.

"Can you believe it?" he asked of the entire room. "Look at this signature!"

He went up and down the rows, pointing to one signature in particular.

"*Bobby Orr writes like a girl!*" Mye bellowed.

"Yeah!" we shouted back. "*He writes like a girl!*"

The reality was he simply wrote neater and clearer than any of us who scribbled our names without much thought. Bobby Orr had clearly practised and practised his signature, thinking of the future autographs he might be signing, just as Rocket Richard and Gordie Howe and Jean Béliveau and Bobby Hull had done when they were young and dreaming.

The mighty Pill Rollers hit the ice fired up as never before. Bobby Orr was on for the opening faceoff. The arena was packed. Even my father had come in from the Algonquin Park bush for the game. "I want to see that kid from Parry Sound everybody's talking about," he said.

We learned almost instantly that Bobby Orr wasn't playing hockey with a ballpoint pen. He scored on his first shift.

In grade six, our quiet little neighbourhood was rocked to a point that Huntsville landed on front pages from the *Toronto Star* to the *Police Gazette*. I read every word of every *Star* story. Perhaps it was here that I got the newspaper bug—without even realizing it. I carried the *Star* up Lorne Street and around Reservoir Hill Mondays through Saturdays, saving the last paper along the route to be devoured in our living room. The "taxi murders" story mesmerized me.

Directly across from Winnie Trainor's brown clapboard house on the corner of Minerva and Centre Streets, C&H Taxi had established a stand in an empty lot back of Parker's Bakery. Cars came and went all hours of the day and night. Winnie had railed against this development, but the town took no action.

"No good will come of this," Winnie told our mother. How right she was.

In 1959, the year of the family's final all-summer-long stay at Lake of Two Rivers, two drivers from C&H went missing: twenty-nine-year-old Francis "Fritz" Grosso and twenty-two-year-old Bruce Spiers. There was instant concern when they failed to return from what should have been a routine trip to Dwight. Grosso's 1959 black Meteor had been last spotted heading north on Highway 11, the taxi roof sign removed.

Late in June, just before we left for the summer, the bodies of the two drivers were found in a sand pit off Birkendale Road, which runs from Highway 35 to the east of town. Two locals were arrested and charged with murder. One was Wayne Sluman, a skinny little seventeen-year-old the *Police Gazette* would tag "Babyface," and twenty-year-old Marvin McKee, a local tough who Brylcreemed his hair into a James Dean ducktail and kept his smokes in a rolled-up sleeve. Sluman sat behind my brother Jim in school. McKee's younger sister had been in my class that year, Joe Caern's grade six.

Local gossip had it that the younger man, Sluman, had cracked under questioning. He had taken the police to the gravel pit where the bodies had been hidden under brush. He also had provided details of the murders. The intention had been to rob the drivers, but all they had was twenty-seven dollars and a wristwatch. A furious McKee, who carried a sawed-off rifle, shot Grosso in the head, killing him. Spiers had been shot but also had a fractured skull. Sluman told police that Spiers had actually survived the night after being shot. McKee and Sluman and McKee's girlfriend had returned the following day to check matters, finding Spiers barely alive. McKee forced the much smaller Sluman to finish off the cab driver by dropping an eighteen-pound rock on his head. They then buried the two drivers in shallow graves deeper in the bush.

Sluman decided to hitchhike back to town. McKee and his girlfriend fled north in Grosso's car. She had family with property at Elk Lake, near New Liskeard. Aware that the police were now looking for them, McKee and the girl stole a boat from her uncle and tried to make their escape via the Montreal River. The uncle reported the theft and police found the boat abandoned. The two runaways were soon captured, badly bitten by mosquitoes and blackflies.

At the end of the Labour Day long weekend, my family returned from Two Rivers so that the four of us—Jim, Ann, me and kindergarten-age Tom—could start school that Tuesday. I was met by Brent and Eric, who could talk about nothing but the taxi murders. They had even watched while police divers searched the reservoir pond up behind our houses, where they found the barrel of a sawed-off .22, just as Sluman had told them they would.

The trial took place that fall and was a sensation. I was delivering the *Toronto Star* after school again and could hardly wait to get home and start reading the latest news of the murders. A friend carried the *Toronto Telegram* along roughly the same route, and since we picked up at the same spot we often compared the coverage. "Couldn't Club Dying Cabby Boy Quoted," shouted the *Tely*'s headline for Tuesday, November 3, 1959. "Told me to get a rock" read the story subhead. I was fascinated by the reporting, never for a moment thinking that one day I'd be a byline myself.

Pale and weighing just 110 pounds, a nervous Sluman pleaded guilty to a reduced charge of manslaughter and was sentenced to fifteen years in penitentiary by Justice René Danis. McKee chose trial by jury. The twenty-year-old claimed that the attacker was, in fact, Spiers, the taxi driver. Spiers had the gun and McKee tried to wrestle it from him, causing the weapon to go off accidentally. McKee told the jury that the dying man "gurgled the way my mother did when she died."

Justice Danis would have none of it. He told the jury: "It strikes me that the story told by McKee is not the story of an honest man. It doesn't seem reasonable to me. I don't like his evidence. I don't accept it." The trial ended with the judge reminding the courtroom that hunting season was opening on Monday and many of the people involved in this trial had commitments to hunting camps in the area. The jury took forty-eight minutes to decide and came back with a guilty verdict.

"And you call this justice?" the shackled McKee muttered as he was ushered from the court. "Don't worry—I'll be back!"

McKee was sentenced to die in the midst of what would become the great Canadian debate on capital punishment. An appeal to the Supreme Court of Canada was denied in early February and McKee was hanged in the Parry Sound jail on Monday, February 8, 1960, at midnight. The front page of the *Star* I delivered the following afternoon had a photo of his brilliantly lighted cell as the time approached.

"May be the last to hang," said the huge headline. McKee was supposedly singing hymns loudly enough that those standing outside could hear. They buried McKee in a pauper's grave by the Parry Sound jail when no family would claim him. The young man had even requested as much, so that his grave might serve as a deterrent "to others who choose to live dangerously." McKee's last wish, the newspaper reported, was that his eyes be donated to the blind. His last words, they said, were "God bless you all."

Oh, the power of journalism in the imagination of a ten-year-old who up to now had been interested only in sports.

Brent, Eric and I came back together in hockey one last time in the mid-1960s. We were all seventeen or eighteen and a few of the small towns around were forming an "outlaw" league, but they didn't seem able to decide whether it should be called "Juvenile D" or "Juvenile Z." Baysville came after Brent and he talked Eric into going out as their goaltender. I joined after their first few games. It was, as they say in that part of the country, a real "woodchoppers' league," with fights as common as goals and precious few fans in the stands.

By the time the first—and only—season was through, we had won the district championship against Gravenhurst, but the winning is not what I remember most. I don't recall the goals scored or the ones Eric stopped, but I do remember that one of the players on our team was in his early twenties and played on a younger brother's birth certificate. I remember he kept a lighted cigarette on the boards during warmup. I remember two brothers on the team and their father in the stands, all three of whom stank of beer. I remember our sweaters—big yellow Bs for Boston, of course, but we were the "Baysville Bruins." And I remember the team rage was chewing tobacco and how I figured I'd rather try backchecking than dip my finger into one of those black tins and then put the disgusting tobacco in my mouth.

The most spectacular game we played in the playoffs was against Bracebridge. In the first period, I was caught with my head down and hit so hard at centre ice that I turned a complete circle in the air before landing again on my skates and falling hard. That seemed to set the tone. I remember Brent getting into a fistfight that lasted all of one punch—Brent's.

But above all I recall the one move I will regret to my grave. I was racing a Bracebridge defenceman named Dave C.—I remember his last name, but think it best not to add it—for the puck in his end and decided, given what had happened at centre ice in the first period, I'd better hit him before he killed me. There was no glass around the boards at that time, nothing in fact until the icing lines, where thick wire screen was strung from beams attached to the top of the boards. Somewhere around the corner faceoff circle I hit Dave C. from below and drove him up into the boards. But instead of flying into the seats, he hit right where the trussing began for the screen. It was a sickening sound. I heard a loud snap, but it wasn't the two-by-four holding the screening. He slammed into the wood and went instantly limp, falling back down onto the ice with a blood-curdling scream.

Much later we would find out he had a broken elbow, a twisted knee, and cracked ribs, but as I say, that was much later. First, there would be a riot.

Perhaps you have seen film footage of the "Punch-up in Piestany," back in 1987, when Team Canada juniors and Soviet Union juniors brawled until organizers turned out the lights, and both teams were subsequently disqualified from the world junior championship being played in Czechoslovakia. This was a mini-Piestany in Bracebridge with the lights on. Before I knew it, the Zamboni doors were swinging open to admit an ambulance.

About two dozen fans were climbing over the boards—remember, there was no wraparound glass—and coming to join in the scrums that had formed around the fallen player. I noticed one older man with two others—the father? brothers?—taking dead aim at me. The older man grabbed a stick from one of the Bracebridge players and came running and slipping across the ice toward me, the stick pointed in my direction like a flamethrower.

Suddenly, the older man went down hard. Eric, alone and ignored while standing in his crease at the far end of the ice, had seen what was developing and decided to take action. He skated hard down the ice and, with his mask and gloves still on, took out the attacker with a single swing of his goalie stick.

With the older man crumpled and moaning on the ice, one of the younger men took up the stick. Eric took him out, too. I could hear sirens in the parking lot. Two Ontario Provincial Police officers were hurrying in the large doors that let the Zamboni out to dump the snow it had scraped.

Eric, fortunately, had the good sense to keep on skating. Out through the doors the Baysville Bruins' goaltender ran, his goalie skates screeching and sparking across the concrete floor of the lobby.

Out into the parking lot he headed in full equipment. He ran past one row of cars and found the car we had driven from Huntsville unlocked. He dove into the back seat, locked all the doors and ducked down.

Inside the rink, the ambulance was leaving and the police were settling things down. Some of the Bracebridge gang were yelling "Assault!" and other silliness, but there was really no doubt this had been an unfortunate accident. We had the right to try to bump each other off the puck. It just happened that my bump sent Dave C. flying into the post that anchored the heavy screening that ran behind both nets.

The game was called. The police waited for us to change and escorted us out into the parking lot, where a seething crowd of Bracebridge players and supporters had gathered.

"*We want the goalie!*" they chanted.

"*We want the goalie!*

"*We want the goalie!!!*"

A window rolled down in a dark car in the second row, a light dusting of snow falling as the glass receded into the door.

Sitting there was Eric. No mask. No sign of equipment. Just an innocent-looking Eric trying to be helpful.

"He's already gone home!" he shouted to the gathering crowd and quickly rolled up the window.

The police escorted our cars to Highway 11 North; we took the cloverleaf toward Huntsville and Baysville, cranked up the radios and cheered Eric all the way home.

People who grow up in small towns like to say "stories like this you can't make up," but in fact, they do. Many years later I would write a screenplay called *Cementhead* for the CBC docudrama series *For the Record*. The scene of Eric taking out the man swinging the stick was a highlight of the story of a senior hockey team out of Sudbury that won through intimidation. Martin Short, in his very first film, played Eric. Many years beyond that, I ran into Short at a fundraiser in Toronto and asked him about the film.

"Loved that character," the now-famous Hollywood actor said.

So did I, Marty. So did I.

THE WORLD'S GREATEST TEACHER

I recognized the handwriting even before the envelope was opened.

Staring at those same perfectly formed vowels and sure consonants on the grades three, four and five blackboard will do that—even if the time gap is now half a century.

The note came from Mern E. Parker—Miss Parker then and forever—who may well be the greatest teacher who ever lived.

She taught those three grades at Huntsville Public School for forty years, ending in 1975. She passed away peacefully in her sleep just before Christmas 2014. She was 102, sharper than tacks right up to when she switched off her night light.

Miss Parker taught what was then called an "accelerated program." Three grades in two years, and the greatest honour she could bestow on her charges on the small yellow report cards we took home three times a year to be signed was a single "Keep up the good work."

I would like to say that I did, but it would be a lie. What was gained by acceleration in primary school turned into deceleration by midway through high school when I flunked, dramatically, grade twelve.

It would be wrong to blame the teachers for that spectacular failure, but it is still remarkable how few Miss Parkers one encounters on the long journey through the Canadian educational system. By the time a student leaves high school, he or she has likely been taught by forty to fifty different teachers. Most students, if they are fortunate, count two or three who truly touched them and affected their entire lives in doing so—but there should be more.

She lived on Lorne Street just two houses up from us on the edge of Reservoir Hill. She was all alone in a house that once also held her parents. She taught Sunday school at our church. Our mother and Miss Parker served on the Ladies' Auxiliary together. They were good friends.

Miss Parker obviously felt close enough to strike a secret deal with me halfway through grade four. She took me aside and quietly told me that if the class won the upcoming music festival, she would ask me to go up and receive the plaque. In exchange for this honour, she said, I would have to do something for her: only *mouth* the words, not sing. I agreed, and somewhere there is a black and white photograph of me proudly receiving the plaque.

Another incident occurred after I had left grade five and moved on to splitting my time between grade six and the principal's office. Miss Parker came one day and asked if she could borrow me to remove, quietly, a large garter snake that had somehow found its way to the back of her classroom and was terrifying the children. She knew I came from a family of rangers and loggers and would know how to handle a snake that was causing her class to shriek and run. I have never been so proud.

She was an extraordinary person. She walked to school each day down Lorne Street and across Main with as many as a dozen little kids trying to hold her hands or, if denied, a part of her coat or umbrella. Like a mother duck with her ducklings. She had as many as forty-eight students in her class at one time, never an assistant, and never a moment's difficulty with discipline. She never raised her voice, never, ever raised a hand.

"I had no problems," she said after I called her to thank her for the note concerning a small award I had been given. "If someone was being bad, I just went and stood beside him until he settled down. If he was really bad, I might put a hand on his shoulder, but nothing else."

She liked to hug children. "Some of them didn't get it at home," she said. "That's often all a child needs, a little pat or a hug."

She despaired that today teachers dare not even touch a child, and she considered herself fortunate to have taught when she did. "I had a very good principal, and good parents," she said. No one spoke of "burnout" back then. Teachers retired more often with satisfaction and even a little sadness, not, as now, because they want to get out as soon as possible, too often with accompanying bitterness toward a system that no longer makes much sense to them.

She said with regret that if she were starting all over, she doubted very much she would have gone into teaching.

Something has changed.

But some things, mercifully, remain the same. The small card that came in the mail—the one with the perfectly formed vowels and the sure consonants—contained the one sentence that any student of Miss Parker's would die for, no matter what age, no matter how long ago the school doors closed forever behind.

"Keep up the good work."

2

Finding a Passion

"Going—going—_____!"

That, in five-alarm, fire-truck-red ink, was scribbled at the bottom of my 1964–65 grade twelve report card by D.C. Stone, principal of Huntsville High School. A red F for history (37 percent), red F for algebra (47 percent), red F for chemistry (49 percent), red F for French (37 percent), red F for Latin (31 percent). I stood twenty-ninth in a class of thirty-two—*who, who, who could possibly have done worse?*— with a 45.4 percent overall average. I passed only health and phys. ed. (64 percent) and English, with a bare pass: 53 percent. Under "teacher's comments," the English instructor wrote, "slipping badly."

In some ways, I never felt more like I belonged. It is not unusual for small, isolated towns to celebrate failure over success, especially if your group is also floundering. Brent and Eric had already failed several years. Brent took five years to get through grades nine and ten, grade ten being required for those wishing to join the Ontario Provincial Police. Eric had failed twice before finishing his grade twelve, after which he headed off to work at various ski resorts in Canada and Europe, drive a cab in Jasper, Alberta, and eventually, as he always knew he would, join the family clothing store on Main Street.

Struggling in school was very much a tradition in our small town. Older brother Jim, who would go on to a fine senior management career in banking, took seven years to get through the five grades that in those days led to graduation from grade thirteen. Huntsville High rarely produced Ontario Scholars, recipients of a small scholarship going to those who scored 80 percent on their grade thirteen provincial exams. These "departmentals" were written in the provincial schools but independently marked in Toronto. Sister Ann was almost certainly going to win one of the coveted scholarships, only to be waylaid by appendicitis the week before final exams. She had to repeat her year, there not being much mercy in those days.

Given my dreadful showing in grade twelve, I was duly ordered to the office of Mr. Stone, a tall, lanky man with a shoulder shrug that made it seem as if he was hiking up an invisible backpack. Doug Stone was known to everyone by his first and middle initials, D.C. He had previously been vice-principal, the authority in charge of discipline, and he could be a hard-ass. He had become principal when Harry Thornton, closing in on retirement, had slipped on ice leading into the school, cracked his head and never recovered. Chubby "Pot" Thornton had been easygoing and friendly, a man whose harshest words were, "If you can't keep up, you can't catch up." I would far rather have faced the wrath of Pot.

D.C. was not amused. He chewed me out about lack of effort, laziness and hurting my parents. He wanted me to leave school voluntarily and, though it remained unsaid, the message was clear that I could offer to leave or I could leave on the end of his size-eleven oxfords. A year in the workforce, he argued, would make me appreciate the value of an education. I could come back in a year if I promised to smarten up and apply myself.

I sat there shaking, certain that this was the end of the road. What would I do? The only jobs I had had were pruning Christmas trees and working in the plumbing and hardware departments in the basement of the local Eaton's. Would I have to head into the park and beg to get on with the McRae mill, where my father worked? I sat there dreading the future, unaware, obviously, that many years down this crooked line I would be asked by the Stone family to deliver the eulogy at D.C.'s funeral. I began my eulogy, of course, by reading from my grade twelve report card . . . "Going—going—_____!"

What stroke of luck brought Clyde Armstrong, the English teacher, into the office at that moment? He asked if he might join the dismissal meeting. Mr. Armstrong, boyish-looking with his horn-rimmed glasses and dark, curling hair, was the only teacher who had passed me—gym hardly counting—and he was also a neighbour on Reservoir Hill.

Mr. Armstrong had always been friendly and had even recruited some of us during the last federal election to distribute campaign literature for the New Democratic Party. We cared nothing for politics but were happy to have an excuse to be out on the streets on a school night, so we had blanketed the neighbourhood with brochures that would, in the end, have no effect whatsoever on a rural riding that voted Conservative decade upon decade.

Whatever the reason, Mr. Armstrong was in the principal's office. He told D.C. that he, too, had grave concerns about my dedication to education but said he had an idea that might provide a solution. D.C. shrugged his shoulders mightily and told him to go on.

"I want to start a magazine at Huntsville High," Clyde said. D.C. stared at him blankly, wondering what this had to do with the MacGregor issue. "And," Clyde continued, "I want *you* to be the first editor." He stared straight at me. I was still shaking. *Me? With a 53 in English?* What madness was this? There were scores of kids with higher marks in English. There were even some who thought Shakespeare relevant. All I was known for was arguing that Bob Dylan and Phil Ochs were the most important poets of the present and that Jack Kerouac was the world's greatest writer.

"You think he can do that?" D.C. asked skeptically.

"I do."

D.C. hunched his shoulders again, stared at the both of us, unsmiling, and finally nodded. "Okay," he said. "But you two better prove me wrong about this."

When high school—for me, grade twelve 2.0—resumed in the fall of 1965, Clyde Armstrong was eager to launch the school's first-ever publication. A contest was held to come up with a name and Jamie Jordan's suggestion, *The Pundit*, was chosen. It would have a rather curious, somewhat pretentious, and ultimately ironic, motto: "A pundit develops on the anvil of criticism." Mr. Armstrong named me editor-in-chief and another favourite of his, the talented and very smart tenth grader Edie Van Alstine, from the village of Port Sydney, as the magazine's features editor. When I finally graduated in 1967, Edie became editor-in-chief of *The Pundit* and did a splendid job. (She would remain a very close friend and, years later, while working for an Ottawa-based international writing, marketing and design firm, would help edit several of my books, this one included.)

We sold subscriptions for *The Pundit* before we had anything but curiosity to sell, and about half the school population of roughly five hundred signed up. The Pundit Publishing Corporation was financially successful from the very first issue. The magazine, sold before it was written, designed or published, would have news and commentary, short stories, poems and illustrations, all by students. Edited copy would be carefully typed onto master sheets and each page run off on a Gestetner, a rather ancient printing machine that, at the time, seemed absolutely magical. It was noisy with its rollers and rotating drums, stinky with its sharp smell of solvent and slow in that it produced but a single page at a time, but eventually the yellow pages piled up and could be sorted and stapled together. *The Pundit* was now a reality. Principal Stone was impressed—and likely more than a little surprised.

Appearing three times a year, the magazine proved very popular with the students right from the start. Mostly it was quite harmless stuff, simple short stories, bad and sometimes good poetry, ink drawings, always on dark yellow paper. The second issue of the 1966–67 school year had a theme, "spotlight on youth" (of course!), and a cover illustration by our art director, Larry Cockrame, of singer George Olliver, his band and the go-go dancers at Hidden Valley, the nearby ski resort that, come summer, transformed into a Saturday night dance venue. The huge chalet had three floors, with the centre open to all three. The bands played on the middle floor while couples danced on every level, and the awkwardly single, mostly young males lined the walls and pretended they were there only for the music.

It was an unusual situation in that this little town each week would play host to the very bands that we were listening to on Jungle Jay Nelson's morning show on Toronto's CHUM radio. Canadian and international rock bands that would normally play Montreal and Toronto would head north to Muskoka and play for the rich kids staying at their parents' cottages as well as the not-so-rich kids who just happened to live year-round in cottage country. The bands might be from England (the Hollies, Peter and Gordon, the Yardbirds with Jimmy Page on guitar, the Jeff Beck Group, a very young Tom Jones), from America (Neil Diamond, the Association, the Troggs, the Turtles, the Young Rascals, Sly and the Family Stone, the McCoys, the Left Banke, Brian Hyland) or, of course, from Canada (the Stampeders, the Mynah Birds, Terry & the Pirates, Mandala with George Olliver, Major Hoople's Boarding House, Five Man Electrical Band, the Stitch in Tyme, the Guess Who, the Staccatos, the Big Town Boys, Crowbar and Lighthouse). Three of these bands—Lighthouse, the Big Town Boys and the Stitch in Tyme—served as Hidden Valley house bands at various stretches.

Overly conscious that we were developing "on the anvil of criticism," I decided to take a run at Hidden Valley in the fourth issue of *The Pundit*. "Huntsville," I wrote, "is the home for the struggling, the poor; a sleepy hamlet in a never-never land. Hidden Valley, however, is the sandbox of the aristocracy, a kaleidoscopic empire that must consume huge amounts of money to survive. Part of this food comes from the poor hamlet and is forever gone. Hidden Valley may well be the worst enemy Huntsville has."

Overwritten, juvenile and downright silly—but it was my name, my *byline*, and it was intoxicating. It was also ridiculous and wrong—resorts brought money *in* to a tourist town—but I didn't realize it at the time. I went too far, calling the bands second rate and dismissing the go-go girls. I even called for the Seagram family, which then owned the ski resort, to open a whisky distillery in "this industrial-deficient community" so they could return some of our money in wages. Absurd, I know, but it provoked debate in the school, some for and many against, and word even got back to me that the original owner of the resort, Mr. Waterhouse, was furious. I, of course, was delighted.

The magazine had other attractions, however. There was a lovely short story by Ellen Griffith, who was also serving as business manager of *The Pundit*. Ellen and her sister, Jacqueline, were new to the school, Ellen in grade eleven and Jackie in grade nine, and they had come to Huntsville from St. Catharines, a small city on the shores of Lake Ontario southwest of Toronto. The Griffith sisters called Huntsville "Hicksville" and weren't at all impressed. We hicks, on the other hand, were mightily impressed. I had first noticed Ellen in the hallway on the way to the cafeteria. She was talking with her new friends and I was smitten with the long, straight, blond-brown hair, the long neck and the most intoxicating laugh I had ever heard. It was part giggle, part chuckle, and as bubbly as a forest stream. Glenn, a good friend of mine in grade twelve, was going out with one of the girls the new girl was talking to, and through Glenn I was able to get her name and a few details—the most significant one being that her father was the new chemistry teacher . . .

I cringed. Chemistry was one of those bright red Fs I had received only the previous June—and it currently appeared I might be headed for another come the next June.

Glenn made enquiries and word came back through his girlfriend that if I went to the upcoming sock hop this girl would agree to a dance. I wore my thick glasses, greased my hair with Brylcreem, had acne and believed that the sole reason for this unexpected turn of events was that we would be working together on the magazine. I was far from the only boy in town trying to get noticed by one of the new girls. We met at the sock hop and danced awkwardly to, of all songs, Gene Pitney's "Town Without Pity," and the dance ended with me wanting to spend as much time as possible with this lovely girl from the south with the long hair and the great laugh.

We began going to the Friday night teen town dances on the top floor of the town hall and once in a while to the costlier dances at Hidden Valley, which, of course, I had ripped in the editorial. Hypocrisy is irrelevant where falling in love is concerned. I used to walk her back to her family's apartment in the west end—the Griffiths were renting that first year while house hunting—the wind whipping across Hunters Bay and over the rail tracks and straight into our faces as we pushed our way west. I would visit a while and then, in the dark, head back along the open sidewalk toward Reservoir Hill. Often, on the coldest days, someone would honk and stop and offer the frozen kid a lift.

I tried to pick up my marks in chemistry but it was not easy. There were others in the class scoring regularly in the nineties while I struggled to hit the sixties. Lloyd Griffith was not impressed by my schoolwork and decidedly not impressed by my regularly showing up at his front door and, whenever I had the chance, helping myself to whatever might be in the Griffith refrigerator.

Mr. Griffith, a native of Manitoulin Island with a work ethic inherited from his blacksmith father, was always polite and even offered to tutor me in chemistry in the hour before the school day began. I took him up on it, in part to pick up my marks, in part to ensure that I didn't land further on his bad side. It helped and I managed to pass all courses in grade twelve, chemistry included.

Somehow, I made it to grade thirteen, which no longer exists in the province of Ontario. Those who passed through this fifth grade of high school and moved on to university are in general agreement that they never had a year more difficult than grade thirteen. Final exams were marked in Toronto by teachers who had not taught you and did not know you. Marks were delivered by mail later in the summer, hopeful graduates and, often, their parents waiting at the post office to learn whether they were headed off to university—or back out Brunel Road to Huntsville High School to try again.

Before the final departmental exams, Clyde Armstrong drove me out to the village of Dwight, where, in a professional photography studio, a formal portrait of the editor of *The Pundit* was taken. I wore a white shirt, tie, sports jacket and shorts—the photograph mercifully taken from the chest up. Once framed, it was hung in the ground floor hallway not far from the official portraits of Queen Elizabeth II, Prime Minister Lester Pearson and Ontario premier John Robarts. I could not believe that two years earlier, in an office just down the hall from these portraits, I had been on the verge of being kicked out of school.

We had to apply to universities or colleges in the spring. Some applied to Queen's University in Kingston or the University of Toronto; both required at least an 80 percent average to have any hope of getting in. Having barely cleared 65 percent in my departmentals, I knew my choices were limited. Some Huntsville students were heading for Sudbury, where the relatively new Laurentian University was growing. There was also Carleton University in Ottawa, known as "Last Chance U" for its low admission requirements. Carleton, however, had a journalism department and the two years running *The Pundit* suggested I should go there.

Both Laurentian and Carleton accepted me. I chose Laurentian on the immature basis that so many other Huntsville kids also chose it. My friend Ralph Cox was already there, as was his older brother, Peter, and they always had a used car from West End Motors, their father's Dodge dealership. I'd have rides home for holidays and the odd weekend. Despite Mr. Griffith's wishes, Ellen and I were still together, and she was only now entering grade thirteen. By choosing Laurentian, I would get back to Huntsville, and Ellen, far more often.

My mother drove me to Sudbury in a borrowed car. It was one of several periods when the family was carless. Let's just say our father, like many bush workers, couldn't resist penny mining stocks that were a "guaranteed sure thing" by whatever huckster was shopping them from bush camp to bush camp. Mr. Cox of West End Motors had generously offered Helen MacGregor a vehicle to take me, my little brother, Tom, and two suitcases full of clothes, boots, LPs and books off to Laurentian. I had about five hundred dollars in summer savings from my job at Eaton's. In my application for a student loan and grant, my father wrote that his salary was four thousand dollars a year, and I was duly awarded a student loan of six hundred dollars that would have to be paid back and a grant of another six hundred dollars that had no strings attached. The money would cover enrolment fees, a shared room in the Thorneloe Residence and a full three-a-day, seven-days-a-week meal ticket.

We drove north on Highway 11 to North Bay and then took 17 west to Sudbury. The landscape changed gradually from lush forests, lakes and rivers to stunted spruce and stark Canadian Shield. We passed through Sturgeon Falls, which I would soon learn everyone called "Virgin Falls," as if they knew something that no one else possibly could. We passed through Verner, Warren, Hagar, Markstay, Coniston, Wahnapitae . . .

Gradually, the stunted trees also vanished until there was nothing but bare rock, the terrain around Sudbury hard and bald and so much like the surface of the moon that the astronauts of Apollo 11 had come here to train. There was not a leaf to be seen, though it was early fall and the maples and birches around Huntsville and North Bay were just beginning to take on their autumn colours. Off in the distance, we could see the stacks of the Inco and Falconbridge mines, high trails of thick white smoke rising into the sky. In 1967 no one had even heard of acid rain.

Laurentian University is built high on the rocks above Ramsay Lake. When I arrived it had three residences: Thorneloe, which had an Anglican Church connection; Huntington, connected to the United Church; and Université de Sudbury ("U de S"), which was tied to the Catholic Church. Thorneloe held about sixty students, all male, most sharing a room. Huntington was coed, with about two hundred students, and another two hundred or so were at the Catholic residence. Rules were strict—no girls allowed anywhere but the common room at Thorneloe, no opposite sexes behind closed doors at the other two residences. Not that it really mattered: the male to female ratio was eight to one.

The culture was very much northern Ontario, small town, working class, more English than French. But French had a presence, as there was a strong contingent of Franco-Ontarians, as well as a requirement that every first-year student take a course in conversational French. All signage and announcements were in both languages, though official bilingualism in Canada was still years off.

The "Summer of Love" was behind us, but you wouldn't ever head for Sudbury with "flowers in your hair." Hair was certainly getting longer, but the drug of choice—really, the only drug—was beer. With the campus's lopsided student body, drinking far outranked sex.

Sudbury had a population of about 150,000 in those years. The two main employers, Inco and Falconbridge, were both mining companies working the Sudbury Basin, a vast valley formed 1.8 billion years earlier when a massive meteor crashed into earth during the Paleoproterozoic era. In 1883, during the building of the transcontinental railway, silver deposits were discovered, and today a massive five-cent coin—a Canadian nickel—stands at the city entrance as a reminder of why this community came into existence.

Inco then employed a quarter of the city's workforce. Its stacks and slag heaps were among the most identifiable features of Sudbury's rather bleak landscape. The downtown was ugly, but the many surrounding lakes, including Ramsay, and the stark Canadian Shield terrain gave the area a certain beauty. Those who lived there loved their city, and students who came from elsewhere soon developed a deep affection for Sudbury.

One of the older students at Thorneloe, Jim Miller, was a bit eccentric—his nickname was "Wiley," after the cartoon character Wile E. Coyote—and had calling cards that identified him as the president of the "Stompin' Tom Connors Fan Club." Stompin' Tom was such a minor figure in the Canadian music scene in those days that many of the students had never heard of him—even if from time to time he crashed at the residence while playing Sudbury-area bars. He was much loved by the miners, however, especially with his most popular song, "Sudbury Saturday Night," which he sang in that oddly nasal voice while his cowboy boot stomped the plywood "floor" he carried on stage with his guitar: "Da girls are out to Bingo and the boys are getting stinko / And we think no more of Inco on a Sudbury Saturday night."

The students frequented the hotel beer parlours—the Nickel Range, the Coulson, the Caswell—but going out required someone who had a car, downtown being several kilometres from the campus. There was also the matter of false ID, as the Ontario drinking age was then twenty-one. More often there would be beer runs, either to the nearest Brewers Retail or all the way out Lorne Street to Doran's Brewery, where a case of twenty-four could be had for less than five dollars. The basement of Thorneloe Residence had a makeshift bar, a fridge and a sound system. Volunteers tended bar. For a quarter, you could have a cold pint of Doran's Northern Ale. It wasn't as much fun as a downtown bar, and women guests were beyond rare, but the price was right. We were there to learn, and we learned to drink.

I arrived at university convinced that it would prove too hard, but at least I would be able to say I went to university. I signed up for English, history, political science, religion, philosophy, biology and French. Along with conversational French at least one science course was also required. I believed my major would end up being English. It wouldn't.

My roommate in first year was Bill Western, from the southern Ontario town of Grimsby. He chain-smoked, rarely studied but was great fun. Everyone called him "Junior" because his older brother, John, was a year ahead and one of the student leaders at Thorneloe. The day I first met John he and another council member sat at a table with suits on and wrote down on a thick pad of paper the names and physical measurements of each cute coed filing out of the bookstore. Most happily offered their measurements. The college called its various sports teams—I played hockey—the "Nads" so that those in the stands, should there ever be anyone there, could shout "go Nads go!" It was very much a different time.

I was already friends with the Cox brothers, but soon had great new friends in Terry Kohls from Pembroke, a small city north of Ottawa along the Ottawa River, Peter Simpson from Chapleau, a town even farther to the north, and Jack Andrews from Cochrane, another northern town. Kohls, already in third year, was a gentle soul who had the first Leonard Cohen album any of us had heard. Simpson, a brilliant musician who would go on to tour the continent in a Vegas-style band, was in most of my classes. We all wore bulky blue leather jackets—the school year was *cold* in northern Ontario—with "LAURENTIAN" in large yellow letters across the back, our department in smaller yellow letters below, and our expected year of graduation in yellow numbers on our right sleeves. Mine said "Laurentian Arts" on the back, "70" on the arm.

Thorneloe had its own little publication, *The Thorne*, which appeared irregularly and was distributed about the campus. I signed up and began writing opinionated columns. Early on, I attacked the head of the Student General Association for his terrible choice in music; he brought in a 1940s-style swing band for a school dance when the students were far more interested in the Rolling Stones than Glenn Miller. I wondered what the reaction was going to be and soon found out.

The phone in the first-floor room I shared with Junior rang. I picked it up and a harsh voice said, "MacGregor?"

"You got him."

"*This is a warning,*" the angry voice hissed. "*You're going to pay big time for that bullshit you wrote! We're going to kick the living crap out of you!*"

The phone slammed down at the other end. I sat there in shock.

"What was that?" Junior called from his fog of smoke on the other side of the room.

I told him what the caller had said. He listened, nodded and asked, "You think it was serious?"

"Very."

"*Jesus!*" Junior shook his head.

We went off to the common room, where there was a television— *Rat Patrol* was a residence favourite—and tables and chairs for card playing, mostly hearts. As Junior and I related what had happened, Terry Kohls came in from a class in the portables at the bottom of the hill. He interrupted us when the name of the student union president came up. "He's in my poli-sci class," Terry said. "And is he ever pissed about the article you wrote."

I was suddenly frightened. I knew the power of words from that childish editorial on Hidden Valley that appeared in *The Pundit*, but no one in Huntsville had ever threatened to "kick the living crap out of" me. Sudbury was a hard-rock town. "We had a good fight," Stompin' Tom sang, as if fisticuffs were an essential part of the Saturday night entertainment.

"You think he's serious?" I asked Terry.

Terry's eyebrows rose. "He's really mad at you," he said. "And so are some of his buddies on council."

"Don't sweat it," Jack Andrews advised. "It'll all blow over. In the meantime, don't be alone walking to class, okay? We'll stick with you."

Bless Jack's heart. Along with Terry and Junior and some of the others, the young men of Thorneloe formed a small militia that would defend the press and freedom of expression. They sat with me in the cafeteria for every meal. They formed what Jack tagged "the flying wedge" to walk me to classes, with me in the middle surrounded by fit young men in their blue leather jackets. I felt safe, but still worried.

By the third day, the flying wedge was starting to fray. My concern grew. By the end of the week, all would be forgotten—except by the union president and his honchos. I mentioned this to Terry and Jack as they and two others saw me to the portable where I was taking the required philosophy course.

"You have nothing to worry about," Jack said with a huge smile.

"Why's that?"

"Because," said Terry, with a straight face, "I'm the one who made that call."

Instantly, his voice changed to that threatening voice. Same tone, same words: *"We're going to kick the living crap out of you!"*

"You?"

"Me," he nodded.

"You knew, too?" I said to Jack, my other best friend who would die for me and my right to freedom of expression.

Jack nodded and burst out laughing, as did the others.

"How many knew?" I asked, feeling my face turn the colour of a stop sign.

"Everyone," said Jack.

"Everyone?"

"Everyone. We all knew. The flying wedge was just a joke. We wanted to see how long we could keep yanking your chain."

It was, admittedly, a brilliant joke they played on me, but it was also an accidental lesson: Know that words written down have a different power, a far more lasting power than those spoken. Be aware of possible repercussions before they happen. Think about what you say if it's going on paper.

In second year, I went to the offices of *Lambda*, the official student newspaper, and signed up to volunteer. I wrote some columns on music—this year, the student union brought in the Lovin' Spoonful, which made me think perhaps my controversial editorial in *The Thorne* had had its effect—and also some bad poetry, which the paper published alongside all the other bad poetry being written by students.

Lambda had real clout, not the fancied clout of those putting out *The Thorne* on a Gestetner machine. It was on real newsprint and printed at a proper shop. It had photographs and art and was, at times, an excellent publication with which I was proud to be associated. And it took up causes.

The university had a cause. A real cause of real concern to the student body. Much was written and much said about this cause, and soon the students were ready to march in support of it.

This was 1968, remember. It has been called "the most tumultuous year" in history. Everyone in the world seemed to be marching, and rioting. The war in Vietnam was a disaster, the year opening with the Tet offensive. The North Vietnamese and Viet Cong were launching attacks so vicious—in one week alone in February, American losses were 543 dead, 2,547 wounded in action—that the American stomach for war turned abruptly.

In early April, Martin Luther King Jr. was assassinated in Memphis, his death sparking riots in dozens of cities across the United States. Students at Columbia University in New York City occupied buildings for days until police broke up the demonstrators, beating and arresting hundreds of them. Out of this grew a massive, worldwide student movement, with huge demonstrations everywhere from Mexico City to

Poland. In Paris, students and police clashed in the Latin Quarter on "Bloody Monday" (May 6), leaving hundreds injured. President Charles de Gaulle threatened to send in the military against the students, dissolved the National Assembly and called an election that he won by basically bashing student protesters.

In early June, Robert F. Kennedy, then running for president, was assassinated in Los Angeles. Two months later, when the Kennedy-less Democrats gathered in Chicago to choose a new nominee—they chose vice-president Hubert Humphrey, who still supported the war—tens of thousands of students descended on the city along with the Black Panthers, the Yippies and the strident SDS (Students for a Democratic Society). Mayor Richard Daley called out the police and television cameras rolled as bloody clash after bloody clash churned through downtown Chicago.

That was the student mood of North America in the fall of 1968 as Laurentian University again filled up with students. Most were from northern Ontario, which seemed a far, far place from Chicago. Yet the residences all had televisions. We saw and read the news. Most were watching that fall when the Olympics were held in Mexico City and American athletes Tommie Smith and John Carlos raised their black-gloved fists during the playing of the US national anthem. Black power was a reality. Student power was sweeping the globe. And Sudbury, isolated as it was, was part of that globe.

We felt the movement.

Word got out to the local media that the students of Laurentian were secretly planning a huge protest downtown, in front of city hall. The secret planning suddenly went into the open, with *Lambda* fully in support of such student action.

That Saturday, hundreds of us made our way downtown in cars, half-tons and the city bus service. The police, well alerted, were out in force, some in riot gear. They would not stop us so long as we protested nicely, as Canadians are wont to do. They had closed off the nearby streets and they stood off to the side, armed and ready, and simply stared at us. Uniforms and weapons versus long hair and attitude.

We were nervous but determined to speak out about the enormous injustice that had been served on the student population of Laurentian University. We had signs and fists to pump and we had our voices. We formed into groups and began walking toward city hall.

We chanted, loud and clear. Not about Vietnam. Not about assassinations. Not about student bashing. Not about Black Power or Student Power, but about Beer Power.

"We want a pub!" we roared in unison.

"We want a pub!

"We want a pub!

"We want a pub!

"WE WANT A PUB! . . ."

In second year, you had to choose your major, and I went with political science. Anyone who read newspapers was already near a passing mark in the subject, and a B average could be had with precious little work. That appealed to me, as it left lots of time for far more important subjects, such as quaffing beer, consuming seventeen-cent hamburgers from the DeLuxe fast-food outlets and reading books by Kerouac, Kurt Vonnegut Jr., Ken Kesey and Hermann Hesse, not to mention the innumerable soft-porn paperbacks that were traded about the residence like we had once exchanged comic books.

The original plan had been to get a four-year honours degree. I had the marks but hardly the interest. In the spring of 1970, I decided to graduate with a three-year general degree instead and travel to Europe—more on that later—not returning to Canada until early 1971. Ralph had an uncle and aunt in Toronto who were spending winters in Florida and unwisely offered their handsome north Toronto bungalow to us if we would keep the drive shovelled. We did, but it surely would have cost less to hire a ploughing contractor than it did to clean the drapes and furniture of all the smoke, legal and otherwise, that we and our Toronto friends blew into that little home.

With a place to live, I now set about looking for my first post-university job. McGraw-Hill Ryerson, a publisher of educational texts, had an advertisement in the *Toronto Star* for copy editors. That sounded promising. I took the Bloor subway east and then a bus near the end of the line that dropped me off at the company's old Scarborough address. They had me do a short grammar test, which I passed easily, and then I was interviewed by a woman who spoke as if self-editing—"whom" rather than "who"—with nothing even close to a dangling participle. In the end, she offered me a job: a hundred dollars a week, two weeks holiday a year. I was ecstatic. For the next five months, I edited and often rewrote textbooks prepared by high-school teachers on topics as varied as war and nutrition.

Over-editing is a curse in all levels of writing, whether books or newspapers. Those who over-edit would rather be the writer and, clearly, I was one of those villains. I was rewriting virtually everything that came across my desk. It was unfair to those who had submitted the material; it was wrong, and I knew it. I would not be long in the book publishing business.

My cousin Don McCormick was now teaching at Huntsville High, running the science department, where Ellen's father still taught. Don had a good friend in the school's English department named Wayne Lilley. Wayne was a hockey and lacrosse player and we got on well from the very first meeting. Wayne also had ambitions to write and had been looking at a graduate diploma course in journalism offered at the University of Western Ontario. He sent away for information and shared it with me one weekend when I was back in town visiting the family. I shared the Western journalism material with Ralph, and all three of us ended up applying for the course and all three were accepted.

And so, in September of 1971, we all set off for London, Ontario. Wayne had his own car—as well as a wife and two young children back in Huntsville—and Ralph again had a used car, an Austin Mini Cooper, courtesy of his father's dealership. Ralph and I rented a walk-up apartment in the city's east end and began checking around the campus before classes were officially to begin. We dropped in on the campus paper, *The Gazette*, which had a sign outside its offices saying they were looking for volunteer reporters, designers and columnists. Thanks to clippings from *Lambda* and some fast talking, we were taken on as record reviewers. All we had to do was contact the major record distributors, and they were more than happy to send us their newest releases, as college newspapers were then considered an ideal way to reach a most coveted target group. By evening, we would be listening to the latest music. By day, we would be taking classes in what turned out to be a completely bizarre program in journalism.

There were more than fifty of us in the University of Western Ontario's graduate program in journalism. The students came from all over the country. It was a cockeyed situation where, generally speaking, the students were far superior to the teachers when it came to practising their trade. Many of these gifted students moved on to careers with the CBC (David James, Robbie Robertson), *Maclean's* magazine (Hal Quinn, me), broadcasting (Cheryl Hawkes), business writing (Wayne Lilley, Ralph Cox), and international television reporting and teaching (Jacques Grenier). Many had long careers at the same outlet—Greg Burliuk, for example, retired as a columnist after forty years at the *Kingston Whig-Standard*. Several others landed excellent jobs in Canadian media.

The professors, on the other hand, were mostly aged newspapermen; they liked to call themselves, with a touch of irony, "ink-stained wretches." Many hadn't worked on newspapers in years and even then had had short careers before moving on to teaching. There were two instructors the students adored—former CBC radio reporter Ron Laplante and former newspaper reporter Mac Laing—and the rest were mostly dismissed. The elderly gentleman teaching the history of journalism course droned on about carrier pigeons and was soon speaking to empty classrooms. Just before final exams, Ralph took the textbook this guy had been using, read it in an all-nighter, wrote the exam and passed by a fair margin. His returned paper came with an attached note: as the professor was heading into full retirement, perhaps Ralph would consider teaching this course next year as a seasonal lecturer.

Our entire class agreed that the most annoying lecturer was the man charged with teaching us magazine journalism, the course in which I was most interested. Tall, chrome-domed and constantly snapping his gum, Prof. Wilson Bryan Key opened his very first class by blasting a student for daring to record the lecture—a curious reaction given that we were all starting to work with recorders and would be using them during interviews. He then rearranged the seats so that no one could sit behind him, where he might not see exactly what they were up to. There was always an air of paranoia with Professor Key.

Wilson Bryan Key was an American, and he was then working on a book on subliminal advertising. It was his contention that all successful ads contained hidden sexual signs designed to arouse your interest and drive you to desire whatever was being advertised. He would begin most classes with a slide show on a projector, putting up various advertisements that allowed him to show the class which ad for underwear had a clear erection going and what a woman putting on lipstick was really up to. We rarely missed a class.

One morning we arrived to see that he had already set up the projector and was showing the cover of the October 1971 issue of *Playboy*. A beautiful young woman with a huge Afro was lounging, presumably stark naked, behind a white chair shaped in the form of the *Playboy* bunny.

"Does anybody see it?" he asked, grinding his gum.

No one said a thing.

"It's so *obvious!*" he barked.

Then, using a pointer, he went over her backlit Afro curl by curl. He said the magazine artists had manipulated the curls so that they spelled out a very clear message: "I am a virgin and I want you to fuck me!"

Professor Key insisted we put subliminal sex into our writings, no matter what the topic, and gave failing marks to those stories in which he could find none. He hated being challenged, let alone taped. One of the students wanted to know what, exactly, he had written that qualified him to teach long-form writing. He said that much of his work had been in defence. He had, for example, written the manual for NORAD, the Canadian-American joint defence system for the North. Asked if we could see it, he shook his head: "Sorry, it's top-secret classified information. I'm not allowed to show it to anyone without clearance."

An early magazine assignment for us from Professor Key was to defend Canada's defence policy in the pages of *Chatelaine*. One of the students quickly fired off a pitch letter to Doris Anderson, the long-time editor of the publication that promoted itself as "A magazine for Canada's women." Anderson replied, "You must be joking."

Key did eventually publish his "findings." *Subliminal Seduction: Are You Being Sexually Aroused by This Picture?* came out a couple of years after we graduated. There were other books—including *The Clam-Plate Orgy and Other Subliminal Techniques for Manipulating Your Behavior*—and there were even books published debunking his wild theories. There were so many complaints about his teaching at Western that the university soon shook free of him, and he returned to the United States. In 2008, he passed away in Reno, Nevada, at the age of eighty-three.

The students were so profoundly unimpressed by the diploma course that in the lead-up to the Christmas break we openly discussed hiring a lawyer to fight for refunds. It got no further than the discussion stage, though. Professors Laplante and Laing were actually teaching something of value. And besides, it would be only a few more months until the students would, at least, have a piece of paper to argue that we were trained journalists.

Then we could see about actually becoming journalists.

In my final year of post-secondary education, such as the diploma in journalism was, Ellen and I returned to Huntsville at Thanksgiving. She had finished high school in five years with excellent marks. She was named class valedictorian and soon was off to the University of Guelph for a four-year course in fine art. For one of those four years I was in London, roughly ninety minutes away, and we spent many weekends together in either London or Guelph.

Ellen's summer jobs had been at Camp Tawingo, a popular children's summer camp on the north shore of Lake Vernon, a brief ride from Huntsville out Ravenscliffe Road. She was hired to teach crafts, and her background in fine arts made her perfect for the job. She was instantly tagged "Crafty Lady" and became very popular with the staff and the Pearse family, who owned Tawingo. Jack Pearse, head of the camp, had a strict "no facial hair" rule for all male staff. By now I had long hair and a full dark beard, but he never said a word about me showing up a couple of evenings a week and on weekends.

Thanksgiving weekend of 1971 saw Ellen and me now very seriously into a sixth year of "going steady." I was working up the courage to ask the obvious question. With the families gathered in Huntsville and everyone in a good mood, it seemed the ideal opportunity.

The evening before the big Sunday dinner, several of us were at the "Rock," a motel and popular dance bar south of Huntsville along Highway 11. There was beer and much laughter and dancing to a small local band.

Ellen knew the question was coming and said an immediate "Yes!" which was followed by a kiss. Others at the table knew exactly what had happened. We all celebrated long into the night. The following day we told our families and knew that we had just had the greatest Thanksgiving gathering ever.

Years later, the Rock was torn down and demolished. The Ontario Department of Transportation and Communications brought in bulldozers and graders, cleared the site and turned it into a roadside rest area, complete with picnic tables and outhouses.

Once our children were old enough, I delighted in taking them to this spot, pointing to the outdoor toilets and saying, "This is where I proposed to your mother."

"*Ooooohhhhh . . . disgusting! . . .*"

If every person has a story, so does every place.

SUMMER JOBS

Classes wrapped up by the end of May, which meant you had a good three months in which to earn the thousand dollars or so you'd need on top of your student loan and grant to carry you through the school year.

After my first year at Laurentian I actually landed a job in journalism—sort of . . .

Another teacher pal of cousin Don McCormick had the contract for delivering the *Globe and Mail* to carriers and businesses throughout Muskoka and points north. I landed the most northern route: the town of Huntsville, up Highway 11, to Burk's Falls, including drop-offs at Novar, Emsdale, Kearney, Sundridge and various gas stations and resorts along the way. I set out each morning before dawn in my mother's new little four-cylinder Simca and was done in time to get in eighteen morning holes at the Huntsville Downs golf course.

My most unusual summer job, however, followed graduation from Laurentian University, when I saw an advertisement in the *Huntsville Forester* for a "tap man" at the Empire Hotel on Main Street—a bar locally known as the "Snake Pit." I was now old enough to be in a bar; I applied and began work the next day. The salary was eighty dollars a week and tips, though the tap man was never tipped as much as the servers.

I learned to "run twenty" by reaching for one glass with my left hand while filling another glass in my right, then spinning the empty glass under the tap just as the first glass filled. I learned to scream "*Is Gordon here?*" when I answered the phone, even though Gordon was sitting directly in front of me. It was invariably Gordon's wife calling and Gordon always tipped if someone could yell "*No!*" and hang up.

One slow Saturday afternoon, a stranger came in with two bags packed full of greenish clear plastic sheets. He walked up to the black-and-white television and slapped one of the sheets over the picture. Then he stood back and pointed. "There you see it, gentlemen, instant colour. Surprise the little lady tonight. Give her blue skies and green grass for *Bonanza*. Turn that old black-and-white into a colour TV for a mere five bucks. Whaddya say?" The bags of clear plastic emptied quickly, the man walked out with a roll of fives and I ran twenty just to make sure I was awake.

The best nights were always when Philip, 250 pounds and gentle, would drop around. Philip sounded exactly like Elvis Presley and was so shy he'd join the country band on stage only after several drinks and on the condition that he could keep his eyes closed.

One *very* slow Saturday, we were asked if we'd host a wedding reception. The couple, like so many of the rural people around Muskoka, Ontario, were dirt poor, and the bride was underage, but we said why not and figured we'd have a few laughs. The groom, hair unruly as a haystack, was resplendent in a new Eaton's suit with but one tag still attached. The bride was in her grandmother's satin wedding dress, which she'd updated by taking scissors and cutting across about three inches above the knees, no hemming, and it was fraying at a shocking rate. Over her left breast she wore a large black handprint, hopefully her new husband's.

The money from the newlyweds and their families ran out within the hour, but by then the Pit had taken their happiness to heart. As the place filled up so did the beer kitty on their table, and the night wore on through endless toasts and dancing. Around midnight the groom was located in a familiar spot, asleep on a john in the men's washroom, but the wedding party got him away into the night. Not, however, before the tearful bride kissed her thanks to everyone in the place.

On my final night of that summer, after last round had been called and served and after the last drunk had been spilled out onto the sidewalk, the boss ran twenty himself and brought them over to a table. We drank and reminisced, and later we all wandered off to the home of one of the waitresses, where we stayed up till dawn singing and drinking and saying goodbyes.

When someone noticed the sky pinking over the town, we all went out into the backyard. And as the sun rose, big Philip set his bottle down in the dew, closed his eyes, and sang the Lord's Prayer in his best Elvis voice. Several of those gathered began to weep.

I knew that night that you could find a story anywhere, and where the very best would come from would often surprise you.

CANOE CRAZY

The canoe was a favourite early date for us. Ellen and I would borrow cousin Don's red cedar and canvas canoe and paddle down the Big East River to Lake Vernon, where we would picnic on a long, very private sandbar, perfect for skinny dipping. We also canoed in Algonquin Park, little aware that canoe tripping would become such an important and beloved part of our lives together.

We loved to paddle and did so every summer from university on.

In the annoying pandemic winter of 2020–2021 there was much talk about the high value of therapy pets—dogs and cats that would be taken to long-term care homes to provide a little emotional support and comfort. I found mine in my garage. I would go out, periodically, and let the stress and anxiety ooze out by patting and petting and stroking my . . . canoe.

It hangs upside down from the ceiling, a cedar and canvas Northland canoe built by Albert Maw of Huntsville and painted fire-truck red by his summer assistant, my younger brother Tom. It is still, more than four decades on, in magnificent shape, with but one small patch from a foolish run down a swollen spring creek a few years back with our daughter Christine and her young children, Fisher and Sadie. The canoe cost $750 in 1978, money that came from a gold medal entry for politics in this country's very first National Magazine Awards.

On a shelf behind where I type this today is a framed photograph, taken by my daughter Jocelyn, of the Northland canoe sitting empty by a campsite on Burnt Island Lake, the water so calm at dawn it looks as if the canoe has been pulled up onto a mirror. On the wall in front of me is a copy of a brilliant magazine illustration by Peter Swan. It was done for the first magazine feature article I ever wrote, "The

Great Canoe Lake Mystery," for the September 1973 issue of *Maclean's* magazine. Peter did a perfect copy of Tom Thomson's famous *West Wind*, but then deftly added in a ghostly addition: Tom kneeling in his canoe, paddling hard against the churning whitecaps.

It seems I can't escape canoes. But I also use canoes for escape.

Our mother canoed to get away. At one point, she was raising four children under the age of seven—her own three (Tom would come along later) and a nephew whose mother had suffered a postpartum breakdown. Where she lived in winter and where she moved to in summer had no running water, and in the summer home, no electricity. She paddled in the evening after all the cooking, washing and caring for four unruly youngsters.

Helen McCormick MacGregor taught me to paddle. Her J-stroke was like a whisper, mine like a fender bender as I clunked the paddle's edge along the gunwales.

But I soon learned to paddle the length of Lake of Two Rivers without ever once having to extract the paddle completely from the silky, still waters. Eventually I would paddle much of Algonquin Park. I would move from flatwater to whitewater. I would cherish rolling down the mighty Petawawa with my friend Phil Chester, running Quebec's magnificent Dumoine with Wally Schaber, dancing effortlessly down British Columbia's Kootenay with Ellen and Jocelyn.

Canoes have given me so much I like to think I was able to return the favour in the spring of 2007.

I was coming to the end of a five-year, five-column-a-week stint on the treasured page 2 spot in the *Globe and Mail*. The idea—to tour Canada almost endlessly, writing about the people and places—had been the brainchild of then editor Ed Greenspon, as had been the title for the column, "This Country." It was this unelected "office," surely, that led the CBC to ask that I serve as one of the jurors for a contest the public broadcaster was launching to identify the Seven Wonders of Canada.

The exercise began innocently. It had come out of a story meeting for CBC Radio's morning show, "Sounds Like Canada," and host Shelagh Rogers had invited listeners to send in their submissions. She would later say they were looking for a couple of thousand, at best, and were overwhelmed to discover they had tapped into something Canadians felt so passionately about that the show received some twenty-five thousand entries.

Many of the nominations were obvious, such as Niagara Falls, the Rockies, the CN Tower, but some others were delightfully eccentric and personal, such as "Mum's house in Scarborough." The CBC would first measure the nominations by number of votes, then pare the nominations down to fifty or so before bringing in a panel of judges to determine the final seven. Seemed simple enough.

The two other judges asked to preside—no pay, but inside work and no heavy lifting—were Ra McGuire and Roberta Jamieson. Ra, leader of the legendary Canadian rock band Trooper—hits such as "Raise a Little Hell" and "We're Here for a Good Time (Not a Long Time)"—came from British Columbia but knew the country intimately after more than thirty years of touring. Roberta, a former ombudsman of the province of Ontario, was a Mohawk from Six Nations in southwestern Ontario and head of the National Aboriginal Achievement Foundation. The judging panel was far from perfect—no francophone, no easterner, all from roughly the same age demographic—but the three of us were about as familiar with the country as it is possible for any three citizens to be.

Throughout April and May the CBC continued to receive nominations and then, in house, pared down the master list to fifty-two. These included such obvious choices as the Rockies and Niagara Falls and Old Quebec City, but also such familiar landmarks as Gros Morne National Park, Percé Rock, the Cypress Hills, the Northwest Passage, the Cabot Trail and Haida Gwaii. There were human creations as well as the natural wonders: the Vimy Memorial, the Rideau Canal, the Manitoba Legislative Building, the Stanley Cup. From that long list of fifty-two wonders, listeners were asked to vote on their favourites. And this is when it really got wild. CBC received more than a million votes. At times the voting was so heavy that the computers doing the calculating crashed.

The greatest vote-getter of all turned out to be the Sleeping Giant, a rock formation on a Lake Superior peninsula that, viewed from the harbour of Thunder Bay, looks eerily like a giant in repose. The Giant tallied 177,305 votes to finish first overall—an uncanny display of community involvement considering that the population of the Thunder Bay area was then listed at 120,370. The tally outraged the people of Niagara Falls, who had presumed—a bit arrogantly, a bit with cause—that their world-famous natural wonder would lead the pack. The famous falls, it turned out, had received less than half the number of votes that had gone to the Giant (81,818), leading to accusations from Falls supporters that there was chicanery at work at the Lakehead. The Falls group even produced an expert in information technology who claimed that he had a "confession" from a fellow IT expert in Thunder Bay that a computer program called "Ghostmouse 2.0" had been used to vote in a continuous loop with a single click of a mouse. The Thunder Bay people denied any such nefarious plan, and eventually the "cheating" fuss died down.

CBC Radio's "Sounds Like Canada" and CBC Television's *The National* announced what the public voting had determined to be the Seven Wonders of Canada: (1) the Sleeping Giant (177,305), (2) Niagara Falls (81,818), (3) the Bay of Fundy (67,670), (4) the Nahanni River (64,920), (5) the northern lights (61,417), (6) the Rocky Mountains (55,630) and (7) the Cabot Trail (44,073). We three judges were then to winnow the top fifty-two down to fifteen and then to the final seven. While the public's voting was to be a significant factor, it was not to be the deciding factor. The final decision would lie with us.

Peter Mansbridge was hosting. He introduced the judges and ran a short clip of each talking about the challenge.

We fairly easily got the list down to a final fifteen—the Bay of Fundy, the Cabot Trail, Cathedral Grove, Gros Morne, Haida Gwaii, the Nahanni, Niagara Falls, the northern lights, Old Quebec City, Pier 21, Prairie skies, the Sleeping Giant, the canoe, the igloo, the Rockies. That evening I scanned down the final list and, frankly, could easily have voted for all fifteen of them. One, however, struck me as being easiest of all to embrace—it had, after all, no actual *location* and it was becoming obvious that geographical correctness was going to have a say. Yet this homeless nomination might, in many other ways, be most symbolic of all of Canada and Canadian history. It alone covered both history and geography and was, to me, the greatest wonder of a wonderful country.

The canoe.

I was happy to champion this nominee. After all, as legendary paddler and outdoors filmmaker Bill Mason liked to say, "First God created a canoe—then he created a country to go with it."

The great stories of Canada—Champlain's voyage, David Thompson's map-making, the Hudson's Bay Company and the Company of Adventurers—all were written by canoe. The great art of the country—Tom Thomson, the Group of Seven—was painted by canoe. Let the American silver dollar say "In God We Trust." Ours had a canoe on it for largely the same reasons—trust and faith.

The next evening, part 2 of the contest opened *The National*. We began by laying down our cards. Each of the final fifteen had been given a large card and we had to lay down our personal seven. Roberta opened with Pier 21, the igloo, Haida Gwaii, the Cabot Trail, the canoe (!), Niagara Falls and Prairie skies. Ra followed with Haida Gwaii, Niagara Falls, the Rockies, the igloo, (and then, so quietly I didn't quite hear he added) the canoe, Old Quebec City, and the Bay of Fundy. I laid down my first card, the canoe, then added the Rockies,

Niagara Falls, Old Quebec City, the Nahanni, the Cabot Trail and Prairie skies, arguing that with the skies we got two for one, in that we could also use this to cover the northern lights. We were already in the process of killing off.

It was remarkable how much in accord we were. But it was also remarkable that this accord spelled the end of the Sleeping Giant. I had actually been the one to do the dirty work, removing the Sleeping Giant card and replacing it with the canoe, which all three of us had chosen as a wonder of Canada. We put the chosen cards down. Pier 21 in the east, Old Quebec City, Niagara Falls, the canoe, Prairie skies, the Rockies, and high above all the others, the igloo.

As Peter Mansbridge announced the final results, photographs of the seven went up on a screen behind him.

And number one was the canoe.

In a remarkable coincidence, I was headed, days later, to Thunder Bay for, gulp, the Sleeping Giant Writers Festival. I had committed to this event months before the CBC had even dreamed up the Seven Wonders contest.

I was met at the airport by a local camera crew demanding that I explain myself, which I did rather badly.

I was in the news business. But this time on the wrong side of it.

3

The Grand Tour(s)

We had the travel itch—bad . . .

It was 1968 and I had just turned twenty. It was the end of first-year university, first summer after the "Summer of Love." Remember singing along with Scott McKenzie? "If you're going to San Francisco be sure to wear some flowers in your hair . . ."

It seemed to our tight group of Laurentian friends that the whole world was happening somewhere other than Sudbury. As mentioned in the previous chapter, Bobby Kennedy and Martin Luther King Jr. had been assassinated. Young Americans were taking to the streets of Chicago to protest the war in Vietnam. Rock music was in its prime—the Rolling Stones released "Sympathy for the Devil," the Beatles answered with "Hey Jude"—and marijuana was everywhere, it seemed, but on that bare rock hill up from Sudbury's Ramsay Lake.

And yet, we were still plugged in, thanks to radio stations and record stores and subscriptions to publications like *Creem* and *Rolling Stone*. We sat with our stubby beers and listened to Bob Dylan and Joan Baez. Terry Kohls played Leonard Cohen's "So Long, Marianne" and "Suzanne" on the portable record player in his second-floor room—

and a few of us went to Toronto to see Phil Ochs play the Riverboat.

On a clear Sunday evening in Huntsville, the little transistor radio would sometimes pick up the signal from WBZ Radio in Boston. With luck, Tom Rush would be singing "Urge for Going" by Canada's Joni Mitchell, whom Ralph and I and a couple of friends had seen the year before at the Mariposa Folk Festival. The song could well have been about our hometown: "I awoke today and found the frost perched on the town / It hovered in a frozen sky, then it gobbled summer down / When the sun turns traitor cold / And all the trees are shivering in a naked row." It could have been about us when next she sang: "I get the urge for going."

We wanted to be Sal Paradise in Kerouac's *On the Road*, living out treasured quotes, like "there was nowhere to go but everywhere" and "nothing behind me, everything ahead of me, as is ever so on the road." We thought the Zen of *The Dharma Bums* was beyond profound. "Ah Japhy you taught me the final lesson of them all, you can't fall off a mountain." Doesn't matter that I haven't a clue what that means today, in my seventies; in the first year of my twenties it meant everything and more.

All winter of my first year Ralph and I talked about hitchhiking around Europe. Jack Andrews, the wavy-haired sports nut from the northern Ontario town of Cochrane, said he'd like to come along, and we were delighted to have him. Our travel talk was not, however, met with much enthusiasm by our families or girlfriends. Some thought it foolish; some worried it would be the end of a relationship, as it would prove to be for Ralph and his girlfriend, Robin, a close neighbour of mine back in Huntsville. I had only one year of university under my belt; Ralph and Jack had two, but we wouldn't listen to those who wisely advised first getting our degrees.

We figured we could save up a minimum of a thousand dollars from our various summer jobs and have enough to survive the winter in

Spain or Portugal, where it was said you could live for pennies a day. Okay, "5 dollars" a day, as the Arthur Frommer book we carried with us put it.

We decided to drop out of school for a year and hit the road.

Good thing we didn't buy return tickets . . .

It was Ralph who found the advertisement in the student newspaper. Transglobe Airways was offering an opportunity to "fly to Europe for $108!" Bus transportation would be provided from Toronto to Buffalo International Airport, with departure slated for 3 a.m., September 7, 1968, landing at Gatwick Airport, London. We immediately sent away our cheques for tickets. No one had credit cards at that time.

Less than three months later, Transglobe Airways would cease operations. But first it would get us to Europe.

In Buffalo, we boarded Transglobe's old Bristol Britannia turboprop for an excruciating ten-hour flight to England. We sat in seats 6D, 6E and 6F, far enough from the overflowing toilet that somewhere over the Atlantic had to be shut down entirely. We landed at Gatwick and took the train into London, heading straight to Misses Reese's hostel, where a place to sleep was advertised for less than a pound a night.

"A place to sleep" did not necessarily mean "bed," as bodies so badly outnumbered mattresses that eight of us slept on a floor in a room that didn't even have a bed. Jack Kerouac would have been proud.

We stayed two nights at this rat's nest of a hostel and spent our days walking around London, taking in the obvious sights: Speakers' Corner, Hyde Park, Piccadilly, Regent's Park Zoo . . . We ate and drank our meals in whatever pub we came across while hungry or, more likely, thirsty. We talked endlessly about where we would go—the Lake District, Scotland, France, Spain . . .

Only . . . how . . . were . . . we . . . going . . . to . . . get . . . there?

We were, if I may remind you, young and foolish—perhaps even idiotic. While we balked at paying forty pounds for a rundown Vauxhall van that had a For Sale sign taped to a side window, we raced to pay 128 pounds each for small motorcycles. The *idea* of a motorcycle delighted me, as I had never forgotten the joys of that little Honda 55 Brent and Eric and I took to North Bay and back . . . well, almost back . . . That evening we drank at the Windsor Hotel and talked about how sweet it would be to feel the wind in our faces and how cool our Laurentian U leather jackets would be on a bike and how the "birds" of England would, naturally, be all over these handsome Canadian bikers in their Laurentian colours.

Next morning we took the tube to the Elephant & Castle stop and walked to a dealership where we paid for three brand-new BSA Bantams, 125 cc, helmets thrown in free. Jack had one caveat: "I've never driven a motorcycle." No problem, the salesman told us, we'll get you practised up out back.

And so, after a half-hour of instruction, three motorcyclists from Canada struck out into the London traffic having never driven on the other side of the road, with one so unsure of himself that, on the advice of the wise salesman, we actually tied a rope from Jack's bike to mine so that he could follow me, the most experienced biker of the three.

Somehow, with one of us weaving through traffic like a leashed puppy, we made it out of London. Once free of the city, we cut Jack free, literally, and he was able to negotiate UK traffic fine. The bikes were not large but they could cruise at 100 kilometres an hour, meaning we never held up traffic. We rode 120 kilometres that first day to Sittingbourne, slept in a trailer and had a great breakfast for seven shillings. We moved on to Canterbury, where we toured the cathedral where Thomas Becket had been murdered in 1170.

We ran into flooding at Three Bridges that had been so severe three lives had been lost the night before. We encountered cold weather that made the rundown van seem like a lost dream. We toured cathedrals and ate in pubs and increasingly argued over who would find the coming night's accommodations. On a windy day in the Cumberland Mountains heading for Scotland, we got into such an argument that Ralph went on ahead and was lost to us—we didn't see him again until we were all back in Canada.

Jack and I continued on to Edinburgh and then to Newcastle, where we boarded the *Braemen*, sailing for Oslo, Norway. For fourteen pounds each, we had a stateroom to ourselves, and the price included shipping the motorcycles. We passed into Sweden, where they were in the process of moving to driving on the right rather than the British left. We ran into war games in the city of Strömstad. By the time we reached Göteborg, we figured we were spending money so fast we'd be home well before Christmas. We were, but for other reasons . . .

Denmark, Germany, on into the Netherlands where, near the small town of Goor, Jack braked hard but still slammed into the rear of a red car that had jammed on its brakes after missing a turn. He hit the back bumper so hard that he flew high over the roof of the little car and landed, miraculously, on his back in a soft grassy knoll by the side of the intersection. Unfortunately, the bike also flew over the car, bouncing a couple of times before it ploughed into Jack, fracturing his collarbone.

We flew home the next day, the kindly Goor police having offered to package up and ship our bikes back to Canada. Jack was in considerable pain, and the Goor hospital had pumped him full of painkillers for the trip home, where they said he should immediately go to a Canadian hospital. He was operated on at Toronto General a few hours after we landed.

The trip had been a colossal bust.

Jack headed home to Cochrane to recover from his surgery, and I headed for Sudbury to see if it was too late to register for the current school year. It wasn't. I had missed a month of classes but they not only let me in but also found me a place in residence, as a homesick first-year student had bailed that very week. Ralph had come back earlier and was already taking third-year classes in his history major. Soon he, too, was back in residence. In time, our spat with Ralph was forgotten, and it was not long before we were talking once again about going to . . . Europe. No motorcycles, though. We swore a pact on that.

The standing joke was that the 1960s finally got to Sudbury in the 1970s. Late, perhaps, but we were cool with it. I had moved on from Jack Kerouac to the likes of Ken Kesey. My hair was well over my ears. I had wire-rimmed, John Lennon–style granny glasses and bellbottoms the colours of the American Stars and Stripes. We now smoked marijuana.

Ellen was loving her art courses at the University of Guelph. I wrote to her about thinking of a return to Europe, but she wasn't impressed, for good reason. I was being self-centred and selfish and at twenty-one years old would have to make a later date to grow up. I am surprised to this day that we stayed together after this.

Ralph was also keen about redoing Europe and getting it right. His first-year roommate, John Western, was so keen to join this new travelling group that he broke off his engagement to a lovely Laurentian girl. (They never made up. John would eventually marry another Laurentian graduate, Linda, who became a great friend of us all.)

We were headed out on our own grand tour, with inspiration taken from an August 10, 1970, edition of *Newsweek*. The magazine contrasted the legendary grand tours of previous centuries—rich offspring seeing the sights of Europe, usually in the company of a chaperone—to the youthful and carefree travellers of the day. "Elaine, 23," told the *Newsweek* reporter, "My total assets are a bedroll, a single change of clothing and $6.15. . . . For the first time in my life, I am truly happy."

Europe, the magazine said, was being invaded by recent graduates and dropouts, with their folding maps and copies of *Europe on 5 Dollars a Day*. With the Vietnam War still grinding on and anti-war sentiment—even anti-American sentiment—still high, many young Americans had Canadian flags stitched on their backpacks. "It's a cool place," one traveller said of Canada, "neutral, and people over here seem to like that."

Most of the young travellers interviewed seemed to be headed for Barcelona, and from there by ferry to the Balearic Islands, which *Newsweek* referred to as "a magnet for the footloose of almost every nationality."

Hold that boat while we get our tickets!

This time, before we left, I did something I had neglected to do for the first trip: I bought a journal and several pens. I pasted a school photograph of Ellen inside the back cover of the green datebook. Each day I would fill an entire page, writing down observations and even recording conversations as I remembered them in the evening. A few years before my diploma, Europe became my first journalism course—and I wasn't even aware that I was taking it.

The second trip to Europe began on a much better note. Not a turboprop but an Air Canada passenger jet with fully functioning toilets. We landed in Amsterdam and found a youth hostel with plenty of beds and a (sometimes) diaper-wearing, masturbating monkey in a cage by the front desk. This was rather appropriate behaviour, given the number of longhaired, unattached North American males who had never heard of sex shops or walked down a street where every window held a woman for hire.

Even though we were now somewhat familiar with recreational drugs, we were astonished by stores openly selling hash and marijuana, bongs and hookah pipes and roach clips. At cafés along the canals young people openly smoked what would get you a jail sentence back home, the air thick with that slightly skunky, sweet-sour smell of burning cannabis.

We boarded a train in Amsterdam that would take us to Paris, where we would then take another train to Barcelona. We had a three-hour wait at Gare du Nord, so we threw our backpacks against what seemed a wall and prepared to grab a nap. We were instantly confronted by two police who informed us we could be arrested for desecration of a war monument. We apologized and moved to another part of the station, eventually boarding a train for the eleven-hour trek to Spain. We shared a compartment with four young African-American women, all gorgeous and friendly, and they shared their chicken sandwiches with us.

This trip was already everything the first one wasn't.

At Barcelona, we did all that was recommended by Arthur Frommer: walked up and down La Rambla, toured the Basílica de la Sagrada Familia and other neo-Gothic creations by Antoni Gaudí, marvelled at the sheer historical sweep of the Gothic Quarter. We ate paella and drank copious amounts of beer and wine that cost a small fraction of what they cost back home or in Northern Europe.

Down at the harbour we bought our tickets for the Balearic Islands, that "magnet for the footloose," and headed for the small island of Ibiza, where practically everyone we had met on this trip said they planned to spend the winter. We sailed through the night, the Mediterranean smooth. We stayed in the ferry bar until closing time, then slept on our packs in the hallways.

Nine hours after departure, we pulled into the island harbour. It was dawn, the sun just hitting the brown walls of the Old Town high above the small, whitewashed village that seemed to sprawl around the feet of the old fort. Never had blue been so blue, white so white, the Mediterranean light bringing everything into sharper focus, much like when the eye doctor asks, "Which is better, one or (switching lenses) two?" This was pure "two" from every possible angle.

We found lodgings at a small hotel that first night and then, next day, began looking for an apartment to rent outside the town. We walked out past the airport to a long beach known as Playa d'en Bossa, saw a sign saying "Apartamento en alquiler," which we correctly took to mean "apartment for rent." It was above the home of a young family with a friendly German shepherd dog. Three bedrooms, a sitting room, bathroom and our own entrance—we took it immediately. Cost would be around sixty dollars a month. Grocery store, tapas bar and pub within easy walking, beach a five-minute walk to the end of the street.

We stayed on Ibiza for nearly three months. We wrote to our girl-friends back in Canada and to our friends from school, swooning over our good luck and how cheap and wonderful it was on this spectacularly beautiful island. We invited everyone to come. Little did we know so many would . . .

Though we had no sense of this then, Ibiza was starting to get a bit fed up with the invading hippies. *Newsweek International* would publish another feature in the summer of 1971 headlined "Ibiza is 'in'—and wants out." Tourism had been a factor there since the days of Homer—the spectacular and rocky small island of Es Vedrà, just off the coast of Ibiza, was where the sirens and sea nymphs who tried to lure Odysseus from his ship lived—and had been popular with Americans since the beatniks of the 1950s "discovered" it. But our invasion was different: a million or more young North Americans were making their way there at the same time we were setting up the apartment we had lucked into.

"For this year," the upcoming *Newsweek International* article would say, "Ibiza has become the 'in' place for freaked-out young Americans." The famous *ibicenco* tolerance was being sorely tested. The magazine would quote British comedian Terry-Thomas, a long-time resident of the island: "Right away they distract from the beauty of the island. They want to make themselves look ghastly. I've talked to a number of these chaps and I haven't really gotten very far with them. They talk about returning to the land. They don't know the difference between a violet and a hollyhock."

We stayed on, swimming in the cool, green Mediterranean and playing Frisbee on the beaches, hiking in the hills and drinking at the Tavern, a pub owned by a Brit named Martin. Mostly we drank English draft beer but also a local sweet liqueur called Hierbas (pronounced "yar-boss"). From a strange American girl, we purchased "golf balls"—small, foil-wrapped balls of tightly packed hashish that she kept in a bread basket covered by a red tea towel.

We made new friends—Dick from Chicago, Fred from LA, Gilda from El Salvador—and spent hours walking along the beaches or deep in the hills surrounding the finca that Fred and Gilda rented near San Rafael.

And then came the old friends. We knew that Jack Andrews was coming, and he arrived along with a couple of Laurentian pals from Chapleau, Peter and Frank. John Western flew to London on his own, connecting there with Robert "Paul" Wilson from Boston, who had travelled with Ralph the year before.

Paul and John surprised us as we walked along the close confines of the old part of Ibiza, but the greater surprise was still lurking in an alley. As the four of us passed by a narrow opening in the street, all talking excitedly about how the newcomers had gotten here, I was suddenly taken out by a tackle.

Eric!

I was stunned. Here I was in a bear hug with a huge, fire-haired, screaming lunatic—the same person I had headed off to kindergarten with so many years earlier.

"What the hell are you doing here?" I screamed at him.

"*I came to see you!*" he roared, the big Ruby voice rattling off thousand-year-old walls.

Eric was at the moment a "ski bum," a rather pejorative term that doesn't fairly describe those who fashion their work calendar around mountains and snow. He had worked at Huntsville's Hidden Valley, both in the family boutique store and in the ski rental booth, skiing before and after work and on his days off. He had now done the same in Leysin, Switzerland. Soon he would be returning to his Leysin role as the "Mad Man of the Mountain," but it was barely November now and first he would go and find the friend who had sent postcards of the idyllic life on the island of Ibiza. He and Paul and John had met on the ferry from Barcelona. (On the way back to Leysin, Eric would somehow end up part of a street fight with locals in Barcelona and spend most of a week in jail, an experience that quite rattled him.)

There is only so much beach Frisbee one can play, however. Only so much bodysurfing in water that was fast cooling. Only so much one can smoke—especially for a non-smoker when it comes to tobacco. And little to no interest in hallucinogenic drugs for most of us from northern Ontario. John and I began to talk about going to Morocco. On Ralph's previous trek to Europe, he and several friends from the Willowdale area of Toronto had made it all the way to Marrakesh, which *Newsweek* claimed had become another must-see destination for the young hippy trekkers. It was so popular that in another few months Crosby, Stills & Nash would release their big hit, "Marrakesh Express"—"Wouldn't you know we're riding on the Marrakesh Express . . ."

The idea took hold during an evening of draft beer at the Tavern. Dan, a guitar player from Colorado, wanted to join the three Laurentian travellers. Ralph, having been to Morocco only a year earlier, wasn't going again. Eric would soon be heading back to Switzerland.

We came up with a plan. Ferry from Ibiza to Barcelona. Train to Malaga and then hitchhike or bus to Torremolinos, a small tourist community on the Costa del Sol where my cousin Carrol Anne and her Danish husband, Storm, had been living for some years, selling real estate and arranging rentals for Brits and Northern European clients. I had been invited months earlier to come and visit if I did make it back to Europe.

We spent nearly a week in Torremolinos, drinking in the bars at night and playing football on the beach during the day. Storm and Carrol Anne were remarkably generous and welcoming—having invited one, ending up with four—and we even ran into two Huntsville High School grads, Peggy and Anne, who were on their own tour of Europe.

When the time came to head for Morocco, I went to a local car rental and paid upfront for a week's use of a small Fiat—called a "SEAT" in Spanish—that would carry four of us and our backpacks. I had to produce the international driver's licence I still had from the motorcycle tour, and I also had to pay upfront for the very important green card that would prove to authorities that the car was owned by the agency and fully insured.

"Do not lose this," I was told by an English-speaking clerk. "It is very important that you keep this in a safe place."

"No problem," I promised, not thinking twice about it.

Full of wild imaginings—"charming cobras in the square"—we set out after thanking our gracious hosts, Carrol Anne and Storm, who surely chugged a few breaths of relief as we backed out of their small drive. We drove along the coastline east, past Fuengirola and Marbella, and eventually reached the port of Algeciras, where we booked the ferry for Tangier, Morocco.

We were nervous in the crossing. None of us had ever been to a Muslim country before, let alone to Africa. We North American university punks might be tolerated in places like Amsterdam and Ibiza, but how would we be received in Morocco? Ralph had said there would be no problems, as all they were interested in was your money, not your political bent or anything else that you might think mattered. We had our traveller's cheques. We'd be just fine . . . we hoped.

We docked at Tangier, just across the Strait of Gibraltar in that strategic funnelling that separates the Atlantic Ocean from the Mediterranean Sea. We easily found lodgings—there were dozens, hundreds of young North Americans already there—and set out for the Grand Socco marketplace, where we found more noise and smells and curiosities than any of us had ever before known. The pungent smell of tanning leather was cancelled by the sickly sweet aroma of jasmine. Candles were for sale everywhere, the mixed odours of sandalwood, rose, cloves and ginger strong and seductive. Our stomachs rumbled when we neared the food vendors, but we avoided the grilled meats and, instead, ate our fill of delicious, dripping oranges and blocks of creamy cheese.

John was determined to buy one of those bulky sheepskin coats that were then the rage. There were racks of them set up in the market and he began picking through them as a very loud woman vendor followed him shouting out prices.

"Hey, mister—you need some help?" a young teenager called out to John.

"I don't understand what she's saying," John confessed.

The boy took over gracefully, moving in with a studied look that suggested he had been running auctions since he was in diapers. He would shake his head, shout back at the woman, then walk away.

"She wants too much," the young man said. "Come with me. I will help you."

The young man said his name was Abdullah. He spoke fairly good English and had a great, infectious smile when he wasn't wearing his serious businessman face. He worked the stalls brilliantly, taking John along and then instructing John how to shake his head no and walk away, knowing the vendor would chase you down with a better and better deal. John soon had his treasured coat, and at an excellent price.

Jack, Dan and I all bought *"striped djellabas we can wear at home!"* and Jack would not take his off for the remainder of the trip. (We would, of course, never wear them back home.)

Abdullah could not have been more helpful. He got us great prices on the djellabas and took us to a specialty shop where we bought a beautifully crafted hookah for smoking.

"You want the best hash in all of Tangier?" he asked. Of course we did.

With Abdullah leading the way, we left the main market area and piled into our car. He sat up front with me and guided me where to drive in the town. Soon enough he told me to park the car and we all got out. With him leading the way, we wound through some narrow alleys where children were kicking balls, old men lay sleeping against the walls and women were preparing meals in the open over small fire pits.

We came to a small building, almost a shack, where Abdullah walked in without knocking. He was greeted with a nod by an older man. Abdullah bent behind a table and came up with a block of hashish that was approximately the size of a paperback. John asked him, "How much?" and Abdullah shook his head, saying, "You will want to try some first."

Again, Abdullah was looking out for us. He shaved some of the hash off one end into a small pipe, lighted it and began passing it around. After two inhales we knew this was quality smoke and were keen to buy.

Abdullah argued with the hash seller for a few moments, seemed even to grow angry at one point and stomp away, only to return to nego-tiate a far better price.

We had our Moroccan clothes. We had some quality hash. We had our car. It was time to explore.

We slept that night on a beach beside the car, the softly lapping surf sending us into a deep sleep, no doubt helped along by smoking with Abdullah before we departed Tangier. We were headed for the Atlas Mountains and the town of Chaouen in the Rif Mountain range. The small city was said to be spectacularly beautiful, with its casbah includ-ing a fifteenth-century fortress, dungeon and museum.

I drove up through the foothills, heading into the high Atlas range. The little SEAT ran beautifully and we stopped often to walk along the edges of the road and take photographs of the spreading countryside below. We could not have been happier. We stopped and filled the pipe and smoked. I declined, knowing I would be driving roads with hairpin turns and narrow ledges.

Rounding the next turn and passing over a bridge that spanned a deep gully, we nearly ran into the Royal Moroccan Armed Forces— there was a green military vehicle blocking the road and three soldiers, one holding an assault rifle, one standing well back and the third an officer who approached our car.

John was carrying the block of hashish and rammed it down the front of his pants. I rolled down the driver's side window and smiled. The soldier spoke French and we were able to make ourselves understood. This was merely a routine checkpoint. The officer was not unfriendly, but also not openly friendly. He seemed rather bored.

"*Où est votre carte verte?*" he asked.

The all-important "green card" that I had been advised to guard carefully and not lose?

I had placed it in a small pocket area at the bottom of the driver's door. I confidently reached for it.

It was gone!

"*La carte est partie!*" I said, feeling my heart fall into my stomach.

The two backup soldiers moved closer. The officer indicated we should all get out of the car, which we did.

Later, John would tell us that he momentarily considered making a run for it, thinking he could leap down into the nearby gully and be gone before the soldier with the assault rifle could bring him down. John, you must remember, was still stoned from Abdullah's pipe of high-quality hashish.

We got out and the soldiers went through our car with a fine comb, checking even our packs. They did not, mercifully, frisk us. Cannabis and hashish were illegal in Morocco, though some parts of the country were said to turn a blind eye to the law.

The officer asked again about the green card and I swore that we had it, that it was put in a special place and that somehow it must have fallen out. I had proof that the car was a rental and also my international driver's licence. He examined all the documents carefully, the two backup soldiers waiting patiently.

Finally, the officer nodded and returned with the documents. He handed them to me. He said I must contact the rental agency as soon as we returned to Tangier and they would arrange for a new card. The card, he emphasized, was very important, and we were lucky that he didn't impound the car and charge us.

I do not think I have ever expressed such gratitude in my life.

The officer waved us on, the two soldiers stepped aside, and we set off again for our destination. It was now that John decided to tell us his escape plan.

"You could have been killed!" Jack yelled at him.

Dan was giggling madly. "They probably would have shot all of us!"

I said nothing. My heart was pounding, my face burning red with a combination of relief and terror.

Up, up, up we climbed through the spectacular mountains. We could see snow at the highest levels. We passed by villages and roadside vendors. We crested one tall climb and, instantly, the white glory of Chaouen revealed itself to our mutual gasps.

We headed for what we could see and it seemed to take forever to reach the actual town, so twisting and convoluted was the road in. But soon enough we were there and we found easy lodgings.

After a magnificent day of exploring the town, the casbah and the torture chamber, we returned to our small hotel, where much to our delight, several young Moroccans were sitting around a table passing a hookah. Some of them spoke passable English or French, and they invited us to join in. We were only too happy to.

John wanted to share some of the glorious hashish we had obtained in Tangier with the help of our friend Abdullah. He laid it on the table and we took a knife to shave off a good amount, which we placed in a couple of pipes and fired up.

After several passes of the pipe, I felt nothing. No, I felt rather queasy—was it the altitude? The scare with the military? Something I had eaten?

I was talking to Jack about all this when, suddenly, he leaned toward me and stared hard at my mouth.

"Your tongue has turned green!"

"What?"

"It is!" shouted John.

Dan was giggling hopelessly.

"*Your tongue, too!*" Jack shouted at John.

There was a cracked mirror on the ottoman back of where we were sitting and the four travellers were all trying to see what had happened to their tongues.

They were all green as frogs.

One of the Moroccans leaned over and picked up our treasured block of hashish. He rubbed it. He spit on his thumb and ran his thumb along the side we had shaved our pipeful from—and then he started giggling.

"Come with me," he said to the four of us.

We followed him toward the kitchen area. He turned on a tap and leaned over, rubbing the block as the water splashed onto it.

The water draining was bright green.

He looked at me and stuck out his pink tongue.

"This is henna," he said. "A dye. People use it in their hair or on clothes."

"*Hair dye?*" I flinched. "Impossible—we smoked some of it before we bought it. It was good stuff."

"I think maybe you got tricked," the Moroccan said sympathetically.

"A bait-and-switch!" Dan giggled. "Abdullah *played* us."

I could hear the light click on in my head. Abdullah had indeed played us. He'd either stuck some real hashish onto the end of this bar of henna or he had somehow switched the hashish block for this block of hair dye when we did the deal.

Abdullah had our money.

Abdullah had our hash block.

Abdullah, I realized with a deep wince, had our green card.

What was it Ferlinghetti had written?

"If you're too open-minded, your brains will fall out."

BOB DYLAN GOES ELECTRIC

She called my bluff.

Daughter Christine has had to put up with Bob Dylan since she arrived home in a basket, just like the rest of the family, just like our poor mother who could not bear the caterwauling and nasal whining and incomprehensible lyrics flying out of the little Viking portable record player with three pennies taped to the top of the needle arm. "I ain't gonna work on Maggie's farm no more . . ."

Bob Dylan had been a constant in my life. I had written about him in *The Pundit* while in high school. I had listened to him—hell, worshipped him—through university. I wrote about him in school publications at Laurentian and Western. I wrote about him in *Maclean's* and other national publications. I listened to him as I wrote my books. He has been very much the soundtrack to my life and career.

Now Bob Dylan was coming to Ottawa. "We'll get tickets," Christine said. "You'll love it."

"Seen him," I said, rather too worldly. "Saw him years before you were even born."

It was mid-November 1965 and Bob Dylan was coming to Toronto to play Massey Hall. We were six young teenagers from a small northern town, and we were able to order tickets by mail. We went to Toronto by train and headed for Massey Hall wearing our Sunday suits, not having a clue how to dress for a folk concert in the big city. We looked like idiots.

But we were all Dylan fans. My older brother had purchased the very first Bob Dylan album to reach the little town, back in 1961. We knew all the words to "A Hard Rain's A-Gonna Fall." We had no idea whatsoever what "Love Minus Zero/No Limit" meant.

It was one of Dylan's first concerts after his famous electric outing at the Newport Folk Festival that summer. He'd been booed off the stage.

Pete Seeger, the story went, had been seen running around backstage looking for an axe to hack through the microphone cable. Dylan was selling out on his folk roots. Bull—we loved the new sound. It combined the music we all loved, rock and folk, into one fabulous mix.

Dylan played the first half of the Massey Hall concert with nothing but acoustic guitar and harmonica. The people in the audience— as only folk audiences can—took on that angelic choir look as they mouthed the words to "Blowin' in the Wind" and other old Dylan standards.

He took a break and came back with an electric guitar and five soon-to-be-famous sidemen and almost blew the doors off with "Maggie's Farm," the same song he had opened with at Newport.

Some booed. Some walked out. Someone threw pennies at the stage—perhaps hoping to short-circuit the guitars—but the rest cheered. Even the goofy teens in the dark suits.

It wasn't as if I hadn't kept up on Dylan since. I'd purchased the subsequent albums, even the awful ones. I repurchased the good stuff on tape, then CD. I went to see him a second and third time in concert, once during that black era when no one could make out a word and once when, happily, he actually tried to enunciate.

He was to play Scotiabank Place in Ottawa in the spring of 2002. We went, tickets ten times what they cost in 1965, and sat to the side of the stage staring straight at him—not that he stared back. In fact, he didn't even seem to notice there was anyone there to see him. That's just the way he was. No banter. Not even a turn to the side so those on the far side could have a look.

The most surprising thing about the simple stage was that the six tight suits of the 1965 teenagers from the small northern town were now on the band—six musicians in dark jackets, pants and thin ties.

Perhaps he had noticed us in 1965 and realized how far ahead of the fashion curve a northern Canadian town can be.

There is no point in pretending it was a great concert. The music was driving but failed to lift the crowd even as high as the opening act, Foo Fighters, had managed. In typical Dylan fashion, the old songs weren't old anymore, but arranged so differently that identifying phrases was difficult—making out words was, at times, impossible.

For me, it was a trip back in time, back to the *Thorne* days at Laurentian when I had slammed the student council president for his terrible taste in music. Music had been my first real journalism in newsprint, columns for *Lambda*, reviews for Western's student paper. Ridiculous in that I am virtually tone-deaf—but where has it ever been a crime to write about something of which you know nothing?

"Man," said an older gent sitting behind us during one of the song breaks, "times sure have changed." They sure had. At that particular moment, Bob Dylan was the sixty-third best golfer among entertainers, according to *Golf Digest*. He no longer trusted anyone over 130.

But he was still Bob Dylan.

And no matter how strange the cadence, no matter how mumbled the words, they were still there, familiar phrases triggering memorized stanzas and complete songs that, for reasons unreachable, mean so very much to those who still fall back on them.

Dylan sang and I thought about Eric, my best friend from kindergarten who could recite Dylan the way others have been known to recite Shakespeare, or Robert Service.

I thought about those silly suits in 1965 and how I still hate wearing a jacket and tie.

"Is it as thrilling this time as last time?" Christine asked, her interest totally flagged by now.

"Yes," I said. "It is."

But I could not explain why.

4

First Job, First Disaster

When Ellen and I decided to marry in the late summer of 1972, Camp Tawingo owner Jack Pearse gave us a remarkable wedding gift. He knew that I had graduated from Western with a diploma in journalism and hoped to find work in newspapers or magazines. He knew, as well, that Ellen, now with her art degree from Guelph, hoped to find design work in advertising. He gave us an introduction to an old friend from his University of Toronto days, Senator Keith Davey. We were to set a date to have lunch with the senator in Toronto.

We met Senator Davey at his chosen location, a Holiday Inn restaurant not far from the Don Valley Parkway. The man was known in Ottawa as the "Rainmaker" for his abilities to bring success to Liberal campaigns. Large, handsome, friendly, with bushy sideburns and, as *Toronto Star* columnist Richard Gwyn once wrote, a predilection for loud suits that Nathan Detroit might have worn in *Guys and Dolls*, Davey had been in radio sales in Toronto while also serving as campaign manager for Lester Pearson. Prime Minister Pearson never did win a majority government, but he held onto power through two elections, rewarding his campaign manager with a 1966 appointment to the Canadian Senate. Davey, the son of a *Toronto Star* production manager, had a lifelong fascination with newspapers and soon was chairing a Senate commission examining mass media in Canada.

The Davey report—actually called *The Uncertain Mirror: Report of the Special Senate Committee on Mass Media*—was published as a book in 1970 and immediately became a Canadian bestseller. The report warned that "public confidence in the press is declining" and claimed plumbers had a more professional approach to their profession than journalists did, plumbers requiring at the very least a minimum standard of training. It called for the establishment of standards for journalism training and for the creation of press councils with real powers. It warned about a growing concentration of ownership in the news industry and cautioned that further concentration would not serve the public well. And yet, through all the criticism, Davey's deep love of newspapers came through. "Journalism, however humble, is a sort of art; there can be very few occupations that are so demanding in terms of speed and judgment," the report said. "The wonder is that newspapers are as good as they are. They really are a daily miracle."

The three-volume report had been required reading at Western, so I was familiar enough with it to be able to chat lightly with the senator once the three of us were seated. We spoke little of Ottawa politics, which was a blessing. Davey was not part of the inner circle of then–prime minister Pierre Trudeau, but soon would be. That fall, Trudeau would barely win a minority government over Robert Stanfield and the Progressive Conservatives. Davey and his protégé Jim Coutts brought a little welcome rain to a Prime Minister's Office that had turned rather fallow in the four years since Trudeaumania had swept the nation.

Davey was aware that prospects were dim in the newspaper world of 1972. The *Toronto Telegram* had folded the previous fall, putting eight hundred employees out of work. A new upstart tabloid, the *Sun*, was publishing in Toronto, but it was staffed mostly by *Telegram* cast-offs and had far fewer positions to fill. He did not hold out much hope that I'd find a newspaper reporting job in the city. He "interviewed" us over the lunch, periodically scratching shorthand notes on small pieces of paper that he peeled from a copy of the *Star* he had been reading when we arrived. It was, all in all, a most enjoyable meeting.

Within a couple of days, I had a call from Senator Davey's office in Ottawa. I was to take down a list of meetings for the two of us, Ellen with a couple of advertising agencies the senator had worked closely with on Liberal campaigns, me with a list of names that left me shaking with apprehension: Arch Mackenzie, head of Canadian Press; George Gilmour, head of the Maclean-Hunter business magazine division; and, gulp, Peter C. Newman, renowned editor of *Maclean's* magazine.

This unexpected opening of doors had nothing to do with my immature poetry or tone-deaf music reviews; it had everything to do with "Crafty Lady" being a favourite staff member at Camp Tawingo. Jack Pearse had done us a favour by introducing us to Senator Davey. The senator easily got me in the various doors, but now it would be up to me to close one of those doors from the inside.

Arch Mackenzie was very kind but very straightforward about the state of newspapering and wire services. There was a glut of seasoned reporters available following the demise of the *Tely*. No one was hiring the untried. He suggested, wisely, looking for a job in a small town— Huntsville, for example—and putting in enough time there to be able to sell myself as an "experienced" journalist. He thought the farther north you were willing to go, the better the chance at finding work. I closed the door behind me as I left.

George Gilmour showed me around the huge Maclean-Hunter offices on the corner of Dundas Street and University Avenue. The Dundas Street side entrance led to a small elevator that went up to the likes of *Chatelaine* and *Maclean's*. The University Avenue main entrance opened to a large lobby of green marble, with a security guard manning an information desk. Past that were eight floors of magazines, designers, secretarial services, managers, publishers and M-H executives. The *Financial Post* was on one floor. On others, there appeared to be a magazine for every imaginable product: shoes, clothes, cars, heavy equipment, hardware, forestry—some 130 magazines in all. That was then; today virtually every one of them has vanished.

Gilmour advised me to apply for a job through "editorial services," a unit in the middle of the vast building where copy was turned out by several "writers" for the various magazines. I said that I would, though I knew I'd far rather be a real reporter for, say, Canadian Press, or—beyond all imagining—a staff writer for *Maclean's*.

My final appointment was with Peter C. Newman. I took the side elevator up to the seventh floor, tentatively walked out and was met by the smiling face of Elda Tilbury, Newman's personal secretary. She had been expecting me. She called into the corner office and was told to bring me in.

Peter Newman was already, at forty-three, a legend in publishing. The Vienna-born business and political journalist had been editor of the *Toronto Star*. He had written national bestsellers—*Renegade in Power*, a devastating dissection of the John Diefenbaker years, *The Distemper of Our Times* and *A Nation Divided*, books that captured Ottawa in the tumultuous 1960s and the arrival of Pierre Trudeau—and his bald pate, dark eyebrows and ever-present pipe were familiar to both readers and television viewers. He was the most famous Canadian journalist of the day, in charge of what was, then, the pre-eminent publication in the land.

His office was vast. One wall was papered with covers of the magazine, beginning with his arrival and ending with the very latest. A brooding Leonard Cohen, shirtless, with a white towel draped around his neck, had just been posted on the wall beside the May cover featuring singer Anne Murray. The most dominant object in the room was not his typewriter, but a large turntable on which he would play his Stan Kenton jazz music, usually listening through large headphones as he wrote. There were photographs of his family—he was then married to Christina Newman, one of the magazine's senior writers—and a picture of his sailing yacht, which he kept at a marina on Centre Island, a short journey by ferry from the quay at the bottom of Yonge Street.

"I had it all figured out," he told me as I admired the yacht. "I was editor of the *Toronto Star*. I was going to live at Harbourfront. From my office I would be able to see where I lived and where I had my boat. It didn't work out and here I am—with an even better job. I just can't see my boat from here."

He could, however, see the mushrooming Toronto skyline. And he could, by turning, see dozens of famous faces staring back at him from the covers of the monthly magazine he had been running since 1971: Gordon Lightfoot, John Turner, Pierre and Margaret Trudeau, René Lévesque, Bobby Orr and Gordie Howe, Bruno Gerussi, JFK, Queen Elizabeth . . .

Newman had resuscitated the magazine that had launched as a business journal back in 1905. It had soon become a general magazine, publishing writers such as Robert Service and Lucy Maud Montgomery and illustrations by members of the Group of Seven. *Maclean's* glory days had been the 1950s, when Ralph Allen had been editor and writers included the likes of Pierre Berton, W.O. Mitchell and Blair Fraser. In the 1960s, with television sucking so much advertising from general interest publications, it had struggled under editors Peter Gzowski and Charles Templeton. Newman's hope was to raise it once again to the exalted position it had held in the 1950s, and to a large extent he succeeded.

Newman talked about the magazine in a voice so soft I wasn't always sure what he'd said. He asked about my work at the college papers—curiously, none of the interviews ever touched on my marks or the journalism program, just on the campus newspaper work—and I told him about doing music and record reviews. This led to a long discussion of Stan Kenton, about whom I was utterly oblivious. Newman suggested I go see him next time Kenton's band was in town and I eagerly agreed.

There was no job he could offer me at the magazine. He did promise, however, to put in a word for me with the business magazines. He thought the Maclean-Hunter editorial pool would be a good place to start, given the current state of newspapers. I left his office thrilled that I had met the great Peter C. Newman, crushed that there seemed nothing there for me.

Within another couple of days, I had a call from Maclean-Hunter, asking me to come to the third floor of 481 University Avenue for an interview with C. Frank Turner, who was head of editorial services. I showed up at the appointed hour, had a nice chat with Mr. Turner and Jean Portugal, his assistant, and was offered a starting salary of seventy-two hundred dollars a year. That was two thousand a year more than I had made at McGraw-Hill Ryerson. I had taken a small apartment on Lonsdale Road near Toronto's Forest Hill district, and Ellen would join me there right after our September wedding.

Each morning, wearing a jacket and tie, I would pass through the front doors of the University Avenue entrance and immediately purchase a coffee and a raisin-laced tea biscuit off the cart that appeared throughout the building for morning and afternoon breaks. I would carry coffee and biscuit to the elevator and rise to the third floor, where editorial services was set up much like a typing pool, with several desks in a row and a small, private office for "Mr." Turner, as we were told to refer to him by "Mrs." Portugal.

It would have made a lovely setting for a British sitcom, except it wasn't particularly amusing. Mr. Turner, a pleasant man with a long face and red hair, spent most of his time behind the closed door of his office working on a major study of the North West Mounted Police. In 1973 he would publish *Across the Medicine Line: The Epic Confrontation Between Sitting Bull and the North-West Mounted Police* and it would be warmly received.

Mrs. Portugal ran the livery of four to six writers like a class. We were to be quiet and diligent. One editorial assistant, Michael Posner, would become a great friend and go on to a terrific career in journalism and books. There was a friendly secretary, Linda, and an equally charming editor of the internal newsletter, Pippa. The writers came and went, usually moving on to become assistant editor of one of the multiple business magazines in the building. Each magazine had a publisher, an editor (sometimes the same person) and an assistant editor. Assistant editor was the lowest you could go, but for us, a first step on the ladder out of editorial services.

A couple of years before I arrived, an ambitious young M.T. (Terry) Kelly went through these same editorial services, quickly left Maclean-Hunter entirely and eventually won the 1987 Governor General's Award for fiction with his third novel, *A Dream Like Mine*. His first novel, *I Do Remember the Fall: One Young Journalist's Search for Truth, Beauty and Wild Sex*, would appear a half-dozen years after I worked for Mrs. Portugal and it would include a ridiculing portrait of editorial services and the matronly woman who ruled over it.

Each morning and afternoon, Mrs. Portugal—dark hair in a bun, sensible shoes, dark nylons, looking as if she had just walked out of a 1950s issue of *Chatelaine*—would distribute our assignments. Almost exclusively, this meant turning press releases into copy. Oddly, we never actually *saw* the shoe or truck tire or drill press or filing cabinet we were telling readers was an excellent new product. We simply took the press release at face value, rewrote it for length and passed it on to whatever magazine the product was intended for. Readers across the country never knew that the person writing about the product had neither seen nor used it.

When the 1972 hockey Summit Series between Canada and the Soviet Union was on, Ellen and I were getting married in Huntsville. We spent our honeymoon at her family's Camp Lake cottage, where we stayed a week in perfect September weather. The night before our September ninth wedding, Team Canada lost to the Soviets in Vancouver. It was the night Canadian fans booed and jeered Canadian players, the night a sweating, exhausted Phil Esposito gave his pained speech to the country from the ice surface. It seemed dire for Canada. The series then switched to Moscow for the final four games. When Paul Henderson scored the single most significant goal in the history of the national game—scoring with thirty-four seconds left in game 8—I was back to work, but in Stroud, Ontario. I'd been dispatched, by bus, by the Maclean-Hunter magazine *Outdoor Power Products* to do a profile of the owner of Sandy Cove Marine, Mercury Outboards' "dealer of the year." There was a television set up in the showroom and I did get to see the dramatic, winning goal. If only my feature on the marine could have been every bit as riveting as the final minute of play in Moscow.

Ellen also worked at Maclean-Hunter, doing paste-up in the design department until a better opportunity came along and she began doing art restoration at Odon Wagner Gallery on Davenport Road. Her sister, Jackie, also a Guelph graduate in art, soon joined her there, the two of them riding their bikes down from our rented home at the bottom of the Allen Expressway and Ralph and Jackie's nearby apartment. They had married two years after us. Life was good for us all.

In addition to my salaried job in editorial services, I managed to land some freelance work from Maclean-Hunter. *Canada & The World* was a thin magazine aimed at high-school civics classes. Harvey Botting, a rising young executive with M-H, was editor and publisher and most of the editorial work fell to a kindly retired teacher named Maurice Walsh. They paid sixty dollars for a feature on religion in popular music. I was later assigned a piece on the theory and practice of communism. There is a copy in my filing cabinets. The lede is "Communism is controversial; some people love it, others hate it." It shall remain in my filing cabinet, thanks.

I was growing increasingly desperate for a creative outlet. The *Financial Post* had its own monthly magazine, called *Impetus*. The editor, Anne Rhodes, was friendly and approachable and came to me with an idea after I had written her a note wondering if there was any freelance work available. She wanted me to move into an old-age residence for a week and just write about what it was like to be "retired" and living in a "home." I was twenty-four years young but jumped at the opportunity to be old. I moved into the "home" in the early fall and "The End of Roy MacGregor's Summer" was published in December 1972. My first real break, and much to my surprise, it led to a very short but positive inter-office note from Peter Newman. He had remembered our meeting!

After spending several months in editorial services, writing for everything from a trucker's magazine to a power tool monthly, I was given the opportunity to move permanently to *Modern Purchasing*, a trade magazine for purchasers, whatever on earth a "purchaser" was. I declined, much to the disappointment of Mrs. Portugal.

"You don't get to pick and choose around here," she said. "We'll allow it this once, but I would strongly suggest you take the next opening."

Soon enough another assistant editor's job came up. It was at a magazine called *Office Equipment & Methods*. The editor was a rather absent-minded Brit who clearly would rather have been working on a Fleet Street tabloid, which is where his interests and ambitions lay. He was jovial and easygoing and had no issue with the long liquid lunches that most of the young assistant editors at Maclean-Hunter enjoyed four or five days a week at various Dundas Street dives. His marriage was not happy and when his wife, who suffered terribly from depression, took her own life, his reaction to various condolences was that, to him, "It's water under the bridge." He was soon gone, off to write for the *National Enquirer*.

Emboldened by the Peter Newman note on my old-age story, I used the inter-office mail to send a cleanly typed memorandum to Newman's seventh-floor office in the adjoining building. I remember whining that I felt "buried on the third floor" and was eager to do some free-lancing for "Canada's National Magazine." Much to my surprise and delight, the following morning my telephone in editorial services rang.

It was Elda Tilbury and she said Mr. Newman wanted to see me that afternoon. I had a dry lunch, much to the surprise of some of my fellow workers. I also couldn't eat.

When the appointed hour rolled around, I walked through the twisting halls of the main building until I came to the single elevator on the Dundas Street side. Already waiting for it were Don Obe and Tom Hedley, two of the senior editors of *Maclean's*. We squeezed on and I could hardly breathe. Hedley was barely thirty years old and a rising magazine star, having worked for *Esquire* in New York City before being lured back to Canada by Newman. He wore his hair like Tom Wolfe and had a scarf wrapped about his neck like Jean-Paul Belmondo. Obe, shorter with wavy hair, was smoking a French cigarette. I said not a word. Inside, I felt I had *arrived*.

Elda Tilbury told me to take a seat. I could hear jazz pounding from Peter Newman's corner office. Stan Kenton, I was sure. I still didn't know a damned thing about jazz, but I knew a small bit about Peter Newman.

Eventually, I was invited in. We made some small talk about M-H business publications—he seemed amused by my account of giving rave reviews to products we never even got to see—and he mentioned that he had been quite impressed by the story in *Impetus* magazine. He had previously worked for the *Financial Post* and remained a fan of the publication.

"What might you do for us?" he asked, tapping his pipe out into the ashtray.

I mentioned the music reviews I had done at college—essentially the same thing I had told him when we first met—and then I threw a bit of a Hail Mary that I had considered, dropped, considered, dropped, but now wound up and threw deep.

"My cousin has a dozen Tom Thomson originals that I don't think anyone has ever seen," I told him. His brown eyes widened. He stopped refilling his pipe from the open packet on his desk.

"Seriously?"

"Well, I know he inherited them. He lives in upstate New York. Our aunt, Winnie Trainor, was Tom Thomson's girlfriend. She lived in Huntsville, just down the street from us. When she died, I helped my cousin empty her old house in town and her cottage on Canoe Lake. Her neighbour told me that Winnie kept a six-quart basket full of Tom Thomson sketches and when she'd go away she'd carry them over to the neighbour's for safekeeping."

"You think we could see them?" Peter asked, tamping down the tobacco and looking for a match.

"I could try. We were very close to this cousin. He and his family used to stay with us all summer. I know I can talk to him about it."

Peter sucked on his pipe and slowly released several clouds of smoke that hung between us. I could see I had his attention. He was probably already seeing that Tom Thomson cover joining all the others on his office wall.

"Why don't you do something in the meantime," he suggested, a big smile on his face. "Something short. Maybe something on the current Canadian music scene. You seem to know that well."

"I'd *love* to!" I said.

We agreed on a length and a fee and I left his office walking on air. I. Had. A. *Maclean's*. Assignment.

Back in the second-floor offices of *Office Equipment & Methods*, my fingers typed fawning words about new filing cabinets and office chairs and mailroom efficiency, but the words in my head were all about what I would write for *Maclean's*. Peter C. Newman had said he wanted five hundred words on the current Canadian music scene, and that is exactly what I would give him.

I worked nights and weekends on the piece. He had asked for the "current state" of Canadian music and I decided, in my great wisdom and extremely limited music knowledge, that it must have gone "stale." I tried to write as if I actually knew something and it came off a bit snobby.

"The emergence of the Beatles back in 1964," I wrote authoritatively, "startled other musicians and dared them to explore new directions in sound. Bob Dylan became a prophet, inspiring the more imaginative, developing a coterie of imitators, and when Dylan went electric, when The Who released *Tommy* . . . those were indeed exciting times."

The short essay went on to mention that the Beatles had broken up, Dylan was no longer the Dylan of old and even the Rolling Stones seemed to have lost energy. In the case of Canada, I argued, "Steppenwolf is already a memory, Joni Mitchell is a musical form unto herself, and she slipped badly, in fact, with her last effort, *Blue*. Only Neil Young and Winnipeg's Guess Who have maintained their reputations, but both defined their creative areas long ago and neither is experimenting."

I delivered the article to the seventh floor and Elda Tilbury said she would get it to the appropriate editor. I soon heard back from the handling editor, Don Obe, that it was fine, with a bit of editing, and a copy was sent back through the inter-office mail for me to approve, which I did immediately, returning my precious first step to magazine stardom.

My piece would appear in the issue of February 1, 1973, which was already in the mail to hundreds of thousands of subscribers across the land. I was going to be *famous!*

The phone on my desk at *Office Equipment & Methods* rang sharply. I picked it up. Elda Tilbury was on the line and she, too, sounded sharp.

"Mr. Newman wishes to see you immediately," she said in the tone of a vice-principal.

I hurried along to the Dundas Street elevator. Perhaps he had a cheque for me? Maybe another assignment? Elda had sounded upset, but perhaps it was something else.

I was immediately ushered into the editor's office. Peter Newman had his pipe glowing, smoke everywhere, and Stan Kenton on too loud for conversation. He quickly lifted the needle from the album and turned off the stereo. He turned and glared at me, the soft brown eyes of a few weeks back now releasing poison-tipped arrows.

The new *Maclean's* issue was on his desk. It had an illustration of Ken Dryden on the cover. But it wasn't waiting there so he could make a gift of it to me.

He opened the magazine to a page marked with a yellow sticky note. He turned it over. There was a large, red, angry circle near the top of the piece that carried my name.

Peter Newman spun the magazine around and shoved it across to me.

"How do you explain *that?*" he said.

I half stood in my chair, leaning to read. It was page 86, my name at the top of the page. The harsh red circle was near the top, right where I had written "when Dylan went electric, when the Guess Who released *Tommy* . . ."

The editor took a hard suck on his pipe.

"We've been getting calls," he said, his anger obvious. "We're going to have to apologize for your mistake."

"But . . . but . . . but . . . *I didn't do it!*"

He tapped the magazine. "It's right there. And that's your name on it."

"I know, I know, but honestly—I didn't do it. No one would ever say the Guess Who recorded *Tommy!*"

"*You* said it. Right here," he tapped the magazine again.

My heart crashed through into the sixth floor, then the fifth, one by one until it sank beneath Dundas Street. "I couldn't have," I pleaded. "I couldn't have."

"You signed off on it. They sent you your piece after it was edited, correct?"

"Yes."

"Then you signed off on a mistake."

"We'll have an apology in the next issue," he said. "But I have to tell you, this is not a good thing. We take accuracy very seriously here."

I was dismissed and almost threw up in the elevator. I made my way back to my desk at *Office Equipment & Methods* and sank into my chair, my head spinning, heart pounding. So much for my first step up the ladder to the seventh floor. I had broken the first rung myself.

Still unable to believe what had happened, I shuffled through my files until I found the carbon copy of my original draft. I swallowed hard and read, "when Dylan went electric, when The Who released *Tommy* . . ."

I had written "The Who," *not* "the Guess Who."

I had it right!

With that in hand, I immediately returned to the seventh floor. Elda Tilbury seemed surprised to see me and puzzled that I had no appointment but wanted a minute with the editor. She told me to have a seat and she would check to see if Peter Newman had a moment.

The editor's door opened briefly a crack, Stan Kenton rushed out, and then the sharp sound of horns grew muffled as she closed the door behind her. The door opened again and I was invited in.

The jazz was still on. He made no effort to stop it or turn down the sound. He simply raised one thick eyebrow, asking without words, *What the hell are you doing back here?*

I laid down my carbon copy. I tapped on "The Who released *Tommy*."

He stared and stared again.

"What the hell?" he asked no one.

"I had it right," I said, near tears. "It wasn't my mistake."

Holding the newest issue of the magazine and my carbon copy—in retrospect, the most precious piece of paper I have ever owned in my life—he marched down the hall past a row of small offices with me trailing behind him. He checked with Don Obe, the handling editor, and Don produced the edited copy I had signed off on.

Once again, it was "The Who" who had released *Tommy*.

"Who had final hands?" Peter asked.

"Joan," the handling editor offered.

We then all three of us marched down to the tiny office of Joan Weatherseed, the magazine's head copy editor. A short, smiling woman with the prim tidiness of a kindergarten teacher, she looked at the magazine, still with the harshly red-circled error. Then she scanned my carbon copy.

"Oh dear, oh dear," she said in a soft Scottish brogue. She read farther down the page.

She tapped on the lower paragraph where I had written, "Only Neil Young and Winnipeg's Guess Who have maintained their reputations . . ."

"Oh dear, oh dear," she repeated. "I must have thought you had simply dropped a word up top. I thought on first reference you should use the band's full name—as you did later on. I'm afraid I know nothing about popular music. I'm soooo sorry about this."

No one, I would soon learn, could be angry with Joan Weatherseed. She was endlessly cheerful and helpful and kind and lovely. Everyone at *Maclean's* adored her. The Who/Guess Who bungle would not become the issue that silly kid from editorial services was fired over, but part of the charming lore of Joan Weatherseed's reign at Canada's National Magazine.

Peter invited me back to his office. I thought I saw a smile from Elda as we passed her desk.

He turned off Stan Kenton, lighted his pipe and invited me to sit down.

"We'll have an apology," he said, removing his pipe. "It won't mention your name. We'll say 'Because of an editing error . . .' or something like that. Joan will be mortified. There's no point in making anything of this other than what it is. A simple human error."

I expelled a huge amount of breath. I thought I was about to break down.

"I'm sorry this happened to you," he smiled. "Not exactly what anyone would want in their very first piece, is it?"

"No," I said.

"Well," he smiled. "Get to work on your second piece for us—talk to your cousin about those Tom Thomsons."

I nodded. "I will," I said. "And thanks for this."

The Dundas Street elevator headed down but my heart and mind were soaring in the opposite direction. I had been saved. I would have a second chance. I was not doomed to spend eternity pushing copy on filing cabinets up the *Office Equipment & Methods* hill.

Early in May, I received a call from the sacred seventh floor. It was again Elda Tilbury, cheerfully asking me to hold for Mr. Newman.

He came on the line and asked a few questions about progress on the Tom Thomson story. I told him I had interviewed a number of people who had known the painter and had their own theories on his mysterious death. I said I had been in contact with my cousin, which was true. I did not tell him my cousin seemed reluctant to talk about his inheritance.

"There's something else," the editor of *Maclean's* said. "We're looking for someone to handle the 'slush pile' here—the manuscripts that come in over the transom, not the ones we assign. It's rare anything comes in the mail that ends up in the magazine, but it does happen sometimes. Would that interest you?"

"*Are you kidding??*" I wanted to scream. Instead, I answered as calmly as I could. "Yes."

"I'll ask them to transfer you over."

Two weeks later I rode the Dundas Street elevator with my very first briefcase, empty but for a few pens. I was going to work.

On June 1, 1973, the latest issue of *Maclean's* came out. The cover had various British Columbia politicians illustrated as totem poles.

Inside, on the masthead, there were two assistant editors listed. My name was one of them.

FINGER LOST IN THE NORTH ATLANTIC

The Universal Helicopters' twin-engine Sikorsky took off from Gander Airport and headed out to sea some 145 kilometres north-west of Cape Bonavista.

We were warned it could get rough. Weather was low and winds gusting. The drills at the airport had been extensive. Each person was dressed in a survival suit and wore headphones in case the pilots had commands. We were shown where the safety raft was stowed and how to release it and trigger the pump that would quickly blow it up.

Once we were strapped into our seats, the pilot issued detailed instructions.

"If there's a problem, you'll hear this sound," he said over the intercom.

An alarm screeched once, twice. Even with headphones protecting our ears, the sound jarred all four passengers: three oil workers and a visiting journalist.

"You hear that," the pilot said into our headphones, "you want to zip up and be ready to bail if necessary."

The huge helicopter roared out over the North Atlantic, headed for the drillship *Havdrill*, a Norwegian vessel built in Rotterdam and contracted out to Columbia Gas Development of Calgary, which in turn had a farming out agreement with BP Canada. BP Canada, itself 65 percent British owned, had been granted exploration rights to a vast expanse of the ocean floor by the Canadian government. It was the mid-1970s, a time of huge optimism for offshore drilling for oil and natural gas. The Canadian Society of Petroleum Geologists had recently estimated the amount of undiscovered oil in Canada to be eighty-four billion barrels, sixty-three billion of which would be found below the sea.

It was early in my career at *Maclean's* and I had been assigned a feature on the men who worked in such isolation so far from land. I was to spend nearly a week aboard the ship and return to Gander on the next run of the big Sikorsky helicopter, which ferried workers and supplies back and forth from June, when the well had been "spudded," to the end of the drilling season, which would come in October. BP Columbia Bonavista C-99 would be the deepest well ever drilled off the Atlantic Coast of North America, down through nearly 340 metres of water before reaching the seabed, ultimately expected to reach more than four kilometres below the bottom of the *Havdrill*.

As icebergs were a serious threat, the forty-million-dollar ship was "dynamically positioned," meaning it used computers and five props (three forward, two aft) to maintain position over the wellhead but could, if necessary, disconnect and telescope the drill, while moving out of the way of a drifting iceberg. Eight hours later, it could be back drilling again in precisely the same position.

It was a fascinating and enjoyable assignment. I interviewed politicians in St. John's who complained that not enough jobs were going to locals, which was true. "There's no one even scrubbing pots in the kitchen," one provincial government employee told me. The "mud men" and "cement men" I met aboard the *Havdrill* who were Canadian inevitably came from the Prairies or British Columbia and had experience in the Alberta oil fields. There were seventy-four workers on the ship—all men—and twelve were Canadians. Two or three were from France, one was a Scot and all the rest were Norwegian. Norwegian was clearly the working language of the ship.

My time was spent with the Canadians, small-towners mostly, who relaxed by playing gin for a tenth of a cent per point and drinking beer. They looked forward to periodic work breaks in St. John's, where BP made a house available to them and gave them twenty dollars a day in spending money. They were young, already making good money for the times (thirteen hundred dollars a month), and as most were single, they talked endlessly about the women they had met—or perhaps imagined they had met.

"You wouldn't believe St. John's," one of them told me. "Down there they know why you're there, by the Jesus, and they want it just as badly as you do—no kissy-face and going around goody-like for three nights before you get a hand on it. It's 'Let's get down to it' from the moment you get there."

Mostly, the men liked the money and were fine with the work. Some disliked the isolation, one in particular saying he hated it so much that he planned to leave on the next flight, having been stuck on board for three months straight. "I hope the bastard sinks," he said.

On my third day aboard the *Havdrill*, I attempted to do a good deed. One of the crew was struggling with two cases of beer, trying to move between two doors on his way to the recreation area, where the bar was.

"Hold on!" I called as I came up behind him. "I'll hold the door for you."

I spoke English. He spoke none. The Norwegian sailor let the door go and it swung back hard.

I did not get my hand back in time. The door, built to seal out the sea if necessary, clipped the top of the middle finger of my right hand, cutting it off as cleanly as a scalpel.

I screamed and blood burst out of my finger. The sailor heard me, saw me, put the beer down and opened the door.

The bloody top of my finger stuck a moment, then fell to the floor.

I had tissue out and was trying to stanch the wound. He ran and got paper towels. He also called for the medic.

The ship medic, also Norwegian, came fast, carrying a first-aid kit. He was able to stop the bleeding, put some sulpha on the wound to prevent infection and wrap the finger in gauze.

The top of my finger was gone, perhaps picked up by one of the many seagulls that travelled with the ship and stayed with it in the hope of scraps—if not fingertips.

The medic and one of the officers spoke English well enough that they were able to map out a plan for my injured finger. The medic would dress it a couple more times and, next day, there would be a helicopter run, so I could get to Gander, and from there to a hospital.

All through the night the finger throbbed. I had painkillers but they didn't seem to help much. This trip had gone so horribly wrong—all because of a case of beer, all because I had tried to help someone out.

The *whuuup-whuuup* sound of the helicopter next morning was the sweetest sound imaginable. I was packed and ready. A few workers got off, some galley supplies and equipment were taken off, and the pilots were ready to head back. I would be the only passenger. The chief pilot was different this time.

I got into our survival gear and strapped in. I waited for the emergency instructions to come over the headphones but none were forthcoming. That made sense. Anyone who was on the ship would have been through the drill on the way out.

We took off and were soon dodging fog banks and fighting against a headwind.

I sat there feeling sorry for myself, wondering how this trip could ever have gone worse for me . . .

. . . when suddenly it did.

The alarm screamed—once, twice, three times. This is what I had dreaded. *We're going down!*

The Sikorsky bounced, then steadied.

The pilot came on over the intercom.

"We got an extra coffee up here," he said. "Can I hand it down to you?"

Different pilot. Different use of the alarm system.

It was an object lesson in feature writing. The assignment is the imagining of the story, the telling is the reality. It rarely, if ever, happens that that story outlined in an office or a memo turns out exactly as planned.

5

The *Maclean's* Years

W*as Adrienne Clarkson wearing a bra?*
　　It was the talk of the Canadian magazine world in the fall of
1972. Not the federal election that Pierre Trudeau came within two
seats of blowing. Not the hockey Summit Series that came down to
the final thirty-four seconds of play in Moscow. But whether or not
a Toronto daytime television star—one day to serve as governor general—was feeling the freedom underneath her blouse.

A young freelancer named Melinda McCracken had pitched a
profile of the rising TV star to *Maclean's* and the editors had liked
the idea. In the issue of September 1, 1972, a sultry portrait of a sitting Clarkson graced the cover beneath headlines promoting works
by three prominent old-school male establishment figures: former
finance minister Walter Gordon, novelist Robertson Davies and journalist Bruce Hutchison. There could not have been a more deliberate
contrast. "Adrienne Clarkson," the cover tag line read, "Scrutinizing
the inscrutable."

Inside, the feature was titled "The Dream of Adrienne Clarkson:
Vichyssoise on ice meets crunchy Granola." McCracken's style was to
place herself in the piece as a natural contrast:

Perhaps she doesn't have to prove that she's liberated herself by not wearing a bra, or not having her hair cut, although it seems to me the fashion trip on any level is oppressive. Maybe she just likes to look nice on television. After all, she, not I, edited the *New Woman* series. And she, not I, covered the conference on women . . .

The reaction to the piece had been strong in both directions, some finding it a fascinating approach, others outraged by what they perceived to be an attack. A letter quickly arrived from Pierre Berton, then widely seen as the leading journalist in the land:

> I opened the current issue of *Maclean's* expecting to read, as advertised, an article about Adrienne Clarkson and, hopefully, to learn something about her that I didn't already know. Instead I found myself reading a piece about the rather dreary life of a writer named Melinda McCracken . . .
>
> I realize that modern journalistic practice insists that magazine writers discuss themselves, their background and their personal prejudices even if it means leaving out material about the subject at hand—but this is ridiculous!

Journalism was changing in Canada. "New Journalism" was a phrase not even uttered at what then passed as a journalism program at the University of Western Ontario. Most of us young print dreamers, however, were very aware of the work of American practitioners of this new style, from Tom Wolfe (*The Electric Kool-Aid Acid Test*) to Hunter S. Thompson, in publications such as *Rolling Stone*. Thompson's *Fear and Loathing on the Campaign Trail '72*, an incisive, often vicious look at the US presidential campaign that pitted sitting president Richard Nixon against challenger George McGovern, had caught the attention of every political journalist in North America. Many loved it. Many despised it.

Maclean's was irrepressibly *Canadian*. Newman was a key member of the Committee for an Independent Canada, a stridently nationalistic group founded by him, Liberal politician Walter Gordon and economist Abe Rotstein. The CIC was co-chaired by publisher Jack McClelland and influential Quebec journalist Claude Ryan (then editor of *Le Devoir*).

The committee's stated purpose was the promotion of Canadian cultural and economic independence—i.e., freedom from the overbearing and overwhelming influence of the huge and powerful country just to the south. Working with leaders such as Edmonton publisher Mel Hurtig and Toronto lawyer Eddie Goodman, the committee pressed the Trudeau government for limits to foreign investment and ownership. It pushed for programs that ultimately led to the creation of the Canada Development Corporation and Petro-Canada. It worked for, and largely achieved, more Canadian content on radio and television, as well as the elimination of tax privileges that had hugely benefited the likes of *Reader's Digest* and *Time* magazines.

Maclean's largely reflected the committee's values. A regular monthly feature was tagged "My Canada" and was invariably a paean to something particularly Canadian, whether a special place or something as simply Canadian as maple syrup. Some of the more sophisticated staff despised the feature. "Goddamn, it embarrassed us," senior editor Don Obe would years later tell the *Ryerson Review of Journalism*. "But [Newman] was right. He struck a tone with his economic nationalism that brought the magazine a solid readership and put it back on its feet."

Obe was a brilliant senior editor under Newman. Half Mohawk from the southwestern Ontario town of Brantford, near Six Nations territory, the short, mustachioed, ragged-haired chain-smoker was forever in search of new ideas. His running partner at the magazine was Tom Hedley, the suave, smartly dressed editor that Newman had hired away from *Esquire* magazine in New York. Hedley would go on to write the ridiculously successful screenplay for *Flashdance*. The two young editors loved to try the improbable. They sent Winnipeg novelist Jack Ludwig, with no former sports writing experience, off to Moscow to cover the 1972 Summit Series. They had the poet Al Purdy profile Toronto Maple Leafs journeyman defenceman Brian Glennie.

I was initially intimidated by such company, though they were very kind and welcoming to me. I had been given a fancy title, assistant editor—of which there were two, Susan Kent being the other—but had only a tiny office next to Newman's expansive editor's office. Most days, I would work to the muffled music of Stan Kenton. I was given no raise as I transferred from editorial services to *Maclean's* and was perfectly content with what I was being paid. My job was to handle the slush pile, mailbags of unsolicited manuscripts that arrived each week from all over the country: recipes for poutine and Saskatoon pie, poetry, cartoons, short stories, essays on everything from abortion to the role of the monarchy.

I would scan each one and then mark the opened letter with a letter, A through E. The letters would then be sent by inter-office mail to the secretarial pool on the second floor, where a typist would take the essentials out of the letter—sender's name and address, type of submission— and then begin typing: "Unfortunately, your short story has not been accepted by the editors of *Maclean's* for publication. We wish you luck with your future writing . . ."

There were other less-expected roles for me at the magazine. Ralph Tibbles, Paul Galer and, later, Angelo Sgabellone in the art department sometimes used me, or part of me, in photo shoots. I once wore a Superman costume while they shot me leaping from window sills, only to have my caped body appear in print with someone else's head. I played a model with a large key sewn into my sports jacket for a feature on programmed dating. I did some rewriting of articles by people who didn't normally write, such as a Saskatchewan flood expert who dealt with an overflowing Qu'Appelle River. I helped the Toronto folksinger

Malka turn taped interviews with the likes of Neil Young and Joni Mitchell into features.

The office might have been small but it had great sight lines. I was first to see not only the morning and afternoon coffee cart as it came off the seventh-floor elevator, but also the steady stream of greats as they filed into Newman's office, often delivering manuscripts. Much of their work I thought brilliant, such as June Callwood ending her opening notes on the 1973 royal tour with a brilliant, "Her Majesty's a pretty nice girl"—perfectly leaving out the Beatles' tag line—"but she doesn't have a lot to say"—as unnecessary. On any one day I might see passing my door the likes of Barbara Frum, Heather Robertson, Christina Newman, Jack Ludwig, Walter Stewart, Jack Batten, Trent Frayne, Harry Bruce, John Gault, Michael Enright, the elfin Robert Thomas Allen and many, many others. Intimidating indeed.

Mostly I worked under the direction of John Aitken, a senior editor who was a nephew of Lord Beaverbrook, Max Aitken, the legendary Canadian and British newspaper publisher. John was very tall, very furrow-browed and seemed in a permanent scowl so long as he kept his pipe in his mouth. Pipe out, he was friendly, quick to laugh and a very kind man. He saved me from being fired.

"Let's go to lunch," he said one morning, catching me off guard. We headed along Dundas Street toward Yonge, walking up a floor on the north side to a Greek restaurant that had no menus. Instead, you were invited into the kitchen, where you pointed at what you wanted and they then carried it to your table.

We talked about all sorts of things before John got around to the main subject. "The boss is concerned that you're not fitting in," he told me. I was shocked. I hadn't seen this coming.

"He says you haven't pitched any ideas."

Now I was stunned. I hadn't—because I didn't think it was my place. After all, there were all these *name* journalists both working there and freelancing. My job, clearly, was dealing with the minor chores.

"I didn't know I was supposed to," I told him. His bushy eyebrows bounced.

"Peter tells me you have a family connection to Tom Thomson," he said. "He thought you were doing a piece on that."

I recounted the details I had previously discussed with Peter: the grandfather ranger who knew Thomson, the great-uncle who married Winnie Trainor's sister Marie, the story Winnie's neighbour had told me about the dozen or more paintings stuffed into a six-quart basket. But so far I had made no progress with cousin Terry, who had inherited Winnie's house, cottage and belongings.

John Aitken's hand shook as he scraped clean his pipe and packed in fresh Amphora tobacco.

"These are Tom Thomson paintings no one has seen?" he asked, brow a ploughed field.

"No one. There are twelve or fourteen, not sure of the number, but my cousin has them."

"Where?"

"Binghamton . . . it's in New York."

John lighted his pipe, drew deeply and exhaled out the side while measuring me.

"Let's get to it, then. That's a hell of a story."

I did press ahead, contacted Terry once again and this time was turned down flat. He said he was writing his own book on his aunt Winnie and Tom Thomson—"the *true* story!"—and he would be using those sketches. (Terence McCormick passed away a few years back without ever producing his book on the romance. Art experts such as Joan Murray and David Silcox believed the sketches had likely been sold over the years to art galleries and private collections.)

I informed John of this unfortunate development and he said I should press on, that there was enough rich material there—the neighbour's story of stashing the six-quart basket of paintings behind her wood stove whenever Winnie travelled—that he believed there was a good feature in it, with or without the paintings.

John then let me in on a little secret. There was a feeling among Newman and senior staff that I wasn't working out. The lunch, in fact, had been to fire me gently. The thinking was I might be returned to editorial services like some minor leaguer who had been called up but hadn't been able to play with the professionals. I will be forever grateful to Winnie Trainor for saving my sorry assistant editor's butt.

With Aitken's enormous help, I did produce a feature on Tom Thomson and Winnifred Trainor—minus the sketches. I interviewed various people, including Winnie's doctor and lifelong friend, Dr. Wilfrid Pocock, who believed he had been screwed out of a promised inheritance of several sketches. In Huntsville, I caught up to Jimmy Stringer, an old family friend who lived year-round with his brother Wam at Canoe Lake. The Stringers made a meagre living by guiding in summer and shovelling cottage roofs in winter.

Jimmy Stringer swore he had once seen Tom Thomson's ghost. He further claimed that there were three Tom Thomson graves, not two. There was the first grave at little Canoe Lake, a second supposed burial in the Thomson family plot at Leith, Ontario, and a third dug by Tom's friends after they had exhumed him from the first grave and buried him again deeper in the Canoe Lake bush. Jimmy even claimed to have Tom Thomson's shinbone hidden in his shed. After two bottles of cheap sherry in the room he had taken at the Empire Hotel, he vowed to show me the secret grave once the snow was gone and the ice off the lake. The spring thaw was then just beginning.

In a bizarre coincidence, the following morning Jimmy collected his groceries and a few bottles from the liquor store and hired a cab to take him back to Canoe Lake, where he had stashed a toboggan by the Portage Store. He put the groceries and booze on the toboggan and set out for the far side of the lake. The ice was soft. He broke through and drowned not far from where Tom Thomson's body had surfaced fifty-six years earlier.

John Aitken was right. Paintings or no paintings, there was a hell of a story there. I became so fascinated with the Tom Thomson–Winnie Trainor tale that, in later years, I would turn it into a novel, *Canoe Lake*, as well as a non-fiction book, *Northern Light: The Enduring Mystery of Tom Thomson and the Woman Who Loved Him*.

The feature took a long time to finish. Peter Newman was still concerned about whether or not I had the right stuff. He knew how much work Aitken was putting in on my Thomson piece. At one point, the editor had Elda, his secretary, call me into his office for a "lesson." Newman handed me a story from an earlier issue by an East Coast poet called Bill Howell. It was about big rig truckers on the Trans-Canada Highway. In his soft voice, the editor pushed the upside-down story across his large desk to me and asked me to read aloud while he scraped and filled his pipe. I picked the issue up and began to read.

"You see the cadence?" he asked at one point.

"Yes," I said, though I wasn't sure.

"You should read whatever you write aloud—it's the best way to get the right rhythm. I play jazz when I write. I think it makes me a better writer."

Writing was almost an ecclesiastical word at *Maclean's*. We weren't *reporters*; we were *writers*. Every so often, someone of vast import would be brought in to give a session on the art of writing. Newman invited the likes of Bruce Hutchison and Hugh MacLennan to hold seminars in the boardroom. Hedley and Obe managed to persuade Tom Wolfe to come up from New York. They brought in Al Purdy, the poet, who began a post-talk lunch by ordering four beers—all for him. Marshall McLuhan talked to us about communication.

Later, when McLuhan had left some of us with spinning heads after an hour of "the medium is the message" theory, Obe and Hedley took their star for a walk down to city hall, where the greatest mind of the moment walked up to Henry Moore's famous sculpture, *The Archer*, tapped hard on it, pressed an ear to the statue and tapped again.

"Why . . . it's hollow!" he exclaimed.

Obe thought this beyond hilarious. Marshall McLuhan, investigative reporter.

As we had no designated sports editor in those early years, I ended up being assigned columns and features on sport, usually hockey. In the winter of 1973–74, I was asked to "ghost" a piece for Ken Dryden, the Montreal Canadiens goaltender who had played such a pivotal role for Team Canada in the Summit Series only eighteen months earlier. I met with Ken—tall, scholarly-looking in glasses, with a sharp and droll sense of humour—and we got on well. I was delighted with the assignment.

This would be no NHL hockey player talking about "stick to our system" or "one game at a time." This was a graduate of Cornell University who planned to move on to law school after a short period of time in professional hockey. He had already won two Stanley Cups, the Calder Trophy as NHL rookie of the year and the Conn Smythe Trophy as the most valuable player of the playoffs. He was erudite and intelligent and clearly had the résumé to back up anything he might have to say about the national game.

Ken had taped and written down his thoughts during the series. He had paid to have the tapes transcribed and kept them in multiple red plastic ring binders. I spent hours wading through them, fascinated by the dedication to detail, and then took a first run at writing his feature. He was a goaltender, after all, not a *writer*.

I do wish I had kept that first draft. I have it in mind that it began something like this: "People see the world in different shades. Some see dark, some light, and some see with more sharpness than others . . ." That, or something equally terrible.

"I'd like to take a run at it," Dryden said after I'd shown him what would surely be his masterpiece. "I have an idea for a lede."

Two weeks later, he was back. This, in part, was his opening:

> People are as important as angles to a goaltender. Players are predictable, and that's why the second-guessing can be just as valid as the goaltending basics. If you know a player well his moves become less surprising, but if you are surprised it takes a second or more to react properly. And you can't afford seconds in a game as fast-moving as hockey. By anticipating what's going to come next you're playing the odds. And educated odds-making can often approach certainty.
>
> Twice now I have faced the Soviet team, in 1969 with the national amateur team and in 1972 with Team Canada. I played four games in the Team Canada–Soviet series—Montreal, Vancouver, and two in Moscow—and was beaten for 19 goals. Oddsmaking can't work when you don't know the people.
>
> That I could get to know them goes back to a moment I had in December of 1969, when the national team was playing the Soviet national team in Vancouver. It was early in the second period and the Soviets had already scored four, maybe five times on me. It was my first game against them, and though at first I was nervous and uncertain, those feelings soon evaporated into angry reality with the suddenness and shock of the endless goals. Anger soon became despair over their effortless passing, the ease of the goals, my own failings. A face-off was called to the circle on my left and Aleksandr Maltsev, whose small stature betrayed his efficiency as a player, moved into the slot area directly in front of me. He was poised to slam the puck my way should it come back to him. I was staring at him, only partly as a goalie fixes on an opponent. He looked back blankly, and brightened.
>
> Then he winked.

It was a brilliant lede. I went to Obe and Newman and showed them and argued that Ken should write his own piece, that he had no need of a "ghost." They agreed to see what Ken could do on his own and the goalie/writer came through. We titled Ken's feature "To Russia with Love: A great goaltender's mission of peace."

Douglas Gibson was then the publisher of Macmillan of Canada and we had periodically met and talked about the possibility of a novel using hockey as the setting. I was still working with McClelland & Stewart editors on my first novel, *Shorelines* (later changed to *Canoe Lake*), but was delighted to consider the possibility of a hockey novel with Macmillan. Doug was quite keen. I told him about Ken Dryden's notebooks and said that I thought Ken had a good book in him. I was able to introduce the two, and though it took several years to finish and a great deal of prodding and pushing from Doug Gibson, Macmillan was able to publish *The Game*, to this day considered the best book ever written on the national game. Contrary to rumours that rise up every now and then, I did *not* ghost Ken's book. Every word he wrote himself.

More and more, I was doing my own features. The magazine sent me to Sweden with a bantam team from Sarnia, Ontario, that featured a young Dino Ciccarelli. I told the story mostly through the eyes of Dino's father, Victor, a welder who had immigrated from Italy in 1955 and now wept openly as the Canadian anthem was played before his son's game in Örnsköldsvik. There were cover features on Guy Lafleur and Marcel Dionne. The Dionne profile is particularly memorable in that it was written mid-season and failed even to mention the young upstart who would catch and tie Dionne for that year's scoring title: Wayne Gretzky. Oops!

The best assignments were the "adventures"—a few of which we will return to later. The magazine sent me to participate in war games with the Canadian Armed Forces in New Brunswick. I went several times to James Bay to write about the Cree and their battle against Quebec hydro development. I went out on the land with trappers and hunters.

I wrote about farming on the Prairies, cruising the Caribbean, tracking acid rain in Algonquin Park. I went on tour in the United States with the Canadian rock band Rush. I wrote cover profiles on Mordecai Richler, Margaret Atwood, Joe Clark, Mila Mulroney, John Crosbie, Flora MacDonald, Jean Drapeau and many others. It seemed I was paid to do whatever I liked. And I truly loved it.

Newman would regularly say that he was in charge of the "world's largest daycare centre." Egos clashed, feelings were hurt, affairs flared. Lots of laughter, lots of cursing, overt fawning and covert backstabbing—it was never less than fascinating. Jack Ludwig, brought in by Obe and Hedley from Winnipeg to do a feature on Ken Dryden, somehow managed to break his arm rolling over in his bed at the nearby Holiday Inn. After he was taken to Toronto General and fitted with an appropriate cast, he returned to the hotel room for several days. I had to take over a typewriter and paper and carbon paper so that he could peck away with one hand at his feature. Somehow he managed.

Hedley could talk a better magazine game than anyone I had ever encountered. He had, after all, worked at *Esquire*, the magazine famous for features such as "Frank Sinatra Has a Cold," by Gay Talese, and Tom Wolfe's "The Last American Hero Is Junior Johnson. Yes!" Hedley was very talented. In the fall of 1973, I had been assigned to edit a Jack Batten feature on quarterbacks in the Canadian Football League and had offered a cringeworthy, pretentious headline—"The Sky Above, the Mud Below," that Hedley took one glance at, crossed out, and replaced with the perfect headline: "Passing Fancy."

John Gault, executive editor of the magazine and pitcher for our press-league ball team, was a master of the story title. He made a sign for his office: "John Gault gives good head." He also gave Newman headaches. When the editor wanted the word "booze" cut from a feature for fear it would upset regular advertisers such as Crown Royal and Black Velvet, liquor ads far outnumbering any other genre, Gault and two other senior editors vowed to resign if the word was removed.

Newman ordered the word deleted; Gault handed in his resignation; the other two turtled.

I had returned to *Maclean's* after a three-year stint at *The Canadian*, the weekly supplement magazine that was now edited by Don Obe and was distributed each Saturday with the *Toronto Star* and a dozen other dailies across the country. While I wrote about hockey stars and baseball and football players, I was increasingly becoming interested in political stories and politicians. A controversial feature on then federal minister of transport Otto Lang won top prize at the first National Magazine Awards in 1978. The story, complete with a caricature of Lang riding a Canadian government transport plan à la Slim Pickens on an atom bomb in the movie *Dr. Strangelove*, was about the minister's use of government jets, which was public knowledge. The story caused a sensation, however, when two newspapers in Lang's home province of Saskatchewan, the *Saskatoon Star-Phoenix* and the *Regina Leader-Post*, refused to distribute the supplement on June 4, 1977 (my twenty-ninth birthday). Two nights running, the magazine feature led the national news. It involved heated debate in the House of Commons. A subsequent lawsuit went on for more than five years before everyone agreed to let the matter drop.

It was an unnerving experience. It would not be my only lawsuit, but certainly the one that dragged on the longest. To my great relief, none ever went all the way to court. MacGregor luck.

Ellen and I now had two very young children, two-year-old Kerry and the baby, Christine. We had earlier made the decision that Ellen would leave her work at Odon Wagner Gallery. She worked in art restoration with a lot of different chemicals and oils, something she wanted to get away from during her first pregnancy. We'd been trying to buy our first house in the outskirts of Toronto—downtown being far beyond my salary reach—and we spent weekends looking around places like Uxbridge and Aurora without much luck. Prices were decidedly cheaper in Ottawa, and with my new interest in covering politics, I requested a move to the *Maclean's* Ottawa bureau. Newman was happy to agree to the change. I was delighted. So off we went, *Maclean's* footing the moving bill. We found a lovely bungalow in Ottawa's Elmvale Acres area, financed its sixty-six-thousand-dollar price, moved in and instantly fell in love with the national capital's parks, rivers and ease of traffic. I even got free parking on Parliament Hill.

Bob Lewis was bureau chief of the Ottawa office in the National Press Building on Wellington, directly across from the Peace Tower. He wasn't pleased to see a Toronto feature writer from head office take up a desk that usually went to someone who would chase MPs after Question Period and contribute to group stories, but I was only too happy to do the grunt work and we eventually became great friends. It was an office of talented, hardworking journalists: Ian Urquhart, Ian Anderson, Susan Riley, John Hay, with others coming and going over the three years I spent as a member of the Parliamentary Press Gallery.

Newman was hiring more and more staff with his master plan to move from a monthly to a biweekly to a weekly newsmagazine. He hired a terrific managing editor in Mel Morris, a classic newspaperman who made the transition to magazines effortlessly. There was another transition going on with the magazine itself as it shifted from an almost exclusively male domain. Many of Newman's hires were young, bright women: Marci McDonald, Angela Ferrante, Susan Kent, Anne Collins, Judith Finlayson, Ann Dowsett Johnston, Elaine Dewar, Erna Paris, Linda McQuaig, Mary Janigan, Val Ross, Barbara Amiel, Rona Maynard, Carol Goar, Joanne Webb, Janet Enright, Linda Diebel, Marni Jackson, Marsha Boulton, Susan Riley, Jane O'Hara, Ann Walmsley, Judith Timson, to mention but a few.

As the magazine shifted to biweekly, Kevin Doyle came on as managing editor and Michael Enright as assistant managing editor. Staff more than doubled as the seventh floor of M-H became more like a busy newsroom than a smoky club where stories took a minimum of six weeks to move from copy-edit to publication. The art department took on a brilliant young designer in Angelo Sgabellone. Carl Mollins joined as an editor and was instantly beloved by the staff for his wise advice and gentle trims. Michael Posner, my old friend from M-H editorial services, joined as both writer and editor. The renovated magazine had accomplished writers like Ian Brown, Michael Clugston and Hal Quinn, Rod McQueen in business, Anthony Wilson-Smith in Ottawa, Graham Fraser in Quebec. Increasingly, the magazine began to spread, with bureaus in Washington and London and correspondents strategically placed around the globe.

For a while, *Maclean's* was a family affair for the MacGregors. Younger brother Tom worked briefly as a reporter/researcher before eventually moving on to a distinguished thirty-two-year career with *Legion* magazine. Our older sister Ann, master of trivia night at her local pub in downtown Toronto, was hired as a researcher and shone in the job. She had sole fact-checking rights for Allan Fotheringham's last page column, at his insistence. "Foth" called Ann his guardian angel. When she died of cancer in 1995 at the age of fifty, the entire staff came north to Huntsville to attend her funeral, then editor Bob Lewis delivering a powerful eulogy before all repaired to the local Legion for drinks—all carefully arranged and paid for by Ann before her passing.

Peter Newman must have decided our little reading lessons on cadence had worked. When he published his memoir, *Here Be Dragons*, in 2004, he wrote, "I mentored many writers, but none with greater satisfaction than Roy MacGregor, who worked for the magazine on three separate occasions. . . . Roy's command of creative non-fiction became textbook perfect. In his columns, articles, and books, his subjects and his country came alive, almost as if he were painting instead of writing."

To me, however, there was no one at the magazine in its monthly, biweekly or weekly form who could compare to Marci McDonald. This vibrant Meryl Streep lookalike could get information from her subjects that no one else could even imagine. I recall her 1975 profile of Defence Minister James Richardson, titled by Gault as "Always the Young Stranger." The detail she somehow dug out of this awkward Winnipeg multimillionaire was simply staggering:

> On his office wall he keeps a copy of Kipling's "If you can keep your head when all about you are losing theirs . . .," beside a chair in his Ottawa office he has fondly placed a sculpture of Jonathan Livingston Seagull and in his left trouser pocket on a leather thong he carries a tiny carved aluminum duck dubbed J. J. after the philosophical seagull. In those awkward Ottawa social pauses when colleagues watch James Richardson fish in his pocket for loose change and in his head for words, he is frequently just fishing for the reassurance of J. J. He reaches for him now . . .

Marci soon left for Paris, where she wrote for *Maclean's* and various other publications as she travelled the world. Her specialty was the long, in-depth feature, and as the magazine morphed from monthly to biweekly to weekly newsmagazine, there was increasingly less room for such work in the new *Maclean's*.

There were certainly growing pains. Early reviews were not always kind. Ian Urquhart, long-time parliamentary reporter for *Maclean's*, told Clive Cocking for his 1979 election book *Following the Leaders* that he considered his own publication to be "Mickey Mouse . . . basically a rewrite operation." Ian left shortly after Cocking's book appeared and was soon a senior editor at the *Toronto Star*.

"Breach of Promise," read a headline in the September 1980 issue of *Saturday Night* magazine. "Two years after going weekly, *Maclean's* still falls flat as a newsmagazine." The article, by Morris Wolfe, traced how lobbying by the Committee for an Independent Canada had led to the passage of Bill C-58 in 1976, taking away the aforementioned mail and tax advantages enjoyed by *Time Canada* and thereby clearing the way for the transformation of *Maclean's* into a weekly newsmagazine.

Wolfe wrote that Newman's first editorial in the weekly version promised "a rough working draft of history . . . a fresh instrument of communications that may change the way this country sees itself." Wolfe was unimpressed, saying this new product on the newsstands "lacks the thoroughness of the American magazines and the thoughtfulness of the British magazines."

Criticism followed about the design and even the writing. Wolfe took a particular shot at Newman's own style concerning a column on Progressive Conservative leader Joe Clark: "He steals into my office like a wild fawn caught eating broccoli." I thought that a pretty accurate portrait of the now former prime minister.

There was some praise in the *Saturday Night* slam. The reporting of Bob Lewis in Ottawa and David Thomas in Quebec was to be admired. "Roy MacGregor turns out excellent essays on a variety of subjects from Mordecai Richler to acid rain. Allan Fotheringham, when he isn't simply sneering, can be superb." Barbara Amiel, he thought, turned out a terrific feature on Leonard Cohen.

What reputation I had came from writing feature profiles. I loved doing them and, it seemed, I was becoming known for them. In a newspaper review of Al Purdy's journalism collection, *No Other Country*, writer Jack Batten asked, "How about a collection of Roy MacGregor's magazine profiles? Good, strong, carefully crafted work that'll stand up over the long haul. . . . Instead, we get Purdy, who's a proven poet and no doubt a prince of a fellow but who, in his most inspired moments, could never make it into the journalistic league with MacGregor, [Christina] Newman, [Heather] Robertson or a couple of dozen other Canadian magazine writers."

I was, however, writing fewer and fewer feature profiles. The changing magazine was more into issues than people. On October 30, 1978, I wrote a rather snivelling note to Peter Newman and Kevin Doyle saying that "A week has yet to go by when I haven't heard 'Features are dead.'" I was overreacting. The magazine was changing but features were not at all dead. Just sick and, it seemed to me, failing.

In late summer of 1981, I received the only Canada Council grant I ever applied for—three thousand dollars. It was enough for me to ask for and receive a three-month leave of absence to finish a work of fiction that turned out to be *The Last Season*, the hockey novel Doug Gibson had wanted for Macmillan. I did not return to *Maclean's*, however. Walter Stewart, that long-time *Maclean's* stalwart, had moved to *Today* magazine (previously known as *The Canadian*) and offered me a substantial raise as well as my own travel budget. Not only that, but I would write nothing but features.

"*Maclean's* is not a place I leave out of any malice," I said in my resignation letter to Peter Newman. "You have been most generous and kind to me since you first hired me from *Office Equipment & Methods* so many centuries ago."

Incredibly, I would return to *Maclean's* for a third round. Working for Walter Stewart at *Today* magazine had been wonderful, but sadly brief. In the summer of 1982, several newspapers closed across the country, leaving one major daily in most markets. There was no more need for weekend supplements to attract weekend readers, so *Today* simply vanished. We were all laid off with severance packages—mine small, as I had been there such a short time—and there was no choice but to turn to freelancing wherever work was to be found. I wrote speeches, articles for sports programs, a few features, but the work was uncertain and the payments irregular. Not good for a young family with a mortgage.

Once again, Senator Keith Davey came to the rescue. He called his friend from college days, *Toronto Star* editor-in-chief Gary Lautens. A single interview with Lautens and I was hired on as one of a handful of columnists sharing the prestigious page 2. Ellen and I moved our four little ones—Kerry, the eldest at six, Christine, four, Jocelyn, one, and the baby, Gordon—to Oakville, just west of Toronto, and I began taking the GO train in to 1 Yonge Street five days a week. Eighteen months later, the *Star* sent me to Ottawa—my employer once again paying all moving costs! It was a great bureau with Bob Hepburn as bureau chief, the renowned Richard Gwyn as national affairs columnist, and several excellent reporters. We were a big bureau with major clout in Ottawa.

It was a happy time—Bob and I even played on the same beer-league hockey team two nights a week—but not a long time. Gwyn announced he was retiring from his political column and veteran Val Sears and I foolishly thought the battle would be between us for the prized post. Much to our surprise, *Star* managing editor Ray Timson announced that the new national affairs columnist would not come from inside, but from outside. Carol Goar, the Ottawa editor for *Maclean's*, would take over the Gwyn space.

I made a career mistake shortly after. I was approached to take over Carol Goar's job and so in 1985 I returned to *Maclean's* for a third run, returning to a magazine that bore little, if any, resemblance to the magazine I had loved.

It was now early 1986. I had spent the last year and a half hiring some superb staff—Ken MacQueen, Paul Gessell, Michael Rose, Hilary Mackenzie, Karen Nicholson—and moving our offices to an open-concept space on the third floor of the National Press Building on Wellington Street, directly across from Parliament Hill.

I had travelled by train from Ottawa to Toronto for a summit meeting with the new *Maclean's* editor, Kevin Doyle, and managing editor, Bob Lewis, who had previously been my boss in our Ottawa bureau. I thought I was about to be fired because of something I'd foolishly put down on paper.

I remember thinking on the four-hour train ride to Union Station that John Turner had it right. The former prime minister and finance minister would tell staff and colleagues to avoid, as much as possible, putting things down on paper. They'll come back to haunt you.

The new hires in Ottawa were struggling to know what the magazine expected of them. I had sold them on the chance to write features, to become better writers, to travel and to cover great stories. I thought they should have their own distinctive "voice"—surely a hope for any magazine that prides itself on its writers and their production.

Kevin, however, had come from *Newsweek* magazine in New York and was determined to turn *Maclean's* into a formula production of meat-grinder copy. There was said to be a Doyle "news-speak" list that encouraged reporters to use phrases such as "for his part" and overused words like "still" and "indeed." The staff quietly ridiculed such verbiage.

There was, as well, a list of words the editor wished all reporters to avoid. The "avoid list" contained something like seventy strict no-nos—never use "perfect" (nothing is perfect), stay away from "probe," "prestigious," "thus," "therefore," "envision," "vow," "viable" . . . Don't use foreign words at all. This applied even to "café," which was to be replaced with "eating place with tables and chairs." Section editors, bless them, fought and won the right to use "café."

Some years later, when Don Obe had moved on from *Maclean's* to *Toronto Life* magazine and then became head of the Ryerson School of Journalism, the school's *Ryerson Review of Journalism* produced a long feature on the converted newsmagazine. Author Andrew Leitch said writers at *Maclean's* bemoaned "what they variously call the 'bizarre,' 'arcane,' even 'byzantine' editing process that has gripped the magazine since 1982, when Kevin Doyle moved into the editor's chair."

Robert Fulford, the erudite editor of *Saturday Night* magazine, penned a very tough article on the current state of *Maclean's*, calling the weekly "a weak magazine by anyone's standard." He quoted me as saying that the newsmagazine's prose had become "a language of its own, a language people neither speak, nor can understand, nor can read."

Reporters knew that their work would be homogenized from the moment they delivered their story. Each piece would go through a long chain up through the system, ending on the desk of either Bob Lewis or Kevin Doyle. The writers all prayed for Lewis, who had the lighter touch and was, in his own right, a fine stylist.

Fulford again quoted me: "The way the process works, says MacGregor, is similar to the way children decide who gets to bat first in a baseball game. 'The last hand on the bat wins.'"

But such harsh comments were not for this day. The Ryerson piece would not appear for some time. I was still at *Maclean's* and still hopeful that some of us there could get Kevin to take a lighter touch, to be more open to varied voices and style, even to a little humour in the copy.

Now, Kevin was a very nice man. He had a face as decidedly Irish as his name. We both had Ottawa Valley roots—he came from Fitzroy Harbour, a small village on the Ottawa River upstream from the capital. He had studied for the priesthood. He was congenial, polite, kind and funny. But he was equally stubborn and determined. Bob Lewis was a friend from our years together in Ottawa. An excellent writer himself, he had, like Kevin, experience with American weekly newsmagazines. In Bob's case, it was *Time*. This was when both US publications were at the top of their game and much admired. Bob, too, could be stubborn and determined. But he did know and appreciate good writing.

My entreaties on behalf of my Ottawa colleagues had had zero effect. I wanted Toronto to ease up on the over-editing. I wanted our Ottawa writers to have a chance to write their own stories rather than "filing" to someone in Toronto who would toss the collected material into that gigantic meat grinder in the copy room and churn out next week's stories.

I also thought *Maclean's* had moved away from being distinctly Canadian. I recalled the glory days of the monthly, when each issue would carry a "My Canada" feature written by one of the brightest literary lights of the day. Now we were, understandably, a publication with international interests—bureaus in Paris, London, Washington, correspondents in capitals around the world—but there was room, surely, for more of a sense of the country we lived in.

Kevin had suggested I write him a memorandum listing my several concerns. I took it seriously. I wrote a seventeen-point memo that I thought argued passionately and correctly for less of a leash on the Ottawa people. I discussed the importance of "voice" and "personality." I went on and on and on . . .

I sent the memo over one of those old, rolling fax machines that took about five minutes a page to send. The following morning the phone rang; I was to come to Toronto to discuss the memo.

This did not look good. I remember buying a new pair of black dress shoes in the morning before our luncheon showdown, and I can still sense how much they pinched as I sat there with Kevin and Bob and we all tried to make merry over small talk and cold beer.

I knew it was coming. Kevin tabled the seventeen-point memo and began going through the points one by one. He and Bob took turns shooting them down in order. They did it politely and nicely and they even partially accepted a few points, but it was growing painfully obvious what was coming.

I listened and nodded. Some of their arguments I did actually agree with, but for the most part I had lost heavily.

They, however, seemed very satisfied with our lunch. Kevin even joked that at one point he had thought the lunch would lead to a dismissal—which, obviously, it was going to—but they felt now perhaps I understood their position better and would be able to adjust everything from my negative attitude to my colleagues' appreciation that "Toronto knows best."

We shook hands and I left on good standing. I flew back to Ottawa and immediately began making plans to leave before anyone could fire me.

I called my friend Susan Riley. We had worked at the *Maclean's* biweekly together and had become close colleagues and even regular Friday guests on CBC Radio's *As It Happens*. She had moved on to the *Ottawa Citizen*, where she was thriving.

Susan acted quickly. I almost immediately had a call from the newspaper's assistant managing editor, Scott Honeyman, who felt me out over the phone and then said he'd get back to me. He called the next day to invite me to lunch with him and managing editor Nelson Skuce.

Again, those handy old Ottawa Valley roots came through. Nelson had family in Barry's Bay, not far from Whitney. We knew lots of people in common. Virtually everyone from that part of the Valley had worked, one time or another, for McRae Lumber, where my father had spent his entire working life.

Nelson thought it was a great idea that I come on as a new columnist. I could even stay working downtown, only now out of the offices of the *Citizen* rather than *Maclean's*.

We made plans for me to meet the *Citizen's* new editor, Keith Spicer.

Another adventure, more strange, more amusing, more fun than I could ever have imagined, was about to begin.

MORDECAI AND THE TAPE RECORDER

It was not my idea.

It was spring 1980 and *Maclean's* deputy managing editor Alan Walker, renowned for his bizarre sense of humour—he kept forceps in his desk for when he had to "handle" sports copy, as well as a real horsewhip to ensure that writers made their deadlines—thought that I, a small-town Ontario anglophone, should be dispatched to Montreal for a cover story they would title "Probing the Jewish Soul."

Mordecai Richler was coming out with his eighth novel, *Joshua Then and Now*, a sprawling 435-page opus and his first published work since returning to Canada from London in 1972, convinced that he was written out. The new book read like an explosion of pent-up imagination: a mother who strips at Joshua's bar mitzvah and blossoms late as a porn star; characters on the Spanish island of Ibiza; examinations of works from the Bible to CanLit; and cameos by the likes of William Lyon Mackenzie King and Gump Worsley. Daunting indeed.

My friend David Staines, who taught (and still teaches) English at the University of Ottawa, gave me a crash course in Richler, as they were friends and David knew all his previous works. It was a great help to me, though I still felt intimidated. Richler, after all, had a reputation for being . . . difficult.

I drove down to Montreal from Ottawa. I took a small, portable tape recorder from the bureau office. I preferred to take notes so I could not only write down quotes but also scribble observations while the subject believed me to be taking down verbatim whatever they were saying. I figured Richler would expect me to record him as I asked the questions I had carefully written down. I checked into the Queen Elizabeth Hotel, and carrying the small tape recorder as well as a reporter's notebook and two pens, made my way to Peel Street and the Montreal Press Club, where the great author had agreed to meet.

He was sitting with a double scotch and smoking a cigarillo when I arrived. A bald man was standing beside him, slapping his own shiny scalp and claiming, "I used to have a crew cut but the crew bailed out!" Richler graced him with an indulgent laugh.

After a couple of beers for me and another double scotch for him, he suggested we go to his apartment on the side of Mont Royal to conduct a proper interview. We left and headed back along Peel Street, where another man invaded his space. "Mordecai Richler!" the stranger shouted. "You write *lousy* books!" Richler ignored him completely.

On the way up the sloping street to the apartment, he stopped at a dépanneur and purchased two bottles of Rémy Martin cognac. At the eighth-floor apartment he introduced me to Florence, also a Montrealer, whom he had met and married in London. She was gracious and said she would be going out while we talked.

I decided to use the tape recorder as well as take my usual notes. Richler opened one of the bottles of Rémy Martin, poured us both a glass, fired up a fresh cigarillo and was ready to go.

We talked for hours. About the book. About the Montreal Canadiens. He was willing to venture anywhere, it seemed, except the topic of his own mother, with whom he was supposedly estranged and not speaking. Anything else, though, was fine. He admitted to never, ever using the stationary bicycle that had sat next to his desk since Florence bought it for him two years earlier. He talked of making the film *The Apprenticeship of Duddy Kravitz* with his friend the director Ted Kotcheff. We talked about his reputation for rudeness. He once told author Richard Rohmer, "If you cared anything at all about letters, you'd never go near a typewriter." He admitted happily to being brusque and often rude.

We talked and he poured. I drank with him because I was nervous and because I wanted him to like me and feel he could be open. I matched him drink for drink—and knew I was drinking far too much.

He opened the second bottle of Rémy Martin. I recall nothing whatsoever after that.

My next recollection was waking up in my room at the Queen Elizabeth.

I was wearing exactly the same clothes I'd worn to the Montreal Press Club. I had fallen asleep—*passed out?*—on the bed without even turning back the covers. My head was killing me.

Panic rose like a tsunami. I had little memory of the interview. I checked my notes and could see that they had turned into a scrawl and fallen off the page like a lemming over a rock cut.

I, too, was drowning.

And then I remembered the tape recorder. It sat on the dresser, though I had no memory of carrying it back.

I went to it as tentatively as if approaching a sleeping bear.

I could see the tape had been rewound to the beginning. *Did I even think to turn it on?*

I pushed the button, praying.

The voice of Mordecai Richler came through loud and clear.

I fast-forwarded the tape to near the end, pushed "play" again.

Mordecai was still speaking. Someone else said something every now and then. Things like "Gee!" and "Is that right?" The other voice was . . . slurring.

But I had my Mordecai Richler interview. No one would ever need to know about the Rémy Martin.

"EXPENSE IT!"

Priorities, priorities, priorities . . .

I was in Winnipeg for the 1975 Manitoba Open. *The Canadian* magazine wanted a profile on a young, up-and-coming Canadian golf professional, Bob Panasik. It was a juicy summer assignment. I was even invited by the organizers to bring my clubs and play in the pro-am that would be held before the weekend tournament.

I had been there only one day when the hotel room telephone—this was well before cell phones or texting—rang. It was my editor, Don Obe, on the line, which immediately spooked me.

"You're going to have to come back," he told me.

Whatever could it be? Ellen had just informed me that she was pregnant. It would be our first child—*had something gone wrong?* Our parents were getting on. Had there been an accident?

"Why?" I asked. *"What's up?"*

"We need you. First playoff game tomorrow at Ramsden Park. Against the *Star*."

The call had nothing to do with family. And nothing to do with journalism. I was needed back in Toronto for a fastball game that no one would watch and no one would ever hear of—but it was a matter of life and death for those of us who played fastball in the Toronto Men's Press League.

The league had been around for years. The three newspapers—the *Toronto Star*, the upstart *Toronto Sun* and the *Globe and Mail*—all had teams. Canadian Press had a team. The CBC had a team. And a sixth team, *Toronto Life*, had been put together using a few scattered magazine types, a handful of advertising copywriters, a few kids and a few old guys.

Obe had recruited me to this grab bag of a team from *Maclean's*, where we had both worked for a few years. One of his pitches—good choice of word there—had been that we could head out after work together to the various ballparks where the league played its evening games, Ramsden Park just off the Rosedale stop along the Yonge Street subway line being one of the more popular.

I first replaced Peter Gzowski at third base. Gzowski was then with the CBC but had begun playing with this group when he was editor of *Maclean's* and had remained loyal to the team, which had gone through various mutations before becoming the *Toronto Life* team. He was retiring from the field. Peter's son, Peter Gzowski Jr., was a mainstay in the outfield, with a great glove and arm. After one season at third, I moved to catcher, replacing Denis Harvey, then head of CBC News, who was also packing it in. Obe played first base. John Gault of *Maclean's* and Bill Durnan of the Vickers & Benson ad agency pitched. Two others from the agency, Terry O'Malley and Terry Hill, held down second base and shortstop, respectively. Third was either John Macfarlane, then editing *Toronto Life*, or Dave Muller, who had a thriving business in sheepskin clothing. Among others joining young Peter in the field were a young Dave Amer, who would later become a formidable pitcher, and a big kid named Byron. No idea if he had a last name. The team was always in flux, with players coming and going. I would soon enough be gone to Ottawa, never to play another Toronto Men's Press League game.

But I would never forget this one.

It was such a different time in journalism. Newspapers had money, lots of it, and they spent it. That meant the weekend supplements had money as well and could spend it as the editor and publisher determined it best spent. As editor, Don Obe was only too happy to approve two return air tickets to Winnipeg, one of them to get me out for the story, one to get me back for the game.

Poor Bob Panasik, the golfer and subject of our profile. We had been running in the morning out by the airport before heading for the Breezy Bend Golf and Country Club out Roblin Avenue and the pro-am round.

"I have to fly back this evening," I told him.

He looked crushed. "What about the story?"

"I'll be back for the final two rounds. Not to worry."

"What's so important that you have to go back?"

Like I could tell him.

The *Toronto Life* ball team was up against their dreaded rivals from the *Toronto Star*. They usually beat us. Their pitcher was Martin Goodman, listed on the editorial pages as the managing editor, called "Marty" and nastier titles on the playing fields of Ramsden and Davisville.

Marty had once played at a high level and now, nearing forty, he was still a fine player. (He would die, tragically, of pancreatic cancer at age forty-six.) Marty had a wicked windmill delivery. He wore real ball pants and had spikes. His son was at most games, assigned to run out onto the field with Marty's warm-up jacket if the *Star* pitcher made it to base on a hit. In a tournament in Kitchener, Marty had soaked his arm in ice between games. In a regular-season game at Ramsden, he had even spiked our shortstop racing to second base to get a forced out. This, in a league where virtually no one else wore baseball spikes. We thought it deliberate. It was a situation where shortstop Terry Hill had to bite his lip as he dabbed at the blood Marty had drawn. The *Star*, after all, was a major client of Vickers & Benson.

Hatred in sports is far different from hatred in politics or real life. Hatred in sports is fun. Players take delight in it. In truth, those who are most hated by other teams are often secretly most admired— players whom others want to beat, humiliate and destroy are the first to be welcomed and embraced should they somehow come to join the team. It is a dynamic unknown in any other world—except, perhaps, law firms.

Obe wanted me back in Toronto for the key playoff game because I had a history with Marty. For reasons unknown, I could hit him. I batted left and that might have been part of it, as most players batted right and Marty pitched right. Whenever I came to the plate, Marty would make a great show of distributing his fielders on the assumption that I would pull the ball to the right if I got a hit. He would realign his second baseman and shortstop and even have the first baseman move halfway down the line in case I hit a grounder to the right of second base.

I got back to Toronto around midnight. Spent the entire next day waiting around our offices in the Simpson Tower on Bay Street until it was time for Obe and me to head to Ramsden and the big showdown.

Terry O'Malley, the head of Vickers & Benson and our team leader, had filled in the lineup card. Gault would be pitching. I would be catching and batting fourth, cleanup. Gault had a nice pitch where he would clip his hip and give the ball a different spin, causing it to curve oddly. Almost a knuckleball. He was fun to catch. He also had a changeup that drove the big hitters crazy. These muscle boys would all but start their swing for the fences even before the ball was released—and couldn't halt their swing as Gault's changeup came floating over Ramsden Park like a white butterfly.

Marty's son, Jonathan, was there with the warm-up jacket ready to rush onto the field to protect the precious arm. Marty would be batting third for the *Star*.

Fastball is a most curious game. It is the only sport I know where the better it gets the worse it gets. Because pitchers are so close to home plate—forty-three feet, versus sixty feet, six inches in baseball—the advantage goes hugely to pitchers with a long reach and step. Pitches actually *rise* from the best of them and are next to impossible to hit. In good fastball leagues, it is not uncommon for the game to go to extra innings and end 1–0 off a home run swing that finally connects with the blur of a ball coming in from the mound.

At my second at-bat, I caught hold of a Marty fastball that I knew was gone. I watched him turn and follow the ball as it sailed, slowly it seemed, over the head of the specially positioned first baseman and all the way across the park to land in the centre of the outdoor hockey rink.

Gault, who followed me at bat, caught the next Marty pitch flush and parked a line drive on the roof of a nearby industrial building.

We had a lead that we never forfeited. We had just put our dreaded rivals out of the playoffs.

Next morning, I flew out early to Winnipeg. I made it to the Breezy Bend course before Panasik's second round was done. The big-hitting pro—regularly outdriving his playing partners by thirty yards—had opened with a 72 and this day's 73. The second-round leader, American Ed Byman, would go on to win. Panasik would one day win the Manitoba Open, but not until 1986.

Back in Toronto I filled in an expense account that included two flights to Winnipeg and two back to Toronto within the week—for a single story.

Don Obe signed off on it and not a word was ever said.

6

_____

Prime Time

I sure never saw a movie coming out of this.

Don Obe, editor of *The Canadian*, thought it might make a nice photo-essay. Freelance photographer Michael Foster had been visiting his parents near the small eastern Ontario village of Madoc and returned to Toronto with a suggestion that the magazine take a look at the current status (circa 1977) of the family farm. He had even picked out a farm and family.

Off we went to visit the Steins of Eldorado in eastern Ontario. Eldorado was now a ghost town, but in the year before Confederation it had been a booming community with four hotels, two grocery stores and two taverns. The 1866 gold rush had turned a couple of farms into an instant town as some three thousand feverish dreamers arrived to stake out the swampy bush and poor farmland northeast of Madoc. There was gold, alright, but it assayed out at a meagre fifteen dollars a ton. Within a few years the hotels closed, the mines closed, the taverns shut and the disappointed prospectors left. Eldorado went back to little more than a few struggling farms.

Fred and Ethel Stein had nine children, five already out on their own and dispersed among the small towns and cities of eastern Ontario.

Fred, sixty-two, was up at five each morning, seven days a week, for the first milking of the twenty-eight cows. Twelve-year-old Calvin would join him Monday to Friday to put in two hours of work before catching the school bus to Madoc with his siblings. On the particular morning the photographer and I arrived, the temperature was minus thirty-four degrees Celsius.

It had been a tough year for the Steins. Their sixteen-year-old dog died. Half the baby chicks they ordered caught chills and died. Seven-year-old Margaret fell under the tractor and, had Fred not immediately noticed and jammed on the brakes, the damage would have been far worse than a badly scraped leg.

Fred did get away for his annual week of deer hunting. "He gets a holiday when he goes hunting," said Ethel. "I get mine when I go into the hospital." Nine children, high blood pressure—her doctor figured she'd already had a couple of heart attacks but had been too busy to notice.

Heart attacks . . . just a couple of weeks earlier a forty-seven-year-old neighbour had been found dead between two cows, the milking stool toppled. The neighbour had been under the same pressures as the Steins: government regulations and milk-board quotas. A year earlier the federal government had determined that dairy farmers were producing too much milk and brought in controls. The Steins had once shipped 277,000 pounds of milk in a year; now they were restricted to 150,000 pounds. If they went over their quota, they were fined $860 per hundredweight. The Steins had made more money milking thirteen cows before the milk board came along than they now made milking twenty-eight.

"It's crazy," Fred said. "It's like putting in a lot of overtime and then having to pay the company to let you work."

The Steins were caught between a rock and a hard place. None of the children were keen on taking over the dairy farm. None could afford it. The farm was worth maybe $150,000 in 1977—Fred and Ethel's pension, if they decided to quit.

"There's no holidays in farming," said seventeen-year-old Allen, "and too much work for nothing. I think my father should get out." Allen planned to finish his grade twelve and head for Belleville, where the steel plant was paying four dollars an hour.

A week after Michael and I visited, Fred suffered a heart attack while pulling down a hundred-pound bag of feed. He survived the attack, and he and Ethel began making plans to sell off the herd.

The Steins' story was titled "A Canadian Tragedy." It wasn't put on the cover of the weekend supplement but it struck a chord with Canadians, especially those who had themselves come from family farms. As the subhead put it, "The harder Fred Stein works his farm the greater his chances of losing it."

That year marked the first annual National Magazine Awards, held May 11 at the Hotel Toronto with Pierre Berton hosting the gala event. The winner of the best general article for 1977, as well as the University of Western Ontario President's Medal, was "A Canadian Tragedy."

Next, Fred Stein's story was going to be a movie.

"*Me?*" I stammered. "I've never written a script." In fact, I'd never even *seen* a script.

The invitation had come from Ralph L. Thomas, executive producer in the CBC's drama department. We met at his office along with another drama producer, Vivienne Leebosh, and they informed me that they'd like to make a film out of "A Canadian Tragedy" and they wanted me to write the script.

"We'll help you," they promised.

Fred Stein was about to become a ninety-minute movie. Thomas had been recruited from CBC current affairs by John Hirsch, head of TV drama. Hirsch had a vision that drama should be as relevant as current affairs to Canadians. He wanted "journalistic dramas"—docudramas, if you will. *For the Record* launched in 1976 and included dramas such as

The Insurance Man from Ingersoll, directed by Montreal's Peter Pearson, and *A Thousand Moons*, directed by Gilles Carle. Reviews were good; audience numbers, great. The series was a hit.

"I want to direct this one," Thomas told me. "Vivienne would be the producer."

And so it began. Someone who had never even seen a script would write the drama. Someone who had never directed a film would direct. Thomas cast a young actor, R.H. Thomson, who had never appeared in a film, as the lead.

We eventually ended up with a script. Its title was simple: *Tyler*, the name of the lead character that Thomson would play. Murray Westgate, famous for his "Happy Motoring" Esso commercials during CBC hockey broadcasts, would play Tyler's father; Sonja Smits was cast as his sister. The whole thing was shot in a matter of weeks, mostly on a farm location not far from Toronto. I recall going to the CBC offices for a pre-screening of the film and shuddering to think that the great Claude Jutra, legendary Quebec director of *Mon oncle Antoine* and *Kamouraska*, would be sitting in on the screening, as he happened to be in the building on other matters. When the film ended, a tearful Jutra hugged everyone in the room.

Tyler was declared "a television triumph" by the *Toronto Star*. The *Globe and Mail* headline read "Farmboy's battle has ring of truth." *Maclean's* thought the film had an "an Ibsenish dramatic quality." It won the International Press Award (Prix de la presse internationale) at the Montreal World Film Festival. It was one of four features Canada chose for submission to the Cannes Film Festival. At the annual ACTRA Awards (later to become the Gemini Awards), the script won the "Nellie" as the top screenplay of the year and Murray Westgate won best supporting actor for his role as Tyler's father. Unfortunately, R.H. Thomson lost out to Gordon Pinsent (*A Gift to Last*) in the best actor category. Thomson, of course, would go on to a stellar career in movies and television.

After such (surprising) success, Ralph Thomas and I collaborated again, this time for a hockey-themed docudrama. *Cementhead* would take a hard look at fighting and violence in hockey, this being not long after the Philadelphia Flyers, also known as the "Broad Street Bullies," won two Stanley Cups with an alarming combination of skill and fists. I did a few drafts of the script and then Ralph suggested he have a go-through, tightening here and there and adding a few new scenes. We would both be given writing credits.

Ralph cast actor Tom Butler as the main character, "Bear" Bernier. An up-and-coming comic, Martin Short, landed his first film role as "Weepy," the team's eccentric goaltender. We were able to give one-time NHL star Eric Nesterenko (Stanley Cup winner with the 1961 Chicago Black Hawks) a cameo. The craggy ex-pro was fawned over in the film by a young woman who said she was majoring in sociology and went on and on about the mystical hold violence has on some people. "You have a beautiful face," she told Nesterenko. He responded by yanking out his false teeth and making an alarming face. "Think I'm still beautiful?" he asked.

The film ran on a night that also featured the first episode of *Roots: The Next Generations*. Still, our show drew an acceptable audience. Reviews were mixed. The *Winnipeg Tribune* said, "*Cementhead* is a solid show worth viewing" and told readers it was "an exceptionally entertaining hour" of television. Reviewer Stan Helleur noted that Ralph and I were becoming an effective team: "We suspect Thomas, who also directed the production, specializes in the dramatic line, while McGregor [sic], who obviously has a Ring Lardner ear for idiom, is responsible for the naturalistic, salty flow of dialogue. They've got something going." The *Ottawa Citizen* was also kind. "Supported by a strong script with believable dialogue," the paper said, "the film's performers carry off their roles with uniform excellence." The *Globe and Mail*, on the other hand, declared in its headline, "*Cementhead* is minor league." Reviewer Ray Conlogue considered it "a watchable show with a few good moments;

but it's still in the minor leagues of dramatic writing and doesn't deserve big league exposure."

This was a different world for me. You write a magazine feature and it appears and, perhaps, a few letters trickle in and might even appear a month or so later. In newspapers, the story appears the next day and reaction can be swift, especially if you have angered someone who immediately fires off a heated letter to the editor. For movies and plays, however, the morning after is simply nerve-racking as you pick through the instant reviews. Not for the faint of heart.

Ralph Thomas and I worked together one more time, on a film called *Every Person Is Guilty*. The title was taken from a line in the War Measures Act. Prime Minister Pierre Trudeau had invoked emergency powers during the 1970 October Crisis, in which members of the FLQ (Front de libération du Québec) kidnapped Quebec cabinet minister Pierre Laporte and British diplomat James Cross. Laporte's body was later found in the trunk of a car; Cross was eventually released. I was tipped off at the time by a friend in Pembroke, Ontario, that the British Special Air Service (SAS) was training with the Canadian military at Base Petawawa, a few kilometres north of Pembroke along the Ontario side of the Ottawa River.

This was at a time of deep national unrest, with a separatist party now in power in the province of Quebec. It was also a time when the Royal Canadian Mounted Police were under heavy scrutiny. The Royal Commission of Inquiry into Certain Activities of the RCMP had been established in 1977 and was still holding hearings. There was national concern that the Mounties were out of control and that the Canadian security system had been politicized. The docudrama related the tale of one man's investigation into curious goings-on at a Canadian military base, where he had been told British commandos were teaching Canadian soldiers "how to murder separatist fighters" without being detected.

The film was considered so explosive that, according to Sid Adilman in the *Toronto Star*, "CBC-TV program chief Jack Craine admitted this week that he urged the drama be postponed if the federal Liberals had called a general election this month or next." *For the Record*'s new executive producer, Sam Levene, was adamant that it run, and so it did in mid-March 1979. "Disturbing film on Secrets Act," read the head-line over Bob Pennington's review in the *Toronto Sun*. Donn Downey, reviewing the film for the *Globe*, found the "tangled tale tedious." The *Star*'s Bruce Blackadar, on the other hand, loved it: ". . . it is pleasing to say that *Every Person is Guilty*, *For the Record*'s final program for the year, is without question the most remarkable, gripping and controversial." Ralph Thomas and I shared that year's ACTRA Award for the best Canadian television screenplay.

Ralph Thomas and Vivienne Leebosh left Toronto for Los Angeles, but the *For the Record* series continued under other producers, such as the very able Bill Gough. Renowned director Donald Brittain and I teamed up for *An Honourable Member*, a thinly disguised look at the trials faced in Parliament by women such as Flora MacDonald, Iona Campagnolo and others. Brittain cast Fiona Reid in the main role with great success. "Fiona Reid superb in splendid drama," shouted the head-line in the *Toronto Star*. "What the drama has going for it is a satirical edge courtesy of director Don Brittain and writer Roy MacGregor," wrote Jim Bawden. "The lines crackle with cynicism. . . . *An Honourable Member* could be a respectable pilot for a series. Reid as Trish Baldwin is too winning a lady to be consigned to political oblivion after just one show." *Maclean's* agreed with Bawden, praising "a delightfully funny performance by Fiona Reid . . . the quietly malicious script by Roy MacGregor skewers the ritualistic backstabbing and bureaucratic lol-lygagging of Ottawa's world."

The final *For the Record* film I worked on remains my favourite, *Ready for Slaughter*, a second script on struggling farm families. This one was produced by Maryke McEwen and directed by Allan King, then legend-ary for his hard-hitting documentaries (*Warrendale*) as well as powerful filmmaking (*Who Has Seen the Wind*). The film aired in March of 1983.

It starred Gordon Pinsent as debt-strapped farmer Will Hackett and Diana Belshaw as Hackett's wife, Colleen. The docudrama was perfectly pegged to the news of the day, as farm bankruptcies were on the rise.

Pinsent and Belshaw were magnificent. Writing in the *Globe and Mail* to recognize *For the Record*'s tenth anniversary, long-time CBC producer Ross McLean said "Gordon Pinsent gave what may be his best performance ever" in *Ready for Slaughter*. "A major ingredient of the film's power is its restraint," Alexander Ross wrote in the *Toronto Star*. "In less skillful hands, *Ready for Slaughter* might have turned out as a televised political tract. But McEwen, MacGregor and director Allan King have shaped it into a moving story about good, ordinary people trapped in a real situation."

The film was shot amidst the rolling green hills of Ontario's Bruce Peninsula. Maryke McEwen was approached on the set by a group calling themselves the Concerned Farmwomen, who were worried that the script would continue the cliché of the good farm wife who stays in the kitchen and leaves the real work to men. McEwen let them read the script, which she had insisted portray Colleen Hackett as a full partner in the farming operation. Satisfied with what they read, the Concerned Farmwomen left. A few days later, while *Ready for Slaughter* was filming around a local bank, area banks became concerned about what sort of story was being told, though it was surely none of their business. Toronto representatives arrived to discuss the situation. "They read the script at that time," Pinsent told the *Globe and Mail*, "and every-thing was okayed. Not the most pleasant situation in the world, but the story is well represented."

Ready for Slaughter went on to win the "Rockie" for best television drama at the Banff World Television Festival.

For the Record wound down in 1985 after producing more than fifty very Canadian docudramas. I was now working once again for *Maclean's*, which had recently made the full pivot into becoming a weekly newsmagazine. As Ottawa editor during this third stint with the magazine, I was far too busy hiring staff and moving our offices to dabble in any further television work. Within months I had switched to daily journalism, moving to Parliament Hill coverage with the *Ottawa Citizen*. I thought the movie ship had sailed. I liked writing for film and had more luck with reviewers than bad luck. Yet I never saw scriptwriting as a career. I was a journalist and that was where I wished to remain.

A few years later, the CBC came knocking again. Drama producer Robert Sherrin wanted to turn my 1983 novel *The Last Season* into a three-part series for broadcast. He had a director, Allan King, which delighted me, and King wanted to cast a young actor named Booth Savage in the lead. As the novel had been set in rural and northern Ontario and Finland, they would be shooting on location. They even signed Johanna Raunio, a former Miss Finland and Miss World runner-up, to play the love interest of Savage's character, Felix Batterinski. The *Toronto Star*'s Roy Shields, obviously writing in a far different time, wrote that if you ran into her on the street you might walk into a lamppost. She has, he said, a "startling beauty. It's more than snow-blond hair, sky-blue eyes and a smile that would crack ice . . ."

The novel had explored much darkness, from hockey thuggery to the deep woods of the Upper Ottawa Valley, where poverty, a dysfunctional family, Kashub superstitions and Catholic religion had produced a troubled young man who had enough talent to play hockey but would be able to play professionally only if he brought violence to the ice. Told through Felix Batterinski's eyes and voice, it had found a respectful readership. The *Calgary Herald* had called it "a classic Canadian novel" when it was published. *Maclean's* deemed it "rich in meaning." The *Globe and Mail* said the description of Batterinski's rural family was "reminiscent of William Faulkner." Lordy, lordy.

Unfortunately, books don't always translate all that well to the screen. Part of the problem was a decision by CBC higher-ups not to run it as a three-part miniseries, but as a one-time broadcast. We had three one-hour productions set to go, but now they would be combined to produce a single, three-hour movie—much too long for anyone to sit through in those pre-streaming days of television.

I confess to cringing when I picked up the January 3, 1987, edition of the *Globe and Mail*, turned to the arts section and was slapped by the headline "Ambitious hockey saga fails to score." Reviewer John Haslett Cuff quickly turned to the essential problem with the movie. "Considering that Canadians generally excel at documentaries and hockey the film should be better. Unfortunately, it contains a rather unlikely denouement to which the entire three hours slowly build, with the result that it is ultimately a letdown. MacGregor's script has none of the eloquence of his book." Fair comment. Allan King's directing was "acceptable," Haslett Cuff wrote, Savage was to be "congratulated" for doing what he could with the main character, and "the much bal-lyhooed import, Johanna Raunio, who plays his Finnish girlfriend, is little more than a pretty plot device." Yikes.

The Last Season fared better with the *Citizen*, with Allan King and Booth Savage praised for their work and the script building to "a power-ful climax." Reviewer Noel Taylor couldn't help but point out that three hours was "a rare commitment of prime time for a CBC film." A rare commitment indeed—and a major mistake.

There would be one more dive into scriptwriting. My agent at the time, Lucinda Vardey, was also the agent for Canadian novelist Anthony Hyde, who had a monster bestseller in *The Red Fox*, a thriller set mostly in Russia. It had been published in 1986 after a bidding war among New York publishers and had become a huge international bestseller. To no one's surprise, Hollywood was immediately interested. A European producer based in Los Angeles came to Toronto, met with Lucinda and me, and proposed that I be the scriptwriter for the screen treatment of a book I had never even read. The money was tempting; the producer suave and persuasive. He had purchased the rights to a Canadian novel. Now he had a Canadian screenwriter.

I suspected I was being offered this work because of my passport, not my résumé. What small reputation I had in film was very much localized, and here was a Hollywood producer with a Canadian book. Both the book's author and I checked off vital boxes when it came to the considerable government funding that was then being made widely available to filmmakers in the hopes of attracting movie production to Canada. Vancouver was exploding with film production, most of it American work headed for international markets. The suave producer had information on a Canadian funding group, the Harold Greenberg Fund, which provided significant financial support as a script moved from first draft to second. We signed a contract for me to write that first draft for the sum of sixteen thousand dollars. Who could resist?

I read the book and worked for three months on the script. When I handed it in, the delighted producer raced off to the Canadian fund, where it is unknown how much he was given to take the script to a second, perhaps final, draft.

The movie of *The Red Fox* was never made. I never saw a penny of the sixteen thousand dollars. Lucinda and I contacted a lawyer in LA and spent several hundred dollars trying to force the producer to pay up. Ontario and fund officials got involved in the chase. But the producer was long gone, vanished.

My one big Hollywood production had been a scam.

As they say, not every script has a happy ending.

THE TRENCHES OF CANNINGTON

Whenever possible, I try to practise what I call "experiential journalism."

There is only so much you can learn from interviews. Subjects know they are being measured and they therefore take their own measured steps to ensure that whatever is said works best for them. Given the chance to paint their own portrait, they rarely colour outside the lines.

If I can arrange to "hang" with a subject for a considerable time, I try always to seize the opportunity. The hope is that as the subject goes about their day, they eventually forget—or at least partially forget—why this stranger with the notebook is there. People let down their guard and the profile becomes much more real. There have been many times when I have sat down with the profile subject for that formal interview out of politeness alone. They expect it, but by then I don't need it.

I spent a long day in the fall of 1977 with novelist Timothy Findley. Alan Walker, managing editor of *The Canadian* magazine, thought a profile to go with the upcoming release of Findley's new novel, *The Wars*, might be timely. It was indeed. The book would become an instant bestseller and, six years later, become a successful movie directed by Robin Phillips.

I headed off to the small town of Cannington, near the Ontario city of Lindsay. Findley and his partner, Bill Whitehead, were then living there in a farmhouse built in 1840. We talked much of the morning and I took notes. Findley told me about a childhood illness he had barely survived, about dropping out of school when he was told grade nine was about the best he could expect, and about becoming a dancer and an actor in England; at one point he even toured the USSR in a travelling troupe performing *Hamlet.*

His life had been a struggle: poor health, drinking (then stopped, at least temporarily), rejection. He thought he could be a writer but Canadian publishing houses hardly agreed with him. At one point, when he called a major Canadian house to inquire, again, about the manuscript he had submitted, the voice at the other end of the line screamed at him: "*Nobody here has ever heard of you. Who could care less about who you are, you little crapper?*"

"I was destroyed," he told me. "Totally destroyed."

With Whitehead, Findley turned to writing television series, such as *The Whiteoaks of Jalna* and *The National Dream*, but his personal dream was still to be a novelist. Two earlier attempts had been published outside the country, but inside Canada he continued to be the "little crapper" no publisher wanted to touch.

"There's some kind of funny disease in Canada," he said. "If someone starts making it here, dump on them."

In the afternoon, we went for a walk around the farm. He showed me some of the thirty-five cats that had free run of the barn and, mostly, of the old house. He showed me some old farm machinery and talked about how this had worked into his own life and his new novel: the hero of the book, twenty-year-old John Ross, is the scion of the Raymond-Ross farm machinery fortunes. Findley's grandfather, also named Timothy Findley, rose to the top of the Massey-Harris farm machinery business. His grandfather went off to fight in the Great War, just as the hero of the novel does. Fictional hero and real hero trained at the same base in Alberta, sailed on the same ship, fought in the same battles.

The Second Battle of Ypres, fought in the spring of 1915, figures heavily in the novel. It was the first major battle for Canadian troops and the losses were heavy, with more than sixty-five hundred soldiers killed, wounded or captured. Many drowned or suffocated in the mud, as heavy, heavy rains had turned the battlefield into a sucking muck.

Findley's descriptions of the battlefield were vivid in *The Wars*. I asked him how he was able to research it so well.

"You see that field," he said, pointing to a large, empty field of black soil on a far corner.

"Two falls ago, it rained almost every day. It turned that field into pure, deep muck. I came out here, fully clothed, and for the entire day I waded through it and rolled in it. I didn't come out until I had a sense of the horrors they must have felt."

Experiential fiction writing. It was something I would practise myself a few years later when writing *The Last Season*. (More on that later.) I would also try, as much as possible, to experience a profile subject's life rather than depend solely on that perfunctory sit-down interview.

Had Findley and I not had that walk, had we not come to that field, this singular, most powerful image would never have come up; certainly not in a formal sit-down interview. Serendipity at its best.

Clarke, Irwin & Company didn't call Findley "a little crapper" when he submitted the manuscript of *The Wars*. The Canadian publisher loved it. So, too, did readers, the novel rising to the top of the bestseller lists and winning the Governor General's Award for fiction. The Robin Phillips film was also a great success.

But the greatest honour came from Findley's own father, himself a war veteran.

"Son," he told the author, "millions of men have just stood up in their graves and saluted you."

OPENING WORDS

They are the first words of any book: the title.

I have never been great with titles—how I pray this one is the exception—and have long envied writers such as Katherine Govier, who seems to have a special gift for grabbing the fleeting attention of those passing quickly along the shelves. Her novel on family and memory she called *Random Descent*. *Going Through the Motions* is her novel featuring a stripper. Her study of romance was titled, brilliantly, *Between Men*. Who could resist?

There have been many great Canadian titles: Ernest Buckler's evocative *The Mountain and the Valley*, Timothy Findley's *Famous Last Words*, Jack Hodgins' *The Invention of the World*, Margaret Laurence's *A Jest of God*. These, and many others, stand tall with those magnificent titles of international renown: Gabriel García Márquez's *Love in the Time of Cholera*, William Faulkner's *As I Lay Dying*, even such attractive novelties as Mark Haddon's *The Curious Incident of the Dog in the Night-Time*.

My first venture into the book titling world was a disaster. I knew that I wanted to write a novel and I knew that I would draw from a family connection with the greatest Canadian mystery of all—the 1917 death of landscape painter Tom Thomson. Anna Porter, then an editor at McClelland & Stewart, knew that I had written previously about the connection for *Maclean's* magazine and was happy to draw up a contract with a handsome advance: $250 when I completed the manuscript, $250 more if M&S chose to publish, which they did.

I called my first novel *Shorelines*—no mention of Tom Thomson, no hint of the romance that touched on our family and may or may not have left a child behind.

The book was published in the spring of 1980. On Saturday, May tenth, it was the feature review in the *Globe and Mail*, a savaging of the novel by Marian Engel. The reviewer—known then for her best-selling novel, *Bear*—appears in retrospect to have been in a bad mood. She dumps on the Tom Thomson prints that were in most Canadian schools. She says Thomson's creations "lack the looping energy of A.Y. Jackson's" (a most curious analysis indeed).

She wonders "if it is possible to invent an artist in fiction at all." There are no novels or films based on Cézanne's life, she claims—correct at the time, but no longer. She finds a main character, Russell Pemberton, not very bright. I am so grateful my father never saw the review, as Russell was clearly based on Dunc MacGregor. She tallies the number of times a character is ill in the book and says, "there's enough vomit to fill Canoe Lake."

The closest she comes to a compliment is a single line: "The tension between Tom and the lumbermen is well drawn, there are pretty passages, but on one level it's as naive as *Anne of Green Gables*." (I should be so lucky!)

With such a launch, it was no surprise that the book bombed. M&S sent me a cheque for $250 and I figured that was the end of that. Having seen it briefly in bookstores, the next place I would see *Shorelines* on display was in . . . Loblaws. Jack McClelland was bringing out a line of M&S books that had flopped and he thought might have a second life if they were wrapped in yellow covers and marketed as one of the grocery chain's "No Name" products. The marketing plan was a flop.

Shorelines would appear once more in bookstores when my second novel, *The Last Season*, was published in the fall of 1983. Penguin brought my first novel out in paperback, only to watch sales collapse once again.

Then came a new title . . .

Anna Porter had started as the editor of the book but had moved on to establish Key Porter Books. Ellen Seligman had taken over the editing of the book and saw it through to publication. Over the years, the gifted young editor had risen higher and higher in the M&S empire. The McClelland & Stewart imprint also had a new publisher in Douglas Gibson, who had published *The Last Season* when he headed up Macmillan.

Doug and Ellen came to me with a suggestion. Ellen had always felt that *Shorelines* had been dismissed unfairly. They thought the book could be retitled and, therefore, reborn. A second chance. Ellen thought it should be called *Canoe Lake*. Two simple words, yet they conjured up so much—the Canadian wilderness, escape, even Tom Thomson for the many who knew his tragic story.

In the spring of 2002, *Canoe Lake* appeared, the new cover featuring an evocative sepia photograph of an empty canoe. Without a single review, it rose to number two on the *Globe and Mail*'s bestseller list. The *Toronto Star*'s book editor, Philip Marchand, did a feature on the phenomenon, as at that point the book had sold some ten thousand copies.

Today, sales of the Book that Bombed are well in excess of twenty thousand. In 2006, to celebrate its hundredth anniversary as "the Canadian Publisher," McClelland & Stewart released its list of what the publisher considered the hundred "essential books" of Canada.

Canoe Lake made the list.

WELCOME TO THE GULAG,
STUPID CANADIAN REPORTER

How could I have been so stupid?

I am in a small room at the Leningrad airport and I am buck naked. Grim-faced Russian soldiers have stripped me, checked every orifice of my body, and are now going through my luggage as if it is wired for sound, with a direct link back to the CIA and the Mounties.

Perhaps I should explain how I came to be here, covering my genitals with one hand, and wanting to strangle myself for getting into this mess with the other.

It was spring 1981. I was with *Maclean's* magazine, then a biweekly and based in Ottawa. The group that I had played hockey with in Toronto through much of the 1970s was off on an adventure and invited me to join in, which I did happily. They were lawyers and teachers, people in health care and advertising and publishing, even a handful of journalists. They called themselves the "Writeoffs."

One member of the hockey team ran a small travel agency. Finnair, the official airline of Finland, had taken note of the increasing popularity of beer-league hockey in Canada and wondered if there might be a market for bringing Canadian old farts over to play against Finnish old farts. There would be a practice or two, at least two games against teams in the Helsinki area and lots of opportunity for players and their partners to see the sights. There would even be a side trip across the Gulf of Finland to Leningrad (now again known as St. Petersburg) for tours of St. Isaac's Cathedral, the famous Hermitage Museum and Pushkin's house.

The proposal was met with great enthusiasm. The Canadians had a full roster and only one forward position left to fill when they asked me if I might join them. The opportunity was, at that point, remarkable good luck, as I was working on a second novel and had chosen to centre it on a fading NHL hockey player. Why not have him finish out his career with a stint in Europe, playing for a Finnish team? It was like being handed free research.

But there was other research involved—much to my later regret. I cleared the time off with the *Maclean's* managing editor, Rod McQueen, and he later came back to me with a side proposal: Poland was reaching a boiling point with the electrician-activist Lech Walesa and the Solidarity movement. The Soviet Union, it was widely believed, was on the verge of acting to suppress Solidarity and, once again, jail Walesa.

"If all hell breaks loose," Rod reasoned, "you'd be able to get to Gdansk."

We were speaking on the phone, so he could not see me swallow hard and almost fall off my office chair.

"I guess," I said quietly.

Rod offered to have the office check the paperwork I would need for Poland. I already had a visa for the Soviet Union, as we were booked for that weekend in St. Petersburg.

"I'll have the library put together some research for you," he offered.

"Okay," I said, certain he must be noting my lack of enthusiasm. What was I going to do—pack my typewriter in my hockey bag? (Yes, it was that long ago.)

A few days later the office mail produced a large manila envelope stuffed with clippings on Poland. (Yes, it was that long ago.) I took the package, stuffed it into the front pocket of my suitcase and forgot all about it.

The team flew on Finnair, Toronto to Helsinki. The group that had played "darks and whites" for years now had brand-new jerseys, courtesy of *Toronto Life*, where two of our players were on staff. As there were a few writers on the roster, the name they had gone with for the front crest was the "Toronto Maple Leaves." Get it? Well, Finland didn't. "Toronto Maple Leaves" translated into Finnish as the "ex-Toronto Maple Leafs." They thought our names should be Keon and Bower and Kelly and Horton and Pulford, not Cappon and Zikovitz and Strachan and Macdonald and Tilley and that late addition, MacGregor. That would be Dr. Dan Cappon, Al Zikovitz, Ian Strachan, Ian Macdonald and Tony Tilley. We played in full arenas with officials and scoreboards and between-period floods . . . and we got creamed. Old-timer hockey in Canada is not old-timer hockey in Finland, where the only greybeards still playing the game tend to be ex-national team players and former European pros.

In the small city of Lahti, where the Finn Olympians train, we met a team so strong they deliberately played a man short for the entire game. We lost heavily, but I somehow fluked a hat trick and was chosen "Best Canadian" in a small post-game ceremony. I still hang the memento, a red and white flag of Lahti teams, in my office.

On the weekend we went to the Soviet Union. This time we boarded Aeroflot, the Soviet airline, and flew across the eastern arm of the Baltic Sea to Leningrad, where we disembarked and lined up to go through customs.

I was quietly chatting with linemate Ian Strachan, a lawyer by day, when it came my turn to present my passport and visa and hand my luggage over for checking. It seemed a harmless, efficient process—right up until a soldier unzipped that pocket of my suitcase and carefully eased out a stuffed manila envelope.

I know I went white. My heart yanked all my blood down to the floor. I saw blinding lights exploding before I saw, for the first time, all that was in that envelope. The soldier opened it and poured the contents out, magazine and newspaper clippings spilling from one end of the counter to the other.

Such a jumble of incriminating evidence! One magazine illustration had Soviet leader Leonid Brezhnev as a dove of peace, flying over Poland with a nuclear bomb in his talons. There were flattering profiles of Lech Walesa, articles condemning every aggressive act by the Soviet Union, articles calling for a great people's revolution to come out of Eastern Europe thanks to the Solidarity movement.

I cannot tell you what I looked like, but I can tell you what I looked like to others. Daniel Cappon, a Toronto psychiatrist and senior member of the Toronto Maple Leaves, later wrote a piece for the *Medical Post* in which he said I had "paled to cadaver-complexion and trembled for hours afterwards."

One of the guards picked up a condemning *Economist* cover and called out something in Russian. "He was immediately surrounded by guards," Cappon wrote, "the material confiscated and his passport taken. He was conducted to an inner chamber and searched just short of a proctoscopic examination."

Sorry, Dr. Cappon . . . but that, too.

Dressed again, I sat in a cold, over-lighted room while two soldiers stood to the side and a man with a gold tooth and a much fancier uniform thumbed through the confiscated documents. He was not smiling. He kept speaking to me, and the tone rather than any translation told me that I was being lectured, warned, and that terrible things awaited me.

A knock at the door produced another Russian, with Ian Strachan in tow. This Russian spoke some English and indicated that Ian might sit with me. "I'm his lawyer," Ian said, which was in a way true. Ian had helped me set up a small company to handle my meagre freelance income. We had been friends for years.

Ian informed me that the hockey group was moving fast on this. Ian Macdonald, a player who also happened to be president of York University, was on the line to the Canadian embassy in Moscow. Someone else was getting in contact with foreign affairs in Ottawa.

The "general" with the gold tooth now had documents in front of him and was filling in sections. He took the incriminating evidence and stuffed it back into the envelope and handed it to one of the guards, who walked over and set it on a desk.

Gold Tooth turned the document he was working on around and pushed it toward me, at the same time holding out a pen. He said something and wiggled the pen, indicating I should sign.

"What's going on?" I hissed to Ian.

Ian shook his head. "Looks like they want you to sign that," he said.

"But what is it?" I asked, again feeling the blood drain from my face.

"I don't know," Ian said. "I don't know Russian."

"If it's a confession, I don't want to sign it."

Ian turned to the soldier who spoke a bit of English.

"My client won't sign what he cannot read," Ian told the translator.

The translator turned to Gold Tooth and said something lengthy in Russian. We understood not a word.

Gold Tooth sighed, then smiled so wide that light bounced off his tooth. He picked up the document, turned it back to himself and nodded.

"What's he doing?" I asked Ian.

"I think he's going to read it to you," Ian said.

Gold Tooth began reading. We had no idea what he was saying. I was confessing to being a spy? I was going to prison? I was in such deep doo-doo that neither the Canadian embassy nor foreign affairs could throw me a lifeline. All because of one incredibly stupid mistake on my part. *Why hadn't I left the package back in Helsinki with our hockey equipment?*

Gold Tooth stopped reading, gave one more high-glint smile, placed the document on the table, turned it toward me and, once again, wiggled the pen.

"*What should I do?*" I whined to Ian. "*You're the lawyer!*"

Ian shook his head and shrugged his shoulders. "I'd sign."

And so, under legal advice, in a foreign country, staring at a document I could not read and could not understand when it was read to me . . . I signed.

And never heard another word about it.

Mind you, for every tour of St. Isaac's, the Hermitage, Pushkin's house, for every meal and walk through the lobby of the international hotel, we felt we were being watched.

Very, very closely.

I HAVE LOST MY FATHER

There is an unwritten rule in journalism that says, loosely, any time you can make your work carry your play, go for it. Usually this amounts to little more than stretching the expense account around the restaurants and bars. But it can also mean combining a personal side trip with a business trip. I spent a dozen happy years at the *Ottawa Citizen*, and editors there allowed me to write about not only family holidays—at one point even renting a luxury van so the entire family, and dog, could spend two weeks exploring the East Coast—but also personal experiences.

My father, older brother Jim and I shared a deep love of sports. We fished and hunted together. Duncan MacGregor's great sports passion was baseball, ours more hockey. I took him to the Hockey Hall of Fame in Toronto and wrote about it. For an assigned feature to run on Father's Day, I took him to Cooperstown, New York, to see the Baseball Hall of Fame . . .

. . . and thought I lost him forever.

"Dunc" was a character. He lived most of his life deep in the bush, never finished high school, yet was as well-read and informed as anyone I have ever known. There were always stories, some of which ended up in print. One that didn't, until now, was the fact that he was banned for life by the local Legion—when he was already into his eighties! He was quite proud of this.

There was a certain irony here, in that the Legion had helped him get back his life only a decade earlier. At seventy-three our father was still working full time at the McRae Lumber Company, then owned by the family of his nephew, Donald McRae. The mill at this point was located near the village of Whitney. It was early December, 1980, on a bitterly cold day, and a logging truck lost its grip on the ice, slid down a small hill and slammed into him as he was making his way back to the cookery. The sliding truck carried this elderly man on its grill down, down, down and slammed him into a snowbank. The blow broke his right hip and crushed his pelvis.

Not sure what to do and without an ambulance in the area, the men at the mill hoisted him into the open back of a pickup and carried him forty-plus kilometres to the hospital in Barry's Bay. It was twenty degrees below zero. From Barry's Bay they transferred him, in a heated ambulance, to the hospital in Peterborough and from there to Wellesley Hospital in Toronto, where they operated. He was told by the chief of surgery that he would have to quit smoking. He told the doctor he'd think about it and had an orderly wheel him down to the front entrance, where he bummed a cigarette off another patient and did indeed think about it—for a moment. A few weeks later he was transported home to Huntsville Memorial Hospital, where he was to recuperate. Doctors said he might never walk again.

The doctors, however, had no idea of the resolve of this man to have his rum and Coke. He passed from wheelchair to walker to cane, and within the year was hobbling down Lansdowne Street from his home on Reservoir Hill to have his daily libations at the local Legion.

Never one to resist penny stocks or lotteries, he would daily buy a few Bonanza tickets that he would slowly crack open as he sat with his drink. He hit the jackpot one afternoon, winning the maximum fifty-dollar prize, and he called over the waiter to cash it in for him. The waiter left with the winning ticket and returned with the old man's winnings: two dollars.

"That was a fifty-dollar winner," he told the waiter.

The waiter shook his head. "No, just a two-dollar winner. I cashed it in."

"*Fifty!*"

"*Two!*"

They argued. The waiter was clearly treating him like a daft old man who was imagining things. That's when the old man decided to rise from his seat and go after the cheating waiter with his cane. He never got his fifty bucks and was banned for life. He thought it well worth it.

Retired now, whether he liked it or not, he had time on his hands. He fanatically watched the Blue Jays, every inning of every game. All his life he had been a baseball fan, having scoured the sports pages for game accounts. He knew all the greats—"Honus" Wagner, "Hack" Wilson, George Sisler, "Wee" Willie Keeler, "Home Run" Baker, Walter Johnson, Rogers Hornsby. He hated Ty Cobb and loved "Nellie" Fox. In 1928, when he was twenty-one years old, he had travelled to Hull, Quebec, where he watched Babe Ruth and Lou Gehrig play an exhibition game during a rare barnstorming tour that included Canada.

He had once met Mickey Mantle's sister when he was sent on an airplane to Dallas to find out about a shipload of lumber from the mill that had been either mislaid or stolen. It was the only trip he had ever taken outside Canada. The only time he ever flew.

Jim and I first discovered the world beyond Algonquin Park through Dunc's car radio. On a hot summer night, he would grab a lantern and head off through a long dark path to the highway where the old Pontiac was parked. And here, when the clouds were kind, he would walk the radio dial through the static and the fading signals until he found the sounds of a distant ball game, with luck Mel Allen calling the Yankees, Red Barber doing the Dodgers.

We would sit, the windows often rolled up against the mosquitoes and the plastic seats sticking to our backs, and after he and Jim had debated, once again, who was the greatest player of the day—Mantle or Willie Mays—he would often take the flashlight and head off into the tiny creek that ran along the road and return a few minutes later with a couple of cold green bottles, the slightly skunky smell of beer cutting through the citronella as he cracked the caps with his knife.

He could recite, from heart, Ernest Lawrence Thayer's *Casey at the Bat.*

> Ten thousand eyes were on him as he rubbed his hands with dirt;
> Five thousand tongues applauded when he wiped them on his shirt.
> Then while the writhing pitcher ground the ball into his hip,
> Defiance gleamed in Casey's eye, a sneer curled Casey's lip.

He had never been to Cooperstown, New York, to visit the Baseball Hall of Fame. It being an easy drive from Ottawa, I suggested we take a trip there, see the hall, stay overnight, and drive back the next day. He was immediately enthusiastic.

This being 1990, long before 9/11 and long, long before the border tightening of the Covid-19 pandemic, crossing the border was a very different matter. We crossed at the Thousand Islands bridge and all the border guard asked was where we had been born.

"Whitney," I answered.

"Eganville," said the old man.

He had never owned a passport. His wallet carried no credit cards. He had a health card and a driver's licence . . . somewhere.

We drove through the Adirondacks while he calculated the board feet in the pine forests we passed. He asked if the soaring hill to the left was a "mountain." I checked the map and told him "Yes, it's Mount Matumbla."

"Tch-tch-tch-tch-tch," he answered. He had never seen a mountain before.

Coming into the town of Old Forge, I spied the golden arches rising on the right and put on the turn signal. "We'll grab lunch here," I said.

"Think I can get a drink?" he asked.

"Dad, it's a McDonald's! They have Coke. Or coffee."

"I'd like a real drink."

I could take the hint. Back out onto Highway 28 and a few blocks away, a diner out of the 1950s presented itself. Sliced lemon meringue pie under glass. Metal containers for the milkshakes. Burgers and bacon sizzling on the grill. A place he could handle.

"What can I start you fellows with?" the middle-aged waitress asked, pencil poised over her pad.

"Rum and Coke—a double, if you don't mind, dear. And one ice cube—just one, though."

"Right away, darlin'," she promised with a wink, as if there were some conspiracy between the two of them. And perhaps there was. A half-hour later I had finished my egg-salad sandwich and he was finishing a second drink.

"Aren't you going to eat?"

"Get me a chocolate bar."

There was no point in arguing diet. He was eighty-three years old. His favourite meal was overcooked beans and gristly bacon. His breakfast of choice was kippers, fried and fuming. Toast had to be burnt. Fifty shakes of pepper over each egg. Thirty shakes of salt over everything. Whisky straight from the bottle when you had it. Rum stained with Coke, one ice cube. Cold lozenges, Scotch butter candies, sponge toffee, chocolate bars, Tums. Cigarettes all day long for more than seven decades, roll-your-own whenever possible, with the strongest tobacco. Into his eighties and he didn't need glasses for distance, didn't take a single pill.

We reached Cooperstown and had a fabulous tour of the hall. "I knew them all," he kept saying as we wandered through the displays. "I knew them all." We also visited the home of James Fenimore Cooper, author of *The Deerslayer* and *The Last of the Mohicans*, two of the old man's favourite books. And we found a room at the Lake Shore Motel on the shore of Otsego Lake, which Cooper called "Glimmerglass" in his many books.

It had been a full day and I could tell he was exhausted. Once we got into the room at the Lake Shore he was keen to go to bed. He pulled back the cover and settled in over the blanket and sheets. I didn't bother correcting him. He was soon asleep and so, soon enough, was I.

Sometime late in the night I was awakened by a sense that something was wrong in the room. It would be some time before I knew what Cheyne-Stokes breathing was, but having heard dying family members go through it now, I realize that this is what had awakened me: the old man breathing so deep it seemed it was coming from under the floorboards; lips, nose and lungs rattling like some ungreased mine-shaft hoist, then suddenly stopping dead, the air utterly silent for what seemed minutes.

That our father snored was part of family lore. It was almost impossible to sleep through a night at Lake of Two Rivers without the thin cabin walls shaking until we could hear our mother slap her elbow against his shoulder, his grunts of surprise and her sharp "*Dunc— you're snoring again! Turn over!*" But this sound was not the snoring we all remembered. This sound was different, frightening.

I lay there a long time, listening to this strange breathing and wondering if he was alright.

Suddenly, he went completely quiet.

A minute passed, then another, then it seemed five minutes had passed in utter silence.

I began to panic. I couldn't shake the possibility that I had worn him out and that something had gone badly wrong. I got up and went to his bed, leaning over to see if he was breathing, but could hear nothing whatsoever from those nicotine-coated lungs. I touched his shoulder, but he did not move. He felt soft and warm, and I wondered if this was how someone would feel if he were dead.

I went into the bathroom and washed my face. There was a small mirror there, the kind women use for makeup and men for bald spots, and I picked it up and carried it out into the bedroom with me. I switched on the reading light. I leaned over him, placing the mirror directly below his hairy nostrils. I placed it in as tightly as I could, waited a moment, yanked it away and checked it against the light.

There, on the bottom edge of the little mirror, was a slight trace of condensation.

He was alive.

His entire body suddenly jerked and he began snorting again, falling back into that loud, rattling snoring that meant he was asleep.

But only he could sleep. For the longest time, I lay there unable to drift off and thinking far too much about life and death and family. I could see through the motel room window that dawn was washing pink with the first light of day. I dressed and went out and walked to the end of the dock, where I sat on a bench next to an ancient mahogany boat and stared out over the still, crack-of-dawn waters of Cooper's Glimmerglass.

Knowing he was safe, I sat there on the dock bench imagining him dead, and I thought about how terribly he would be missed. He had, obviously, never been the easiest person in the world to live with, but he would be harder to live without. No one to set you in your place with a sharp, gentle crack. No one to bring the past alive when you least expected it. No one to ask when you needed to know things like Casey Stengel's managerial record versus his playing record, or why there are no walnut trees in Algonquin Park. Sometimes you need to know such things.

The sun rose high enough to begin baking the small bench I was sitting on. I stayed a while longer and then thought to go back and check on him one more time. I knew I wouldn't be getting back to sleep.

I entered the room as quietly as I could. It was once again silent . . . *dead* silent.

His bed was empty. The cover was crumpled back, but the blanket and crisp sheets were still untouched apart from random creases from his weight.

Where was he?

He wasn't in the bathroom. He wasn't on the dock. He wasn't at the little motel office. He wasn't by the water.

Had he wandered off? Was he lost? He had no identification, no credit cards. The only money he carried would be the product of the strange habit he had of folding twenty-dollar bills in half, then quarters, then eighths and stuffing them into a deep corner of his wallet.

How would I explain to the police? Hell, how would I explain to the family that I had lost our father?

I broke into a run until I reached the main drag of the little town. I was the only person on the street. There was a small diner on the corner. And it was open.

He was there, sitting at the counter. He had a glass of dark liquid in front of him.

The waitress noticed this frantic stranger coming in through the front door. She smiled at me.

"Your father?" she asked.

"Yes."

"He always order a double rum and Coke for breakfast?"

7

Newspapering

I was leaving the world of magazines for newspapers, never to look back. It was early 1986. Managing editor Nelson Skuce had booked a lunch meeting where he would introduce me to Keith Spicer, Nelson's boss and the new editor of the *Ottawa Citizen*. Nelson did such a great job of selling me, at a restaurant within walking distance of the newspaper, that I hardly needed to say a word. Spicer spun his second glass of white wine, smiled that slightly cockeyed grin of his and asked, "How soon can you start?"

We agreed on two weeks.

The two weeks passed quickly and I rose early, dressed in tie, jacket and those pinching dress shoes from my final Toronto meeting with the now-weekly *Maclean's*. I drove from Kanata to the *Citizen* offices on the south side of the Queensway at Pinecrest. I was early, as I'd been told I would have to see human resources and fill in a bunch of forms for matters such as pay, insurance, benefits, etc.

I walked in, carrying my briefcase, just as Spicer whirled out of his office, tie looped over his shoulder and a sheaf of notes in his left hand.

He saw me and stopped. I presumed it was to shake my hand and welcome me.

"Can I help you?" he asked.

He had no idea who I was.

And so began a dozen absolutely treasured years at the *Ottawa Citizen*, the first three of which were spent with Keith Spicer as editor. The end of his tenure, however, would not be the end of my relationship with this delightful and fascinating man.

Spicer was flamboyant in a newspaper world largely populated by introverts. He wore a wide-brimmed panama hat and safari suits to work. He quoted Greek and Latin, and was so fluently bilingual in French and English that he had served as the country's first commissioner of official languages. His newspaper experience was minimal—some column writing for papers like the *Globe and Mail*—but new *Citizen* publisher Paddy Sherman saw something in Spicer that could bring a new spark to the 140-year-old Ottawa newspaper.

A spark? How about a firebomb?

I was not at the paper when he was introduced, but the moment was captured in a later parody of the *Citizen* by my friend and *Citizen* colleague Charles Gordon. In his comic novel *The Grim Pig*, Charlie has a flashy guy given to Hawaiian shirts introduced as the new editor of the *Grand Valley World Beacon*. (Charlie tells me the character was a combination of Spicer and the equally eccentric Neil Reynolds, the *Citizen*'s next editor.) The editor, very Spicer-like, begins his presentation by writing the word *destiny* across a flip board.

"Destiny!" he tells the assembled editors and reporters.

"Destiny," he says again. "That's what our readers want. They want to be connected with their destiny. They need a sense of how their lives will intersect with the final things in our existence, the spirits that will accompany them on their next journeys, as well as with the spirits and demons they meet in their everyday comings and goings."

Nothing about classifieds or car sections or subscriptions—everything about destiny. It was certain to be a different ride.

We had a great downtown bureau in the National Press Building on Wellington Street, with a rear entrance onto the Sparks Street Mall. Among those who rolled through this large bureau over the years were Susan Riley, Jane Taber, Debbie Dowling, Jim Robb, Mark Kennedy, Wendy Warburton, Greg Weston, Paul Gessell, Daniel Drolet, Ian Hunter, Kathryn May, Stephen Bindman, Jack Aubrey, bureaucracy columnist Frank Howard and his assistant Mary Bland, feature writer Robert Mason Lee and the aforementioned humour columnist Charles Gordon, long a treasured friend from Sunday-afternoon softball. It was a lively, fun bureau filled with some of the best talent of the Parliamentary Press Gallery.

One of the reporters, Greg Weston, had written a book, *Reign of Error*, on the 1984 federal election campaign and had been very tough on John Turner, the Liberal prime minister who lost that election and was now in parliament as the leader of the official opposition. It was the time of the great free trade debates. Conservative prime minister Brian Mulroney, who had won a majority government, was leading the charge in favour of a free trade deal for North America, Mexico included. Turner was very much against any such deal. Parliament was not the only place in Ottawa deeply split on the issue, which would dominate Canadian news for months on end. The Mulroney pro–free trade argument was that the economy would grow, consumers would benefit and red tape would be sharply reduced. Protectionists like Turner, however, wanted to save vulnerable jobs and ensure that certain industries, from food production to steel, would be strongly protected to ensure that Canada could be self-sufficient in a shifting world order.

Shortly after hiring me, Spicer announced that he had hired yet another national columnist—throwing several noses, including mine, out of joint. The new hire was Marjorie Nichols, an Albertan who had previously worked for the now-defunct *Ottawa Journal* and who had, in 1967, become both the youngest member of the Parliamentary Press Gallery and its only woman.

Marjorie was a fierce competitor—understandably so, as she had had to fight for every opportunity in that male-dominated gallery of the 1960s. Loud and as flamboyant as Spicer, she was a close friend of Allan Fotheringham, the long-time *Maclean's* back-page columnist and *Vancouver Sun* icon. John Turner also had deep roots in BC, his father-in-law once serving as lieutenant-governor, and he now represented the riding of Vancouver Quadra. Nichols had lived in Vancouver prior to taking on the job in Ottawa and considered herself a good friend of the former prime minister.

No surprise, there was instant friction between Greg Weston and Nichols, so much so that she refused to work out of our bureau, choosing instead to work from the old "hot room" near the public gallery entrance in the Centre Block. The hot room, once infamous for its noisy rows of parliamentary reporters, smoke, and cooler filled with beer, was now relatively quiet, smoke- and cooler-free, and had become the domain of freelancers.

It was the golden era of newspapering, though no one at the time realized this. Newspapers made big money, the *Ottawa Citizen* one of the richest in the country, and Spicer seemed determined to spend as much of it as possible. Spicer not only hired Marjorie Nichols but also gave Jacques Parizeau, the former Bloc Québécois minister of finance, a once-a-week financial column. Then he hired the most unusual columnist ever to appear in the nation's capital: Ilya Gerol.

Gerol, a Russian émigré, was to serve as the paper's "international columnist." Gerol had been born into a wealthy family in Riga, Latvia, early in World War II. He and his mother escaped the city when the Germans moved in and the SS death squads began killing the Riga

Jews. He eventually became a Russian journalist but ran afoul of the Kremlin following the invasion of Czechoslovakia. He was able to get his young family to Vienna, and from there they made their way to Vancouver, where he soon began writing columns on international affairs for the *Province*.

Citizen publisher Paddy Sherman and Spicer brought Gerol to Ottawa and immediately sent him off to Reykjavík, Iceland, to cover the October 1986 summit meeting between Ronald Reagan and Mikhail Gorbachev. Spicer then dispatched his newest toy to the Middle East, convinced that only columns filed back to Ottawa and read by Ottawans could somehow solve international tensions. Gerol obviously had clout. He was able to get interviews with the likes of Poland's Lech Walesa, Israeli prime minister Yitzhak Shamir, Austrian president Kurt Waldheim and Soviet dissident Andrei Sakharov.

On his international trips he had to be accompanied by a *Citizen* reporter, usually Chris Cobb. Gerol had trouble meeting deadlines and, rumour had it, couldn't type. Many evenings he could be seen and heard walking about the Baxter Road newsroom, pipe in mouth as he dictated a column in his strong Russian accent to a poor intern trailing behind with pen and notepad. There was some debate, as well, as to whether Ilya could drive, as he seemed to find himself in various situations with those bright yellow *Citizen* cars that were available for staffers needing to get to interviews. There were multiple complaints about the driving skills of our international affairs columnist.

Gerol and the *Citizen* eventually parted ways over a curious incident in which some American investors showed up at the Baxter Road offices wishing to speak to "Mr. Gerol" about a lucrative chicken importing-or-exporting business Ilya was supposed to be setting up for them in Russia. They had stopped hearing from him and wanted to see for themselves the vast operation he had sold them on. This became known around the office as the "Chicken Kiev Affair."

Gerol left the *Citizen* after a few years and moved with his wife, Marina, to Montreal, where he published a foreign affairs newsletter and served as a consultant for companies hoping to do business with Russia. He died of heart failure in the summer of 2022. He was eighty-one.

Spicer was nothing if not inventive. He published a special section on the two-hundredth anniversary of the French Revolution, an expensive enterprise that attracted little advertising. He didn't care. He put out another special section, this one on the seventieth anniversary of the October Revolution. He was saved from acute embarrassment by a staff member who, at the last minute, pointed out that "Bolshevism" was misspelled in the main headline.

He sent me to China for a month. It was to be an exchange between the two then fairly friendly countries, Canada hosting a couple of Chinese journalists while China hosted a francophone reporter—actually, a priest—from Montreal and an English columnist, me. We travelled all through the country, from Shanghai to Beijing to Harbin to the oil fields and the mountains. I wrote glowingly of the progress I saw first-hand. About eighteen months later, Tiananmen Square happened . . .

Spicer sent our fashion writer, Nancy Gall, to cover the spring showings in New York and Paris and Milan. He wanted the *Citizen* to be seen not just as a vital national newspaper in Canada, but as a paper with international ambitions.

He launched the *Sunday Citizen*, a seventh daily edition that he envisioned a couple might read on a Sunday morning in their brass bed, the newspaper a vital part of their breakfast of café au lait and croissants. He wanted that Sunday paper to include a weekly essay that he described as "an elegant canter through an educated mind." The first one had a headline in Latin, and when Jay Stone, our design editor, pointed out to him that, uhh, most of our readers weren't fluent in Latin, Keith said that was alright—the few who could read it in Latin would appreciate the gesture.

Spicer hired several mentally challenged adults to work in the mail-room and other jobs on the paper—and he paid them real salaries. On the day of his farewell to the newsroom—he was off to chair the CRTC—one of these employees walked out in front of the entire assemblage and gave Spicer a huge hug in thanks. There were many tears shed.

As editor, Spicer held irregular "retreats" at Le Cercle, a red-brick mansion on Laurier Avenue close to the University of Ottawa. Le Cercle Universitaire was the club he belonged to and it was old-worldly, sophisticated and refined—hardly the sort of place to which ink-stained wretches would be attracted. But Keith liked to celebrate the launch of special sections there and would prepare his own invitation list.

He decided to have a "columnists' dinner" at Le Cercle to thank them for their good work and to thrash out ideas for new newspaper adventures. He invited managing editor Scott Honeyman and a variety of writers and columnists—Charles Gordon, Frank Howard, Tony Cote, Marjorie Nichols, George Grande, Lynn McAuley, Greg Weston, Ilya Gerol, me—and another recent hire, sports columnist Earl McRae, my friend from our days at *The Canadian*.

The dinners were long and boozy affairs. They quietened down after one of the senior editors got nailed for impaired driving on his way home, but this was still the 1980s, still macho-driven, hard-drinking, chain-smoking newspapering. We were encouraged to take cabs, which we could expense.

Spicer had clearly wanted this columnists' dinner to be an intellectual exercise, an exchange of high ideas and smart sentiment. But it was a bit of a bust, with most just wanting to gossip, and Marjorie wanting to kill Greg for what she considered a hatchet job on her friend John Turner. The 1988 federal election was on, with Turner and Mulroney once again going at it toe to toe in debates and on the campaign trail. The singular campaign issue was free trade, and much to Marjorie's regret, Mulroney seemed to be winning. She was in an understandably foul mood. Only months earlier, she had been diagnosed with cancer and had been undergoing chemotherapy treatment, yet never took medical leave. She covered her head with flamboyant scarves, scheduled her medical appointments around her work, and never missed a deadline. (Three years later, sadly, Marjorie Nichols would be gone at the young age of forty-eight.)

Earl decided the head waiter was the spitting image of actor/comedian Martin Mull and would refer to him only as such throughout the evening—"Hey, Martin Mull, can you bring us another bottle of that red plonk!"

The unsuccessful evening eventually wound down and Earl and I found ourselves leaving at the same time as Keith. Earl, well lubricated, was into his interviewing mode, asking question after question of Keith as if he were doing deep background research for a two-hour documentary. Keith was loving it and expansive about his unusual background that had eventually landed him at this job.

Keith invited us over to his place, which was nearby, for a nightcap. He had a walk-up apartment where he lived alone with a cat, Charlie, and an old dog, Shay, who seemed part beagle and had lost virtually all movement in his back legs. Keith would not hear anything about putting the old dog down, though. He sometimes pushed him around in a cart. He carried him up and down the stairs so the dog could poop and pee.

"I'll just take him out," Keith said. "Won't take but a minute."

He leaned down and scooped up Shay like a baby. The dog rolled over in Keith's arms, all four paws in the air. Contented as a baby.

Earl was still firing questions at Keith about his past. They were talking about Keith's days as a student in Paris now and Earl was on a roll. He insisted we accompany Keith down to the street so that Shay could do his thing and Keith could keep answering the questions that were coming at him like tennis balls out of a serving machine.

While the dog sniffed along the curb and piddled here and there, Keith began telling Earl of an early infatuation he had in Paris with then French prime minister Pierre Mendès France, at that time a pivotal world leader hugely admired by the young students of Paris.

"'PMF,' we all called him," Keith said. "I practically stalked him. I took photos of him with my little Brownie Kodak. I even tried to walk like him."

"*What??*" Finally, Earl had what he'd been prodding for. Something unbelievable.

"You tried to *walk* like him?" Earl prodded again.

"Yes," Keith said, smiling and picking up Shay, who had finished his toilet.

"Show me how he walked!" McRae pleaded.

"It was kind of like an orangutan," Keith said. "Head down, hips swinging, a bit of a crouch."

"Show us!"

And so, Keith Spicer, putting the dog down like a baby into a crib, began walking in PMF's strange gait. Crouched, head down.

Earl fell in behind his editor, imitating the walk of Pierre Mendès France.

"You have to have your arms dangling down like an ape!" Keith shouted back.

Earl let his arms dangle.

I joined in.

The future of the *Ottawa Citizen*: three overly refreshed men walking like Pierre Mendès France well after midnight on the back streets of the nation's capital.

Spicer eventually left the *Citizen*, but we would soon meet up again. In July of 1990, not long after his departure, Oka exploded in southwestern Quebec. A peaceful occupation by Kanesatake Mohawks to protest a proposed golf course turned violent, leaving one officer of the Sûreté du Québec dead. Building the golf course would have destroyed an ancestral cemetery of the Mohawks, and even after the army moved in the Mohawk warriors stood their ground. The actual firefight lasted all of twenty seconds, but the standoff would last seventy-eight days and shake Canadians to the core.

Several of us reporters were quickly dispatched to the village, known until this point for the soft-rind cheese originally manufactured by Trappist monks in a nearby monastery. The quickest route from Ottawa was down the east side of the Ottawa River to the Quebec town of Hudson to catch the towed ferry across the river to Oka. One of the *Citizen* reporters, Ian MacLeod, spent nine weeks covering the standoff, often sleeping in his car. At one point the newspaper rented a large and very comfortable trailer, and several of us camped out at Oka for days at a time.

Canada was in a frail state. Only two weeks earlier, the Meech Lake Accord had collapsed. And the news business was changing, changing fast, and changing more than any of us at that time could have foreseen. I had joined the Parliamentary Press Gallery in 1978, a time when television reporting was cumbersome, slow and definitely considered lower in the food chain than the important columnists who typed up what Canadians knew, or should know, about their politics.

A television report from Ottawa required a reporter, a producer, a cameraperson and a sound person. Video—"film," they called it— needed to be taken to the television headquarters so it could be edited and, later that night, be part of the news package.

No longer. Not only was equipment fast changing—reporters using cameras, live reports possible—but the delivery of news was fast changing. The United States had long had all-news channels, and now Canada was entering that world through the CBC Newsworld channel.

From the moment a single captivating Canadian Press photograph was taken of soldier Patrick Cloutier standing face to face with a bandana-covered warrior, Brad Larocque (calling himself "Freddy Krueger"), Oka became prime-time viewing for Canadians.

The warriors played to the media—and by media, I mean the cameras. Television. There were gripping images daily. When the warriors had anything to say, they walked to where the cameras were set up, their words and complaints carried live on Newsworld's 24-hour channel.

Ian MacLeod kept an "Oka diary" for the *Citizen* during the many weeks he spent behind the lines. He saw what was happening to news. "We have to ask permission to use the payphone inside the Mohawk headquarters," he wrote in one entry. "Otherwise we are pretty much left to ourselves. The Warriors really cater to the TV people."

Near the end of his long stay, MacLeod wrote in his diary that "We sat watching *The National* tonight. The announcer mentioned the CBC had pulled out, but there was no mention of us. It's like we don't exist now that the cameras are gone." In a very short time, I would see first-hand how dramatically news was changing in Canada, as what was said to the cameras and microphones often had little to do with what was being said to print reporters.

Shortly after Oka, starting in the fall of 1990 and running through late June of 1991, Spicer and I would meet again, though working for different employers. I was still with the *Citizen*. He was now with the government . . . sort of. In response to wide public outrage over the handling of the Meech Lake constitutional accord—remember Prime Minister Mulroney talking about how he had "rolled the dice"?—the federal government had moved to set up the "Citizens' Forum on Canada's Future" and named Keith Spicer as its chair.

Spicer had a good sense of the country, having previously served as commissioner of official languages, chair of the CRTC and, of course, editor of the capital city's main newspaper. He was good with catch-phrases—he tagged wealthy Montreal anglophones "Westmount Rhodesians" when serving as language commissioner—and had unusual talents, such as being able to quote Shakespeare at length or play on the piano, by ear, a variety of national anthems. Years later, in *Life*

Sentences, the memoir he published in 2004, he would say he was chosen to run the Citizens' Forum because he was the only high-profile Ottawa type "crazy enough" to take on such a "bizarre adventure."

Twelve commissioners were named to the forum, with Spicer as head and eleven others representing regions and special interests. Their assignment, as best determined by a suspicious media, was to reach out to "ordinary Canadians," hear them out and then prepare a psychiatrist's report on the general state of a depressed nation.

The smart set—the privileged and well-positioned who make up the news panels and fill the opinion pages—thought it ridiculous. To many, "ordinary Canadians" was a euphemism for "stupid, dull Canadians"— citizens with little education and lacking in everything from personality to worth. The very phrase, to them, called up images of farmers with flat, uninteresting faces, suburb dwellers with insignificant jobs, seniors more worried about their lawns than their country, truck drivers wondering if their bladder would last till the next stop, airport security workers bitching about who's late coming back from break . . .

It was a stunning misread of their own country.

With much embarrassment, I am here to confess today that I initially chose the sneering route. I began signing off my *Citizen* columns as "Commissioner 13." I structured the columns so they would look like inter-office memos, Commissioner 13 reporting privately to the "Chairman." Insider stuff that I was, at first, simply making up to mock Spicer and his commission's take on the country.

The forum did, however, supply a steady stream of real material for reporters and columnists. The selected BC commissioner, broadcaster Jack Webster, bailed almost instantly. There were immediately rumours of disorganization and ballooning costs, which Spicer himself had joked would fall "somewhere between a shoestring and an orgy." Spicer set off for Tuktoyaktuk in the Northwest Territories and told a *Globe and Mail* reporter that he had prepared for this first trip into the Far North by reading Inuit poetry. Satirical editorial cartoons instantly followed.

Commissioner 13 wrote in the Southam newspaper chain that "the wheels have all but fallen off"—not even giving the forum a chance.

"I thought I was singing 'This Land Is My Land,'" Spicer wrote in his memoirs, but "media and public heard the theme from *Looney Tunes*."

Slowly, however, the forum began to take shape. David Broadbent, a senior public servant with impeccable organizational skills, came in as executive director to run the office. Laurier LaPierre, an excellent communicator, took on the task of training the moderators. Patrick Gossage, once Pierre Trudeau's press secretary, came in to talk publicity and planning. And Spicer himself hired on some gifted advisers and writers, among them magazine writers Martin O'Malley, Nicole Bourget, who had worked with Spicer at the CRTC, and Nancy Gall, the excellent reporter who had worked for Spicer at the *Citizen*.

The *Citizen* was now getting such good reaction to the "Commissioner 13" columns—Southam papers across the country began regularly carrying them—that they sent me on the road with the commission, assigned to cover it full-time until Spicer tabled his final report.

It was an education the likes of which I could not possibly have imagined. The forum began in Charlottetown, Prince Edward Island, the "Cradle of Confederation." The crowd that came to listen to Spicer—in the very room where John A. Macdonald and the "Fathers of Confederation" had gathered 127 years earlier—was mostly white-haired and concerned, though one elderly man told Spicer if Quebec decided to leave it would "sure as heck shorten up the drive to Toronto."

Another older man, a blueberry farmer named Angus MacLean who had once served as PEI premier, said, "I'd have to say, in hindsight, the Fathers of Confederation botched it."

"Like a dying person clinging desperately to the life he knows," the Charlottetown *Guardian* ("Covers Prince Edward Island Like the Dew") editorialized the snowy day Spicer rolled into town, "Canadians have sunk their claws into a nation of the past, and perhaps even of the imagination . . ." A letter to the editor wanted the prime minister charged for what he had brought about with the failure of Meech Lake. A wire story carried a survey claiming that Canadians were so anxiety-ridden over the state of their frail nation that they had stopped having sex.

There was indeed a sense of apocalypse in early 1991 as Spicer took his commission about the country. For the two hours Spicer and a few commissioners stood and listened in Charlottetown, "ordinary Canadians" railed against the GST, the Quebec language bill, sovereign-tists, the handling of the Oka standoff between Quebec Mohawks and the army, the prime minister, the bungled accord and even the media.

The meeting was about to close when an old man with soaring black-grey eyebrows took to his feet from near the back of the room. He had not said a word beforehand. He said he was a farmer from Pownal. He said he was a father of twelve. He said he had been born dirt poor and was still dirt poor. He spoke with such incredible calm and certainty of voice that the entire room stilled as he stood, carefully unfolded his scarf and placed it around his neck. He was preparing to leave even as he addressed the gathering. He put on his coat and held his gloves in his hand, a man dressed for the cold as he spoke under hot lights.

Leo Cannon had a story to tell about his garden. He talked about the magic he felt when he took a small carrot seed into his huge hands and poked it down into the soil and how, a few months later, thanks to a lot of care and a little faith, the next time he moved the earth aside it revealed a beautiful, full-grown carrot.

"The problem with this country," Leo Cannon wanted the Citizens' Forum on Canada's Future to know, "is that we have lost our faith. This country is morally bankrupt. It's about money and profit and greed. We are morally bankrupt, and unless we are willing to change, there's not a hope in hell of it."

And with that he pulled on his gloves and walked away, off into the night where the snow was just beginning to swirl again along Charlottetown's University Avenue.

———

Leo Cannon's unusual speech changed my attitude. I stopped laughing and began listening. After Charlottetown, nothing seemed quite so funny any longer about the Spicer Commission. Ordinary Canadians, most so angry they visibly seethed, were being listened to by Spicer and his eleven real commissioners. And these people—most often older, most often white, far more often in one official language than the other—had a great deal to say.

Far too often the ones not listening were the media, and to some extent it was not entirely the media's fault. It struck me during the Spicer hearings that Canadians do not speak as themselves when television cameras are around. For whatever reason, the presence of a television camera has a profoundly different effect on Canadians than it ever seems to on Americans. Americans seem eager to reveal, to star in their own fifteen-second movie; Canadians seem keen to conceal, to let stardom remain with the television interviewer.

Spicer was attuned to media and wanted television to be a part of his travelling circus. He himself was superb on television, a master ad libber, capable of saying things like "I'd like to make four points" and then actually making four. He was equally comfortable in French and English. He liked the camera and the camera liked him. He was hardly an ordinary Canadian himself, yet he thought that televised "town hall" meetings would be able to draw out the thoughts of these real ordinary Canadians and that the little community centre or church basement they might be meeting in could somehow, magically, be electronically transformed into some huge "meetin' tent" that would cover the entire country.

Spicer did not yet understand the ordinary Canadian. One bright light, one camera, one earplug connecting these people by satellite to some distant interviewer and they instantly changed. Rather than say what they thought, they would say what they thought they should be saying, what the interviewer wanted to hear. Instead of the anger pouring through, reason seemed the order of the day. On television they sounded tolerant, reasonable, hopeful, resigned; off camera, and in the sessions where no cameras showed up, they seethed, they accused, they threatened, they swore to avenge and punish those politicians who had been involved in the whole sorry process leading up to the Meech Lake debacle. Ontario premier David Peterson had already paid the price by losing an election; others would follow. Even the prime minister, master of two jaw-dropping majority wins, would have the sense to bail before daring to face such wrath. Brian Mulroney's once-dominant party was pounded and pummelled to an astonishing two seats in the 1993 election.

Commissioner 13 started to argue that the televised town hall meetings were a disaster and not at all reflective of what people were feeling. What television—particularly the then-powerful CBC news program *The Journal*—had done, even if inadvertently, was create a *third* official language, which I termed "BarbaraSpeak" after Barbara Frum, then host of this program and by far the most recognizable news media personality in the country. Since the media elite, like the political elite, had been so intensely behind the accord—many of the leading media lights, from old Bruce Hutchison out in Victoria to the young national news managers in Toronto, were convinced that the country would fracture and likely die if Meech did not go through—the discussions they led had a discernible edge to them. When ordinary Canadians responded on camera in their small broadcast voices, the result was an inaccurate portrait of the country's state of mind.

The commission swept across the country, television paying only periodic attention. Hardly a night went by when there wouldn't be a meeting, somewhere, on the *meaning* of Canada, the current state of Confederation, the constitution and how to fix things through everything from Senate reform to, as many favoured, a full constitutional assembly that would, in essence, be starting from scratch to redesign this improbable country called Canada. There were official meetings and unofficial meetings, meetings in people's houses over wine and cheese, meetings in community centres over tea and coffee.

In Brandon, 472 people showed up to talk to Spicer, a crowd so large the organizers thought to bring in uniformed Canadian Tire cashiers to act as ushers. It all gave new credibility to the old joke that a Canadian coming to a fork in the road with a sign in one direction saying "heaven" and a sign in the other promising a "panel discussion on heaven" would head straight for the panel discussion.

Commissioner 13 stopped in Edmonton to spend a day with Fil Fraser, the human rights activist and filmmaker who was one of Spicer's eleven commissioners on the Citizens' Forum on Canada's Future—or, as Fraser preferred to call it, the "Yo-yo Commission." One day up, one day down; one day filled with hope, one day filled with despair.

In Fraser's opinion, what the Spicer Commission had done, if nothing else, was show that there was "a quiet revolution going on in the country." The anger against the prime minister—complete with "Impeach Mulroney" bumper stickers—was merely the opening salvo in a battle still being played out. "Maybe people aren't marching in the streets," he told me, as he slipped his black Jaguar through the Edmonton traffic, "but the amount of emotional energy being expended is similar."

Fraser conceded that he himself had fallen into a pit of despair over the country. As little as three weeks earlier, he had admitted to himself, and then to those closest to him, that the country was finished, done, over with. But then, he said, the beginnings of a "sea change" had started. The national venting was having an effect, and a good effect.

"If I had to tell you when I realized how important it was," Fraser told me over lunch, "I'd pick the time I went into northern Saskatchewan. I flew in to Île-à-la-Crosse, the most unbelievably beautiful but poverty-stricken place you ever saw. The village is all Natives and Métis. They used to run traplines but now there's no point, the fur industry is dead. They used to fish, but now the fish are mostly gone. They've got 80 percent unemployment and Third World birthrates.

"We sat in a circle and they handed around an eagle feather. Whoever held it got to speak. It took three hours and they just spilled their guts on the floor. One young man said he was going to burn down the whole northern forest because he had nothing to lose. Old people talked about there being nothing for the young but welfare and despair.

"When it was over they came up one by one and some of them shook my hand, but most of them hugged me. Hugged me.

"And you know what they told me? They said, 'Go and tell them.'

"'Go and tell them' . . .

"We're going to do that. We're going to tell what people said. Not how many people said this or how many people said that—but what they said.

"We're going to say what we really heard . . ."

In Vancouver, I ran into Elijah Harper Jr. by accident; both of us were staying in the same downtown hotel. He was the member of the Manitoba legislature who, over and over, refused the unanimous consent required for debate on the Meech Lake Accord to continue. His refusal, and the subsequent refusal of Premier Clyde Wells to continue debate in the Newfoundland House of Assembly because Manitoba had already said no, had led to time running out on Meech Lake and the accord had died on the table.

Wells had received the greatest official blame, though Harper had been the key player. Politically, however, it was far easier to blame a reluctant premier than a rebellious Indigenous MLA. "We know the truth," Harper said over coffee in the Hotel Vancouver. "We know what really happened. The prime minister continues to deny us, who we are and what we did. He can't give us the credit we deserve. He can't deal with us.

"When he spoke the day after he didn't even mention us. He had to point to Clyde Wells for political reasons. He had to portray what had happened as rejection of the accord by English Canada.

"Besides, he couldn't blame us because everyone knew that we were morally right."

Since the future of Quebec was a central focus of the commission—the theory being that, having been snubbed by the collapse of the accord, Quebeckers would now choose to go their own way—Spicer was keen to head straight into the province and find out what "ordinary Quebeckers" were thinking. Wearing his signature trench coat and wide-brimmed black fedora—looking more like he was tromping around the set of *Casablanca* than Canada—Spicer took his commission into Saguenay, straight to the heart of *bluet* country where the sovereigntist movement had long been strongest. At a radio talk show, he was asked what he had gained by bringing the topic of Canadian unity into the heartland of Quebec separatism. Spicer considered a moment, placed a finger over his mouth, then lifted the hand away and held the finger almost tight to his thumb.

"About two millimetres," he estimated.

It may have been a generous estimation. Quebec was in turmoil and paid scant attention to the Citizens' Forum. It seemed every day produced a new idea, each one banging its head against the rising prospects of an independent Quebec. One man was proposing the "corridor option," which would allow most of the province to go its own way but would provide for a superhighway running south of the St. Lawrence between the Ontario border and New Brunswick, with a wide ribbon of Canadian territory surrounding this preserved corridor. A political movement calling itself the Equality Party was calling for the creation of the "Republic of Laurentia," an idea that would have Quebec returning to its tiny New France borders as they existed before the 1759 conquest. Another group wanted to create the "West Island Nation," a sort of Luxembourg that would hold the West Island of Montreal, where most of the Anglos, most of the businesses and much of the wealth were to be found.

All this, of course, was without even getting to the growing topic of Western separatism. The farther west Spicer ventured, the greater the fury over whatever it was Canadians believed had happened when all those middle-aged men in suits, equally wired on coffee and their own sense of self-importance, closed the doors at the Ottawa Congress Centre and hammered out an agreement they claimed contained no "egregious" errors and was, therefore, not even open to discussion by those who would be most affected by it.

The sense was growing, fast, that the line down the centre of the road could not possibly hold under such traffic.

What Spicer gave all these different elements was an opportunity to vent. I had created the "Commissioner 13" persona as a lark, but it quickly became something quite apart. Commissioner 13 began receiving inside material on the forum and, in particular, information on what direction it seemed Spicer might be heading. Spicer would later say in his memoirs that this little joke, Commissioner 13, had somehow "become nationally known as the Forum's ultimate, well-informed quasi-insider."

I cannot say who, exactly, was involved, largely because it seemed, at times, like everyone was involved, from the highest to the lowest level. Those who were working for the commission had noted the same phenomenon—that the "ordinary Canadian" was absolutely in a shit fit over the country.

The commission came out with an interim report that touched on the fuming anger toward politicians but gave little indication of which way the final report would go. There was a split in the forum's office and splits among the commissioners. Spicer often seemed to be waffling, members of his own staff unsure which way he would go and several of them trying, desperately, to prod him to go the distance.

There were those who wanted Commissioner 13 to keep the hot coals tight to Spicer's heels. There were rumours around, and widely believed, that Spicer had been offered the ambassadorship to France if he played along and reported back, mildly, that ordinary Canadians had vented their anger and were now feeling much better about things, thank you very much. Spicer had once lived in France, was a known francophile and, in fact, would later return to live in Paris, so the rumour certainly had legs. In his memoirs, published fourteen years later, Spicer would recount a telephone conversation with the prime minister in which he said Mulroney promised him any embassy he wished—"Just name it and we'll work out whatever you like." Spicer says he politely told the prime minister, "Thanks, but I don't really want anything. Let's just get on with the job."

Commissioner 13, by now, had turned into something never intended and certainly never expected. What had begun as a farce was now a force. I became convinced that Spicer would buckle. The pressure on him was building, and it was very clear—even if France was not in the works—that he could personally benefit by largely clearing the government name on this file. Spicer had always been both an iconoclast and a survivor, and it seemed these aspects of him were running at cross purposes to each other. If he chose to mollify, he would lose the respect of a great many then close to him, but if he chose the path they wanted him to take, he might lose his own future prospects—something anyone entering the last decade of a career would surely consider. Spicer was then fifty-seven years old. He was eating poorly and drinking too much. His assistant, Barbara Ursel, forced him to see a doctor, who wanted to hospitalize him for burnout and advised him to stop working for a two-year period. Hardly something Spicer needed to hear with only two months left before he would have to report. Instead, he promised to cut back quietly, go for a daily walk, and restrict his daily red wine intake to two glasses—as he put it, "minimum and maximum."

Through May and the first part of June, Commissioner 13 regularly berated Spicer about following through, about telling the truth, about not letting down the four hundred thousand "ordinary Canadians" who had come in some contact with the forum. Spicer had not said a word about what he had found but already the case against him was building in the media. There were, of course, exceptions—the *Globe's* Michael Valpy, for example—but for the most part the Ottawa media bought into the elites' line that Spicer was a bureaucratic joke. They said the expense of his commission, $27.4 million, required its own commission of inquiry. They laughed at his figures; they said the forum was unscientific (*of course* it was); they said Spicer was more interested in finding an apartment in Paris than the pulse of the nation he wished to leave behind. They said he would be offering no solutions without realizing that solutions had never been part of the mandate. The role of the forum had been merely to listen—and then to report back.

As Spicer later revealed in his memoirs, the government made sure to get certain discreet messages to him that if he played the game right, he could be in line for a nice posting or, as he claimed, a four-hundred-thousand-dollar golden handshake that "nobody would find out about." None of this, of course, was ever put in writing. Nor, however, was it ever denied.

Commissioner 13 was no longer among those who had ridiculed Spicer's commission in the early going. In late June, only days before he was to table his report, the column struck hard, telling Spicer—whom I quite liked and admired—that he had a "sacred pact" with those four hundred thousand that could not be broken. He was advised to forget the media response because they were only going to laugh anyway. And if there was widespread knocking because of the forum's failures in Quebec, go with the four hundred thousand rather than deny them, and let it be known that this would be the first time ever that the voice of the "rest of Canada" had come through so loudly and so clearly. Canadians—and this included Quebec and the chortling elite—needed to hear that voice.

What Commissioner 13 did was supply his own "minority report." I wrote that Keith Spicer knew better than anyone else that Canadians everywhere talked about their love of their country and their utter incomprehension concerning what had happened to it. They were ashamed of their political leaders, the prime minister in particular, and they had lost faith in the political process. Having been excluded by a process that wanted nothing to do with them, they wanted in on whatever process might follow. They had no interest in abandoning the fate of a country that, in their minds, had once worked wonderfully and must be made to work again. I told him about a very short note I had received that said it all. "Let me put it to you this way," the handwritten note said. "If Canada dies, then I die." It was signed "Pete."

Spicer's job, then, was to speak for all the Petes. And Pete lived in every region of the country, was both man and woman, white and Indigenous, of colour, new Canadian and old Canadian, young and elderly and everything in between, spoke not only both official languages but many other languages. When asked by the commission before each session to list the things those present most treasured about Canada, all those Petes across Canada had listed medicare first and, to the great surprise of many, but not all, hockey second.

In the days leading up to Spicer's June 27 release of the report, there was panic in his office as he seemed to vacillate. The official report had gone to the printers and couldn't be called back. It would contain two dissenting reports, one from Quebec publisher Robert Normand, one from Newfoundland union leader Richard Cashin, largely questioning the validity of the exercise. There would not be 100 percent agreement among the commissioners.

On the day of the report's release to the public, Spicer was said to be carrying two speeches in his jacket pocket, still uncertain as to which way he would go, though his press secretary, Nicole Bourget, had strongly advised him to ignore the speaking notes he had been working on and, instead, just speak "from the heart." The official report had been written up, and enough had been leaked to let people like Michael Valpy know that unless Spicer came through, it would quickly find that infamous Ottawa shelf that holds hundreds of unread and instantly forgotten commission and parliamentary reports.

After 241 days of pulse taking and pointless busywork, Keith Spicer delivered his report on Thursday, June 27, 1991, in the Grand Hall of the Museum of Civilization on the side of the Ottawa River opposite Parliament Hill. It was, as the *Ottawa Citizen* reported on page 1, nothing less than the "Scream of a Nation." If he did indeed carry two speeches into the building, he elected to go with the one that would take no prisoners. He laid the blame for what had gone so terribly wrong with this country's spirit squarely at the door of Prime Minister Brian Mulroney.

It could hardly have been a more dramatic setting. Spicer stood nervously on a tall stage in front of the West Coast totem poles, the assembled cameras and media below and, through the vast glass walls opposite, dark clouds gathering over the round Library of Parliament, the sky rumbling and periodically flashing with lightning.

Spicer's personal "Chairman's Foreword" became the story of the nine-month Citizens' Forum on Canada's Future. It was Spicer's Hail Mary pass, a play kept from the other commissioners when the official report was sent off to the printers—thirty-five hundred words only, but every single one of them lacking the bureaucratic governor that had been applied to the official report.

Spicer called the current state of the Canadian spirit "a pessimist's nightmare of hell." He said, "Our democracy is sick. Citizens do not accept their leaders' legitimacy. This begins with the prime minister, but does not end with him. It includes leaders of the Opposition and provincial leaders . . ." He said Canada had become a country "dying of ignorance, and of our stubborn refusal to learn." He said Canada faces "twin crises—one of structure, the other more profound and delicate, of the spirit." He said people were losing faith in the symbols and institutions that made a country and made a country's people believe in it. He slammed the "consensual editing" of the official report that had muted the degree of fury out there toward the prime minister, who had become a "lightning rod" for all the anger Spicer said he had encountered. "From most citizens' viewpoint," Spicer said, "our report lets the PM off too lightly. At least for now, there is a fury in the land against the Prime Minister."

Canadians, he said, had become "the wind that wants a flag."

Spicer finished up as, outside, the storm broke, thunder and lightning over Parliament Hill, rain pelting the high windows of the Grand Hall.

And then the power went out. The sound system that had carried Spicer's words had blown its circuits.

Several weeks later, I got a call from Spicer suggesting a lunch with him and David Broadbent, the bureaucrat who put the forum back on track and carried it through to the end. We met across the river at Café Henry Burger and, at the end of a lunch in which some astonishing stories were told of government interference and internal fiascos, Spicer reached down behind the table and pulled up a framed certificate. It looked official, complete with the Canadian coat of arms embossed at the top. It read: "Commissioner 13—Roy MacGregor: In recognition of your valuable contribution to the work of the Citizens' Forum on Canada's Future" and was signed by both the chairman, Spicer, and the executive director, Broadbent.

It hangs today above the desk in my office.

What had started as a joke had turned into a transformational experience. I had always felt a special bond to the country, especially the small towns and rural routes. The Citizens' Forum took me deeper into that world, where, off-camera, Canadians were furious with politicians. They felt they weren't being heard and were being ignored, perhaps even ridiculed, by those in power. This has happened in waves over our history—recall the anxiety over Quebec separation a generation earlier?—and seems in the early 2020s to be rising again. The bumper stickers that shouted "Impeach Mulroney" are now screaming "Fuck Trudeau."

There is a marked difference between farmer Leo Cannon quietly folding his scarf in Charlottetown and telling the crowd, "We are morally bankrupt, and unless we are willing to change, there's not a hope in hell of it" and convoy horns blasting through the night in Ottawa in the early weeks of 2022, but there is also a similarity that should not be denied. Riled Canadians act. We are a country that so often seems much better at kicking someone out than putting someone in.

A month or so after Spicer delivered his dramatic "wind that wants a flag" speech at the Museum of Civilization, a surprise envelope showed up in the morning mail bag at the *Citizen*'s Parliament Hill bureau. The envelope was addressed to me. It had no return address.

Inside the mysterious envelope was a copy of a letterhead from the Office of the Prime Minister.

> 02 July
> P.M.
>   Attached is a printout of the article written by Commissioner #13 which appeared in the Ottawa Citizen on Wed. Nov. 9, 1988—less than two weeks before Nov. 21st election!
>   Proof positive of how wrong one can be.

High in the top-right corner of the single page of letterhead a scribbled note read "This is for P+P on Monday," signed with the initials "BM"— which would appear to be Prime Minister Brian Mulroney. Priorities and Planning—the only cabinet committee chaired by the prime minister—would be discussing a nearly three-year-old column of mine on Monday. "Priorities and Planning" indeed. Someone in the PMO wanted me to know.

Spicer's speech had mentioned "a fury in the land" that was, obviously, directed at the prime minister, the lead player in the push for the failed Meech Lake Accord. And he had taken it personally. Who wouldn't? And the PM wasn't just angry with Spicer; he was furious at those he thought had pushed Spicer, which would seem to include me, in the guise of Commissioner 13.

Attached to the PMO note was a printout of the column referred to—an *Ottawa Citizen* column from November 9, 1988. It had been written in the heat of a bitter debate over free trade. Liberal leader John Turner, who had stumbled terribly in the 1984 election—Mulroney's famous "You had an option, sir" destroying Turner in the televised debate—had seemingly found his feet as he railed against the free trade proposal. Polls were shifting. PC staffers aboard the Mulroney bus were unnerved. Commissioner 13 announced that, among the people, free trade was a dead issue. "The people have decided," Commissioner 13 wrote with certainty.

Twelve days after that 1988 column appeared, Mulroney won a second straight majority. Free trade went through. The people had decided—the opposite of what the column predicted. Hey, this is someone who said Wayne Gretzky would never be heard of again after the Oilers traded him to LA.

Throughout all this, unbeknownst to all but the parties directly involved, my old boss at *Maclean's*, Peter C. Newman, was conducting taped interviews with Mulroney. They spoke at least once a week, and the intention was that, once Mulroney was no longer prime minister, Newman would publish the official history of those transformative years in office when Meech Lake failed and free trade succeeded. The two men had long been close, and there was great trust between them.

Fourteen years after that P+P meeting over Commissioner 13, Random House Canada dropped a book-publishing bombshell. The years of taping that Peter C. Newman had done with then prime minister Brian

Mulroney had resulted in an explosive book titled *The Secret Mulroney Tapes: Unguarded Confessions of a Prime Minister.*

Mulroney and his supporters were outraged. Through a spokesman, the former prime minister said he was "devastated" to learn that the tapes were being made public and felt "betrayed" by his now-former friend. He claimed to have been unaware that their conversations were being recorded. Poppycock, responded Newman, saying they had a clear deal that he would write the definitive account of the Mulroney years after the then prime minister had left office. The deal included a promise to make available certain cabinet documents and other materials. When that didn't happen, Newman decided to publish the tapes as insight into the workings of a man who would go down in Canadian history as a most significant prime minister.

With word out that such a blockbuster publication was coming, the race was on to get an early peek at the contents. That, however, seemed impossible, as Random House announced that *Maclean's* magazine had obtained exclusive rights to the book. *Maclean's* would be publishing excerpts in the September 19, 2005, issue, which would appear on September 12, Random House's official publication date. Everyone would have to wait to see what it was that had so excited and upset the Canadian political world.

I was now at the *Globe and Mail*, my final, eighteen-year-long stop of full-time employment. There was a package waiting for me at the downtown *Globe* bureau. It held an early copy of the book. There was also a letter attached. The letter detailed exactly what chapters were reserved exclusively for *Maclean's*. The *Globe and Mail* was free to make whatever use they liked of those chapters not committed to the newsmagazine.

Maclean's knew they had something very special. It was, of course, the main feature for the issue that was in the mail to subscribers on Monday, September 12. The cover had a fine photograph of a smiling Brian Mulroney. The headline shouted "EXCLUSIVE—The Secret Mulroney Tapes," and the cover lines continued the theme:

On Trudeau: 'A Coward and a Weakling'
On Chrétien: 'F****** Stupid'
On Clark: 'He Blew the Whole Goddamned Thing'
And On His Successor: 'Keep Your Pecker Up, Kim'

That very same morning, Monday, September 12, 2005, the *Globe and Mail* published a thirty-four-hundred-word feature on the contents of the book. Having access to all but the two chapters exclusive to *Maclean's*, we found more nuggets than could have been imagined:

- Brian Mulroney believed he would go down as the best prime minister since Sir John A. Macdonald.

- He blamed Pierre Trudeau for the undermining of the Meech Lake Accord— "Nothing has ever compared to the lack of principle of this son of a bitch."

- He dismissed Kim Campbell, his successor, as "a very vain person" who blew the 1993 election because she was too busy "screwing around" with her Russian boyfriend.

- The Ottawa press corps was a "a phony bunch of bastards."

- Former Ontario premier David Peterson, a Mulroney supporter throughout Meech, told Newman that "I would never trust or respect him. He's a pathological liar . . ."

The newspaper publication was an instant sensation that Monday, while most issues of *Maclean's* were just beginning to cross the country by delivery truck and snail mail. The *Globe* owned the sensational story—and had not paid a cent for it.

Word came very quickly that *Maclean's* publisher and editor-in-chief

Ken Whyte was furious at the *Globe and Mail*, as well as at Random House and Peter Newman, the person he had to think had provided the material. Who could blame Ken? He had hired me when he and Conrad Black founded the *National Post* in 1998 and we had been friends and gotten on well through four glorious years of the early *Post*. But there would be no backslapping and reminiscing over good times after this shocker. At least not for a time.

To no one's surprise, two days later, on September 14, a letter was faxed to Edward Greenspon, the *Globe's* editor-in-chief and the one who had hired me away from the *National Post* in the summer of 2002. It was from the Random House head office in New York and was signed by corporate counsel.

"Put as simply as possible," the counsel wrote, "your unauthorized and excessive use of material from the Work violates Canadian copyright law, and no reasonable interpretation of the fair dealings justification can excuse that conduct." The counsel went on to state that we had no authorization to use such material and that publication of information from the book was "a violation of the author's and our rights . . ." Furthermore, "The *Globe and Mail* has not compensated neither [*sic*] Mr. Newman nor this company for its use."

"Let me make myself clear," the counsel continued. "We do not dispute your right, and even your obligation, to report on newsworthy matters, including obviously the Work and its contents." Two paragraphs later he went on about the "long standing and collegial relationship" that the publisher has with the *Globe and Mail*, as well as being one of the newspaper's leading advertisers. "Given the nature of that relationship," he concluded, "we would ask that you let us know how you intend to rectify this matter as soon as possible."

Naturally, the *Globe's* legal people wanted to know how it was that I came into possession of the book. I was able to produce the book, as well as a letter from the publisher itself outlining which chapters *Maclean's* had exclusive rights to and which we might use should we choose to. I had even been provided with three pages of indexed "highlights" to help us find the juicier parts.

There would be no lawsuit. The *Globe* had done nothing wrong in taking a gift freely given and running with it. Not a word was said after the initial outrage from the New York offices. *The Secret Mulroney Tapes* by Peter C. Newman flew to number one on the bestseller list and stayed there all fall and through Christmas.

One passage in the book that was not used by the *Globe* concerned that long-ago P+P committee meeting where the shortcomings of Commissioner 13 had taken up valuable cabinet time.

The creator of Commissioner 13 was called "one of the leading Mulroney haters," a columnist who had taken control of Spicer by attacking the Citizens' Forum on Canada's Future. "To buy his peace with him," Mulroney said on one tape, "Spicer engaged in this little secret, denouncing me for all the country's problems."

As Mulroney had recounted to Newman, that 1988 column wrongly predicted that the people would vote against free trade. In telling the tale, the former prime minister wildly rewrote much of it. He said the column was "about being on the Conservative bus, saying that all the journalists knew that Mulroney was finished. [Commissioner 13] wrote, 'We knew all along that this lousy mediocre guy from Montreal's right to lead the Conservative Party was a one-termer. We knew he was possessed by the Americans. I fall asleep on this bus tonight knowing full well that this is the end of the Mulroney government.'"

Not quite, sir, but close . . . touché.

(A personal note: When an unexpected passing struck our family in the spring of 2021, one of the first calls of condolences came from . . . former prime minister Brian Mulroney. Much appreciated.)

For months, I remained working on the Hill, but nothing could match the adventure of Commissioner 13. I had been covering politics for the best part of fifteen years. Life was routine. Get in the car early each morning, drive down the Ottawa River Parkway to Parliament Hill, turn through the Wellington gates and down the hill to the small lot by the water where the Press Gallery members enjoyed free parking.

Times were changing. The *Citizen* had a new editor in James Travers, who had previously served as a Southam columnist. He was a fine editor and we got on well. There was a small Press Gallery movement under way that argued we should not be accepting the free parking at the back of the Centre Block, as it made us somehow beholden to the government that granted us this privilege.

Few of us had any interest in paying a monthly parking fee and having to find space in one of the many private lots that dotted the downtown core. I sent Travers a memo arguing that this was unfair to those of us in the bureau, as all the other *Citizen* employees had free parking at the paper's offices on Baxter Road.

The next day I got a call from Jim. He was friendly and suggested lunch.

We met at a bar near the *Citizen* offices. We ordered drinks and chatted easily about the biggest story to hit town since free trade and Meech Lake—the surprising and rather unlikely arrival of the Ottawa Senators, the National Hockey League's newest Canadian franchise.

Our food arrived and after a few chews, Jim smiled, swallowed and announced, "I think I've solved your parking problem."

I hadn't expected this to be so easy. I startled and was lost for words.

Jim Travers smiled even wider.

"You'll be parking at the Civic Centre," he said. "I want you to cover the Senators for us."

SLEEPING WITH
ELIJAH HARPER'S FEATHER

I felt like I had fallen into a spy novel.

"*Meet us there*," the voice at the other end of the telephone said after he had passed on the coordinates of a downtown Winnipeg intersection. I could have sworn he whispered when naming the streets.

It was June, 1990, and the Meech Lake Accord had only days remaining until the deadline for ratification ran out. The recently elected Newfoundland premier Clyde Wells had been one face of the opposition. Another was Elijah Harper Jr., a New Democratic Party member of the Manitoba legislative assembly who had objected to the accord on the grounds that Indigenous groups had never been consulted. Between June 12 and June 21, Harper had said, "No, Mr. Speaker," eight different times to deny the unanimity required to table the accord for its ratification. Manitoba had been unable to follow the eight other provinces that had already ratified.

On June 22, with only Manitoba and Newfoundland outstanding, there would be one final chance before the legislatures rose for both provinces to come on board at the final minute. The pressure on Harper in Winnipeg and Wells in St. John's was almost unbearable.

The national media, naturally, flew off to both provincial capitals for the showdown. It was expected that Manitoba would go first, and if the accord fell in the Manitoba legislature, the actions of the Newfoundland House of Assembly would be rendered academic. If Harper buckled and Manitoba approved the accord, then the pressures of the entire country would fall on Wells, and no one was certain which way he might go.

The *Ottawa Citizen* dispatched me to Manitoba for the showdown. But it seemed every other media outlet in the country sent someone.

Not only was the national media taking over most of the downtown Winnipeg hotel space, the Prime Minister's Office had sent an entire team of legal arm-twisters to try to talk some sense into Elijah Harper Jr.

Trouble was, no one could find him.

Indigenous leaders from across the country, as well as Manitoba leaders and Harper's own extended family, had also descended on the provincial capital, and they had ensconced Harper somewhere far away from both his apartment and his office, where no one could reach him.

I called my old friend Billy Diamond, the former grand chief of the Cree of James Bay, at his northern Quebec home in Waskaganish. Billy put in a call to Ottawa and Ovide Mercredi, then with the Assembly of First Nations (AFN), and Mercredi then contacted Phil Fontaine, the Manitoba leader in the AFN and a close friend of Elijah Harper's. I was lying on the made bed of my hotel room, wondering what one might write about with absolutely no access to the main story, when the telephone rang.

"Meet us there" turned out to be mere blocks from my hotel. I dressed, packed my laptop with notepads and pens and hurried to meet whoever was going to be there.

Three men were waiting for me. Two were Indigenous leaders and the other a white lawyer, all seeming tense and serious. We shook hands and they walked me to a hotel several blocks away from the legislature. We got in the elevator and rose to a high floor with a huge, multi-roomed suite in one corner.

There, sitting in a chair by the window, holding an eagle feather in his hand while reading quietly from a black Bible, was Elijah Harper Jr. He did not look up, did not acknowledge my arrival.

"You can stay the night," I was told. "No one's going to get any sleep around here."

It was a remarkable experience. The man who—some were saying—held the very future of his country in his hands, was holding, instead, a large feather, periodically spinning it. He sat, for the most part, quietly, though the large room was anything but quiet. There were Indigenous leaders everywhere, leaders like Fontaine and Chief Gary Potts of the Bear Island band in northern Ontario, cousins and brothers of Harper, Cree down from Red Sucker Lake, national leaders, lawyers, friends and the curious. The only ones missing were the federal negotiators, who kept calling and demanding a meeting they never got—and the national media, with one lucky exception.

There was room service food and coffee. Elijah finally closed his Bible and came to chat. He spoke so softly it was sometimes difficult to hear him. What was clear, however, was that he was interested in talking about anything but the pressures and the accord, and so we talked about residential schools and hockey and his own fascinating life.

Like Billy Diamond, Elijah Harper Jr. had been born on a trapline in the winter of 1949. Elijah was forty-five days older than Billy. He had been the second of the thirteen children of Allen and Ethel Harper of Red Sucker Lake, an Oji-Cree community some seven hundred kilometres northeast of Winnipeg. Allen and Ethel would have so many children that Elijah was raised by his grandparents, who clung to the "heathen ways" of the Cree traditional teachings. At age eight, again like Billy Diamond, he was sent off to residential school, but, unlike with Diamond, it didn't much take. He lasted eight unhappy years and then returned to Red Sucker Lake to take up what he believed would be his life calling: trapping.

Like so many who came through this experience, he found he was straddling two worlds, with his footing unsteady in both. Like the others, he believed, wrongly, that he was alone. It is the mark of his generation to feel that way initially, only to discover that others of similar experience feel much the same. The story of the residential schools in Canada is one of shame and abuse, sexual and psychological, none of which can be denied. There can be nothing said in support of wrenching a child away from his or her family, yet it speaks to the power of the spirit that so many of those who survived the horrors of residential school became future leaders: Nellie Cournoyer of the Inuvialuit, Bill and Georges Erasmus of the Dene Nation, Jim Antoine of the Northwest Territories, Fontaine, Mercredi, Diamond, Harper . . .

Elijah Harper Jr. gradually grew so upset with conditions back on the reserve that he decided to forgo trapping and its miserable financial returns and instead go back to school, this time of his own volition. He took courses and eventually was accepted by the University of Manitoba, where he soon linked up with another angry young Indigenous student, Ovide Mercredi. They created an ever-widening circle that would include the likes of Phil Fontaine and Moses Okimaw, all of whom would end up in Winnipeg in the third week of June 1990. Together, they formed an Indigenous association and almost immediately engaged in battle with the University of Manitoba itself. The engineering students ran a satirical newspaper, and one week ran nothing but photographs taken of drunken Indigenous people in downtown Winnipeg. The Indigenous association forced an apology but fell short when they then set out to impeach the university president for allowing this to happen.

One winter in the late 1960s, when the group had been to Brandon to organize a similar organization for Indigenous students attending Brandon University, they ran into a blizzard driving home from the small city, more than 200 kilometres west of Winnipeg. Cars and trucks were everywhere off the highway. The others wanted to quit, but Mercredi and Harper refused and took turns running out in front of the headlights so the car could stick to the pavement. Police and stranded truckers yelled at them to give up, but they believed if they just kept plugging away eventually the storm would lift. They ran for 30 kilometres before the weather let up, but they'd made it through when no one else could.

Such sheer stubbornness would pay off twenty-two years later when they hit another bad patch.

The Meech Lake Accord had been passed in secret by eleven first ministers who couldn't spare a thought for Indigenous people and their position in the Canadian constitution. Indigenous leaders—First Nations, Inuit and Métis—had fought against this omission for the past three years. A parliamentary committee looking into the accord had recommended it be opened for their inclusion. Various politicians, including all three Manitoba party leaders, had called for a change to accommodate Indigenous people, but nothing had ever been done. The official contention of the Prime Minister's Office and its legal minions was that the accord held no "egregious" errors and could not, and must not, be reopened on any account.

The door was slammed.

The same gang that had gone up against the University of Manitoba in the late 1960s was now going up against the federal government of Canada. But they were no longer kids. Mercredi was a lawyer and deputy chief of the Assembly of First Nations. Moses Okimaw was now a lawyer. Phil Fontaine was the Manitoba regional chief for the Assembly of First Nations.

But only Elijah had the clout to actually do anything about it.

Elijah Harper Jr. had gone home without his degree. He had worked and then become chief of his band. He had been one of the Canadian chiefs who had travelled to London to ask the Queen to ensure that Indigenous people were treated fairly when the constitution was repatriated, as the Trudeau government intended to do. In 1981, he became the first Treaty Indian to be elected to the provincial legislature. He was elected again in 1982 and served, briefly, in the cabinet of Howard Pawley. That same year, he refused an invitation to attend the Parliament Hill ceremony when the Queen came to Ottawa to sign the Constitution Act into law. She had done nothing to ensure that the original nations be treated fairly by the ones who called themselves the "two founding nations."

It was not an illustrious political career for Elijah Harper Jr. He got in trouble instantly when on election night a man with no patience for Harper's noisy victory party tried to put his fist through the new member's nose. He got in financial trouble. He was arrested for failing to take a breathalyzer test. His marriage faltered. His four children suffered. His party was tossed out of office, though he held his own seat.

But then, around the beginning of the Meech Lake discussions, Harper began to pull himself together. He quit drinking. And he started planning how he might somehow stymie this runaway train of an accord that appeared to have a "No Indigenous" policy when it came to assigning seats at the table.

The moment Harper saw the full details of the final Ottawa deal, he called his old friend Gordon Mackintosh, now a lawyer but once clerk of the legislature. A procedural expert, Mackintosh helped refine Harper's notion to block it. They discovered, much to their delight, that the Gary Filmon government had incorrectly introduced the Meech Lake motion, meaning they would have to reintroduce it until they had unanimous agreement in the chamber to consider the matter, or until time ran out, whichever came first.

For all those days throughout June that Elijah Harper Jr. kept saying "No, Mr. Speaker," he held an eagle feather in his right hand. It soon became the symbol of his defiance, a feather that could appear in the backdrop of an editorial cartoon and instantly remind readers that, somewhere out in Manitoba, one lone "Indian" just might have the power to derail the whole thing.

The feather had been found by Elijah's older brother, Saul, a trapper who quietly followed the traditional ways. Saul believed he was being told to walk out to a clearing in the woods not far from his home in Red Sucker Lake. When he got there, the eagle feather was lying in the very middle of the open ground. He took it and gave it to younger brother Darryl, who followed more Christian ways, and Darryl brought it down to Winnipeg, where he gave it to Elijah to give him strength to get through this difficult month.

In the middle of this pivotal final week, the Red Sucker Lake band had gone back to the clearing where Saul had found the feather and stood in a circle, held hands and asked the Maker to give Elijah strength.

"Look," Chief John Harper, a cousin, cried, pointing into the sky.

High above, circling slowly in the drafts, was an eagle.

"The eagle is on Elijah's side," Chief John Harper told the gathering. "He's going to win."

While we were sitting in the hotel suite talking, Darryl Harper began flipping through the Bible that Elijah had been reading and opened it to the Book of Isaiah, chapter 40:30-31. He read the section quietly to himself, then aloud to everyone gathered there.

> Though youths grow weary and tired,
> And vigorous young men stumble badly,
> Yet those who wait for the Lord will gain new strength;
> They will mount up with wings like eagles,
> They will run and not get tired,
> They will walk and not become weary.

Later that long night, when Elijah Harper Jr. finally decided to try to get a little sleep before the day of decision, he took the eagle feather and placed it over these words, then closed the Bible.

The following day, at 12:24 p.m., Manitoba time, the feather was once again in his right hand as the motion was made and Elijah Harper Jr. killed the Meech Lake Accord with a single word.

"No."

OLD MEN YELLING AT CLOUDS

"You see the world through rose-coloured glasses."

I have heard this all my life and have even come to take it as a compliment. My family says it, friends say it, colleagues agree and social media is quick to ridicule. When I hit my seventies, I became acutely aware that a car accident or falling off a ladder or merely wandering off and getting lost in a park would see me described in the local press as an "elderly gentleman." I began to wonder at what point, exactly, do aging males become the cartoon character Abe, grandpa in *The Simpsons*, raising a fist to the sky over that perfect headline: "Old Man Yells at Cloud."

Twice I have seen this happen, in both instances the raised fist belonged to those whose observations had for decades been held critical to the understanding of Canada. For most English-speaking and -reading Canadians, they had been fundamental instructors. The first was Hugh MacLennan, whose 1945 novel, *Two Solitudes*, became the high-school text for students seeking to comprehend how a nation claiming two official languages and two separate codes of law could ever hope to exist for long. Second was Bruce Hutchison, whose 1942 non-fiction look at Canada, *The Unknown Country*, was first published in the United States as sort of a primer to the great unknown north but became, instead, the first detailed mirror Canadians were able to hold up to their often confusing face.

Both men ended their days under heavily overcast skies.

In the summer of 1980, *Maclean's* dispatched me to North Hatley, a charming little town in the Eastern Townships of Quebec. The story peg was MacLennan's upcoming novel, *Voices in Time*, which would also prove to be his last. He was seventy-three years old, in good health but bad humour, though you would never guess on first meeting this tall and elegant man with the soft and cultured manner of speaking that hinted at both his Cape Breton roots and his Oxford education.

He and his second wife, Frances (his first wife, American writer Dorothy Duncan, had died of cancer in 1957), were, as I'd expected, welcoming and gracious. We sat in the garden of their lovely country home, acorns periodically falling into the flower beds, as he spoke of his grave disappointment in a world that seemed, to him, to have lost its bearings, its grounding.

The five-time winner of the Governor General's Literary Award had been greatly celebrated in Canada and, in turn, had greatly celebrated his country, writing moving novels (*Barometer Rising, The Watch That Ends the Night*) and producing loving coffee-table nonfiction offerings on matters such as the fall colours and the rivers of the nation.

MacLennan had, however, slowly fallen out of critical favour in his own country. His previous novel, *Return of the Sphinx*, had been slammed by the critics. His long-ago bestsellers, novels that had largely defined his country, were out of fashion, dismissed by students who thought any "Two Solitudes" interpretation of French and English Canada was, well, rather facile and quaint. He, in turn, was dismissive of his fellow writers. He said his colleagues around the world were wasting time and talent by "devoting their immense technical abilities to the dissection of cowards, drunkards, weaklings, criminals, psychotics, imbeciles, deviates and people whose sole common denominator seems to be a hatred of life and terror of living."

What had happened to this polite, dapper, distinguished and reserved Scots-Canadian was the 1960s. Hugh MacLennan turned sixty in the centennial year, 1967, and he felt that the Canada he had been born into—at Glace Bay, Nova Scotia, a decade before Ypres—was now gone forever. The sixties had not been kind to this old-world soul. Student unrest, assassinations, the war in Vietnam, nuclear fear, the music, drugs, the dress and the manners of the youth coming to, and skipping, his classes at McGill upset him greatly. He couldn't tell boy from girl. One of his own students came to his office braless, "nipples at the salute," and he was convinced that had she walked down the street dressed this way only a dozen years before she would have been arrested.

"It was the fate of my generation," he wrote in *Rivers of Canada*, a glossy 1974 production that featured the photography of John de Visser, "to have been born in the death throes of a civilization that had supported the west for two thousand years. It was our tragedy that hardly any of us understood what this had meant."

Such lashing out—especially in a *gift book*—appeared unseemly for such a courtly, reserved man. He said the bright promise of the centennial year and Expo 67 had not even lasted a year. He said the Beatles were now "forgotten" within a few years of claiming they were more popular than Jesus Christ. He believed the world had been turned upside down by a movement no one seemed able to stop.

"In those years," he wrote, "I literally swam in the broth of students in the most harassed university in the land and I could not have dodged their anger if I had tried, which I didn't. I learned that they were rejecting, either with fury or with despair, nearly all the values and many of the methods which had produced the stupendous power of humanity in the mid-twentieth century."

One young man had told him the students were against "the whole God-damn phony mess." He found them to be "the weirdest-dressed young generation there ever was. Its worst members, and they were many, were so soft, spoiled, and self-degraded that when you saw them on city streets you could weep for them . . ."

Looking back on his diatribes in *Rivers of Canada*, it is possible today to see an angry early environmentalist venting. The rivers he had first written about in the 1950s, first in a series of essays for *Maclean's*, were often polluted and dammed. He implored Canadians to learn to "think like a river." If they could, he believed, they would then understand and appreciate "the overwhelming significance of waterways in this vast country." The rivers needed help, but he had little faith that they were going to get any.

By the time *Voices in Time* was being printed and I was sitting with him in his North Hatley garden, it seemed Hugh MacLennan had abandoned all hope for humanity. The new novel was set in 2039, fifty years after nuclear war had destroyed civilization. All cities, including his beloved Montreal, had been vaporized and there were precious few survivors. All knowledge gained over centuries had been wiped out. There was no respect whatsoever for the knowledge of the few elders who had survived. They had so much to offer, but no one was listening.

It was hardly surprising that John Wellfleet, the main character in *Voices in Time*, is very much like the disenchanted author sitting that day in the garden.

On a rainy day in the spring of 1991, I headed off to Victoria, British Columbia, to pay a visit to Bruce Hutchison. I was then with the *Ottawa Citizen* but my columns were carried on the wider Southam chain. It was the year following the failure of the Meech Lake constitutional accord and for much of the previous nine months I had been on the road "taking the pulse of the nation." Who better for a wandering journalist, holding a stethoscope instead of a pen, to call on than the one they called "the conscience of the nation"?

Hutchison had written millions of words trying to come to terms with this country and its people. Some might even say *he* invented us. He had written more than anyone before or since on the elusive Canadian identity. In thousands of columns and several books he had sought to analyze and advise this country, its politicians and even its people. His writing was vibrant, his optimism renowned. Peter C. Newman had once called him "the eternal optimist."

For someone setting out to travel the country in search of answers, Bruce Hutchison was an obvious destination. He was, after all, author of *The Unknown Country*, surely the most important book published in this country over the previous half-century. Three times he had been awarded the Governor General's Award for non-fiction. He had been named to the Privy Council and made an Officer of the Order of Canada.

In 1942, the year he published *The Unknown Country*, Bruce Hutchison was forty-one years old. It wasn't even a book Hutchison intended on writing. He said that it came out of a liquid lunch— Hutchison was a very light drinker—with a New York publisher who kept pushing drinks and kept insisting, "We ought to have a book about Canada and *you* ought to write it."

Hutchison wasn't convinced but agreed to write something. He decided to do it somewhat as a travelogue. He and his wife, Dorothy, visited the Maritimes and then Quebec, where they were hopeless with the language. They stopped off in Ottawa, where Hutchison attended Question Period and described the House of Commons as "the true heart of Canada." In his opinion, "It reflects every passing mood, sensation, pleasure, and pain in the vast, sprawling body of the nation, and articulates it within a few hours."

Such description would invite ridicule at the time of such Meech Lake discord and anger toward all politicians. On the other hand, in 1990 he would surely have been applauded for adding "Yet Parliament, on its green hill, lives strangely aloof, floating in a warm, comfortable vacuum."

Right from the well-known opening paragraph of *The Unknown Country* there is a sense of this country's new spirit and the author's great optimism for what was to come:

No one knows my country, neither the stranger nor its own sons.
My country has not found itself nor felt its power nor learned its
true place. It is all visions and doubts and hopes and dreams. It
is strength and weakness, despair and joy, and the wild confu-
sions and restless strivings of a boy who has passed his boyhood
but is not yet a man.

Hutchison wrote about a then-young country, eleven million strong,
but spread so thinly in such an impossibly large space that the real
story of the eleven million was an uncanny "loneliness"—the people
huddled around the lights of little towns and a few cities, the country
forever beyond. "All about us lies Canada," he wrote, "forever
untouched, unknown, beyond our grasp, breathing deep in the darkness and we hear its breath and are afraid. No, they could not know
us, the strangers, for we have not known ourselves."

In this journey across a country no one really knew, Hutchison
discovered the source of optimism that he would become renowned
for in the eyes of younger writers such as Peter Newman. The country,
like Hutchison himself back then, was young and filled with energy.
Psychologically, the country was in his mind just coming out of the
muffling snows of the past and into a promising new season: "Wondrous
and very sweet is our name. *Canada!* The very word is like a boy's
shout in the springtime, is like the clamor of geese going north and
the roar of melting rivers and the murmur of early winds."

Surging with optimism, Hutchison wrote, "The war has remade
Canada economically and industrially. It has built a stronger nation
than we ever thought possible in our time. Greatly led, Canada can
play its great part in the next peace, as the hinge between the democ-
racies which will have to shoulder, whether they want to or not, the
load of a ruined world."

"Now our time is come," he believed, "and, if not grasped, will be
forever lost."

It was as if he could hardly wait to see what was coming for his young country.

But that was then, and this was now . . .

Bruce Hutchison would turn ninety during the year of Meech anguish. He was still writing a weekly column for the *Vancouver Sun*, still living on his small acreage just outside Victoria and still obsessively splitting firewood at his rustic cabin retreat farther up Vancouver Island at Shawnigan Lake.

The *Vancouver Sun*'s Jamie Lamb, a fellow columnist, and I had come to Victoria by rented car, taking the ferry from Vancouver to the island. We joined up with Vaughn Palmer, the fine legislative columnist for the same paper. Despite an age difference of half a century, Palmer was then Hutchison's closest friend and very much treated as a son by the older man.

The three of us drove up between the tall Lombardy poplars that Hutchison had planted as seedlings sixty-five years earlier. We approached the small bungalow, knocked on the door—the knocker a smiling William Shakespeare in brass—and were greeted by a small, wizened old man with large black horn-rimmed glasses and a turn-of-the-last-century British wardrobe that made him seem more a character out of P.G. Wodehouse than a resident of the laid-back Canadian West Coast.

Bruce Hutchison—Palmer, like other friends, called him "Hutch"—had a cane in his hand and its presence clearly embarrassed him, but the endless damp of this disappointing spring had turned his sciatica leg pain "excruciating." Up to now, the old man's health had always been excellent, but during his annual visit to Ottawa over the past winter—a visit that invariably included a private tête-à-tête with whatever prime minister happened to be in office, from Mackenzie King to Brian Mulroney—he had ended up in an ambulance rushing him to Ottawa General. There, doctors had determined he had suffered a small but worrisome heart attack.

"You know," he said to the three of us at one point, "there is noth-ing about old age to recommend it. Avoid it. *Avoid* it."

He needed the cane to get about his garden, which he insisted on showing off even though the tulips were bent over from an overnight pounding of rain.

"It's not what it used to be," he said, waving the cane over the expansive gardens while his spit-and-polished black shoes sank in the long, wet grass, "but then, what is anymore?"

And that, of course, was exactly the question I had come to ask.

He was, in many ways, the personification of "the pulse of the country" that I was supposedly taking. Four decades after writing *The Unknown Country*, he had written a follow-up whose essence could be found in the title alone: *The Unfinished Country*.

"*There won't be a third!*" he shouted. I swear he raised a fist to the clouds.

The four of us headed back into Victoria for lunch at the Union Club. He sat in the passenger seat while I drove. To passersby who happened to peer in at this shrunken little hawk-nosed man sitting there, his tie perfectly knotted, his black hat fitted so tight it seemed threaded on, he would have looked like a frail senior being taken for a ride by his grandsons. They would not have realized he was the one in charge, barking out directions and condemning a "Road Closed" sign as simply one more reminder of the housing developments and the world beyond closing in on him.

Once at his club, he moved into his familiar seat at the very same table former British Columbia premier W.A.C. "Wacky" Bennett had eaten lunch at for twenty years—"a *sacred* table!"—and imme-diately began railing about the country. He barely paused in his rant to take breath or bite. There was no pretending he had not lost his once-great faith.

"This is a *country* we're talking about here!" Hutchison snapped at one point when the discussion wavered off into individual politicians.

But he himself then swept it back into personality when he began to talk about the death of the constitutional accord and the role played in its death by the likes of Manitoba legislator Elijah Harper Jr. and, of course, the accord's most vocal critic, the premier of Newfoundland, Clyde Wells.

"That *bastard!*" the grand old man barked at one point.

Vaughn Palmer said later that day that he had never seen Hutchison so black and pessimistic. On the ride out to pick him up, Palmer had warned that the old man had taken "personally" the crushing blows dealt by Harper and Wells nine months earlier when they refused the accord its required unanimity. The accord had been well received in Quebec for its reference to the French-language province as a "distinct society" and Hutchison was one of many who believed this was the only way to keep Quebec in the fold. Instead, an angry Hutchison argued across the lunch table, it was "rejected without serious thought by an English-speaking majority who had not bothered to learn its contents."

Not surprisingly, Hutchison's opinion had not been well received by those who had opposed Meech Lake. Some recalled how much Hutchison had always admired Pierre Trudeau—and hadn't the former prime minister said the accord, which he opposed, could be rejected without consequence?

"*Balderdash!*" said the old man. In his mind, Quebec could not now be stopped from leaving Confederation, having been dealt such an insult by this rejection. Canada's justification for existence, Hutchison argued, lay in the experiment it represented: different languages and different cultures coexisting peacefully and prosperously under one flag. If Quebec were to go, the rest must follow.

"People who think the rest of Canada can survive are mad," he said over dessert. "You can't have a 'scarecrow' nation. It would simply fall apart if the Maritimes and Ontario and the West tried to stick it out. The others couldn't deal with such a strong Ontario. The Maritimes would be the first to petition to join the United States and it would be over for everybody else very soon after."

Over coffee, he spoke to no one in particular: "Democracy is such a dirty, dirty business, isn't it? *How* does it go on? *How* does it keep working? I honestly don't know. It wouldn't matter if Lincoln or Ben Franklin was sitting down to write up a Canadian constitution right now. It wouldn't work. It *can't* work. The country is in too bad a temper.

"This country has lost its soul—it's like they took you and they ripped out your heart, that's what it feels like."

He predicted that he himself likely had a year or less, the way things were going with his health. The country that he had spent his life defining had, at best, he believed two more years left. It was also finished.

Bruce Hutchison would miss both predictions. He would last another two years, passing away on September 14, 1992.

And Canada would shake off its sciatica attack and hobble on.

Canada can sometimes seem like the land of Grumpy Old Men. Bruce Hutchison and Hugh MacLennan were hardly alone.

Robertson Davies, at one time Canada's best-known author internationally, was so put off by the 1980s rush to enter free trade with the United States that he became convinced "this is the worst this country has ever seen." Historian Donald G. Creighton had died in late 1979, mere months before the first referendum on Quebec sovereignty. He had come to regard the country he spent a lifetime writing about as "a good place to live, but that's all Canada is now, just a good place to live."

Such failed doom-and-gloom scenarios are why I eventually came to think of Canada as the bumblebee of nations.

Scientists have gone to considerable lengths to show how bumblebees do actually fly, despite the impossibility suggested by fixed-wing aerodynamic calculations. Poor Canada, however, has yet to find its Cambridge zoology professor who can explain the secret. For bees, it might well be the extra lift acquired by the air expelled during rapid wing clapping, hence the buzzing sound.

The forces that keep Canada airborne, on the other hand, are rather more elusive. Apart from rumours of cabinet shuffles and possible hockey trades, Canadians emit no buzz.

And yet the country these Canadians call home flies on, seemingly without a plan, flitting from one distraction to the next.

While working on this memoir, I reached the age Hugh MacLennan was when we sat in that garden at North Hatley and talked about his dystopian vision of the future.

It is one I've never been able to share. Canadians have a curious way of working things out, even when everything seems to be flying in opposite directions.

We did, after all, invent the centre line in highways for exactly that purpose.

And, apart from some troubling blockades during the long Covid-19 pandemic, the highway is still mostly open.

Pardon me while I reach for those rose-coloured glasses.

There's always sun beyond the clouds, is there not?

My father and me, 1950.

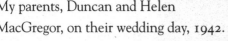

My parents, Duncan and Helen
MacGregor, on their wedding day, 1942.

Ann and Jim with me at
Lake of Two Rivers, 1951.

Duncan with my sister Ann and
brother Jim.

The Huntsville neighbourhood kids (I'm the little guy—always was—second from the right in the back row, Brent and Eric to my right).

Hockey had me from the beginning (second from the right in the back row). Huntsville peewee All-Stars.

I got many black eyes, metaphorically, as a journalist. As a kid, I got a few real ones.

When I wasn't playing hockey or baseball, I played lacrosse. Here with provincial-champion Huntsville Green Gaels (second from left, front row).

"Going, going…" but surprisingly not gone. Report cards could be harsh in the 1960s.

My first magazine as editor, *The Pundit*.

Slinging drinks at the Snake Pit, when I wasn't yet writing for a living. But I was learning a lot that nobody teaches in school.

The book that gave one of my journalism-school professors his credentials to teach.

A late morning with Ellen.

With old friend Ralph Cox (back) and new friend Dick (from Chicago, front right) on our Ibiza adventure.

Travelling across Morocco with Dan (a new friend from Colorado, middle) and university pal John Western (right).

Gathered in Spain in 1970 (I'm dressed like a local, second from left, old pal Jack Andrews is in the middle).

Seeing the Mediterranean from the south shore, on the beach in Morocco.

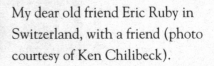

My dear old friend Eric Ruby in Switzerland, with a friend (photo courtesy of Ken Chilibeck).

Anything for the story. Mucking stalls at the Stein family farm.

The—if you can believe it—scandalous Adrienne Clarkson *Maclean's* cover.

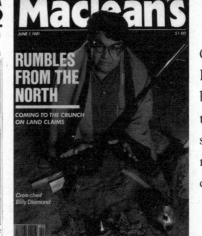

Chief Billy Diamond brought me the story of a scandal much more worthy of the term.

My modelling days at *Maclean's* didn't last long.

A little sightseeing while on assignment in China.

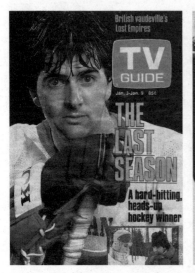

Tyler, my first screenplay, was directed by a first-time director and starred an actor in his first film role. Critics loved it.

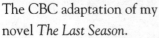

The CBC adaptation of my novel *The Last Season*.

Another critic of my work, Prime Minister Brian Mulroney, is less complimentary in this staff memo.

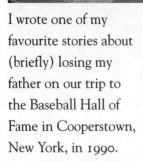

I wrote one of my favourite stories about (briefly) losing my father on our trip to the Baseball Hall of Fame in Cooperstown, New York, in 1990.

MacGregor family headed for "assigned" PEI vacation, 1988 (Roy, Jocelyn, Bandit, Gordon, Christine, Kerry and Ellen.)

Between my lifelong friends Brent Munroe and Eric Ruby.

Spending the day with Prime Minister Jean Chrétien, waiting to see if he'd announce his resignation. (Photo appears courtesy of Dave Chan)

Making some writing suggestions for first-time author Prime Minister Stephen Harper. (Photo appears courtesy of the Prime Minister's Office)

ST GEORGE'S CHAPEL, WINDSOR CASTLE

Morning Prayer
2 June 2002
Jubilee Thanksgiving
attended by
HM The Queen and HRH The Duke of Edinburgh

Entrance by
SOUTH DOOR
From 10.00 am

Please be seated
by 10.30 am

An unexpected invitation to meet the Queen of England.

The final resting place of Chief Billy Diamond, a dear friend and hero.

With a very happy Brent on his wedding day.

Ellen at her cottage on Camp Lake. "You and me, buds forever."

If cousin Don McCormick hadn't introduced me to a friend, I might never have gone to journalism school.

Ellen and me, with daughters, son, sons-in-law and grandkids. MacGregor luck.

8

The Sporting Life

"Maybe Rome was built in a day."

So read the *Ottawa Citizen*'s banner headline on page A1, October 9, 1992, the morning after the reborn Ottawa Senators met the Montreal Canadiens on opening night of the 1992–93 NHL season. "Senators in stunning 5–3 debut victory over Habs," read the subhead over sports reporter Wayne Scanlan's story; "10,499 fans went wild and it was magical."

It *was* magical. No longer worried about my Parliament Hill parking problems, I now had a pass to the Civic Centre's media lot, as well as a pass—my 1992–93 NHL credentials—to a world I barely knew but would come to love. I was no stranger to the NHL, having profiled the likes of Guy Lafleur, Marcel Dionne, Börje Salming, Gilles Gratton, Bryan Trottier and others over the magazine years, but this was different. I would not be dipping in and out, barely noticed and quickly forgotten, but would be full-time with the team as the *Citizen*'s sports columnist. That meant covering every practice and every game, riding the bus and charter aircraft and staying in the same hotels as the team.

I had long been a fan of great sports writing. I read Milt Dunnell, Frank Orr, Jim Proudfoot, Red Fisher, Trent Frayne, Dick Beddoes and

Scott Young when I was growing up. In my era, there was such a wide variety of talent, writing mostly on hockey. Montreal, for example, had Jack Todd for informed opinion and Michael Farber for exquisite storytelling. Toronto had Stephen Brunt and many others. Women journalists who periodically turned from their columns to the sports pages—Christie Blatchford and Rosie DiManno come to mind—excelled. Canadian sports readers were well served by beat teams in Winnipeg, Vancouver and, of course, Ottawa. They might lack the high profiles of the Reds and Milts, but they were, and remain, high talents. I was excited to be asked to join this world.

The *Citizen* had a sports department run by Graham Parley, a Brit with unruly hair, an abiding love for Chelsea Football Club, and a mischievous streak. He was also a fine editor who would go on to shine at the *National Post* and *Toronto Star*. Like me, Parley had been shifted over from national affairs coverage. Tom Casey, once a fine junior hockey player, was Parley's assistant and would eventually take over his job. John MacKinnon was then the columnist, and Wayne Scanlan, Rick Mayoh, Kenny Warren and Martin Cleary were all reporters assigned to various beats—high-school sports, junior hockey, professional football, minor league baseball and the Olympics. It was very male-selective, as was most hockey coverage in those days, and this changed at the *Citizen* only when Lynn McAuley, known as a superb features editor, took over the sports column long after I had moved on.

Editor Jim Travers was switching me over to be the new columnist to follow the team and write everything from player profiles to columns about league issues. MacKinnon would become the paper's lead hockey reporter, handling game stories and off-day reports. It was a most uncomfortable situation for the first several weeks, but eventually John and I became good friends and have remained so.

I quickly discovered that the "sports family" is far more welcoming and warm than the "politics family" on the Hill. Political reporters are always suspicious of what others are up to away from the House of

Commons and Question Period. Sports reporters cover events that everyone gets to see equally, and while, from time to time, a sports journalist might break news ahead of their peers—a firing, new contracts, trade demands—the sports crowd is far, far more congenial. Sports journalists also spend far more time on the road, meaning rivals are also travelling companions. The *Citizen* reporters and those from the rival *Ottawa Sun*, Chris Stevenson, Don Brennan and Bruce Garrioch, were good company, as were the reporters for *Le Droit*, Pierre Jury and Marc Brassard. Tricia Boal, Brent Wallace and Ian Mendes from local outlets and wire-service freelancer Lisa Burke were fun but rarely travelled. The radio and television play-by-play broadcasters, Dean Brown and Gord Wilson for TSN 1200, Christian Doucet for RDS, were good road companions—and there would be lots of road.

The original Ottawa Senators had played in the NHL from 1917 to 1934, when financial losses caused the franchise to be moved to St. Louis. The Senators became the Eagles, failed again and were ultimately disbanded. Many decades later, in 1990, when the NHL announced that it would expand by two teams, multiple cities expressed interest. The Ottawa bid was the brainchild of three young business partners—Bruce Firestone, Randy Sexton and Cyril Leeder—who conjured up their impossible dream over a few cold ones after a beer-league hockey game. They announced their intention to "bring back the Senators." No one believed they had a prayer.

If Canada was going to get another franchise, it was expected it would go to Hamilton, which had a fine rink in the Copps Coliseum and financial backing from Ron Joyce, then owner of Tim Horton's. There was also a growing regional population. A franchise in Hamilton would make for a great rivalry with Toronto, which was already solidly in place through the CFL Tiger-Cats and the Argonauts.

The three young men pitching Ottawa to the NHL had no rink, and their team would have to begin play out of the 10,500-seat Ottawa Civic Centre, home of the Ottawa 67's major junior hockey franchise.

No matter, they said, their company, Terrace Investments, had a brilliant plan. Firestone said they would build a rink and, critically, that rink would be the core of major development—housing and retail—that would grow up around the NHL facility, which did not, at the time, even have a property. While the Hamilton bid had irked the NHL by asking to be allowed to pay the fifty-million-US-dollar expansion fee in instalments, the Ottawa group made no such request. No one checked to see if they had the money; they did not.

There were other interested cities with far better financial backing—Miami, St. Petersburg, San Diego, Anaheim, Seattle—but the NHL board of governors seemed taken with Terrace Investments' vision of a new rink creating a new city. (Others ridiculed it at the time, but this is pretty much exactly what came about over the ensuing decades, though not without the three young men losing their prize to a wealthy entrepreneur who ended up declaring the franchise bankrupt and losing it to yet another wealthy owner. But the rink is there, on the outskirts of Kanata, retail has run wild and there are housing developments as far as the eye can see from what is now called the Canadian Tire Centre.)

In late 1990, the NHL met in Palm Beach, Florida. The Ottawa group, complete with a marching band and more than a hundred supporters, dazzled the NHL owners and, following a secret vote, the Ottawa Senators were reborn, back in Ottawa and the NHL after a fifty-eight-year hiatus. The NHL board of governors also approved the application of Tampa Bay, the Lightning, fronted by Hockey-Hall-of-Famer Phil Esposito. Hamilton did not make the cut.

No surprise, but there were problems from the start for the reborn Senators, and not just financial troubles. The NHL held an expansion draft that offered dozens of aging players and struggling journeymen—Esposito likened it to being offered "snow in winter." The inexperienced Ottawa management team arrived at the expansion table without a cord to plug in their laptop computer and subsequently screwed up their selections so frequently that "Ottawa apologizes" (for selecting ineligible players) became a punchline that to this day requires no explanation in hockey circles.

Mel Bridgman, a former captain of the Philadelphia Flyers who had gone on to earn an MBA from the Wharton School of the University of Pennsylvania, was named the new franchise's first general manager after the job had been turned down by Scotty Bowman and others. The coach was Rick Bowness, a former player who had gone on to coach the Boston Bruins. His assistants were Alain Vigneault, E.J. McGuire and Chico Resch. Director of player personnel was John Ferguson, a former tough player with the Montreal Canadiens and former general manager of the Winnipeg Jets.

The management group cobbled together a team and, miraculously, the Senators won that very first game. They lost their next game, against the Quebec Nordiques, 9–2. They then flew to Boston, boarded a bus and got hopelessly lost in the fog. It was the perfect metaphor for a team that would go on to set new records for futility on the road.

But that doesn't mean they weren't entertaining. They were, in fact, hockey's equivalent to the '62 Mets—baseball fans may remember manager Casey Stengel saying his best fielders were sitting in the upper deck—and the stories from that first Ottawa Senators' season, 1992–93, are today the stuff of legend:

- When young defenceman Darren Rumble, previously a minor leaguer, showed up for the first plane ride out of town, he carried his own pillow and a bag of sandwiches. Told by one of the broadcasters that he should sign up for Aeroplan, he asked what that was. When the travel points program was explained to him, he went wide-eyed and exclaimed, "If they'd had 'bus-o-plan' when I was in the minors, I could go around the world."

- Another rookie, Darcy Loewen of Sylvan Lake, Alberta, became a fan favourite for his wild style of play—the other players called him "Taz"—and even his mother said he had "cement hands." She also said if the circus came to town, "Darcy'd be the one they'd shoot from the cannon."

- Veteran Andrew McBain, a fine player, became the only Senator to make the ESPN "plays of the year"—by falling down the steps leading to the old Chicago Stadium dressing room.

- To take his mind off the team's woes, assistant coach Alain Vigneault took up running. By Christmas he had dropped thirty pounds.

- The Senators had to fire their mascot for "abusive conduct," only to have him flee Ottawa with the car they'd rented for him.

- Thieves broke into the Senators' practice facility and made off with all their video equipment but left behind the game tapes. "Burglars with taste," said assistant coach E.J. McGuire.

The losses, particularly on the road, became so regular that those of us on the Senators beat decided to spice things up by taking our skates on the road. Ed Georgica, the team's equipment manager, offered us space on the road trips for our hockey gear, and soon enough, following the team's morning skate, we were playing full games of shinny in places like Madison Square Garden and the Philadelphia Spectrum. A couple of twenty-dollar bills to the Zamboni drivers and we could usually arrange a fresh sheet of ice.

Others began joining us—equipment handlers, media personnel, players about to come off the injury list, even the coaches and General Manager Bridgman. One late morning at the St. Louis Kiel Center, Bob Bowness, Rick Bowness's father, laced up with us. Senators forward Mike Peluso dubbed us the "dream team"—and while we wouldn't dare compare our morning shinny matches to the NHL games scheduled on those evenings, they were often much more fun.

That opening night victory over the Canadiens would stand as the year's high point, as the Senators went on to win only nine more times, while losing a stunning seventy games and tying four times for a total of twenty-four points. They won only once on the road, still an NHL record for futility. In truth, the franchise *wanted* to lose, despite the frustration and humiliation it brought upon the players. The owners wanted as high a draft pick as possible, a marquee player they could market—and they knew exactly the player they wanted: Alexandre Daigle.

Daigle was tearing up the Quebec junior league while starring for the Victoriaville Tigres. He was a lock to go first in the June draft, the number one pick in the draft then going to the team that finished last in the standings. The Quebec Nordiques badly wanted the francophone superstar to build a new arena around, and they told the lowest teams in the standings that they would gladly trade their best players for a chance at selecting first.

As the season wound down, it was clearly a race to the bottom between the Senators and the San Jose Sharks. Parley, the *Citizen's* sports editor, began running a daily feature he called the "Yelnats Puc" (Stanley Cup reversed) and treating the race to last place as an exciting spectator sport.

The Senators did land Daigle, but not without controversy. Remarks by Firestone at a draft day celebration in Quebec City led some reporters present to believe that the team had been willing to strategically tank so they would end up in last place, get the first pick in the draft and choose Daigle. The NHL launched an investigation following a *Globe and Mail* column suggesting that the *Citizen* was already working to confirm this interpretation of Firestone's remarks. The *Globe* column was true, as I had been working on a book about that first season and Parley and Casey had been kept informed every step of the way. The league hired Arnold Burns, former deputy attorney general of the United States, and Yves Fortier, former Canadian ambassador to the United States, to probe these allegations. The *Citizen* could have refused to participate but decided to agree after grilling me and studying my notes. Publisher Russ Mills and editor Jim Travers felt we were on solid ground and agreed to let me be interviewed by the league.

For my session, I was accompanied by Travers and lawyer Rick Dearden. What I believed I had heard in Quebec City was happily confirmed by a young woman reporter who was not with the *Citizen*. Firestone maintained that the group had been having a few beers—true—and his words had been misunderstood. Regardless, the NHL deemed his conversation "intemperate" and fined the franchise. The league ultimately changed the draft into a lottery system that meant no team could deliberately end up in last place to claim the top pick.

Alexandre Daigle would never become the superstar he was supposed to be—but he would certainly leave his mark on the National Hockey League.

That first-year team was entertaining even if not winning and regularly sold out the small Civic Centre. They had found property—an old cornfield far out Highway 417 between two small suburbs, Kanata and Stittsville—but had made no progress on building a new rink. Strapped for money, and in the midst of a recession, the franchise survived only because a well-heeled entrepreneur, Rod Bryden, assumed control. A well-known and well-positioned Liberal, Bryden was furious when the new provincial government—Bob Rae's New Democrats having defeated David Peterson's Liberals following the Meech Lake fiasco—billed him twenty-seven million dollars for the construction of an overpass so fans could get to the games.

Bryden ran into multiple other, uh, roadblocks, including a federal government directive that civil servants could not accept free tickets. Corporate ticket sales were largely fuelled by opportunities to do business with invited guests, or in the case of Ottawa, to lobby those government officials with whom the corporate ticket holder might like to land a government contract. Now that was lost. The Canadian dollar was also shrinking and player salaries were being paid in American currency. At one point, in early 2000, the financial situation was so dire that the federal government, then Liberal, was willing to step in and put up a twenty-million-dollar support plan for struggling Canadian teams. The backlash was so livid, particularly in media centre Toronto, where the Maple Leafs had no need of charity, that the government quickly backed off its offer.

As stated, the Senators did "win" the number one pick, took young Daigle as intended and believed they had a sensation in the eighteen-year-old. Not only was Daigle lightning-quick, but also darkly handsome and willing to do anything—even posing for a "hockey card" wearing a nurse's uniform. His English quickly improved and he was an instant fan favourite—until he wasn't. In his rookie year, he played well but not as well as another Senators rookie, Alexei Yashin, who would go on to captain a quickly improving team. Daigle would become more interested in acting than professional hockey and soon enough was traded to the Philadelphia Flyers. He bounced around the league a few more years and by 2006 was gone from the NHL.

The Senators' coaching staff had been desperate to start winning. By late 1995, they had even assembled candles and a table and were on the verge of holding a séance before an assistant coach, a deeply religious man, panicked and backed out. The losing spell was not so easily broken.

But in early 1996 they had their new arena, a new general manager in Pierre Gauthier and a new coach in Jacques Martin. They had Yashin starring for them and a rising new talent in Daniel Alfredsson who—to give the original managers full credit—had been plucked 133rd overall in the 1994 draft. By 2007 they would be in the Stanley Cup finals, led by "Alfie," now the captain, with Yashin traded to the New York Islanders. The line of Alfredsson, Jason Spezza and Dany Heatley was, for a considerable stretch, the best line in the league.

Bryden eventually lost control of the team. He said if the Canadian dollar rose by just a couple of cents he could stave off bankruptcy, but it didn't and he couldn't. A new owner, Eugene Melnyk, a Canadian billionaire who made his fortune in pharmaceuticals and now lived in Barbados, picked up the franchise and the relatively new rink in 2003 for a mere ninety-two million US dollars. In 2022, following the death of Melnyk, the team was put up for sale—with Sportico, a sports business publication, valuing the franchise at US$655 million.

I covered the team off and on for more than a quarter-century. When I left the *Citizen* to join the newly launched *National Post* in 1998, I was to do a general column with national reach, far more politics than sports. (When editor Ken Whyte asked me to recommend a sports columnist, I immediately answered "Cam Cole," my playoff travelling companion and long-time columnist with the *Edmonton Journal*. Whyte agreed that Cam was his first choice as well, and Cam and I were soon on the same paper.)

Four years later, I was hired by editor Ed Greenspon to do a page 2 national column for the *Globe and Mail*, which I would do five days a week for five years, after which I would shift to doing columns and features on politics and sports. Eventually I was doing far more hockey than elections for the *Globe*, and I was loving it.

The game had me for life.

When Ken Dryden and I published *Home Game: Hockey and Life in Canada* back in 1989, he suggested we add a chapter we could call "The Magic of Play"—our own personal accounts of what the game has meant to us. He had starred in the NHL, of course, and had more Stanley Cup rings than fingers on his left hand. I had played small-town hockey and the only cup I had was to be found in my hockey bag when it wasn't protecting my privates. Now, however, we were both beer-league players, Ken a goalie turned defenceman, I, a checker turned loafer.

This is how I opened my half of that chapter:

> It hits me the moment I awake. I stare out the bedroom window through the gathered frost and the first light is made brighter by the knowledge that today there will be hockey. This knowledge, this heightened awareness, will be with me over breakfast. It will haunt me when I should be paying attention to other matters during the morning and again in the afternoon. I will think of plays over the lunch hour. I will imagine a breakaway and think about the relative advantages of deking over shooting. I will remind myself to knock down high passes with a glove rather than my stick whenever possible. I will daydream about tucking a puck in between a defenceman's skates and coming up with it again on the other side, home and free for the last-minute goal that breaks the tie. I will linger with this fantasy long enough to feel the rap of a winger's stick against my shinpads, the congratulatory cuff of a teammate's glove on my head, the ringing, surprising sound my own name makes when it bursts in a hollow arena. I will not fight it, even if it sometimes distracts me, for this is simply the way it is. On game day, from the moment I wake to the moment I fall asleep, I think about hockey.
>
> I am forty-one years old.

Well, I'm seventy-four years old at the time of writing this. Hockey has taken me all around the world: from Dufferin Street on Reservoir Hill to every NHL city, world championships for men and women, world juniors, multiple Olympics, around Europe with Wayne Gretzky's "99 All-Stars" during the 1994 lockout, once to Scandinavia with a peewee team that featured future NHL star Dino Ciccarelli, once much later to Scandinavia and Russia to play with a beer-league team that featured no one.

The game certainly has its faults. It has been and still can be overly and unnecessarily violent. It has failed miserably to address the concussion issue at the highest levels. It has a heartbreaking history of sexual abuse by predators who hide behind the overly powerful cloak of coaching. There is long-standing homophobia in the language on the ice as well as in the dressing rooms, and that has to change. Hockey needs to be much more inclusive so that the national game reflects the changing country. Never a year goes by without racism raising its ugly head. In late 2021 there was a story out of the Maritimes that a sixteen-year-old Halifax player was repeatedly called the N-word during a game in Charlottetown, the player later told by players on the other side that hockey is a "white man's sport."

Throughout 2022 there were revelations—mostly exposed by TSN's top reporter, Rick Westhead—that the national junior teams from 2003 and 2018 allegedly engaged in inappropriate sexual activities. One woman had filed a $3.5-million lawsuit claiming that eight players sexually assaulted, humiliated and degraded her in a hotel room in London, Ontario, during a Hockey Canada gala event. A settlement had apparently been reached using monies parents across the country believed were going into hockey development. Hockey is a broken culture that has been slow to change, but now knows that it must change. There is no arguing that reality.

The good of the game is also undeniable. For me, the most charming part of hockey is that no one can claim to have invented it, unlike baseball, basketball, football and most other sports. I know the claims. I have stood on an upper floor of Vienna's Kunsthistorisches art museum and stared hard at *The Hunters in the Snow*, which Pieter Bruegel painted in 1565, and I have seen, beyond any doubt, that there are two youngsters in the background playing a game any Canadian would instantly recognize. I have seen the literary evidence that Thomas Chandler Haliburton was writing as far back as 1810 about kids "hollerin' and whoopin' like mad with pleasure" as they cuffed something back and forth with sticks on a frozen pond near Windsor, Nova Scotia. I have listened to the claims of Montreal that the first game was played there on March 3, 1875, listened as well to the claims that the game originated in the small Ontario city of Kingston sometime in 1886—and I have only one response to all of these claims on the Cradle of Hockey. To me, hockey is invented every time someone drops a puck at centre ice or lobs a cuffed-up tennis ball on an isolated back street. Soon enough, someone will yell "*Carrrr!!!*"—the call that is as much a part of Canadian winter as the call of the loon is to summer. Let the game begin. Ever inventing and reinventing itself at every imaginable level.

No wonder hockey has long been Canada's national game. "In a land so inescapably and inhospitably cold," Bruce Kidd and John Macfarlane wrote many years ago, "hockey is the dance of life, an affirmation that despite the deadly chill of winter we are alive."

Think, for a moment, about this game's hold on this country. In what other nation would the news of the world be put on hold each spring until the scores are in?

Where else would you find fewer people knowing the words to their national anthem than to Stompin' Tom Connors' "The Hockey Song"? Let the Americans put "In God We Trust" on their money, Canada put a snippet from Roch Carrier's fabulous "The Hockey Sweater" on its five-dollar bill. Let the Americans boast about how many millions watched man's first steps on the moon. In Canada, we marvel at the six million who tuned in to Salt Lake City in 2002 to watch the women win gold, then the record *ten* million who tuned in a couple of days later to watch the men's final—a victory helped along by a Canadian loonie secretly buried at centre ice.

This is a game I have played, watched, covered and written about for nearly seven decades. If I had to pick one moment in all my hockey life that caught me most off guard, it was in a telephone call back in the early summer of 2012. The caller was Kevin Allen, long-time hockey writer for *USA Today* and then head of the Professional Hockey Writers Association, which I became a member of shortly after *Ottawa Citizen* editor Jim Travers informed me of my new parking situation.

"Congratulations," Kevin said in that voice that seemed to come from the bottom of the ocean.

"For?" I asked, unsure of what was going on. We weren't close. Friendly at press boxes, of course, but we had never before spoken on the telephone.

"You're going into the Hall of Fame."

As Kevin quickly informed me, I was the 2012 print-media inductee into the Hockey Hall of Fame, winner of the Elmer Ferguson Memorial Award, given annually by the Hall "in recognition of distinguished members of the hockey writing profession whose words have brought honour to both journalism and the sport."

Entering the Hockey Hall of Fame was something I had dreamed of since those earliest skates on the Munroes' backyard rink and those marathon road games under the Dufferin Street streetlight. It was a dream shared by every kid lucky enough to make the town's all-star team or one of the city's "rep" teams. If you were already this good, how good would you be when you finally made the NHL?

Reality set in early for those of us who made the Huntsville peewee all-star team. There were games where we were told there were "scouts" in the stands, but that just meant we were playing Parry Sound—the scouts were there to see the one kid who really was living the dream—Bobby Orr.

Personally, I knew by bantam. That was the year I realized I couldn't see the play very well and was endlessly sharpening my pencil in class so that I could memorize the blackboard from up close. Bobby Orr went off to play junior hockey for the Oshawa Generals. I went off to Orillia to have my eyes tested and be fitted with career-ending horn rims.

Instead I got into the Hockey Hall of Fame through the back door. I was one of two non-player inductees that year, the other one being Buffalo Sabres play-by-play voice Rick Jeanneret, winner of the Foster Hewitt Memorial Award for outstanding contributions as a hockey broadcaster. The players—the *real* Hall of Famers—elected that year were Pavel Bure, Adam Oates, Joe Sakic and Mats Sundin, all undeniably deserving of such high honours. Rick and I were floored to be chosen and flattered to go in with such an outstanding class.

The critical signature of approval for the Hockey Hall of Fame in Toronto is the jacket. Just as the green jacket is the symbol of victory at the Masters Tournament in golf and the yellow jersey symbolic of the leading cyclist in the arduous Tour de France, the dark-blue blazer with the bright logo of the Hockey Hall of Fame/Temple de la renommée du hockey is proof that you have made it all the way to that childish dream—even if it required a back-door entrance.

The players were honoured with their Hugo Boss jackets during a televised Saturday afternoon game at the (then named) Air Canada Centre, with 18,800 fans on their feet to cheer Bure, Oates, Sakic and Sundin as they pulled on their coveted blazers. Rick and I received our jackets at a lovely Monday lunch before family and friends, the applause warm and polite. I was given my jacket by my good friend Calgary sportswriter Eric Duhatschek, a previous winner of the Elmer Ferguson. It could not have been more appropriate or appreciated.

A few hours later the six new inductees and their immediate families were herded onto a bus outside the Westin Harbour Castle hotel on the Toronto waterfront and driven the few short blocks to the Hall of Fame at the corner of Yonge and Front streets.

There was a huge crowd waiting and they cheered as we disembarked. Many pressed for autographs. Rick and I trailed the familiar players and listened to fans calling out "Mats!" and "Joe!" and "Pavel!" and "Oatsey!" and we merely followed along, signing whatever books or pieces of paper were shoved in our direction. We imagined the fans, mostly young, wouldn't have the foggiest who we were.

But some did . . . to a degree. This was Toronto, only an hour and a half from Buffalo, and many were familiar with the Sabres' broadcasts and knew of Rick and his signature calls, such as *"May Day! May Day!"* for light-scoring Brad May's overtime winner against the Boston Bruins in the 1993 playoffs, *"La-La-La-La-La-La-LaFontaine!"* any time superstar Pat LaFontaine scored and *"Top shelf—where momma keeps the cookies!"* any time the puck found a top corner on the other team.

Much to my surprise, a lot knew my name. When they saw the magic blazer, they thrust books and papers at me to sign. One fan even told me to keep the black Sharpie he had handed me. A young man reached deep into an envelope he was carrying and pulled out an 8 by 10 glossy colour photo of me and asked me to sign it.

By the time we made it slowly up the steps and into the large hall above the Hall of Fame, security guards were forming human shields to get us through. The fans were calling for autographs. Television cameras were recording, photographers shooting—it had the feel of an important event.

I recognized one photographer, Bruce Bennett of Getty Images, perhaps the best-known hockey photographer in the business. He usually worked Rangers, Islanders and Flyers games, but we had become great friends during the 1993–94 lockout, when Bruce and a handful of hockey writers had joined Wayne Gretzky and the 99 All-Stars for that barnstorming exhibition series through Sweden, Finland, Norway and Germany.

Bruce commanded the whole entourage to stop while he took several photographs of Ellen and me as we made our way along following the players. This stop and Bruce Bennett's interest served only to arouse more interest in the balding unknown in the Hall of Fame blazer who was bringing up the rear.

We were about to be led to the escalator that was taking everyone down to the private reception with the Hall of Fame staff, NHL commissioner Gary Bettman and dozens of previous recipients of the prestigious jackets—legendary players like then eighty-seven-year-old "Terrible" Ted Lindsay, who turned out to be far more gracious than terrible when he was off the ice and out of uniform.

A man was blocking my way. He was smiling and holding his iPhone camera out so that I could see it.

"Okay if I take a quick picture of you with my daughter?" he asked.

My chest swelled enough to pop the logo off the Hugo Boss blazer.

Ellen moved to the side. I moved off a bit to give room to the young girl, perhaps seventeen or eighteen, who seemed rather sheepish to be thrust into this situation by her overly eager father.

The man tried to frame his picture. He was clearly flustered, very nervous.

"Cindy!" he called out to the girl. I could sense her shaking at what he was going to say or ask for next.

"Cindy—move in a little closer to Mr. Ellis, please!"

Mr. Ellis?

He must have meant Ron Ellis, the one-time Toronto Maple Leaf who had won a Stanley Cup and played for Canada in the 1972 Summit Series. He now served as director of public affairs for the Hockey Hall of Fame.

"Uh . . ." I began. "I'm not Ron Ellis."

The man seemed stunned. He looked at me as if I were lying.

"You're not?! Then who are you?"

I could hear Ellen howling with laughter just behind me. That laugh that had first attracted me to her was now humiliating me.

"Roy MacGregor."

Before I could say anything more, he cut me off. "*Whodya play for?*"

"No one," I said. "I'm a media inductee."

"Media??!!!" he shouted, incredulous. Ellen was still laughing.

"I'm a *Globe and Mail* sportswriter."

The man looked like he wanted to deck me. His face was furiously red. He grabbed Cindy by the wrist and yanked her away from me, as if I might be carrying some unknown virus.

"Come on, Cindy!—we're outta here!"

And off they went, the father pulling the daughter along like a reluctant puppy.

There is, alas, no picture to prove this story . . .

THE UNPLANNED PENSION PLAN

In 1994, McClelland & Stewart publisher Douglas Gibson came to me with an unexpected request—would I consider writing a series for children?

Huh?

I had never once thought about writing for children. But Doug wanted to talk about "reluctant readers," a term I had never before heard. I would soon learn that it was merely another way of saying "boys."

M&S had been hearing for years from librarians and teachers who were looking for something boys—sorry, reluctant readers—might want to read. Having passed through Thomas the Tank Engine and dinosaurs, parents and teachers were struggling to find books that would appeal to young male readers in Canada.

"We think a hockey series aimed at eight-to-thirteen-year-olds might find a ready audience," Doug suggested. "We think you're just the author to produce such a series. Will you at least think about it?"

I did. And decided to try. After all, I had a reluctant reader in our son, Gordon, then going on thirteen and at the top end of Doug's target audience. McClelland & Stewart produced a three-book contract, I signed, and then I had to come up with what such a series might be like.

Hockey, I thought, might not be enough. The game is played, one side wins, one side loses, and the players get ready for the next game . . . Zzzzzzzz. Pass the remote, please.

What if I made them hockey *mysteries*, I wondered? My sister, Ann, had been an avid reader of mysteries, and I had been picking up a few out of her wide collection for light reading on the hundreds of flights I was taking each year while covering the Ottawa Senators full-time. Agatha Christie mysteries were short and simple—and you couldn't put them down. She alone must have saved millions of reluctant readers.

There was also the matter of settings. I would use places that I knew personally from my years travelling as a journalist. The characters would play all over Canada, perhaps even the United States. Before too long, they would have tournaments in Japan, Australia, London . . . all financed, of course, by bottle drives . . .

Next, I thought, why not be a lot more inclusive than hockey was in those years. Wanting to put together a team that would reflect our urban realities, I made a list of possible characters, including one of Asian heritage, one from the Middle East, one from the Caribbean, one from the Indian subcontinent, even one from Russia. I added a couple of Indigenous players, as I knew how popular the game was on the many northern reserves I had visited over the years.

Then I did something some might have considered rather daring: I made the best player a *girl*. But why not? Four years earlier, I had played in an exhibition game against Team Canada in the lead-up to Ottawa hosting the first-ever IIHF Ice Hockey Women's World Championship. Many of the players—Angela James, Geraldine Heaney, France Saint-Louis, Vicky Sunohara, Kim Ratushny—had mightily impressed our group of retired NHLers and beer-league dreamers.

Sarah Cuthbertson would be the team's top player. The captain, Travis Lindsay, I modelled on Gordon. A next-door neighbour, Justin Ikura, became the model for Wayne Nishikawa, "Nish," the most mischievous (and soon most loved) of the players. Fahd I modelled on another of Gordon's friends. As I was then coaching a peewee team that included both Justin and Gordon, I had a dozen other handy models. And then, of course, I could also draw from my early years with Brent and Eric and the Reservoir Hill gang—a bottomless well of material involving kids the ages of the fictional hockey team.

What to call this team? I wanted something that kids would remember. I decided to call them the Screech Owls. They would play in a town, Tamarack, very much like Huntsville, where I had grown up. Their coach, Muck, would be modelled on a real coach named Muck.

I contacted Doug Gibson with a rough outline and he got back to me immediately.

"If you get this right," Doug predicted, "this will be your pension plan."

I was confident I could do the three books. If the series went no further than three volumes, no worries—there were always other projects. At least I would have tried.

I set the first one in Lake Placid, located in New York State an easy drive from Ottawa, thinking the publisher might like a US location with potential American sales. *Mystery at Lake Placid* revolved around Sarah's equipment. Someone was gaining access to the team's dressing room and sabotaging her skates and sticks. She had lost all confidence, couldn't score, and the team wasn't winning—at least not until they discovered the culprit was within their own group.

Number two was *The Night They Stole the Stanley Cup* and set in the Hockey Hall of Fame in Toronto. The title alone might attract the Canadian reluctant reader. As a bit of an inside joke, I had Nish race into a Yonge Street strip club, just as Brent and Eric and I had done back when we were of peewee hockey age. Not one reader or parent complained.

The next, *The Screech Owls' Northern Adventure*, was set in Waskaganish, a Cree village in northern Quebec I had visited many times while writing magazine and newspaper articles and finally a book on Chief Billy Diamond and his battles against the James Bay Project.

Much to my delight, and somewhat to my surprise, the books sold well from the start. The Toronto Maple Leafs even did a reading of

Northern Adventure. Players such as Tie Domi, Mats Sundin, Doug Gilmour and others read the entire book, one chapter per player. The team then sent packages including the book and a tape of the players reading it to hundreds of schools and libraries. The Maple Leafs held a pre-game ceremony at centre ice, where they presented Gordon with a Félix Potvin Maple Leafs jersey.

The series was doing well and Doug was keen to talk about another contract, this time for an astonishing *five* more books in the series. We met at the M&S offices and talked about where the series might go next. They loved the different locations I suggested—Disney World and the New England Aquarium among them—and agreed that the mystery element was as critical to the series' success as the various hockey settings.

I said I already had a title for book number four. They were keen to hear it.

"It will be *Murder at Hockey Camp*," I said.

Those gathered at the meeting gasped as one.

Doug cleared his throat. "We're not sure that murder is an appropriate 'mystery' for this age group," he said.

Others agreed with Doug. I told them of a study that claimed by the time a North American child had reached age twelve he or she would have witnessed about ten thousand murders on television and in the movies. I asked if they would reconsider if I went to a class of grade five students and asked what the kids thought of the idea. The publisher agreed and, to no surprise, every hand in the classroom went up when I asked who might read such a book.

From that point on, murders would periodically take place in the books. The team would play in tournaments in places such as Sydney, Australia, Sweden, Japan, Florida, Pittsburgh, New York City, Boston, Washington and all across Canada. The Screech Owls obviously ran the greatest bottle drives in the history of hockey . . .

As the years went by, I would run into NHL players who had grown up with the Screech Owls. Wayne Gretzky endorsed the series because his kids were reading the books. Taylor Hall, a number-one draft pick and winner of the 2018 Hart Trophy as the NHL's most valuable player, provided a cover blurb for the Owls. John Tavares, when he was captain of the New York Islanders, took part in a literacy program by taking his old Owls books to Long Island schools and reading to classes. He told *Newsday* the Screech Owls were his "favourite" reading while growing up.

Eventually the series ran to twenty-nine volumes, thirty if we include *The Screech Owls Scrapbook*, which artist Greg Banning and I produced in 1997. My favourite M&S editor, Alex Schultz, handled more than two dozen of the books and became an absolute expert on the characters and their ways. Thank you, Doug and Greg and Alex.

For the final book, *Reality Check in Detroit*, I brought a co-author aboard, daughter Kerry MacGregor, and we then moved on as co-authors of a new hockey series, the Ice Chips, which involves a similar team that travels back in time to meet the likes of Gordie Howe, Hayley Wickenheiser and Paul Kariya when they were twelve years old.

"The Screech Owls series was a stunning success," Doug Gibson wrote in his 2022 book *Great Scots: Celebrating Canadian Writers with Links to Scotland*. "It was published not only in English. From Canada, the respected centre of the hockey world, it came out in French, Swedish, Finnish, Czech, and, yes, Mandarin. It has sold more than two million copies. Two million!"

Pension plan, indeed.

THE BEST TEN CENTS EVER SPENT

A journalist soon learns there are always stories within stories. It's the serendipity of the profession, gifts that come from the privilege of bearing witness to events big and small. Take, for example, the tale of the dime that bought a legend. It was March of 1992 and my eldest daughter, Kerry, then just turning sixteen, and I were flying west to Saskatoon. We were going to help build the "Rink of Dreams."

This will require some explaining. Three years earlier, Ken Dryden and I had published *Home Game: Hockey and Life in Canada*. It had also been a successful CBC television series that looked into everything from children's hockey to the Wayne Gretzky trade, including an inside look at an NHL game in the old Montreal Forum and an examination of the state of grassroots hockey.

For the grassroots episode, we chose as our location the little Saskatchewan town of Radisson, about an hour up the Yellowhead Highway from Saskatoon. Radisson's Memorial Rink, built in 1961, had recently been condemned as structurally unsafe. Insurers wouldn't touch the old Quonset-style rink, deeming it a fire hazard. The province wanted to tear it down, leaving no place in this community of 434 for the children to learn to skate and play minor hockey.

Radisson's decline wasn't exactly unique. All along the Yellowhead Highway were small towns and villages—Maymont, Fielding, Borden—involved in what the locals called the "survival game." Of the 850 separate communities in Canada's most rural province, some were thriving, many struggling, some barely hanging on, and some were already lost, even if they didn't know it. A generation earlier there had been twelve hundred grain elevators standing high and proud over the flat Prairie province. Now there were eight hundred, soon to be less than half that.

It had long been the story of small-town western Canada. As poet W.A. MacLeod had written many years earlier:

> When the railroad comes—it cannot come to all of us;
> Some will mourn in far-off valleys, some will curse on distant
>   slopes.
> For the tinkling of the hammers filling many hearts with rapture
> May be spiking fast the coffin lid on other people's hopes.

A sign along the Yellowhead as it approached town proudly boasted, "Welcome to Radisson, home of Bill Hajt," acknowledging a local kid who had reached the NHL. No longer a kid, the long-time Buffalo Sabres defenceman had retired five years earlier, but the Radisson rink was where he had played his first hockey.

The town was so proud of Bill Hajt that one of the Main Street fire hydrants had been painted to look like him in his Sabres uniform.

At coffee row out at the Red Bull Café, several of the town leaders, including school principal Walter Kyliuk (also a town fire hydrant), long-time minor hockey coach Scotty Mundt and Bill Hajt's father, Alfons, had been thinking of ways to save the rink or, better yet, get a new one built. They'd held a retirement dinner for Bill and brought in Don Cherry as guest speaker. That had raised eight thousand dollars and the Sabres had sweetened the pot with a cheque for five thousand dollars. More money came from bingos and box lunches. They put on an event they called the "World Mud Volleyball Championships." But they were still hundreds of thousands of dollars away from a new rink.

The book and television series spread the word. A young man from southern Ontario, Joe Tutt, cycled all the way out to Radisson and back, raising thirty-five thousand dollars for the cause. People all over the country sent money, some as little as five dollars, some in the hundreds of dollars, all the little fundraisers adding up to $160,000.

But a new rink would cost five hundred thousand dollars—minimum.

Somehow, the plight of plucky Radisson got picked up by the *Los Angeles Times*. The story was read by Rob Paulsen, an actor then doing voices for the Teenage Mutant Ninja Turtles cartoons. Having grown up in Detroit, Paulsen was hockey-mad and regularly played with a group calling themselves the "Hollywood Celebrity Hockey Team."

Paulsen talked to his teammates and then contacted Walter Kyliuk to see if the town might like the Hollywood team to put on a charity match to raise money for the new rink. Kyliuk, naturally, leapt at the opportunity.

A lot of organizing and a few months later, the game was on. It would have to be held in Saskatoon, where there was a new and large rink. Paulsen put together a team that included actors Alan Thicke (*Growing Pains*), Richard Dean Anderson (*MacGyver*), Jerry Houser (*Slap Shot*), Dave Coulier (*America's Funniest People*), Jason Hervey (*The Wonder Years*), Chip and Pepper Foster (*Chip and Pepper's Cartoon Madness*), Ken Olandt (*The Young and the Restless*), Matt Frewer (*Max Headroom*) and Tom Babson (*Cheers*).

Canadian organizer Bob Strohm put together a team of former NHLers that included sixty-four-year-old Gordie Howe, Hajt, Bernie Federko, Orest Kindrachuk, Tiger Williams, Reggie Leach, Gregg Sheppard, Garry Peters, Dryden and the Pinder brothers, Gerry and Herb. Dryden would play forward, not goal. A few media types, me included, were sprinkled into the old-pros lineup. Former NHLers Dave Schultz, Keith Magnuson and Joe Watson were added to the Hollywood team for depth, as was Quebec's Manon Rhéaume, the first woman goaltender in junior hockey. (Rhéaume would soon become the first woman goaltender in the National Hockey League, when the Tampa Bay Lightning put her in net for a pre-season match.)

The game was a fundraising success (raising a hundred thousand dollars) if not an artistic beauty. I don't even remember the score, but vividly recall Tiger Williams, for no apparent reason, slugging Jason Hervey on the nose before a corner faceoff. Hervey started to cry. Schultz then tried to drive Williams through the boards and the two squared off, a brawl about one punch away from breaking out. The Hollywood team, outraged, left the ice and said the game was off if there was going to be crap like that involved.

The 7,250 people in the stands thought it was all a comedic set-up, howling with laughter as the young actor seemed, to them, to be faking mortal injury, cheering happily as Williams and Schultz squared off. They thought the team leaving the ice was all planned and part of the show. It took Howe and Wild Bill Hunter, our "coach," to go to the Hollywood dressing room and talk them back out onto the ice with a promise that Tiger would behave himself.

The treasured memory of that weekend, however, was something that happened in the afternoon before the charity game. Kerry, who had shown interest and promise in journalism, had come along for the adventure. In the morning, she had been walking around the arena, passed a group of men and suddenly found herself gently hip checked into the inside boards. Surprised, she looked back to see a smiling Gordie Howe reaching out to shake her hand. It was love at first sight.

Kerry and I had eaten lunch and were walking back to the hotel when a white limousine pulled up. A window rolled down—it must have been forty below—and Gordie Howe's long face stuck out, his breath freezing as he invited us to come along for a ride. The organizers had provided him with the limo to go off and visit his sister Joan.

He seemed embarrassed by the limousine. We got in—all luxury leather, a polished bar, tinted windows—and he said he was going to show us Saskatoon.

With Gordie calling directions to the driver, we drove out to where the small village of Floral once stood but was now lost to urban sprawl. It was in tiny Floral that the Howe family lived. Gordie had been the sixth of nine children born to Ab and Katherine Howe. It was the

Great Depression and, more often than not, Ab Howe was out of work, the family struggling to make ends meet. Gordie then had the driver take us to visit his sister in a little stucco house that seemed it could fit into the limo. He showed us the park where he used to play. We drove by King George School, which he attended and didn't much like.

"He was clumsy and backward and bashful," a crusty Ab Howe told a radio interviewer decades back, when Gordie made it to the NHL. "That's why I thought he'd never amount to anything."

He sure amounted to something. Four Stanley Cups with the Detroit Red Wings. Six Hart Trophies as the NHL's most valuable player. Top ten in scoring for twenty-one straight years. A comeback in his mid-forties to play seven seasons with his sons Mark and Marty in the World Hockey Association—and one final year in the NHL with the Hartford Whalers. He was then fifty-two years old and suited up for eighty games, scoring fifteen goals and forty-one points. His hair had long ago turned grey and was now turning white.

"If I dyed my hair," he joked, "they'd want more speed."

We drove back into the city and passed by the park named after him, the skating rink named for him. He told us there was a statue of him somewhere but it looked more like his brother Vic than him. Kerry was interested in how he learned to play the game. It was, of course, on a frozen prairie slough. Did the kids have skates?

"We had two," he said with a lazy, reflective smile. "My sister Edna had one—and I had the other."

The Howes had no money for frivolous matters like sports equipment. One of the poor Floral neighbours had recently had a baby and was having trouble feeding it. She brought a gunny sack filled with various items to the Howes' front door and asked if Katherine might like to buy it. "There should be someone here who can use these," she said, pointing to an old pair of skates.

Katherine wasn't interested in the skates or anything else in the sack, but wanted to help the poor woman out, so she handed over a few coins and then passed the sack back to Gordie and Edna, standing behind her. The old skates nearly fit Edna but Gordie had to stuff extra socks in to get close to a fit. Off they went to the slough, Gordie hopping on one boot and one skate, Edna struggling behind with one boot and the other skate. Edna struggled on the frozen ice, but Gordie was loving it, as he pushed with his one boot and glided with his one skate. He asked Edna if he could buy hers and she looked ready to give up.

"How much will you give me?" she asked.

"I have a dime back home," he said.

"Sold."

And so began what may forever stand as the greatest investment ever made in Canadian hockey.

"SMITTY" THE SNEAK

In midsummer 2020, the *Ottawa Citizen* published a powerful and emotional feature looking back twenty-five years—*twenty-five years!*—on the tragic murder of popular local sportscaster Brian Smith, known to all as "Smitty."

Smitty had been born and raised in Ottawa, and for years had been doing the sports on CJOH, the local CTV outlet. He had played professional hockey from 1960 to 1973, suiting up in the East Coast Hockey League, the American Hockey League, and Austria, and after the 1967 expansion spent time with two NHL teams, the Los Angeles Kings and the Minnesota North Stars. His career ended following a badly broken jaw while playing for the Houston Aeros of the World Hockey Association. His father, Des, had played in the NHL for the Chicago Black Hawks and Boston Bruins. His brother, Gary, had been an NHL goaltender for several teams. Smitty scored only ten NHL goals in total, but the happiest two were against his little brother.

Smitty was popular around town and much loved by the Ottawa sports media. He had been the most ardent supporter of the Senators landing an NHL franchise several years earlier. He was a much-in-demand MC for charity events, always giving freely of his time. On August 1, 1995, he finished his segment on the six o'clock CJOH news and set off to host a Children's Wish Foundation fundraiser in Rockland, a growing community to the southeast of Ottawa. He never made it out of the parking lot.

Heading for his car, he was shot at twice, the first shot missing but the second driving a .22 calibre bullet into his head. The assailant calmly placed the rifle back in the trunk of his car and drove away. Smitty was rushed to hospital but could not survive. He was fifty-four years old.

The attack had nothing to do with the sportscaster. Nothing he had done or said. He was targeted merely because he was a known face. The assassin, a thirty-eight-year-old man, had been waiting for someone, anyone, he recognized. It could have been any of a half-dozen known broadcasters coming to and going from the Merivale Road studio that evening. A classic wrong place at the wrong time story.

The killer turned himself in. It was found he was a diagnosed paranoid schizophrenic who had stopped taking his prescription medicine. Voices had told him to do this. Nearly two years later, a jury would find the man not criminally responsible of first-degree murder. After nine years in care, he was given an unconditional discharge and returned to Nova Scotia, his former home. He would die of heart failure in 2017.

Smitty never had that second chance.

The article's author, Gord Holder, spoke to Smitty's wife, Alana Kainz, who back in 1995 was a *Citizen* reporter. He also spoke to many of the sportscaster's colleagues, including Bill Patterson and James Duthie of CJOH, both of whom would one day take over Smitty's seat. While growing up in an Ottawa suburb, Duthie had idolized Smitty.

Some fifteen hundred mourners came to Smitty's funeral at St. Patrick's Basilica. The pre-funeral visitation line stretched so far down the street that it had to be extended by an hour. They talked about how funny Smitty could be. They spoke of his kindness—one of the mourners was a homeless man who had been handed a five-dollar bill by Smitty the day before he was killed. They talked about how humble he had always been, never wanting to talk about himself, certainly never to brag.

No one mentioned what a sneaky bugger he was.

"Pssst—you got a minute?"

It was less than six months before Brian Smith would be murdered. The Ottawa Senators were on another hapless road trip, with one more match to play Friday evening in Tampa against the Lightning.

The Senators had yet to win a single game on the road, despite having two of the league's youngest superstars in their lineup, Alexandre Daigle and Alexei Yashin.

Head coach Rick Bowness was at his wits' end. In his third season as head coach—the only head coach the expansion team had known—the Senators had never finished better than last place. The 1994–95 season had been half lost already due to a league lockout and the team was headed, once again, to a last-place finale. Bowness had vowed to reporters that the team would not be returning home from this trip without a win.

"Pssst—you got a minute?"

It was Thursday afternoon in Tampa. The team and travelling media—this being when we flew with them, bused with them, stayed in the same hotels—were at a nearby Marriott. It being a beautiful afternoon following a brief practice, I had decided to go for a walk before sitting down to tackle my column.

The *pssst* came from a seat just outside the entrance. It was Cunney—Randy Cunneyworth, the team captain. Sitting with him was assistant captain Troy Murray.

"What's up?" I asked.

"We got a good scoop for you if you want it."

A "scoop"? I had never thought of myself as a scoop sort of reporter. Columnists analyze and try to be cute and sometimes soundly condemn, but we don't often break stories.

"It's big," Cunneyworth whispered.

I went over to be closer to them. They both gave conspiratorial looks in each direction, decided they wouldn't be seen or overheard, and spilled it: Bowness had decided to bench both Yashin and Daigle for the Friday game.

I thought they were pulling my leg. The two youngsters were supposed to be the building team's foundation stones. Yashin had been the team's very first draft pick, taken second in 1992 behind Roman

Hamrlík, who had been picked by the Tampa Bay Lightning. Daigle had been drafted first overall at the end of the inaugural season for both the Senators and the Lightning. Yashin had stayed in Russia for one more season and both had been rookies for the 1993–94 season.

Bowness wanted to make a blunt point. He told his captains that he would be benching the two youngsters for indifferent play. Yashin had been selfish with the puck and selfish with his ice time. Daigle had played well at home but had often not shown up on the road.

I knew I had the sports story of the year for the *Ottawa Citizen*. The Senators were, by far, the biggest story in town. The two second-year players were the darlings of the capital, certain to one day lead the Ottawa Senators back to the Stanley Cup glory days last seen in 1927. I immediately forgot the afternoon walk and raced to my room to phone Tom Casey, who was now running the sports department.

"Are you sure?" Casey said, thinking I was still drunk from the night before.

"Certain," I said. "Cunneyworth told me himself."

"We're going big with this," Casey declared once I had convinced him. "Just make sure no one else gets it."

"No one else will," I promised.

The "no one else" in my mind was Bruce Garrioch, the Senators beat guy from the *Ottawa Sun*. Bruce had become a good friend, but he was a take-no-prisoners reporter when it came to breaking stories. It was what he lived for. He loved it that the players had even given him the nickname he cherished: "Scoop."

Garrioch's nose for news was twitching. He knew something was up but not what. Perhaps he had seen me whispering to John MacKinnon, the *Citizen* beat reporter who was now also writing about tomorrow's benching.

"You've got something, haven't you?" Bruce said to me as a few of us headed out to a local bar for dinner.

"Maybe I have. Maybe I haven't."

"I know something's up. Cunney said you had something big."

"Maybe."

"You're going to bury me, aren't you?" he whined, nearly in tears.

Periodically, as the evening wound on, he would repeat that—
"You're going to bury me, aren't you?"—and as the deadlines for both
papers loomed, I finally looked at him, grinned, and said, "Yes, I am."

"Tell me!" he cried.

"Wait'll the deadlines pass," I said.

Both papers would close their pages around eleven-thirty. After
that, it wouldn't matter. We had only to sit, drink beer and wait.

Several others eventually joined our table. The *Citizen* and *Sun* were
represented, as was *Le Droit* and RDS, the French-language newspaper
and broadcaster. Dean Brown and Gord Wilson were there, the play-
by-play and colour team broadcasters, and even Brian Smith of CJOH,
on a rare road trip with the team.

Bruce carefully watched the clock. At precisely eleven-thirty he
ordered beers for us both and said, "It's too late to file anything—what
do you have?"

Smugly, full of myself, proud of one of the only scoops of my career,
I leaned back and told him. "Bones is benching both Daigle and
Yashin tomorrow." ("Bones" was Bowness.)

"*No way!*"

"Yes, way."

"Someone's pulling your leg," one of the reporters said.

"It's true," Dean Brown said. "It's really going to happen."

"You buried me," Garrioch conceded. He lifted a glass in salute.

Smitty slipped away to the washroom. On the way there, he picked
up a payphone and called CJOH, just in time for the final sports
report of the day. The newspapers might be to bed. The television
station was still up and on.

Brian Smith of CJOH broke the biggest Ottawa Senators story of
the year.

He buried us both . . . in overtime.
Stick taps all around for Smitty.

(The following evening, with Alexandre Daigle and Alexei Yashin sitting in their suits in the press box, the Senators came from behind to defeat the Lightning 2–1. Head coach Rick Bowness was named first star of the game.)

9

The Pulse of America

The *National Post* was changing fast. No longer was there endless
money to spend on any whim—one summer they sent me on a
fly-fishing course with son Gordon, fully expensed—but the early
giddiness was fading somewhat by 2002, my fourth year at the paper.
In 2000, Conrad Black had sold 50 percent of the paper to CanWest
Global Communications, then sold them the remaining 50 percent
in 2001. The *Post* and several other papers in the chain were now
owned by Winnipeg-based Izzy Asper and would be run by his sons,
Leonard and David. Budgets tightened and the editorial direction
shifted. The *Post* had been founded by Black in 1998 as a conservative
voice for the Unite the Right movement, yet the Aspers were long-
time Liberals. When the *Ottawa Citizen* ran an editorial calling for
the resignation of Liberal prime minister Jean Chrétien, CanWest
changed the publisher.

Some of us were looking to get out, and almost immediately I was
handed a chance. I got a telephone call from Ed Greenspon, then editor
of the *Globe and Mail*. He was in Ottawa on bureau business and wanted
to know if I might join him for a coffee in the Glebe area of Bank Street.
We would meet the following day at a small, intimate café. The coffees

were still warm when an agreement was reached that I would join the *Globe* as the page 2 daily columnist.

Ed even had an early first assignment for me. He was well aware that through several elections, the publications I worked for would send me out to, as the old journalism saying goes, "take the pulse of the land." It was something I very much enjoyed.

"I want to send you across America on the anniversary of 9/11," he said, setting down his coffee. "Go wherever you want to go. Just talk to Americans and tell our readers what America feels like one year later."

"9/11"—two numbers, nothing more needed, ever. There are dates that are forever remembered—November 11, 1918, the day the Great War ended; October 28, 1929, the day the stock market crashed; June 6, 1944, D-Day; August 6, 1945, Hiroshima; November 22, 1963, the assassination of JFK—but this is the only date that requires but two numbers and everyone instantly knows the date and the story. At 8:46 a.m. on September 11, 2001, an American Airlines Boeing 767, packed with passengers and carrying twenty thousand gallons of jet fuel, flew into the eightieth floor of the north tower of the World Trade Center in New York City. Eighteen minutes later, a second Boeing 767, this one United Airlines flight 175, flew into the sixtieth floor of the south tower. A third plane ploughed into the Pentagon, in Arlington, Virginia, and a fourth crashed into a field near Shanksville, Pennsylvania, its presumed target the White House.

It was a plan so brazen, so brilliant, that it stunned the world. It had been carried out by nineteen terrorists who used box cutters to commandeer the flights and rudimentary flying skills to change the flight plans. Nearly three thousand people died in the crashes, a miracle that there were not thousands more.

I decided to begin in Oklahoma City, site of the previously best-known terrorist attack. On April 19, 1995, Timothy McVeigh, a twenty-six-year-old veteran of the Persian Gulf War, parked a rented Ryder truck filled with fertilizer in front of the Alfred P. Murrah Federal Building. He set a fuse, inserted earplugs and casually walked away. He set off an explosion so fierce that people living eighty kilometres away felt it. He killed 168 people, nineteen of them children in a daycare centre for federal government employees. He would later call the children "collateral damage."

To get from Oklahoma City to Shanksville, near Pittsburgh, would take a tremendous amount of driving. I would be gone at least two weeks, writing a daily column the *Globe* ran, sometimes on page 1, under a banner calling it "An American Journey." Not sure how I could possibly cover such ground and still research and write a nine-hundred-word column each day, I asked my brother-in-law, Ralph, recently retired after running a successful video store in North Bay, if he might join me. I had so many airline points from covering NHL hockey all those years that I could cover his flights. The hotel rooms, rental car and my meals could all be expensed. I'd cover his meals, as well. All he had to do was the driving, so I could write in the car while we travelled. He enthusiastically agreed.

We flew through Chicago and landed at Oklahoma City on a hot late-summer day, with the cicadas so loud we had to shout to be heard. We went immediately to the Oklahoma City National Memorial & Museum, dedicated to those who were lost that April morning seven years earlier. Here, by a reflective pool, is the most simple, most heart-rending memorial: 168 empty chairs, nineteen of them seats for small children.

If fifty years in journalism has taught me anything, it is that blind luck is often better than hard work. I have stumbled upon more columns than I have sought out, and this day would be no different. We ran into Paul Howell, who volunteered at the museum and often came to hold the empty chair reserved for his daughter, Karan, an angel-faced banker with two young daughters. She was twenty-seven when Timothy McVeigh killed her. Paul Howell was at home, 120 blocks north and five kilometres west, when he felt the explosion rattle his house. He watched on television as the first images rolled in from a news helicopter.

"I knew," he told us. "I just knew."

Paul Howell could never understand the cold heart of McVeigh, who showed no repentance at all, who claimed the score was 168–1 that day in his favour, and who told people to "get over it." Howell was a military man with thirty-five years of service behind him, and he found McVeigh's continuously belligerent manner reprehensible.

"I still can't get over that," he said. "He was brought up on our values."

Timothy McVeigh was sentenced to death and, on June 11, 2001, more than six years after he calmly walked away from that rented truck, he was executed at the federal prison at Terre Haute, Indiana. Paul Howell was one of ten survivors and family members selected to witness McVeigh being given a lethal injection. Prison authorities assured the witnesses that the convicted terrorist would quietly fall asleep and slip away.

It did not go as planned. Defiant still, McVeigh willed himself to scan the windows, at one point staring hard into the camera carrying the execution back to another 232 survivors and family members watching on closed-circuit television.

He died with his eyes wide open.

Paul Howell believes that Timothy McVeigh blinked first. "There was a tear in one of his eyes. I was close enough to see. And I want people to know that he wasn't nearly as tough as he thought he was."

This was going to be different. No longer about the escape of sport; no longer about the often annoying theatre of Parliament Hill. This was about anger—the pure, undiluted anger that could drive a man to commit such a heinous act and show defiance to the bitter end. Where did such anger come from? How could it last with such intensity?

This wasn't the simmering anger against politicians that I had found during the Citizens' Forum. It was a burning fury against . . . *everything.*

From Oklahoma City we drove to El Dorado, Kansas, where we met Dave Clymer, a seventy-seven-year-old war veteran and double amputee who ran a real-estate company called "Oz." His Cadillac had the Tin Man and Scarecrow on the front licence plate over the words "El Dorado, Kansas, The Land of Oz," even though neither the 1939 Hollywood movie starring Judy Garland nor the 1900 book by L. Frank Baum ever specified where in Kansas Dorothy and Toto were plucked up by that tornado. No matter. Dave Clymer knows it to be his town. As Dorothy so perfectly put it, "There's no place like home."

"I've had a heart attack and diabetes," the old veteran said. "I've lost my legs, I take eight pills a day and I walk with a cane—but I'm not going home to sit and wait for something else to happen. I am not afraid."

He admitted, on the other hand, to being profoundly puzzled by what had happened a year earlier in New York City, Washington and Shanksville.

"When you get older," he continued, "you eventually come to realize that everything doesn't quite come together like you thought it would. You take religion. If there's a just God, then where is He? Why would He allow all this killing?

"I have three questions I'd like a chance to ask. Number one, I'd like to know if there is a God. Number two, I'd like to know if there is a Heaven. Number three, I want to find out who gets welcomed into Heaven. Will it include the terrorists and the whole nine yards?"

If the answer to question number one was no, then the other two questions would be meaningless. But this wasn't so much about existentialism as it was about confusion and anger. A terrorist attack—not the first, certainly not the last—had a triggering effect on America. A fury they were not quite sure where to direct.

"The terrorists believe they're doing the right thing," Clymer told me. "Those who are fighting terrorism are convinced they are right. Who decides who's right? The question I ask myself is simple: Why? What has the United States of America done to deserve this treatment?"

Next stop was Branson, Missouri, the "Patriotism Capital of America." Others say it is "where Walt Disney came to throw up." Branson had a glitz equal to Disney World, neon lights everywhere, and movie theatres offering up fare from a world seemingly light years away from terrorists and victims. On this particular day, you could see Bobby Vinton, Glen Campbell, Andy Williams, the Osmond Brothers and even, at least in spirit, Lawrence Welk.

One year after 9/11, Branson was wall-to-wall "God Bless America." *Magnificent America* was on at the White House Theatre. Tourists were viewing replicas of the Oval Office and Air Force One at the American Presidential Museum. PBS was taping Lawrence Welk's *God Bless America* at the Champagne Theatre. We decided to take it in.

The crowd went mad at the first sight of faces once familiar, now decidedly aged: the Lennon Sisters, Dick Dale, Norma Zimmer, Myron Floren, Ralna English. They gave standing ovations to most. They called out, "We love you, Joe!" to Joe Feeney, who blew his song cue. To the music of Gershwin, George M. Cohan, Glenn Miller and others, they marched through both world wars, Korea, Vietnam, and the Persian Gulf. "A country attacked at home, assaulted by the deadliest of enemies," a loudspeaker blared, "an enemy with no regard for life— not even their own." America, they promised, would rise from the ashes of 9/11. "She will never be destroyed—nor her heroes be forgotten."

Then everyone sang. "Amazing Grace." "God Bless America." Then all rose to recite the Oath of Allegiance, hand over heart.

Ralph and I awkwardly got to our feet, placed our hands over our hearts, and mumbled.

On then in our rented Subaru Outback to Memphis, where we of course went to the Lorraine Motel—now the National Civil Rights Museum. It was here, on a cool spring evening in 1968, that Martin Luther King Jr. stepped out on the balcony of room 306 for a quick smoke. An assassin's bullet struck with such accuracy that it blew the knot out of his tie.

Johnnie A. Morton had come to Memphis to see where Dr. King, his hero, died—just as he had been to Atlanta to see where he is buried. At fifty-five, Mr. Morton had lived through most of the stories told at the museum—Montgomery, Birmingham, Mississippi. As a Black American, he had long known the importance of civil rights and the sacrifice of those who fought for those rights and, at times, died for them.

And yet, he wanted to talk about another date in American history: 9/11. With Dr. King's famous words from the 1963 March on Washington—"I have a dream . . ."—echoing regularly from the corridors of the museum, Johnnie began his own speech about the night of September 10–11, 2001.

"I had a dream," he said in a firm, deep voice. "I dreamed an airplane was falling out of the sky. I dreamed it crashed and was burning and a lot of people were dead. It was about four o'clock in the morning, and I woke up my wife and told her, and she just told me, 'You're weird,' and went back to sleep."

But Mr. Morton could not go back to sleep. He stewed through the rest of the night in his home in Greenwood, South Carolina, unable to shake the image, and was up and watching television when the first plane struck the World Trade Center's north tower four hours and 46 minutes after his dream.

"I still feel odd about it," he said. "Maybe if I could have ciphered it out I could have called somebody—but they would have just said I was crazy."

Our most unusual experience came near St. Joe, Arkansas, when we encountered Tony Altman driving down the side of the highway on a lawn mower, a loaded 30-clip assault rifle hanging off his left shoulder and a quart of margaritas cradled in his right arm. He pulled in at the General's Mercantile, a Civil War–themed memorabilia and souvenir store on the side of Highway 65, just north of the Buffalo River and deep in the Ozarks. Tony not only cut the grass, but also manned the store.

He sold replica flags and hats and bayonets, rebel bikinis, Confederate dog collars and even toilet paper called "Johnny Wipes," but the main attraction for most visitors was to have a photograph taken beside a roadside sign saying "Adopt-A-Highway Litter Control. Next 1 mile, Knights of the Ku Klux Klan, St. Joe, Arkansas."

Tony Altman could not have been more friendly, more welcoming. Smiling and joking, the forty-one-year-old former member of the US Coast Guard told us he was a proud Klansman and, in fact, was off to a cross burning that very evening. He was not joking.

"You're more than welcome to come," he said. As a columnist in search of good stories, I was sorely tempted, but Ralph was extremely reluctant. Perhaps wisely so, for once we began talking about 9/11 the tone took a decided turn.

"I think it very possible," Tony Altman said, "that 9/11 could be some kind of covert deal."

His real job was not so much selling Civil War paraphernalia, he said, but in telling what he called "the Truth." By this, he meant facts that he was convinced the government suppresses and the mainstream media ignores, leaving the people ignorant of inconvenient realities. He was not allowed to attend university, for example, because his white skin was not the right colour. Immigrants were ruining America. Lazy government and corporate greed were the reality behind pornography, including that involving children who had been abducted from their families.

There were no good politicians, he said. The Republicans and Democrats were all "weasels" bought and paid for by big corporations. He believed, absolutely, that the country would split again down Civil War lines, with a different outcome.

In his "Truth" about 9/11, President George W. Bush's family and the family of Osama bin Laden had business interests together.

"There's more to this guy than meets the eye," he said, not clarifying whether he meant Bush or bin Laden.

Altman told us he became quickly suspicious when the death counts started coming in. Early reports had been six thousand or more, the reality was around twenty-eight hundred. "The Truth" was not being told here, he was adamantly convinced.

"How many people were told not to go to work that day?" he asked. "It sure looks odd, doesn't it?

"To tell you the truth, I wish they'd wiped out the entire city—I despise New York City.

"You're sure you don't want to come along tonight?"

We stopped in at Monticello in Virginia to visit the home of Thomas Jefferson. Jefferson was the great visionary of the founding of the United States of America, a slave owner who had as much a way with the English language as he apparently did with the kitchen staff. His words from the Declaration of Independence are memorized by Americans— "We hold these truths to be self-evident: that all men are created equal, that they are endowed by their Creator with certain inalienable rights, among these are life, liberty and the pursuit of happiness"—but they have also been twisted by those who would terrorize America. When Timothy McVeigh walked away from that rented truck in Oklahoma City in 1995, he wore a T-shirt quoting Jefferson: "The tree of liberty must be refreshed from time to time with the blood of patriots and tyrants."

McVeigh, however, did not include the full quotation, which also says, "What signify a few lives lost in a century or two?"

Not 168. Not nineteen of them children.

We moved on to Williamsburg, Virginia, where James Southall, the tavern owner, apologized when I brought up 9/11. "I'm sorry," he said, "but we don't know anything about that here."

That would be because it is always November 9, 1774, in Williamsburg, and those who live and work there never leave their role. To suggest all was calm in Williamsburg would be wrong, as the tavern owner was quite concerned about the possibility of war with Britain over unfair taxation. The governor was off fighting "savages to the West," he said, and as for "terrorists," that would be the pirates who make their way up the river and make off with livestock and slaves.

Stopping off in Washington, we ran into Kelly Clarkson and the commercialization of 9/11. At a special event to be held the following day, Clarkson would be singing "The Star-Spangled Banner" at the top of the marble steps leading to the Lincoln Memorial. A week earlier, she had been a virtual unknown, but the twenty-year-old former waitress had just won Fox Network's *American Idol*. The publicity and magazine covers that followed had created an instant celebrity, and she had been added to the special memorial to mark the first anniversary of the attack. Some thought it was all in terribly bad taste.

"There needs to be a drawing back," said Tom Hipple of nearby Baltimore, Maryland, who worked for a brokerage firm that lost thirteen employees in the World Trade Center attacks.

"Something like that," added his wife, Dorothy, "just trivializes the whole thing."

"That" would be the instant booths set up to sell, for example, an orange sign saying "Special Issue USA Permit No. 91101 Terrorist Hunting Permit. No Bag Limit. Tagging Not Required."

A poster calling September 11, 2001, "The Darkest Day in America" went for fifteen dollars, though the vendor claimed, "Seven dollars goes back to the families of 9/11." You couldn't help but wonder . . .

At Shanksville on the actual day of the anniversary, we gathered in a cold, wind-whipped hayfield with thousands of others to honour forty overshadowed, often forgotten victims of the attack. These were the passengers who rallied to Todd Beamer's "Let's roll!" shout, overwhelmed the terrorists and sent United Airlines Flight 93 into this empty field rather than a fully occupied White House.

We had risen well before dawn to make the drive from Pittsburgh. We joined a massive convoy of cars and buses passing hundreds of lighted candles shining from the windows of farmhouses and rural homes along the route. The locals of Somerset County were saluting the families; the families were there to thank the locals who, over the past year, had turned the field into a poignant monument to the final disaster of that day. The families came, as did uniformed colleagues from United Airlines, as did more than a hundred young staffers from the White House, all in dark, fashionable suits—and most in tears.

At 10:03 a.m., the moment locals heard the violent crash a year earlier, a bell tolled for each name read out. Sandy Dahl, wife of Flight 93 pilot Jason Dahl, spoke for the hundreds of family and friends who had gathered so early. "After September 11," she said, "we know there is no shortage of angels."

President George W. Bush and Laura Bush arrived by helicopter to lay a wreath and, later, meet with the families. There was a flypast of huge C-130s, the massive military transport planes, low under a canopy of dark cloud. Then came the air force fighter jets in "missing-man formation." The people on the ground applauded the planes as they passed.

The organizers released forty doves into the sky following a twenty-one-gun salute and the singing of "God Bless America." The small cloud of birds vanished almost instantly in the harsh north wind that had been blowing since dawn.

People were beginning to leave when there were shouts and a lot of pointing to the sky. The doves were coming back, in their own rough formation, and all forty swept directly over the crash site.

The people responded as they had for the formal flypasts: they applauded.

The column that appeared in the September 11, 2002, edition of the *Globe and Mail* was my dispatch from Gettysburg, with the paper also including the full Gettysburg Address by President Abraham Lincoln. A woman standing in front of the cairn holding Lincoln's immortal words sighed and softly read aloud: "The world will little note, nor long remember what we say here, but can never forget what they did here."

Mary Beth Gibbs of Columbia, North Carolina, fought back tears as she read, unaware that that same morning New York governor George Pataki was at Ground Zero in New York City, reading aloud the 272 words that most Americans know by memory: "Four score and seven years ago . . ." ending with a vow that is held sacred—"that government of the people, by the people, for the people, shall not perish from the earth."

Garry Wills, author of the Pulitzer Prize–winning *Lincoln at Gettysburg*, wrote that when the crowd dispersed that long-ago day in Gettysburg, "They walked off, from those curving graves on the hillside, under a changed sky, into a different America."

We left the famous battleground convinced that this was true once again in 2002.

Ralph and I had travelled 5,035 kilometres, through nine states over fifteen days. Looking back now, more than two decades later, it is possible to see the perhaps irreparable rift that would open up on January 6, 2021, when Donald Trump seemed unwilling to leave office after losing the election to Joe Biden. That near insurrection is today seen as far, far more alarming than it seemed even at the time.

Ku Klux Klansman Tony Altman had predicted the country would again one day split along Civil War lines. His "Truth" was far removed from what officials found and the mainstream media had faithfully reported.

And this all came before social media had its own astonishing explosion.

Sadly—hell, chillingly—perhaps Tony Altman was looking into the years to come in America rather than the year just finished.

THE QUEEN AND MY SHORTS

"*Sir!*"

The policeman was following me, but surely was calling someone else. Ever since I had arrived in the lovely British town of Windsor, I had felt like an intruder, an alien. On a bright Sunday morning in June 2002, I was the only one around not dressed as if attending a royal ceremony—which, in fact, was taking place in nearby St. George's Chapel. The archbishops of Canterbury and Westminster were both on hand. The congregation had been arriving over the previous hour or so, mostly elderly men and women dressed quite formally, many of the men with medals and the women in glorious, colourful headgear, perhaps in small tribute to one known more for her hats than for her words.

"*Sir!!*" he called again.

I stopped and turned, half expecting to be placed under arrest for being somewhere I had no right to be.

The British bobby had several small pink cards in his hand. "There are extras, sir," he said as he handed one to me. "Would you care for an invitation?"

The pink card read as follows:

St George's Chapel, Windsor Castle
Morning Prayer
2 June 2002
Jubilee Thanksgiving
attended by
HM The Queen and HRH The Duke of Edinburgh
Entrance by South Door, from 10:00 a.m.
Please be seated by 10:30 a.m.

I was off to church with the Queen of England.

The Golden Jubilee celebrations of 2002 were going ahead despite the bad personal news of the year. The Queen had lost her sister, Margaret, to a stroke in early February, and her mother had died at the age of 101 in late March. There would still be concerts and parades. There would be public appearances most days during the week, and the newspapers duly listed what would be happening where and when. For Sunday, June 2, the papers said that the Queen and Prince Philip would be attending a by-invitation-only communion service at St. George's Chapel, Windsor Castle. It would be a private affair. No press coverage.

Jet lag had me up before dawn on a glorious and warm day. Having nothing better to do, I decided to head for Windsor to see if I might chat to some of the locals before they headed off to the private service at St. George's Chapel. I dressed quickly—golf shirt, shorts, sandals— and headed out for Paddington Station, where I checked the train times and found that one was leaving shortly for Windsor and would take approximately an hour. That meant I could get there early and be back before lunch, giving me the afternoon to write a piece on the Golden Jubilee through the eyes of the Windsor locals.

The train stopped at Windsor and Eton Central station and I had a leisurely stroll to the castle over the cobbled streets. Here, in this small town across the Thames from Eton, England's famous private school, was where the family found its name, dropping the Saxe-Coburg-Gotha that arrived in 1840, when Queen Victoria married her cousin Prince Albert. That family name decidedly fell out of public favour when another cousin, Kaiser Wilhelm II, declared war on Britain in 1914.

Here in Windsor was where the young Elizabeth Alexandra Mary Windsor and her sister, Margaret Rose Windsor, spent the early years of the Second World War away from the bombing, holed up in the thick-walled, fifteenth-century Lancaster Tower while officially described as living "somewhere in the country." Much later in the war, Elizabeth herself served as a truck driver and mechanic.

Here was where Elizabeth had spent so many of her happiest as well as saddest moments, the worst being the 1992 fire—was it a lamp, or did the Queen Mother fumble a cigarette?—that caused forty million pounds in damage and destroyed a hundred rooms.

Once I reached the grounds outside the castle, it was easy to spot who might be going to the church service just by their apparel. I spoke to one such couple, took some quick notes, watched as the town worshippers lined up to go through the security check and when the last ones had gone through, I turned to head back to the train station.

That's when the policeman called out, "*Sir!!*"

I took the pink card thinking I would at least have a souvenir. I went back to the chapel at the side of the palace and found the South Door, where the last of the arrivals were being processed through as if they were entering airport departures. I handed a woman the pink card, she returned it to me and told me to join the line. There was no expression on her face one way or the other concerning my dress. It was the perfect British moment.

The chapel is connected to the much larger Windsor Castle, a magnificent fortress built nearly a thousand years earlier by William the Conqueror, the hero of the Battle of Hastings, and the one who began this long royal line that, forty kings and queens later, had produced the longest-reigning British monarch of all: Elizabeth II.

I got through the security line fine. Nothing was said about the small notepad I was carrying or the two pens. (A smart journalist always carries a backup.) I carried no tape recorder, no camera. I was treated like just another worshipper come to morning communion. I might not know how to dress, but I did know how to behave, having attended hundreds of communion services as a young server in All Saints' Anglican Church in Huntsville.

Entering the larger chapel, I was struck by the size of St. George's. It looked so small beside the castle, seemed so large once I was inside. There were large columns covered in colourful mosaic tiles, twenty-six rows in two sections for the congregation and a stand-apart room for the choir. There was a large marble tomb on the far side that held the remains of King George VI, his wife, Elizabeth (the Queen Mum), and their daughter Margaret. (In 2022 Queen Elizabeth II would be entombed there, as well.)

I was checking out a seat on the far edges near the very back when I detected a small man in full morning dress moving fast in my direction. He carried a distinctive air of authority.

Obviously, he was coming to give the absurdly dressed intruder the boot.

"Are you *alone*, sir?" he demanded in a rather posh accent. Perhaps he was wondering if he needed to call for added security.

"I am, sir," I answered.

"We have an empty seat farther up, sir," he said. "Would you please follow me?"

With me in tow, the man in the morning jacket wound his way through those still finding their seats. Closer and closer we came to the chancel and the cross. Finally, four rows from the front of the church, he pointed to a spot near a distinguished gentleman with white hair and an older woman who seemed dressed more for the Ascot races than morning communion.

People stared at me as I made my way down to the open seat. The very charming Elizabeth Pearce, retired, of Windsor Great Park moved over slightly with a welcoming smile. She introduced me to the white-haired man, who immediately shook my hand. He was James (Jim) Beaton, who in March of 1974 took three bullets—one each to the hand, the arm and the stomach—in thwarting what was either an assassination attempt or a kidnapping of Princess Anne on the Mall, just outside the gates of Buckingham Palace. For this he was awarded the George Cross, and, in 1982, appointed the Queen's Police Officer.

My two seatmates had every right to hold the pink invitation-only cards. Beaton would march in the royal procession on Monday as the royal family paraded to St. Paul's Cathedral for the formal jubilee service; Elizabeth Pearce would be in that congregation, also by special invitation. The true measure of their class, however, was in the polite and welcoming manner in which they dealt with this unexpected Canadian intruder in the golf shirt, shorts and sandals who dared sit near the very front of the congregation awaiting the arrival of the Queen.

And that's when she appeared. All rose as the Queen and the Duke of Edinburgh entered. She was dressed in pearl white, hat included, and made no acknowledgement of anyone. She passed on, with Philip trailing, into the quire and behind a screen while the few hundred sitting in the congregation stood like curious prairie dogs trying to see everything there was to be seen.

The service was slick and economical, the choir in glorious form. The sermon was given by the Right Reverend David Conner and he talked, not surprisingly, about the appreciation this congregation gathered "on home ground" had for the Queen's exceptional lifelong devotion to duty. A man to my left was snoring loudly.

The service over, I stood to go, thinking if I hurried I could still catch that late morning train back to London. But Elizabeth Pearce grabbed my arm. I must stay, she insisted, as there was to be a small gathering in the courtyard outside—and the Queen would attend.

"You come with us," Elizabeth Pearce commanded, making sure both James Beaton and the Canadian were guided through the side doors and out onto the lawn, where the local faithful were already gathering, all talking about the jubilee celebrations.

"She has done an enormous amount for everyone in the entire country," said Elizabeth Pearce, "but they don't all appreciate it."

"It's been half a century," I said. "I can't really put my finger on what her subjects feel about her."

"A very great respect, I should say," added Elizabeth Pearce. "'Warmth' is something I should think you reserve for someone more close to you."

Jim Beaton offered that the key thing the Queen had to offer her people was "stability" and no one any longer expected to see much "warmth."

"She is not 'cold,'" he told me, "but you could say that she is 'reserved,' as the English use the expression—and you can translate that in any way you wish."

Such chatter died suddenly on the courtyard lawn as the Queen entered from the left, Philip trailing behind with his hands locked around his lower back. She came to our little circle, nodded in recognition at Jim Beaton and Elizabeth Pearce . . . and stared at me briefly.

The "reserved" woman who created a long-running family joke when, seeing herself on television, said, "Oh, that's my 'Miss Piggy' face," cracked briefly—one quick smile and she was gone.

Philip, on the other hand, was openly chuckling as he fell in behind her.

"She is looking very happy," said a thrilled Elizabeth Pearce.

More likely amused.

SINKING IN THE FAR NORTH

How, I wondered with a shiver and a shudder, am I ever going to put *this* through on expenses?

Hotel	$169.00
Breakfast	$14.95
Lunch with interview	$36.90
Ski-Doo replacement	$15,000.00

It was mid-June 2005, and the *Globe and Mail* had dispatched me to cover Governor General Adrienne Clarkson's "Farewell Tour" of the Far North. In her five years at Rideau Hall, she and her husband, the writer John Ralston Saul, had developed a deep passion for the North. She would be leaving office at the end of September after serving the full five-year term and being granted a one-year extension by Prime Minister Paul Martin.

Clarkson had been both a popular and a controversial Queen's representative. She was the first visible minority and only the second woman to be appointed to the post. She worked hard, travelling all of the country and much of the world, which annoyed some Canadians who saw her lifestyle as lavish.

The GG role is a difficult one in Canada. Some are admired for the simplest of matters—Lord Stanley offering a hockey trophy after he had already returned to England—and some, like Viscount Byng, are remembered only for their political problems. Canadians hugely admired GGs eighteen (Vincent Massey), nineteen (Georges Vanier) and twenty (Roland Michener), but then ran into a string of difficulties. Number twenty-one, Jules Léger, lost his voice to a stroke but stayed the full five years with the determined help of his wife, Gabby. Ed Schreyer (twenty-two) was deemed boring. Jeanne Sauvé (twenty-three) closed off the Rideau grounds to the public. Ray Hnatyshyn (twenty-four) and Roméo LeBlanc (twenty-five) were seen as nice but little attention was paid to them. GG number twenty-six, Clarkson, significantly raised the governor general profile and largely returned some majesty to the office, even if some didn't much care for it. She was succeeded by Michaëlle Jean (twenty-seven), David Johnston (twenty-eight), Julie Payette (twenty-nine) and Mary Simon (thirty). The affable Johnston was so admired for what he brought to the job he was asked to stay on two extra years. The toxic Payette was so disliked she was asked to leave early and was replaced by Mary Simon, the first Inuk to hold the position.

Clarkson's love for the Far North had raised the profile of this increasingly vital cap of the Canadian land base. It was a story of great interest to me, as well, as I had become so deeply involved with the Cree of James Bay and their battles with the federal and provincial governments of the day. This was a chance to see much more of the North than I had so far visited.

This trip was seen as a last hurrah for Clarkson, who at times had seemed tired as her extra year came to a close. Little wonder—a few weeks following her return from the Far North she was admitted to hospital in Toronto and fitted with a pacemaker.

Travelling in a military Twin Otter, the small group—I was the only journalist along—visited Iqaluit, the capital of Nunavut, as well as the far-flung communities of Pangnirtung, Tanquary Fiord, Pond Inlet, Resolute Bay and Grise Fiord. There were also stopovers at the research station at Eureka and the military base at Alert, the northernmost permanently inhabited settlement in the world. Some sixty people, the vast majority of them in the Canadian Armed Forces, live at the base on Ellesmere Island north of the eighty-second parallel, some eight hundred kilometres from the North Pole.

It was a spectacular week to be there. Thanks to the twenty-four-hour sunlight of the summer solstice, I watched youngsters playing golf in "Pang" well after midnight, their makeshift course with just a single hole laid out along village streets and the rugged coastline. How appropriate, then, that the visitor centre at Pangnirtung contains an ancient club, a very rusty niblick, that had been found in an old Scottish whaling camp.

At Alert, Clarkson and Saul led a work brigade in constructing a rock cairn at the far end of the runway, a point where Canada ends—or begins, depending on which direction you might be travelling. It was a remarkable spot for the cairn, with mountain ranges barely within sight and, across the choppy ice, Russia sitting somewhere beyond the far curve of the horizon. The symbolism did not need to be explained.

At Grise Fiord I spoke with Larry Audlaluk while he skinned a ringed seal. He told me how his community had been torn from their traditional home by the Canadian government during the 1953 High Arctic relocation. They were moved more than a thousand kilometres from their northern Quebec homes. This was a Cold War policy of the Louis St. Laurent government: take several families from a northern Quebec village called Port Harrison, now known as Inukjuak, and have them serve as "human flagpoles" in the High Arctic to underscore Canada's claim to the Northwest Passage. Then, the government brought in a few families from Pond Inlet to teach Inuit hunting and survival skills to those now forced to live in what amounted to a foreign land.

Not residential school . . . not quite.

Larry's father died from heartbreak. The people found the place they had been taken to so dark and desolate that they decided this time to transplant themselves, moving far across the bay to a place where they could catch more sunlight. They could also catch Arctic char, a food staple in their traditional grounds in northern Quebec. When Larry brought the first sparkling char home, his mother broke down and wept at the mere sight of it. When I spoke to Larry, more than fifty years had passed since their forced move north and, as he put it, "People have to move on. The young have grown up here. This is their home. And it's my home now—I love it here."

At Tanquary Fiord, on the far northern edges of Ellesmere Island, we hiked in the northernmost wilderness reserve in the world, Quttinirpaaq National Park, and stared in awe at a remarkable glacier known as the "Hand of God." It is a massive glacier shaped, eerily, like a long forearm reaching down into the fiord, thumb and four fingers tightened as if it were a giant hand seeking a purchase on earth. We saw photographs taken over the years that show the arm shrinking, the fingers appearing to tighten . . . the grip slipping.

At Resolute Bay I thought I might die.

And if I somehow survived, I thought I might still be killed—by the accounting department of the *Globe and Mail*.

Resolute Bay, a small village on Cornwallis Island, was another forced-relocation community. The government-created settlement in the Arctic Archipelago along the Northwest Passage is called Qausuittuq in Inuktitut, which means "place where the sun doesn't rise." It certainly was in the time we were there. No dusk, no night, no dawn—just twenty-four-hour sunlight in this place that lies farther north than any other Inuit settlement but Grise Fiord.

John Saul was in a mood for adventure. On the flight in to Resolute on the Twin Otter, Captain Dominique Lassonde had pointed out a site where a Fokker F27 operated by Great Northern Airways had crashed on approach to the Resolute Bay airport in early June 1968. He pointed it out not to scare us, but to say that, somehow, no one aboard was killed, though the plane was completely destroyed.

John Saul wanted to go to the crash site. There are times in journalism when reporters must make their own managerial decisions. There was no chance to phone the *Globe* to ask permission. I made an executive decision to join the Canadian Rangers who were taking him out to see what remained of the old Fokker nearly four decades after it went down in bad weather.

Sergeant Randolph Idlout and three corporals, Mark Amarualik, Debbie Iqaluk and her son, Joadamee, would lead a snowmobile convoy over the still-thick ice of the harbour that offers refuge from Barrow Strait. Also along would be RCMP constable Glen Fishbook. Each of us had a snow machine to ride. Having spent twenty-some winters in Muskoka, I was familiar with the machines, often heading out with my friend, now brother-in-law, Ralph, on his brother Ted's old snowmobiles. The Bombardier Ski-Doo I would be riding in Resolute, however, was brand new.

We set out over the ice, the pace quickening until we were going faster than I had ever gone before on a snow machine. It was exhilarating, exciting, fun. The group paused only briefly when Amarualik spotted a ringed seal in the distance and took a long-distance shot that missed, sending the frightened seal vanishing back into the hole it had made through the thick ice.

We travelled across the harbour and then left the ice to climb far up a valley to a high, snow-covered plateau. It was here that flight GNA F-F27 ran short of fuel while circling the airport in heavy fog and had to ditch. It was one of those rare times in the Far North when bad luck takes all the right turns. The pilot found an unusually flat and solid stretch of ground; the plane held together well enough to protect the passengers; and the crash took place close enough to Resolute Bay that a rescue was both possible and prompt.

Up here, disaster can strike fast—just keep reading.

At the urging of the southern visitors, the rangers selected a different route back, twisting and soaring through a magnificent canyon with high snowdrifts curling on one side and a small stream just beginning to melt through the middle.

Up ahead, one of the rangers turned his snowmobile across a shining stretch of melting ice, the spray spreading on both sides like instantaneous crystal wings. It seemed like a good idea to follow suit. I aimed my much heavier, brand-new, *borrowed* fifteen-thousand-dollar machine into the same ski slots, skimming out over the wet ice . . .

. . . bogging down . . .

. . . stopping . . .

. . . sinking . . .

Let's be open about this. Mistakes happen—but in this particular person's case, they had usually been grammatical, fatal only in the eyes of certain readers.

The ice seemed to sag, almost as if I were a child walking across a king-size bed. Everything seemed slow. Slow, but also inevitable. I had screwed up—big time. I stepped free of the machine, flicking the engine off as steam began rising as the ice water of the stream found the hot engine. Water was seeping into my right boot.

Had I been alone, I would have been doomed. Boots wet and still eight kilometres from the village. Southerners see Inuit hunters with their thick gloves attached to their coats like the mittens of a toddler, unaware that this is life protection. Were a glove to blow away while a hunter cleans a seal or sets a trap, not only fingers would be lost.

But you can also get lucky—just like the crew and passengers aboard GNA F-F27. Blind dumb luck in this case was John Saul riding a more powerful Ski-Doo than any of the rest of us. Ranger Mark Amarualik sprang into action, grabbing a long rope from the pack on the back of his machine and easing out onto the ice close enough to the slowly, slowly, slowly sinking machine that he was able to loop the rope around the handlebars. Racing and slipping back to shore, he then attached the rope to the rear of Saul's machine, replaced Saul as driver and slowly, with a great roar of the engine and grind of the treads, extricated the sinking machine from certain doom and reporter damnation.

The machine was saved! There would be no career-ending expense filing.

MacGregor luck.

RESIDENTIAL SCHOOL REALITY:
PHIL AND DENNIS FONTAINE

It was the day before the National Day of Action, late June 2007, and the Fontaine brothers, Phil and Dennis, had come to the Sagkeeng First Nation to talk about something they had avoided most of their lives.

It was a beautiful day at this point where the Winnipeg River empties into the southern basin of Lake Winnipeg. There was a light wind playing in the nearby alders and a new family of geese out on the light chop of the river. The sun sent shadows racing across the tall prairie grass as small clouds drifted across the sky.

Phil Fontaine was sixty-two years old and in his third term as grand chief of the Assembly of First Nations. For years he had been giving speeches almost daily, yet this day he was speechless. When he tried to talk, his throat choked, his eyes brimmed with tears, and all he could do was turn and walk away. Dennis, four years older, was openly crying.

They had come, they said, to once again see "Canada's dirty little secret," the residential school system that existed from the late nineteenth century until, unbelievably, 1996, only eleven years before the Fontaine brothers came back to revisit their own demons at the mouth of the Winnipeg River.

There were once residential schools across most of the country, some 130 in total, housing 150,000 First Nation, Inuit and Métis children who had been forcibly taken from their parents and communities and sent off to live at and attend schools such as the one that once stood here, on the reserve formerly known as Fort Alexander.

In 2021, evidence was found that suggested hundreds of unmarked graves of Indigenous children might be found at closed residential schools in places like Kamloops, British Columbia, and Marieval,

Saskatchewan. These lost children would be lying in graves that hadn't even the courtesy of a marking. The story grew into a national shame virtually beyond understanding, with searchers spreading out across the country looking for further evidence. There were calls, often by the grand chief of the Assembly of First Nations, for government compensation and church apologies, some of which came—but never fast enough for those who had survived the schools.

Phil Fontaine had come home to attend the funeral of a first cousin who had died from complications arising from diabetes, the scourge of older Indigenous generations, only to learn that his brother Dennis's fourteen-year-old granddaughter had taken her own life, the scourge of younger Indigenous generations.

The two grieving brothers had gone together to the reserve cemetery, where so many family members, including two infant brothers, are buried. They wanted to pay their respects.

But not to all who were buried there, at the cemetery next to where the residential school stood for so many decades. This quiet, wind-blown cemetery is also where priests who once ran the mission and the Fort Alexander Residential School lie beneath weathered stones.

Some of those priests were Phil Fontaine's abusers.

Three generations of Fontaines went to this school. All that stands today on the property is the Notre Dame de Lourdes grotto the oblate brothers built, in no small part on the forced labour of small boys they made ferry the large rocks up from the shoreline of the river.

Earlier, the brothers had stopped to visit their ninety-three-year-old uncle, Albert Fontaine, himself a former chief of the Fort Alexander band and also a "graduate" of the Fort Alexander Residential School. There was talk about compensation coming to those who suffered in the system. If everything went as hoped, Phil told his uncle, there should be a cheque for around thirty thousand dollars coming to him.

"Is it enough?" he was asked by the visiting journalist.

"Not for the years I put in at that place," the old man said.

His lower lip quivered. He stared out the window for what seemed a very long time before speaking again.

"You know," he said, "we had cows at that place—but I never got a drop of milk in all the time I was there."

Dennis Fontaine, moving ahead on the gently blowing grass, came to a halt. It was at this precise spot, more than half a century back, that twelve-year-old Dennis held the hand of his bawling little brother and told him not to worry, that everything would be alright. Even though Dennis knew it would not be. Not ever.

Dennis had reached grade six. It was time for him to move from the Little Boys' side of the school dormitory into the Big Boys' side. He desperately wanted to be with his friends; his eight-year-old brother desperately needed him to stay.

The priests, one in particular, wanted the big brother gone, out of the way.

It was a moment of sheer terror for Phil. The only prayer he had been saying for months was that Dennis would be allowed to stay with him, protect him.

Phil Fontaine still cannot speak about what happened after that separation.

Dennis Fontaine could barely talk of it and did so only after his younger brother had wandered off into the tall grass, his throat pinching, his eyes stinging. Dennis might have been only twelve years old, but he knew what was happening. He had seen it before. He knew and yet he also knew he was utterly helpless when it came to preventing the obvious.

"I knew," he said, the tears now flowing. "I knew . . .

"I knew what was going to happen to him and I did . . . nothing."

Which is all the more reason why everyone from today's children with their Orange Shirt Days, federal and provincial politicians, church leaders from around the country and across the ocean, as well as those of us fortunate enough not to have gone to such schools, must now do . . . *something.*

JACK LAYTON AND
THE LOST MOUSTACHE

"I'll meet you just outside of Crossfield at the rail crossing at 1 p.m."

It was early June 2004, summer coming on and a federal election under way. I had been criss-crossing the country for weeks on end for the *Globe and Mail* and this particular day hoped to call on Myron Thompson, the member of Parliament for Wild Rose.

Most MPs will meet you in an office or a restaurant. Myron Thompson insisted on a gravel pull-off just outside the small town of Crossfield, a farm community about a half-hour drive north of Calgary.

His dusty Buick was there when I pulled off Highway 2A toward town. He was standing, back to the passenger-side window, leaning against the car and waving at all who passed by. He needed no sign to identify him or his Conservative Party. The big white cowboy hat was all the signature required in Alberta. Not a vehicle passed the man in the stetson and the balding reporter with the moustache without a vote by honk, many of them winding down their windows on the dusty road to shout encouragement at their grinning, barrel-chested, accidental politician:

"Hey, Myron!"

"How ya doin', Myron!"

"Good luck, Myron!"

How he got to this spot was itself a story. He grew up in Colorado and was good enough at baseball to be invited to the New York Yankees' spring training camp. He played catcher, but unfortunately so did Yogi Berra, who had the job, and Elston Howard, who wanted the job. "I didn't have a chance," he admitted.

He became a teacher, moved to Canada and ended up in the nearby community of Sundre in the late 1960s, soon becoming principal of the school.

He was outspoken and opinionated. Hated metric. Hated bilingualism. Hated the GST. Stay away from my guns, he'd say. Finally, one of the lads on coffee row said he should think about running for the Reform Party, to which Myron responded "What the hell's the Reform Party?"

He ran for Reform in 1993 and won the Wild Rose riding. He won it for the Alliance and, following the Alliance–Conservative merger, won it for the Conservatives and was about to win it again. He was now a career politician, what he called "the occupation that's the most hated in the entire country."

No one, however, seemed to hate Myron Thompson.

"How ya doin', Myron!"

"Afternoon, Myron."

"Myron!"

We talked baseball and health. First heart attack at forty-four, second at forty-eight, big one at fifty-four, another at sixty-one and a minor one at sixty-four. Brand-new pacemaker was doing wonders, he claimed. (He would live to eighty-two, dying in 2019.)

All the while, vehicles kept passing by, some honking, some yelling. Eventually, an empty flatbed truck passed us, the window rolled up tight in the dust. No honk for Myron Thompson.

Down the road a bit, the driver suddenly slammed on his brakes, gravel pebbles flying in all directions. Slamming the truck into reverse, the driver snaked back to where we stood talking. He rolled down the window to reveal an older farmer, baseball cap pulled down to the eyebrows, mouth cradling a lighted cigarette, which he removed before leaning out of the window.

"Myron Thompson!" he shouted, glaring first at the MP for Wild Rose, then at the reporter from another world.

"What the FUCK are you doing talking to Jack Layton?"

Myron Thompson grabbed his ample gut, bending over double and rolling along the side of the Buick until it seemed he would spin off into the ditch. He was howling with laughter as the farmer yanked out his smoke, spat, rolled up the window, and gunned the flatbed, wheels spitting up gravel like shrapnel.

Immediately upon my return to Ottawa, I shaved off the moustache.

1 0

———————

Unforgettable Characters

Over a half century of journalism, you are bound to meet a great many people. You become friends with some, enemies of some, reach mutual indifference with others. You will most certainly meet those who are simply unforgettable—talented colleagues who inspire you, feature subjects who change you, stories that rock you, shock you, amuse you and, yes, serve you well for a lifetime of chatter with friends and family.

These are a few I met along the way that I will never forget—and never wish to forget.

Christie Blatchford

She was the most difficult person I ever worked with, whether together or against each other. She was the hardest worker I have ever known in the business. She was also the softest person I have ever known—especially when it came to dogs.

Christie Blatchford, the late, legendary newspaper columnist, spent time at the *Sun* papers, the *National Post*, the *Globe and Mail* and PostMedia. We worked together at the *Post* and the *Globe* and knew each other since the mid-1970s. In the fall of 2000, we were colleagues at the *Post* and both of us were assigned to cover the Sydney Olympics.

She flew to Sydney from Toronto, I from Ottawa. She flew business class; I didn't. On that trip I learned to book along with her if going on any assignment together and, sure enough, when the next Olympics came around, Turin in 2006, we both had glorious business-class "pods" for the flight.

The Sydney Games would deliver great competition—Canadian Simon Whitfield winning gold in the triathlon, American Marion Jones winning three golds in track (only to be stripped of them years later after admitting to using performance-enhancing drugs in the lead-up to the Games)—but those matches would pale at times beside the battles that took place in the Main Press Centre. The only thing missing was a podium, but we all knew who would take the high middle seat if there were medals to hand out.

On September 15, Christie, Cam Cole and I went off to watch the opening ceremony. Cam, as our lead sports columnist, had been assigned to write a front-page piece on the event. First, however, we had to pick up our special passes at the Main Press Centre. Inside an envelope marked "National Post" were four passes—though we were only three.

There was no way to give the extra ticket back, so we decided to search for someone who would appreciate it. We found the perfect candidate taking a photograph of the stadium with one of those disposable cameras you no longer see. She had a tag around her neck identifying her as a volunteer. Her name was Dawn Gavin, and she was from Melbourne. Her husband, a retired firefighter, had stayed home to volunteer at the preliminary soccer matches being held at the Melbourne Cricket Ground. They were proud grandparents.

She thought we were pranking her. Tickets for the opening ceremony had been posted for sale for more than fourteen hundred Australian dollars. We convinced her it wasn't a prank. Blatch laughingly told her we'd tell people she was our "interpreter." She took the ticket, covered her mouth with her empty hand and slowly began to weep. She would cry again when Australian folk singer John Williamson led the 110,000-strong crowd in a powerful rendition of "Waltzing Matilda." So, too, would Blatch.

I gave Dawn my cell phone so she could call home. "You'll never guess where I am, Barry!" she shouted into the phone. "*I'm in the stadium.* Yes, at the opening ceremony. Yes, I am. *Really.* I'll wave to you on TV."

And so began a brilliant evening. It unfolded with a tribute to the stock horse, a domestic animal much admired and respected in Australia for its work ethic and pivotal importance in early ranching. A lone rider rode in; the horse, called Ammo, reared high, the rider cracked his whip like a rifle shot and suddenly 120 other stockmen and their horses roared into the stadium, the horses doing intricate steps and eventually forming the five Olympic rings.

Blatch melted. As she always deprecatingly said of herself, she was a sucker for puppy dogs and men in uniform. Military first and foremost (she would later win the Governor General's Literary Award for non-fiction for her book *Fifteen Days*, recounting her time reporting on the Canadian military's involvement in Afghanistan). After military came hockey players, first love of her sports reporting. Then came baseball and football. And today, from the moment she first laid eyes on them and squinted her nose in approval, the Aussie stockmen.

"I *have* to write this!" she shouted over the music—I think it was the music from the film *The Man from Snowy River*—and began flipping a notebook open and fumbling in her purse for a pen.

"*I have to do this story!*"

Cam looked at me wide-eyed. He was already taking notes. Blatch had to have noticed that he was the one who would be writing on this. I looked back and flinched. We had seen this before. In the business it is called "bigfooting," meaning a reporter or columnist higher up in the food chain will, from time to time, decide that a story is much too important to be left in the hands of those at a lower pay grade.

When it came to the Big Story, the front-page piece that everyone would be reading the next morning, Blatch would fight to the death to see her byline on it before anyone else's. She was simply being Blatch. She needed that front page the way others needed food, or blood—and from time to time blood would be at least metaphorically spilled. This looked like one of those times.

Blatch worked furiously on her notes as the opening ceremony continued. The Indigenous of the continent were celebrated with two hundred Indigenous women from central Australia, the "heart" of the country, dancing to protect the Games.

These were early days for cell phones for reporters, but Christie had flipped hers out and was calling back to the *Post* desk, demanding to speak to editor Martin Newland, a Brit beloved by Blatch as much for his handsome looks as for a foul mouth that was every bit the match of hers. Newland was an avid Blatchford fan but he also knew that, from time to time, issues could arise and mediation was required.

As Christie kept up her note-taking and calls back to the desk, Cam kept working. He had decided he would not back down. There would be no calls back to head office from Cam. Instead, he would continue working on his story, which would be told through the eyes of our guest, the weeping grandmother from Melbourne.

Then came the dramatic parade of the athletes: 199 nations, the athletes all fit and waving as they marched in behind their countries' flags. North and South Korea entered under a unification flag. The Olympic flag was then carried about the arena by eight former Australian Olympic champions before it was raised while the Olympic hymn was sung by a huge choir.

It was time for the lighting of the Olympic flame. To celebrate a century of women participating in the Games, the torch was handed from Australian woman Olympic medallist to medallist until, finally, it was placed in the hands of track star Cathy Freeman, world champion in the four-hundred-metre race. A woman, and Indigenous, Freeman was striking in a silver track suit as she leaned down and lit the cauldron, the flame fast rising until a computer error caused it to stall, suspended in mid-air, for more than three minutes before roaring up a water ramp to burn high above the stadium. The delay only added to the drama.

Blatch, too, was on fire. She had called and called and even screamed and cursed, but whoever was calling the shots back in Toronto stuck by the original plan: Cam was writing the opening ceremony. There would be only the one piece.

The following day, Cam's brilliant piece began on page 1 and turned inside. Christie was on page A20 with a diary of her arrival in Sydney, beginning with a trip on a curb that had sent her into a face plant; one hand bleeding and the other sprained. It had not been a good start.

She would not be beat again.

On the final day of the Sydney Games, Christie and I were walking together toward the Main Press Centre when, in tandem, our cell phones rang. My caller was Graham Parley, our beloved sports editor. Her caller was Martin Newland, the managing editor.

We were to catch the first available flight home.

Pierre Trudeau was dead.

In Ottawa, the lying in state was already under way when we arrived. Crowds were lining up well past the Centennial Flame to spend a few moments honouring the most colourful, controversial and longest-serving prime minister in generations. He had been Canada's major personality of the twentieth century and his passing was not only news, but also a once-in-a-lifetime national event that any reporter would kill to cover. In other words, Blatch would be on full attack to gain, and hold, the strategic hill that is the front page.

It was going to be a tough week. I knew that even before our plane touched down. Journalism history counts few victories such as Cam Cole scored at the opening ceremony. Far more often there would be a body count of those run over by the most driven reporter in the country.

Perhaps because I had served so many years on Parliament Hill, I was assigned the plum task of riding on the train that would carry Trudeau to Montreal for his funeral and burial. Blatch was enormously put out, even pointing out that family members had worked the rails and so it was in her blood. No, the editors said, we want you in Montreal for the arrival and the funeral. I got the train; she got the church. It was, to them, the logical choice, as no one had ever done weepers better than Christie Blatchford. She, on the other hand, had the perfect nose for news—and knew instinctively that the funeral train would be a most powerful experience.

Probably even page 1.

VIA train number 638 left Ottawa for Montreal. There were six cars: one for the media, one for the Mountie pallbearers, two for various officials and staff, one for family and friends and one, of course, for the coffin. The train would travel slowly—at an "especially dignified pace," as one official put it—passing through various small towns and villages before reaching its destination in Montreal.

It was a gorgeous early fall day, the sun shining, the fields brown. Ottawa civil servants have a natural inclination to control matters, and a decision had been made to bring, one by one, various Pierre Trudeau colleagues—people like former finance minister Marc Lalonde, Senator Jacques Hébert, former governor general Roméo LeBlanc—up to the media car and have us interview them about their thoughts and memories of the late prime minister. The problem was, this had been going on for days, as Pierre Trudeau lay in state. Hardly anyone who knew him had not been interviewed.

But what of those who had not known him? I was staring out the window as the train passed by the Ottawa-Carleton Transpo shops. Outside, standing by the fence in a single line, were a half-dozen mechanics, their grease-covered hands folded in front as if they were choir boys in this vast church that this day was all Canada.

At the small town of Casselman, an old farmer had stopped his tilling and stood dead centre in his field, his cap off and held over his heart. Older couples sat in lawn chairs at rail crossings. One man had climbed a tree and was waving a Canadian flag tied to a hockey stick. A woman stood at the sidings holding up a canoe paddle with a voyageur's scarf wrapped around it. At small towns, cub packs and legionnaires stood at attention and saluted. Justin and Alexandre, the late prime minister's two surviving sons, came and stood to each side of the vestibule between the family car and the domed coffin car and stared down in amazement at those who sometimes clapped, sometimes saluted, often wept.

There was a connection here that surprised many. Pierre Trudeau had been a loner, an intellectual, a millionaire, someone who once said to farmers, "Why should I sell your wheat?" Who once, in a limousine driving him late at night to a rally, stared out at the flickering farm lights and wondered aloud to an aide, "Whatever do they do?"

But they were clearly feeling his passing, both figuratively and literally. At the small eastern Ontario town of Alexandria, the train slowed significantly, there being such a large crowd by the station. There was a squeaking sound not unlike that heard when you dip a finger in water and run it around the rim of a wine glass. The sound grew and grew and we wondered if there was a mechanical problem, an axle grinding or something wrong with the engine.

And then we realized what it was. It was the hands of those in the front lines of the crowd. They were reaching out and touching the slow-moving train, their hands making a squeaking sound as skin passed along metal. They were *feeling* his passing.

Had Christie Blatchford been on board, she would have burst into tears. And she would not have been alone.

But she was not on board.

At least not literally.

Blatch wrote about the train ride anyway. "One hundred and 22 miles of Canada VIA Rail special train No. 638 travelled," she wrote, "a speck on the slender track which first stitched this frail and immense country together, and which, in its strange and singular way, did so again yesterday."

She wrote about the eastern Ontario and western Quebec country-side, the cavalcade of colour that is fall in those parts. She described "the light dappling painterly in the trees, the grasses this time of year wet until noon, fog hiding in the low places of farmers' fields." She even talked about the two engineers, Raymond Saumur, the lead engineer, Barry Halverson, the second engineer, both wearing dark funeral suits rather than their usual work clothes.

She found two people, Danielle Villeneuve and her aunt, Saundra Landriault, who had parked their car near the small town of Vars so they could see the train pass, and she described, in exquisite detail, "The white light first; the sounding of the whistle; the ding-ding of the wooden gate falling, its red light flashing . . ." As if she had been there.

I filed my piece about "The Hands of Alexandria" and the response from head office was enthusiastic. I knew I had the story of the day. But then Christie got on the phone, calling the editors, publisher—for all I knew even the owner. She *had* to have the front page.

This time they caved. The front was simply a powerful photograph of the train. My story was on A2, hers on A3, side by side, two stories of a single train ride by two reporters who had to have been there.

That's the sort of formidable force that was Christie Blatchford, the best reporter of her generation.

Billy Diamond

"There's a man here—and he insists on speaking to a reporter."

It was spring 1981 in the *Maclean's* Ottawa bureau. Our receptionist, Julie Van Dusen—who would soon move on to a fine career at the CBC—had opened the door to my office and somewhat sheepishly

stepped inside. She needed rescuing. It was unusual to have an unexpected visitor show up. As often as not, they were themselves unusual.

I left my office and found a large man with thick black hair and thick
glasses sitting on a chair by Julie's desk. It was our first meeting, neither
thinking this would become a friendship for life and an encounter that
would profoundly change my sense of the Canadian north. The stranger
stood quickly and introduced himself with a voice that seemed to
explode from the depths of a coal mine.

"My name's Billy Diamond," he said. "And I have a story for you."

He handed me a single sheet of paper. It was an announcement from
Indian and Northern Affairs Canada. "For Immediate Release," it said
at the top. "Agreement Reached on Yukon Indian Elders' Program."

The press release quoted the minister, the Honourable John Munro,
as saying, "I am extremely pleased with the progress of the Yukon Land
Claim negotiations to date and am particularly pleased with this opportunity to provide benefits to Yukon Indian elders."

It was obvious that this Mr. Diamond was himself Indigenous. I mis-
takenly thought he must be from the Yukon. Why else would he be
showing me this routine press announcement?

"I am the grand chief of the James Bay Crees," he thundered. "We
have had a land-claims settlement since 1975 and it has been broken
by this same federal government that is bragging about its settlements."

He shook the paper as if trying to snap the neck of a snake.

"John Munro is bragging about what Indian Affairs is doing for the
elders of the Yukon. But they are doing nothing, absolutely nothing,
for the Cree children of James Bay.

"The federal government is killing our children."

Two hours later, we were still sitting in my office. The grand chief of
the Crees of James Bay had come to Ottawa to raise an alarm over
children dying of a disease more common in developing countries. He
had gone first to the CBC, then to CTV. Neither gave him the time

of day. He had dropped in to *Maclean's* only because he saw the sign on the door as he made his way through the corridors of the National Press Building.

I was vaguely aware of the James Bay Agreement. Years earlier, the Quebec provincial government of Robert Bourassa had proudly announced the "Project of the Century," which would involve hydro-electric dams along several of the great rivers of northern Quebec. The dams would flood vast areas that for ten thousand years had been the traditional lands of the Cree—and no one had even bothered to ask the Cree what they thought of seeing whole villages, their traplines and hunting grounds and the graves of their ancestors under a man-made ocean of water.

The Cree, led by Billy Diamond, in 1975 a twenty-one-year-old chief from the village of Rupert's House (Waskaganish to the Cree), had led the fight against the project. At one point, with the help of dedicated Montreal lawyers, the Cree even had a court injunction to stop con-struction, forcing the federal and provincial governments to negoti-ate. In 1975, the James Bay and Northern Quebec Agreement became Canada's first modern land-claims settlement, with the Cree receiving $135 million and the Inuit of northern Quebec $90 million for allowing Hydro-Québec's massive project on the La Grande River to proceed.

But if they'd been happy with the settlement, why six years later was the grand chief calling foul?

Sitting in that little office off Sparks Street, Billy explained. The agreement had, in fact, been working just fine. New houses had been built in several of the villages. One of the villages had been relocated. Cree who wished to live on the land were actually being paid a per diem to trap.

All might be fine in Cree territory, but they were far from fine in Quebec City and Ottawa. As happens so often in this bumblebee of a country, a squabble broke out between the two governments, which had been working jointly on the construction of new housing and waste and water systems in the villages. The new homes had been completed and ditches had been dug for the sewer lines, but then, with everything ready for one final push to completion, all work had come to a halt just because the feds and the province got into one of their constitutional hissy fits over which government had jurisdiction over what.

The two levels of government stopped working together. The Cree were forced to resort to outhouses the first winter of the work shutdown. The outhouses worked fine in winter, but when the spring thaw came the frozen outhouse sludge melted, ending up in the ditches that had been dug the previous summer. The sludge worked its way, by gravity, down to the main town well and into the water system.

Just as women in some developing countries had been encouraged to do, the Cree women had turned away from breastfeeding and were using formula, which had to be mixed with water. There were "boil water" orders in effect, but there was also slippage. People began suffering from diarrhea; babies began to fall ill.

Billy and Elisabeth Diamond's fifth child, Philip, had become so ill that he had been transferred by air ambulance to the Sainte-Justine mother and child care centre in Montreal. The diagnosis for Philip confirmed the others: gastroenteritis infection. At one point, the parents were called into the room to say their farewells to the toddler. Billy had spoken to the semi-conscious baby in Cree, miraculously causing the child to rally. Philip was one of the lucky ones.

On August 10, 1980, Tommy Wapachee, a four-month-old baby from the village of Nemaska, died. Soon there were others. Five more babies were dead. Their little bodies were taken away for autopsies. One of the dead babies, the Cree claimed, had been returned to the family for burial wrapped in a green garbage bag.

I sat there stunned as this large man with the deep voice told the story that the CBC and CTV had passed on.

"We'll tell the story," I said to him. We exchanged contact information and he left. I immediately made a pitch to the Toronto office, where
editor Peter Newman and managing editor Rod McQueen decided
the right way to tell this story was to send me and photographer Brian
Willer to James Bay and report it properly.

Brian and I met at the Val-d'Or airport in northern Quebec, where I
had booked a single-engine plane to take us farther north to Waskaganish.
The snow had melted enough that the small planes had switched from
skis to wheels, and this would be the first flight in on tires. Word had
come by radio telephone that the runway was clear and solid.

The plane was a Piper Cub four-seater, Brian and I in the back seat
and the young male pilot alone in front. We took off and climbed high
over the endless stands of black spruce and what seemed like more
water than land as bogs and wetlands sent sunlight sparkling everywhere as we looked down and headed out over a string of twisting lakes
and rivers. The currents below were visible in the white jumble of rapids;
the currents above were kicking the little plane around like a kid with
a soccer ball in the driveway, but soon we climbed through the pockets
and levelled out into a smooth ride with the roar of the engine making
conversation difficult, if not impossible.

We had been flying for a couple of hours before Brian poked me and
indicated that I should check out the pilot.

"*He's asleep!*" Brian mouthed.

I leaned forward and turned for a proper look. The pilot was indeed
asleep, his eyes closed tight—yet the plane was flying perfectly in a
locked-in position.

I tapped the pilot's shoulder hard a couple of times and he jolted
awake and went back to checking instruments and looking busy, as if
nothing at all had happened.

Welcome to air travel in the north.

———

We landed at Waskaganish on the gravel runway. The pilot turned the Piper around and taxied back to the small Quonset-style shed that served as the hangar. No one was there to greet us, but the hangar manager had information for us.

The grand chief and his entire family were out for the spring goose hunt. We asked if we could drive to it and he shook his head no. "It's on an island," he said.

I panicked. What were we to do? I had personally made arrangements to arrive on this day and thought that it was all set.

"Billy says you can come out by helicopter."

"Helicopter? *Where are we going to get a helicopter?*"

The hangar manager pointed to the other side of the shed, where a helicopter sat idle. We were told it was mostly used by Hydro-Québec for checking hydro lines, but that the pilot was in town and was only too happy to rent it out. He often flew families to their hunt camps and traplines.

We spoke to the pilot and he agreed to fly us out to the island. It would take about an hour both ways and the price of rental was $572 an hour. I made an executive decision to do it, there being no way to call Toronto and ask permission.

We were soon flying low over the village, the tiny white church and the graveyard on the edge of the bay, where the Rupert River empties into the yawning mouth of James Bay. It was quick and exhilarating and Brian was getting quite excited about the possibilities for powerful photographs.

Billy Diamond and his father, Malcolm, came walking to greet us as the helicopter landed and we disembarked, the chopper immediately taking off again to get back to the village. We were introduced and Billy advised us that Malcolm spoke only Cree.

Billy suggested we go into the cabin and have some tea, then go out on the frozen bay to a place where the family had built a large goose blind out of snow and ice. Brian said he'd stay outside and set up for some photographs.

We were inside barely sipping our tea when Brian suddenly appeared at the doorway. He had a light and an extension cord wrapped about his shoulder.

"Where can I plug in?" he asked.

I thought the grand chief of the James Bay Cree was going to split a gut laughing. So, too, was Malcolm howling.

"Plug in?" Billy howled. "You think we have electricity out here? James Bay may be the biggest hydroelectric project in the world—but we're still on propane!"

We stayed for days on the island. We huddled in the goose blind, surrounded by goose decoys, and Billy told his whole long story between periodically holding his hand over his mouth to form a trumpet and sending long "*Krrraaaack!!! Krraacckk!!*" calls into air in the hopes of luring one of the dozens of flocks of Canadian geese passing overhead to come back down to earth. If they came close enough, Malcolm and Billy wheeled onto their backs and fired their shotguns into the landing chevron, invariably killing two or three that Malcolm would then gather up while Billy returned to his tale.

He told me he had been born Bileesh Diamond on Malcolm's trapline, it being too late in the spring for the family to cross the frozen Rupert River and back to the village for the birth. Malcolm had cut the umbilical cord with his hunting knife. Billy talked about growing up on the trapline and about his time at residential school in Moose Factory. He, of course, had not wanted to go and had to be forced onto the float plane and tied into a back seat for the flight to the school. He hated the residential school, where the Anglican Church teachers had forbidden him to speak Cree, only English, of which he knew little. They refused to let him see his older sister, who had gone to the residential school the year before him. The first evening at the school, the nuns had tried to force him to eat his vegetables by not letting him leave the table until he had—as a stubborn eight-year-old, he had outwaited them and won his first serious negotiation.

Billy told me he had dreamed of becoming a lawyer and had, in fact, been lying in a goose blind right here in the spring of 1970 when Bourassa announced the "Project of the Century." Quebec, the premier announced, would flood eleven thousand square kilometres of northern Quebec and build a massive, sixteen-billion-dollar, sixteen-thousand-megawatt hydroelectric plant and dam on the La Grande River.

Billy had come back from high school in the northern Ontario city of Sault Ste. Marie with a little transistor radio and had been listening to the CBC newscast. It was the first the Cree had heard of any such plans. As he and other Cree would say, "Only the beavers have the right to build dams in our territory."

Malcolm, known as the "Shouting Chief" to the people of Waskaganish, pushed his son to run for chief and, at twenty-one, Billy suddenly found himself leading the Cree charge against Bourassa's grandiose hydro scheme. Billy and his friends Robert Kanatewat and Ted Moses organized a meeting of the leaders of the seventy-five hundred Cree along James Bay. They held it at a one-room schoolhouse in Mistassini. Some came by canoe, some walked. It was the first collective meeting of the five Cree communities in their living memory.

Billy spread out maps he had acquired and began to show the assembled leaders where traplines and ancestral graves would be lost—only to be interrupted by an older man standing at the back of the room.

"First thing we have to do," the older man told the gathering, "is buy an electric typewriter."

"But none of us even knows how to type!" Billy protested.

The man looked at him, incredulous: "And that, Billy, is why we need an *electric* one."

From that little gathering the James Bay Cree gradually became a force to be reckoned with. When Billy arranged for elders to come to Montreal and testify as to where the ancestral lands were, the elders refused to get on the jet that had been chartered to pick them up. This being the start of the 1970s, most northerners were familiar only with the bush planes that serviced isolated communities. The older Cree pointed at the jet and laughed, one of them explaining to Billy that there was no way any of them were going to board a plane "that has no propeller!"

Eventually, however, the groundbreaking settlement was reached. The Cree had their $135 million and now had their own school board and were making great progress in health care. They were looking at creating their own airline and would, eventually, find great success with Air Creebec. They had new housing being built—right up until construction stopped and the babies began dying.

As Billy told me his astonishing story over a long couple of days, Brian Willer took spectacular photographs of the island, the hunt camp and the surrounding landscape. He finally persuaded Billy to pose with his shotgun, sitting by a blazing fire at the camp on a dark evening, the scene eerily lighted from the front by Brian's use of lamps and, mercifully, a battery, courtesy of the goose camp.

Billy looked fierce and determined, the gun threatening. Inside, he was laughing so hard at the image that it required multiple takes.

Maclean's loved the story and Brian's photographs. They put the menacing Billy photo on the cover and titled it "Rumbles from the North." Peter Newman wrote a scathing editorial to go along with it. The Cree were getting nowhere with their lawsuits against the Quebec government or through meetings on Parliament Hill, one of which ended up with Billy Diamond screaming at John Munro about "dead babies" being on his conscience. The Cree managed to meet with Jean Chrétien, formerly minister of Indian Affairs. Chrétien would play a key role in reaching the 1975 agreement.

The *Maclean's* story was seen across the country and could not be ignored by those in a position to do something. It stands, even today, as evidence of what can happen when governments meddle with Indigenous lands in the mistaken belief that they know better than the people who live on that land.

Soon after the story appeared, Grand Chief Billy Diamond set off for Geneva, Switzerland, for what was to be the first United Nations conference on Indigenous people and land. He tabled the *Maclean's* cover story.

The federal government had commissioned John Tait, a lifelong bureaucrat, to conduct a full review of the situation. His report ran to 126 pages and was sympathetic to the Crees' plight. At the end of June 1982, a year after the magazine story had appeared, the federal cabinet voted to pay out $61.4 million to remedy the housing situation.

Billy called that night with the news.

"Congratulations!" I said.

"No," he replied. "Congratulations to you—no *Maclean's* cover, no settlement. That story saved lives."

And so began a thirty-year friendship. Multiple times I travelled to James Bay and often Billy came to Ottawa. We fished together on Gods Lake in Manitoba. We went on a mission across the bay to Winisk on the Ontario side to get supplies after severe flooding had threatened the village and ruined its water supply. His son Sandy and our son Gord fished together and became friends.

Whenever possible, I tried to sell a story on the James Bay Cree to whatever publication I happened to be working for—a typical journalist forever in search of angles to get someone else to pay for your fun. The *Toronto Star* sent me up to Waskaganish to do a feature and editor Lou Clancy came along for the ride . . . and adventure. The *Star* also approved a later business feature on a joint venture between the giant

Yamaha company of Japan and the James Bay Cree to build the sort of seaworthy canoes the Hudson's Bay Company had once built in a now-abandoned factory on the banks of the Rupert River. Only these canoes would be modern, made of fibreglass, and they would be sold around the world.

Billy wanted me to have one of the first runs in the new craft. With Doug Sprott, a friend of mine from Ottawa, and Charlie Diamond, Billy's brother, and Billy's friend Lawrence Katapatuk, we set out to test the boat on the waters of James Bay in late June, only to run into a fierce blizzard late Friday afternoon that forced us to wait it out for three nights on little Obedjiwan Island. The CBC's *Morningside* show had arranged for Peter Gzowski to interview Billy Monday morning about the joint venture with the Japanese company, but when *Morningside* called, Billy had to tell them the boat was "lost at sea." When the four of us made it back to Waskaganish later that day, Billy was standing on the wharf holding his gut he was laughing so hard.

"Weren't you worried about us?" I asked, incredulous.

"Of course not," he howled. "You were with Cree hunters!"

His sense of humour was, in fact, as much a part of his success as his fine mind. People took to him, laughed with him, liked him.

When he retired as grand chief, the people presented him with a set of golf clubs, which he tried out several times at a course at Val-d'Or. He kept losing golf ball after golf ball in the bush off the fairways. "Then I discovered why they get lost in the bush," he laughed. "They're *white!*"

Penguin Books Canada expressed interest in a book on Billy Diamond and his modern leadership. Billy was most agreeable and we spent months talking and interviewing both in Waskaganish and Ottawa. Billy was impressively loquacious when it came to funny anecdotes, political personalities and issues—he had such a photographic memory it seemed some chapters were dictated rather than molded and formed— but each time I approached the deeply personal stuff, he balked.

Finally, Elisabeth stepped in and told him if he didn't tell the whole story there was no point in doing a book. We met for a weekend at his home in Waskaganish and he opened up about his drinking—I had been witness to enough of that to know it was a problem—and his dark side. He talked about how Elisabeth's support, and his experience as part of an Indigenous delegation that met with the Pope, had helped him find God. Now born again, he was finally able to shake free of the demons that he had carried home from residential school.

The book, *Chief: The Fearless Vision of Billy Diamond*, was published in 1989 and was wonderfully well received. It is still used by the Cree as a basic text on the history of the people and, most significantly, on the fight to reach the James Bay Agreement. I will be forever indebted to Billy and the James Bay Cree for letting me tell their story.

In 2009, at the age of sixty, Billy suffered a stroke. To relieve pressure on the brain, doctors in Montreal removed a part of his skull entirely. They kept it and, months later, operated again to put his skull back together. Billy thought it hilarious that he was now the "first grand chief ever scalped."

In September 2010, however, he was watching television in his new home in Waskaganish—the first new home he and Elisabeth would own—when he suffered a second stroke. He did not even close his eyes or slouch in his chair, but he was dead. The reason it was noticed at all was because, for once, he was so quiet you could hear a pin drop.

To the very end of his days, he had never eaten a vegetable.

I returned to Waskaganish for the funeral with Marsha Smoke, Billy's long-time assistant; Jim O'Reilly, the Crees' lawyer during the James Bay battle; Brian Craig and other friends from Ottawa and Montreal. We flew on Air Creebec, the airline Billy Diamond founded with the help of the Deluce family of Timmins and Air Ontario. Both pilots for this flight were Cree, just as Billy had once predicted.

They held the funeral in the Waskaganish Gathering Place, the community hall packed to overflowing. Billy's nephew John Paul Murdoch told the gathering that Billy was so well known for his powerful voice that "even when we were hunting, it was almost as if the geese would line up to be shot, so they wouldn't get yelled at."

Jim O'Reilly spoke magnificently about Billy's achievements from the James Bay Agreement on. He had been the key strategist—dealing with the likes of Pierre Trudeau, René Lévesque and Jean Chrétien—behind the 1983 amendment that enshrined Indigenous rights in the Canadian constitution. O'Reilly listed some of the Cree leader's achievements: their own health board, school board, a per diem for trappers, Air Creebec, and a Cree company to build transmission lines and manage forestry projects in northern Quebec. In 2002 Billy had helped negotiate the Eastmain–Rupert hydroelectric project that led to a $1.4-billion settlement with the federal government. "Negotiating beats blockading roads, it beats blockading bridges, it beats blockading railroads," Billy said when that deal was signed.

Canada had celebrated him with honorary degrees and the Order of Canada. He was made a chevalier of the Ordre national du Québec. He was the first person inducted into the Aboriginal Business Hall of Fame. But what mattered most to him was what his own people thought. Matthew Coon Come, former National Chief of the Assembly of First Nations, said, "My Indian friends from India had Mahatma Gandhi. My American friends had JFK. My Afro-American friends had Martin Luther King. My South African friends had Nelson Mandela. My Cree Nation had Chief Billy Diamond."

Taking turns, they carried his coffin through the streets, past the school that he built to ensure that no one would ever again be flown away to a place where far, far worse could happen than a standoff over vegetables. They carried Billy Diamond to the little graveyard down by the bluffs overlooking the Rupert River's steady roll into James Bay. The entourage walked on paved streets in front of modern housing with full water and waste facilities, all possible because of this one leader. Elders sat in wheelchairs, weeping as the coffin passed. Young mothers held up their babies to see. Teenagers wearing rap T-shirts wiped the sting from their eyes.

They listed eighty-nine pallbearers on the service pamphlet. If it takes an entire village to raise a child, then it seemed only right that it took this entire village to bury its chief.

It had rained heavily during the service, but when they opened the doors, they found a rainbow had spread over the town.

They placed him in a fresh grave with a simple wooden cross and took turns filling in the earth.

In a few months, it would be replaced with a tombstone bearing an inscription on the back side of the stone that he had specifically requested his son Ian to arrange.

"Gone to a meeting—will return."

Postscript: In 2021 a group of Billy Diamond's friends, including Marsha Smoke, executive director of the Grand Council of the Crees of James Bay Bill Namagoose, long-time civil servant David Tobin and two early reporters on the James Bay Project, Bill Fox and me, helped put together the Chief Billy Diamond Scholarship. The initial endowment of $150,000 will be managed by Indspire and is intended to provide support for Indigenous post-secondary students enrolled in business, commerce, management or leadership programs.

Barbara Amiel

In the late fall of 1977, I returned to *Maclean's* for what would be the second of three stints. I was listed as a senior editor along with David Cobb, Robert Marshall and Robert Miller. There were three senior writers on the masthead: Angela Ferrante, Michael Posner and Barbara Amiel.

Peter Newman had been busy hiring as he began the transformation of the old monthly into a biweekly and, ultimately, weekly newsmagazine. The design department was expanding, and space on the seventh floor of 281 Dundas Street was at a premium. Managing editor Kevin

Doyle walked me down the hallway to my new office, which had two desks in it, each with a telephone.

Doyle turned, his Irish roots crinkling his eyes with mischief.

"You'll be sharing your office with Barbara Amiel."

Newman had hired Amiel in the mid-1970s and liked to claim he invented her, turning a relatively unknown freelancer into a national columnist who would go on to become editor of the *Toronto Sun* and later, in London, a highly controversial columnist for the *Sunday Times*. He also liked to say he invented her future husband, Conrad Black, writing positively about the young businessman long before Black became a media mogul and, eventually, Lord Black of Crossharbour— and she Baroness Black. They would be described in the British press as "London's most glamorous power couple."

This, of course, was many years before Lord Black went to prison in 2007 for fraud and obstruction of justice (sentenced in a Chicago court-room to seventy-eight months' imprisonment and later pardoned by US president Donald Trump), and it was long, long before 2020, when Lady Black would publish her 610-page *Friends and Enemies: A Memoir*. She had led, undoubtedly, a fascinating life—but she also was seeking revenge against those she had battled with along the way.

She was young, beautiful and flamboyant when working at *Maclean's*. In his 2004 memoir, *Here Be Dragons*, Newman wrote about hiring so many young writers, mostly women, for his weekly newsmagazine. Amiel, he said, wanted to be taken seriously as a writer but he felt undermined herself with her behaviour. "You don't advertise your intellect by sashaying to work in thigh-high boots, a tight sweater tucked into tighter jeans held up by a heavy leather belt dripping with metal studs," he wrote. "She proclaimed that clothes were her 'sexual armour,' which didn't really justify her wardrobe, since it was a come-on instead of a deterrent."

People, often her colleagues, called her "Babs" behind her back. They whispered that she had had a nose job (apparently true) and a boob job, which she vehemently denied. "If I used silicone," she told one fellow worker, "my breasts would be twice as big. I don't do things by half."

In mornings when we might both be at the office, I could tell if she had beaten me in just by sniffing the air. She wore perfume that would cause a nose with fragrance sensitivity to go into septic shock. Long after she sailed down the office corridor her aroma would linger in the air like a jet contrail on a windless summer day. She wrote about perfume for the magazine ("The Sweet Smell of Decadence," October 22, 1979) raving about Yves Saint Laurent's Opium ($125 an ounce), Bal à Versailles ($175 an ounce) and Jean Patou's Mille ($275 an ounce). When Salon.com profiled her in 2004, the feature was headlined "An extravagance that knows no bounds." After the Blacks' fall from grace in the US courts, a British comedy group produced a parody of the couple selling their own brands of perfume, "Slut" for Barbara, "Vermin" for Conrad.

People joked about her mid-Atlantic accent, dismissing it as phony, but it was, in fact, earned. She had been born in England to a well-to-do Jewish family but spent her teen years in Hamilton, Ontario, where her stepfather (her parents had divorced) struggled with work. She claimed her own mother "loathed" her and she was largely on her own from age fourteen on, picking up part-time jobs and eventually making it to the University of Toronto, where she took philosophy and English literature. She bounced around in various TV jobs—researcher, editor, some on-air work—before Newman offered her a full-time job at *Maclean's* in 1976.

He may well have invented her, but it seemed in his memoir that he must have regretted it. "She was among the most difficult columnists *Maclean's* ever had in its stable, which takes in a lot of territory," Newman wrote in *Here Be Dragons*. "She was a misery for the editorial desk, a second-guesser of headline choices, a whining pest over each lost comma or adjective, and a drama queen who made a point of milking every situation for its maximum emotional impact."

She certainly had an emotional impact on some of the staff. One senior editor, in particular, was like a mooning twelve-year-old around her, endlessly coming to the doorway of our shared office and all but whining like a puppy for attention. She clearly had no interest in him; he was clearly obsessed with her. It was embarrassing to witness.

Sometimes her then husband, George Jonas, would show up dressed head to toe in black leather, motorcycle helmet under one arm. George fancied himself a poet and played the part to perfection, speaking careful English with a Hungarian accent, even smoking through an impossibly long, silver-tipped cigarette holder. He drank the smoke as much as drew it in.

The gossip around the office was that the marriage was in trouble, and they soon divorced, though remained friendly. It was her second failed marriage. A third would also fail in England. Lord Crossharbour would be her fourth, and it would last.

"I just love sex," she happily confessed in her 2020 memoir. "I once counted the number of partners I've had . . . don't even ask!"

She was spending a great deal of time with a Toronto travel agent during the time we shared quarters at *Maclean's*. There were affairs in London that she spoke openly of in her book. One, in particular, was with the elderly George Weidenfeld, Lord Weidenfeld, a well-known British publisher. "Though I loved every minute with George," she wrote, "I not only had no sexual interest in him—I had a positive revulsion. I was trying to hang on to the social advantages he gave me without incurring the payment required sexually. . . . The only way I could deal with it was to avoid actual body-to-body contact and pleasure him orally."

She did indeed have a potty mouth. She was irreverent, funny, shocking at times. Once, after an impromptu staff birthday gathering, she ate some cake and then immediately threw up in a trash can. She talked openly about her insecurities.

I have to say I found her delightful and good company during those few months we shared space on the seventh floor. There was none of the prima donna, none of the drama queen. She was professional and polite and we got on fine.

In June 1978, I transferred to the Ottawa bureau, as Peter Newman wanted a feature writer stationed there for when the magazine went to a weekly format in September.

I left the week that a new *Maclean's* cover was on the stands, a young businessman staring out with a fierce determination.

Conrad Black.

Earl McRae

I formed an early, and very bad, first impression of the person I today think of as one of the greatest friends of my life.

Earl McRae wrote as if he'd been moving about in the back pocket of whatever sports celebrity he was profiling, which seemed to me an impossibility. He put himself into stories—sometimes as the star of the story. He was loud, controversial, an agitator and a character. He was far more in keeping with a flashy style of American sports journalism than the steady, sensible and shy Canadian approach. I now think had he been American he would have been a superstar among the ranks of Red Smith, Jim Murray, Jimmy Cannon, Ring Lardner, Leonard Koppett, maybe even Grantland Rice and Damon Runyon. Americans would have embraced him; Canadians too often dismissed him.

In February 1975 I followed Don Obe from *Maclean's* to *The Canadian* magazine. Don had landed the job of editor at Canada's largest weekend supplement and he wanted me to join him. I would be moving from mostly editing at the monthly magazine to full-time writing at *The Canadian*. Don and I shared a poor opinion of the look-at-me McRae style of writing and I was under the impression that once Don took over at the weekend publication, he would soon show McRae the door.

As I settled into my new job, I would find Earl had the office next to me in the Simpson Building on Bay, where the rotogravure was put together each week. He was friendly when we met. Late twenties, dark curly hair, glasses perched perfectly on his head—something I had never mastered—a bow tie and a flashy sports jacket. His bottom lip usually preceded his upper. In fact, he liked to call himself "the Lip," but that had more to do with mouthing off than with facial structure.

I don't know when he worked. He clearly had ADHD years before anyone used that term. He sat in his office drawing caricatures of the people he was writing about and the people he worked with. He chain-smoked (most journalists seemed to in those days) and he liked nothing better than to burst through your office door and throw you completely off your game.

Earl pestered me incessantly about Don Obe, his new boss and, as he well knew, my good friend. He wanted to know everything: what Obe thought, what he read, drank, laughed at, worried over. Obe and he had been discussing a story—a weeper about some hockey enforcer who'd fallen on hard times—and McRae was on fire with enthusiasm. I thought his excitement kind of sad, a bit pathetic, as I presumed he wasn't long for the magazine.

Two weeks later Don Obe called me into his office, closed the door and handed me a large packet of typed pages. McRae's name was at the top. "Have a read of this," Don said. He left the room then, leaving me sitting there alone to read what was the finest sports profile I had ever read. It was about Reggie Fleming coming to terms with the end of an eighteen-year career as a hockey brawler in the NHL, WHA and, finally, a league no one had ever heard of deep in the heart of Wisconsin. It was, as Don later titled the piece, a "Requiem for Reggie." A true classic in Canadian journalism.

Earl's feature on Reggie was a remarkable study in character and setting. It was also, in retrospect, about forty years ahead of its time in its harsh and riveting detailing of the effect of fist-pummelling on the hockey brain. A generation later, scientists at Boston University would confirm, through research, what McRae had already shown in words. Reggie Fleming had chronic traumatic encephalopathy (CTE)—brain damage.

The profile was so vivid—Reggie's mother, his coaches, his team-mates, even his dog—that I thought much of it had to be fiction. The description of Reggie's twisted and ruined hands alone seemed surreal. But Brian Willer, the superb photographer who had accompanied McRae on the trip to Wisconsin, backed up every detail. I had to concede that the story was brilliant. I also knew, instantly, that Earl McRae was not about to be canned, but would go on, with Don Obe's encouragement, to write many more magnificent features for the magazine.

My dislike of Earl soon turned to envy. Working next door I could hear him working the phones. He didn't make one or two calls extra, as I might have done, and not three, five or ten, either, but twenty and more. I became a better journalist by following the example set by the one they called "Earl the Pearl." We were soon close friends, my ill-considered envy parked and forgotten.

Earl had so many talents. His caricatures were devastating. The morning after then transport minister Otto Lang sued the magazine and me for my controversial profile on him that had been banned in Saskatchewan, I arrived to find a searing portrait of myself shaking behind prison bars. He could do voices and mimic actions. Within a couple of months his impersonations of Don Obe—stuttering, sputtering, always looking for his pack of cigs—had everyone, Obe included, in tears. He liked to call himself the "lippy little shin kicker" and he could be devastatingly funny.

The stories about him were often as good as the stories he wrote. During the 1976 Canada Cup, the magazine arranged to have a young Denis Potvin record his thoughts daily on a tape recorder and produce a "diary" of this first truly international tournament featuring the best hockey players in the world.

Before the tournament began, an earlier McRae profile of Team Canada leader Phil Esposito had appeared—a portrait that several times mentioned Phil's efforts at covering up a spreading bald spot. Esposito didn't like it and, never one to take things quietly, he began calling the magazine's Toronto office—this being in the glory days before e-mail, cell phones or even voice messaging—and Earl simply let the calls build into a pile of ignored pink phone slips. He instructed the magazine receptionist—for those with no historical reference, these were human beings, usually women, who actually answered ringing telephones—to never, ever, allow one of Esposito's calls to go through to him.

At one point, while we were meeting with Potvin at Maple Leaf Gardens to retrieve a cassette (another historical oddity), Potvin warned McRae that "Phil is steaming" and had sworn to get some revenge. By chance, Esposito happened to walk out of the stick room just then and began moving in our direction. McRae bolted, knocking over an elderly Gardens employee as he rounded the corner. I was left to pick up the cassette *and* the poor employee.

Esposito called the magazine again the following day, and finally the receptionist told McRae to "deal with it."

So he did. He had the receptionist put through the next call but persuaded her to tell Esposito that the publisher wished to speak with him. Earl put on the deep voice of a phantom publisher and, in a very grave manner, he informed "Mr. Esposito" that, sadly, "Mr. McRae passed away suddenly yesterday morning."

Those of us standing around could hear the player sputtering over the phone. *"What did he say?"* Earl was asked when he quietly placed the receiver back down.

"He asked that his condolences be passed on to the family."

Earl was a sentimentalist when it came to family. He told me he had but one memory of his father, Earl Piche. He is floating in the air above his father's laughing head as the elder Earl, in army uniform, tosses his little boy over and over and over. The older Earl never came back from the Second World War. He talked about taking the old Ottawa streetcar out to Britannia Beach with his grandfather and how the old man would sit and read a newspaper while Earl played in the sand and swam.

Ellen and I were beginning our family then and Earl and Pat, already with three boys and a girl, made their Bolton home our weekend getaway. I remember how, on Christmas Eve, he went up onto the roof with skis over his shoulder and made ski tracks in the snow so that Jill, Bob, Neil and Dave could see exactly where Santa had landed.

Years after we had moved to Ottawa, I was working at the *Citizen* and the paper was looking for a general sports columnist. Earl's marriage was breaking down and when he heard about the opening he rushed to the capital and landed the job. We were now colleagues. I wrote columns on the new hockey team, and Earl wrote about everything from football to boxing to the Olympics. He became, instantly, the most interesting and entertaining character in Ottawa sports. There wasn't a coach or player in town he couldn't impersonate perfectly, whether it be his great pal, football coach Leo Cahill, or the insufferable goaltender Tom Barrasso, who played briefly for the Senators and ended up looking forward to Earl's out-of-the-blue questions.

He had a style like no one else in the business. Another great Canadian sportswriter, Trent Frayne, once said that "McRae gets a piece of people no one else seems to by hiding behind a facade of helplessness, a sort of blissful ignorance that gets them talking freely."

He could also be tough with his words. In 1988, the day after Ben Johnson was stripped of his gold medal for using performance-enhancing drugs, Earl's column read only, "Thanks, Ben, you bastard!" with the rest of the column nothing but blank space. Protesters filled the *Citizen* parking lot that day, but McRae neither apologized nor backed down.

Earl married again, this time to broadcaster Bev Bowman, and they had a daughter, Caitie. He seemed to his peers to be the only one of us travelling backward in time, never aging, refusing, it always seemed, ever to grow up. He eventually left the *Citizen* for the *Ottawa Sun*, where he wrote a general column.

"Earl the Pearl" was sixty-nine when he died suddenly of a heart attack in the fall of 2011. He had just returned from covering the funeral of a cyclist who had been struck and killed by a motorist. His last word was a loud "*Fuck!*" as he collapsed on the newsroom floor.

Perhaps his heart burst because it was too full. He loved life with a passion that few could ever match.

As David Cobb said when he heard the news: "A light has gone from the lives of all who knew him. He wrote some of the most marvellous stories I've ever read."

Hear, hear—he was brilliant, talented, and so very much fun. At his best, he was simply the best sportswriter in the country.

Val Sears

In early 1984, I was working out of the *Toronto Star*'s Ottawa bureau. *Today* magazine, the new name for *The Canadian*, the weekend supplement carried by the *Star* and Southam papers across the country, had stopped publication on August 28, 1982. There were dozens of us magazine types now out of work. I had freelanced for half a year but pay was unsteady, nerve-racking for a young family expecting another child that fall, which would make four kids under the age of six. I needed to find regular, steady work.

Senator Keith Davey, who had introduced me to Peter Newman a dozen years earlier, called out and offered to connect me with Gary Lautens, the new editor-in-chief of the *Star*. I headed off on the train to Toronto. Gary, for many years a nationally beloved humour columnist at the paper, was warm and welcoming, offering me a three-day-a-week column on the second page of the newspaper. I immediately and gratefully accepted, though the prospect was intimidating. I had at that point never written for a newspaper; nor had I ever written a column. Page 2 already had Joey Slinger and Frank Jones as columnists. And I'd have to move the family from Ottawa to Toronto. For several months, I stayed with sister Ann in her one-room apartment near Allan Gardens. Over the summer, Ellen and I moved our family, now six of us, to a four-bedroom home in nearby Oakville, where I could catch a GO train that would take me almost to the front door of the *Star* building on One Yonge Street.

Working at the *Star* was a delight. I could write columns on any topic I wished—politics, sports, family, absurdities, tragedies, whimsy. A promising young reporter, Lindsay Scotten, invited Joey and me out to dinner early on and we had a fine time. Lindsay told me years later she had been asked by the editor to do this—to make sure there was no friction between the younger page 2 columnists. There was none. We got on wonderfully for the less than two years I worked at One Yonge.

Oakville was fine and the commute easy, but I pined for Ottawa, the rivers, the parks and the small-town feel. An opening came up in the *Star*'s parliamentary bureau and I asked Gary if I might be considered. He was happy to accommodate my wishes. Ottawa bureau chief Bob Hepburn was less happy, not at all pleased to have a prima donna magazine features writer and columnist come to a daily news operation, but we ended up playing hockey in the same beer league and soon became good friends.

The bureau was eclectic. Joel Ruimy, Joe O'Donnell, David Vienneau and Bruce Ward were reporters working the Hill and Question Period. Carol Goar had been part of the bureau but left to become bureau chief of *Maclean's*. The political columnist was the esteemed Richard Gwyn, with his courtly British accent and knowledge of absolutely everything and anyone of any import in Ottawa. The senior political reporter, even more intimidating, was Val Sears, a tall man with silver hair, elegant and well-spoken, with a tongue as sharp as the stylish hats and suits he preferred.

Val had been a legend in Canadian journalism for as long as I had been reading Canadian journalism. He had been a lead character in the infamous "newspaper wars" of the 1950s, when the *Toronto Star* and *Telegram* battled for supremacy in the GTA. It had been Sears who engineered one of the greatest scoops ever in 1954, when his first-person feature on Marilyn Bell's swim across Lake Ontario appeared on the front page of the *Tely*—when Bell was supposedly under exclusive contract to the *Star*. In 1988, he would recount these tales in his memoir, *Hello Sweetheart . . . Get Me Rewrite*.

Val Sears was a role model for a vast array of familiar bylines in this country, a journalist who could report well and write beautifully and was fearless. He was foreign correspondent, political reporter, feature writer and even, for a while, science reporter, who proudly claimed he'd won a National Newspaper Award for "rewriting a news release." He was, above all, a storyteller. He took no prisoners, played no favourites. Covering a federal election campaign back in the Diefenbaker–Pearson era, Sears is forever remembered for his loud challenge to the Parliamentary Press Gallery: "To work, gentlemen, we have a government to overthrow."

Covering Progressive Conservative leader Joe Clark during the 1979 election that Clark won, Val was greeted at the launch of the campaign and asked by the soon-to-be-prime-minister how long he might have the pleasure of Val's company.

"As long as it takes, sir," Val responded.

Invited to my birthday party, he made the long drive from downtown Ottawa to our Kanata suburb, where we still had two of our children in diapers. Asked by Ellen if he had any trouble finding the place, he looked down his long nose and said, "Not at all, my dear—I merely looked for the chlorine cloud above the house."

His wit was renowned. If someone produced a new book, he would say "I will waste no time getting to it." He claimed to read only Canadian political books that mentioned him and would immediately turn to the index of any new book to check for his name. Southam's long-time Ottawa columnist Charles Lynch gave Val a bit of his own when he inserted "Val Sears" in the index of his memoirs, *You Can't Print That*, but when Val joyously flipped to the reference page, his name was nowhere to be found.

Prime Minister Pierre Trudeau had decided to retire, for a second time, and the Liberal Party of Canada would be holding a leadership convention in Ottawa on June 16, 1984. John Turner, the once finance minister and a previous leadership candidate in 1968, when Trudeau had won, was so much the perceived front-runner that the race was seen more as a crowning than a contest. His main rival was Jean Chrétien, also a former Trudeau cabinet minister, but Chrétien was not then seen as much of a threat. (Turner would win easily on the second ballot, but would serve as prime minister only from June 30 to September 17, the second shortest tenure in office of all prime ministers, with only Charles Tupper serving a shorter time. Turner would never get to sit in Parliament as prime minister.)

Gary Lautens had an idea. He wanted me to do the largest, longest profile of the prime-minister-to-be—and we'd run it just before the convention. Gary wanted me to head out on the road with Turner as soon as possible, and I was all for it. Problem was, our senior political writer was already on the road with Turner. I would be travelling with Val Sears, and who knew if I would be welcome? We had gotten on fine in the office, but we had never worked on the same stories. Would he be territorial? Would he help?

It turned out a blessing for both of us. Val, then fifty-six, had only recently returned to work after suffering a stroke. It had affected his speech—he now spoke with a slight slur—as well as his fine motor movements. He actually needed someone like me on the road with him. Each morning I would meet him at his hotel room, where I would tie his tie and do his cuffs. His hands, while improving, could not handle buttons. (He would eventually recover quite well, retiring to the small eastern Ontario town of Almonte with his wife, Edith Cody-Rice, and pass away at the age of eighty-eight.)

We were in British Columbia, travelling by ferry and car from Vancouver to Victoria, where Turner was scheduled to hold a rally. We stopped at a restaurant in Nanaimo and Val ordered sandwiches for us to eat on the road. The sandwiches came in a box, and I had no idea there was also a bottle of wine inside and two glasses. He paid, carefully folding the receipt for future expense claims.

We drove south along Highway 1 and Val, who knew the area, suggested we pull in where there was a small falls and a picnic area. We sat by the falls and he brought out the picnic. The wine turned out to be Greek retsina, which he likened to kerosene, but we soldiered on and had a most pleasant afternoon break at the falls.

From Victoria we returned with Turner to the mainland and off into the Rossland Range of the Monashee Mountains in the BC interior. A young John Turner had lived for several years in the small alpine town of Rossland, where his mother, Phyllis, had been born. John and his sister, Brenda, had been born in England, where Phyllis had been studying at the London School of Economics and married Leonard Turner, a journalist with the *Manchester Guardian*. Widowed at age twenty-nine, she had then returned to Canada with her young children, eventually marrying Frank Ross, a future lieutenant-governor of British Columbia.

Turner's handlers had arranged a photo opportunity at the Rossland Museum & Discovery Centre. All went wonderfully well until Turner, knowing the photographers were awaiting something different, reached out and picked up what seemed a quite heavy rock sample. Turner felt its considerable heft and then leaned closer to check out the label on the rock.

"Imagine that," he told the gathering. "90 percent lead!"

"Much like you, sir," Val cracked from the back of the crowd, causing Turner to turn sharply, his blue eyes drilling for the culprit.

Next day, the wisecrack appeared in the *Toronto Star*, the quip attributed to a local wit under Val Sears's magnetic byline.

David Shoalts

"You've gotta be kidding me!"

It was the spring of 1997, the beginning of the Stanley Cup finals, and Dave Shoalts and I were having a beer at the airport Marriott in Philadelphia. Dave "Shoaltsy" was covering the playoffs for the *Globe and Mail*; I was there for the *Ottawa Citizen* and the Southam chain of newspapers.

Shoaltsy had the sports section of the *Philadelphia Inquirer* open—both of us looking for quotes to steal (in the days before the internet complicated sportswriters' lives) and I was picking through the arts section.

"This is incredible!" I said.

He looked at me as if I had lost it. I tapped on a small advertisement. Ramblin' Jack Elliott was appearing at the Tin Angel in Philadelphia—*tonight!*

"All my life I've wanted to see him," I said.

"A guy whose first name is *Ramblin'*?" Shoaltsy said in his most sarcastic drone, arching one eyebrow in grave doubt. (Yes, sportswriters do pick up on sport's penchant for nicknames.)

Shoaltsy's specialty is sarcasm, delivered in a low, piercing monotone of disbelief. He tends to say out loud what others might only be thinking. Sort of like a cartoon bubble with sound. He's somewhat of an acquired taste, but those who get him love him for it. No one knew back then that one day he'd retire and turn his natural sarcasm into a comedy act.

I tried to explain. My brother Jim bought an album, *The Freewheelin' Bob Dylan*, the year I was fourteen. Hated the sound at first but soon came to love listening to those amazing words spill out of the Viking portable record player that sat on the desk where he should have been doing his homework, but never did. Dylan opened the door to a whole world of folk music: Tim Hardin, Tom Rush, Peter, Paul and Mary, Ian and Sylvia, Donovan, Simon and Garfunkel, and Joan Baez. As years passed, my folk interest became increasingly country, as I began listening to Kris Kristofferson, Willie Nelson, Emmylou Harris, Guy Clark, Townes Van Zandt and, of course, Ramblin' Jack Elliott.

Obviously, Shoaltsy and I weren't in Philadelphia for a folk concert. The Philadelphia Flyers were a new powerhouse in hockey, led by young captain Eric Lindros and his "legion of doom" line featuring John LeClair on one wing and Mikael Renberg on the other. Lindros was perceived to be taking over as the face of NHL hockey, a title long held by Wayne Gretzky, who just happened to be playing for the New York Rangers, the team the Flyers met in the third round.

The Flyers would defeat the Rangers in a tight, exciting series—it was the last playoff appearance for Gretzky—and move on to lose in four straight to the Detroit Red Wings, the Flyers' soon-to-be-fired coach Terry Murray delivering his memorable "choking situation" line following his team's third straight loss.

This night, however, was an off night. No game to cover. We were free to do whatever we wished after filing the mandatory wrap and vacuous quotes from practice.

"I know where that is," said Shoaltsy. "I'll drive us down."

The Tin Angel was in the Society Hill district, near Independence Hall and the Liberty Bell. Both of us had often stayed at the Sheraton there on previous trips to Philadelphia, so we knew the area: cobblestone streets, historical plaques, terrific restaurants. The Tin Angel was on the second floor, above the Serrano restaurant.

We drove down from our airport hotel, parked and headed straight for the venue. The entrance was on the side, with a ticket office right there before the stairs leading up into the concert hall.

"Sorry," the young woman said at the ticket desk. "Sold out."

I was crushed. I had so long wanted to see and hear Ramblin' Jack. Years earlier I had fallen in love with his "talking" song, "912 Greens." I could even recite a good part of it: "Around about 1953 I went down to New Orleans. Perhaps I should say many years ago . . ." It is a lovely, lingering tale of . . . well . . . nothing. A bunch of fellow travellers meet at a house in New Orleans at 912 Toulouse Street that they reach by going up an alley—"And over a fence, by some garbage cans, look out for that rusty nail"—and the story involves a banana tree, a grey cat with three legs and an "ex-ballet dancer" who took off all her clothes and danced around in the August heat. Everyone danced with her around the banana tree and then they left. End of story, end of song, with the final two lines wonderfully enigmatic:

> Did you ever, stand and shiver
> Just because you were, looking at a river?

Elliott had a sequel to that talking song and the story included Jack Kerouac, the author of *On the Road* and a great hero of my younger days. But I had never heard the second version. Now I figured I never would.

Shoaltsy and I repaired to the Serrano, where we pulled up to the bar and Shoaltsy, without even asking, ordered two Jamesons.

"Make it doubles," he told the bartender. "And a side of water, please."

The bartender splashed enough Jameson in to fill half of each glass, a marvellous illustration of the difference between American and Canadian bars. In the United States, they guess the volume, always erring on the side of the customer. In Canada, they measure the ounces out with eyedroppers and bring in the National Research Council to weigh, measure and sign off on each ounce before it is given to the purchaser.

Shoalts poured a little water into his glass and then handed me the water.

"I see you like a little water with your Jameson," a voice said from the other side of the bar.

We looked up and across. The other customer was raising his glass of amber liquid in a salute. "Nectar of the gods," he said.

"'Tis indeed," said Shoaltsy.

"Where you boys from?" the man asked.

We told him. We said we were hockey writers from Canada, here for the playoffs, but on a free night we had tried to go to the concert upstairs but it was sold out.

"I've wanted to see Jack Elliott for decades," I said. "I'm a big fan."

"What about you?" Shoaltsy asked the stranger. "What brings you here?"

The man smiled and sipped his drink. "I'm a musician," he said, placing the glass down on the bar with a rap. "I opened for Jack—I just finished up before you two came in."

"Bullshit!" Shoaltsy and I said at once.

"It's true," the 'tender broke in.

The musician said his name was Eric, no last name. "You want to see the man sing?"

"Yeah," I said. "But no tickets."

"You don't need none," he said. "Finish up your drinks and let's go."

And so, the drinks down, the bar bill paid, the three of us left the bar and went around the corner to the entrance to the Tin Angel. The young girl was still at the ticket office and looked curiously at us.

"They're with me," Eric said. She nodded and smiled.

Up the stairs we climbed. I could hear Ramblin' Jack Elliott singing the last few verses of Bob Dylan's "Don't Think Twice, It's All Right" as we reached another door, which Eric entered with Shoaltsy and me following. An usher nodded at us and stepped aside.

Every seat in the 130-seat hall was taken. It was indeed sold out.

"Follow me," Eric said.

We made our way down the sloping walkway and then turned to the left and walked along the side of the stage until we came to another door. Eric yanked it open and up a small flight of stairs we went until we were standing at the very back of the stage, the singer about four good steps in front of us, the crowd stretching out beyond him—rapturous as Ramblin' Jack plucked the last few notes on his guitar. It looked too beat up to play—a frayed opening even below the sound hole, which would have come from decades of picking—yet it produced the most lovely music.

Jack had noticed us coming up and nodded and smiled back at Eric, who gave him the thumbs up. Jack went back to singing. A couple of Woody Guthrie tunes. Another Dylan. And then he began talking . . . talking . . . talking . . . periodically plucking a single string of the old guitar . . . and I knew that *this was it—the song I had wanted to hear for decades . . .*

It was different, but it was also the same. The story began in New York and was about the same two musicians, Guy and Frank, and they travelled down to North Carolina, went shrimp fishing, ate a bunch of meals, and then headed down into the Smoky Mountains—just as they had in "912 Greens."

I was in heaven. Here was Ramblin' Jack Elliott and he was telling this absolutely rapt audience about the cat with three legs and the climbing over the fence—no rusty nail this time—and had just gotten to the part about the ex-ballet dancer and the banana tree when . . .

. . . Shoaltsy cups his hand over his mouth, leans in toward me and says in that distinctive, often-annoying sarcastic voice . . .

"Now I know why they call him Ramblin'."

Shoaltsy obviously had no knowledge or appreciation of superb concert hall acoustics. The line shot out from the back of the stage like a circus stuntman shot from a cannon.

The worshipping crowd caught its collective breath and gasped.

Ramblin' Jack Elliott stopped plucking the guitar strings, stopped talking and turned to stare back at this interruption.

He paused, seemed about to say something, turned back and decided to continue on with the story.

I was already shaking before he closed off with the final two lines:

Did you ever, stand and shiver
Just because you were, looking at a river?

Graeme Gibson

It was 1969, and I had just turned twenty-one—the age required in those years to buy beer and liquor in Ontario. Ralph Cox and I had come down to Toronto for the weekend, planning to go to the Book Cellar in Yorkville. I had one specific book in mind that I was hoping to find.

It was *Five Legs*, by a Canadian author I had not heard of before this year—Graeme Gibson. The *Globe and Mail*'s book critic, William French, had written a review in which he said Gibson's manuscript had been turned down by multiple publishers as being "too experimental." (Sounded good to me already!) Finally, House of Anansi, a new, small Toronto publisher, had decided to take its chances on the book. It had its flaws, French wrote, but he also said, "*Five Legs*, I have no hesitation in saying, is the most interesting first novel by a Canadian to be published in many years."

The Book Cellar had the book in stock, and now I was carrying it as we got off the subway at Summerhill. We were staying nearby at Ralph's grandmother's place on Birch Avenue, but first we wanted to stop at the beer store, then known as Brewers Retail.

There were only three customers in the beer store: Ralph and I and a tall, balding guy with a Zapata moustache who had just purchased a twelve-pack of Molson Stock Ale and was stuffing it into a string bag. There was something about his face. I thought I recognized him but knew I didn't know him. Then it struck me: *this was the face on the back of the book I was carrying in my bag from the Book Cellar!*

I very nearly said something, but then stopped. This was the city, not Huntsville. You don't speak to others or even acknowledge their existence. City rules. The man with the Molson Stock left the store and I made a rash decision. I would not let such an opportunity pass. I would ask him to sign his book.

I caught up to Graeme Gibson just outside the store. He turned around and saw me holding the book and seemed startled and surprised. I now know why. This never happens.

"Mr. Gibson," I asked in a voice that verged on trembling, "would you mind signing my book?"

It turned out he had a pen. He asked me where I found the book and hoped that I would like it. I loved it even before I turned the second page, as the first page in now said, "For Roy, with best wishes, Graeme Gibson, Sept. 7, 1969."

I held the book as if it were the most precious thing I had ever owned— a book signed by the author himself! I read the blurbs full of praise from the likes of Jack Ludwig and John Robert Colombo. Scott Symons gushed on the back cover that "*Five Legs* has more potent writing in it, page for page, than any other young Canadian novel that I can think of. Or indeed any young American novel—including Pynchon and Farina."

Some comments not included in the blurbs were rather less effusive. M.B. Thompson, a lecturer in the English department at Carleton University, would later review Gibson's second novel, *Communion*, in the *Ottawa Citizen*, and claim that *Five Legs* had been "an absolute disaster. It was literary in the worst sense, reeking with English department-mentry and dotted with quasi-recondite allusions to the Great Masters of Englit." It was the sort of "self-indulgent stuff that gifted adolescents write when they are about 17 and thank providence, at 25, that they never showed it to anyone. Gibson was 34 when *Five Legs* burst upon the unsuspecting public."

I loved the book. It was weird and, to me, wonderful. More than a half century later, when I have culled hundreds—hell, thousands—of books from the sagging shelves of our home, *Five Legs* remains in an honoured position.

Years passed and I was a staff writer with *The Canadian* magazine in Toronto when managing editor Alan Walker assigned me to a profile on Margaret Atwood, then the rising superstar of CanLit. The author of multiple books of poetry, a probing book on Canadian literature, two novels, *The Edible Woman* and *Surfacing*, was about to publish her third novel, *Lady Oracle*.

Walker had been a friend of Atwood's from their days at the University of Toronto and had arranged for me to visit with Atwood at her isolated farm near Alliston, about ninety minutes north of Toronto. I would be welcome to stay over for a couple of days so that there would be plenty of time for interviews. The author was a brand-new mother—little Jess only six weeks old—and would be busy with the baby's feeding and care.

There was one caveat: the magazine would not reveal the location of the farm (long since sold); Walker had agreed to this. Rising celebrity brought with it rising attention, sometimes not wanted. On the previous New Year's Day, a carload of drunken fans had turned up the long drive and laid siege to the farmhouse, demanding that their favourite author sign their books and meet with them. Fortunately, Atwood's relatively new husband—six-foot-four, military-trained Gibson—and Finn, their 140-pound Irish wolfhound, had convinced the rowdy fans to leave far more quietly than they had arrived.

The assignment meant that I would be meeting Gibson again and I could let him know how much I had enjoyed his book. I was as keen to meet with him as I was to interview the reigning queen of CanLit.

Atwood and Gibson were most welcoming and showed me around the property, including the small writing cabin at the back where both worked on their next creations. They had a mare and five kittens. They had help in a charming young woman named Carolyn Moulton, a university student, who was essentially a jane-of-all-trades, taking care of everything from correspondence to telephone calls to sometimes rocking the baby.

Gibson was most welcoming, baking a roast wrapped around chocolate for dinner and showing off the wine he was fermenting using bananas and cherries for flavour. He told me he was busy and happy as chair of the new Writers' Union of Canada. He was writing but clearly not comfortable talking about what he was writing about or how it was going. He would far rather talk about his partner's works. To say Gibson was supportive of Atwood would be a remarkable understatement. He was, I wrote, "the perfect counterpoint to a small, suspicious Atwood whose enormous fame has made her, as she says, 'just a little paranoid.'"

The Canadian put her on the cover of the September 25, 1976, edition. They tagged it, "The Private Life of Margaret Atwood."

Three years later, I was back at the farm. Alan Walker and I were now at *Maclean's* magazine, my second stint there, and Walker wanted me to profile Atwood again, this time for a cover feature that would be pegged to her then latest novel, *Life Before Man*. Again, Gibson was more eager to talk politics than literature—Joe Clark had recently been elected prime minister and the country was obsessed with what Pierre Trudeau would do after losing the election. Gibson did confess to struggling with a third novel, then titled, rather ominously, *The Reckoning*.

Another three years later and, once again, I was back—only this time as a freelancer on the loose since the weekend supplements had folded. *Toronto Life* magazine wanted a profile on Gibson himself. He had finally finished the troubling book, now titled *Perpetual Motion*. It had been a very hard grind for Gibson, but as English professor Eugene Benson had written to him back in 1960 in a letter Gibson had kept and treasured, "If you are having a good time, you are not writing."

Atwood, it seemed, was both writing prolifically and having a very good time of it. She enjoyed the literary life and was good at it—a charming, often funny interview, a grounded person despite her rising international fame. Gibson had charm and was very down to earth, but it was clear that writing to him was not a good time—it was difficult and perhaps even torturous.

Perpetual Motion could not be further removed from *Five Legs*. It is a fictional account of an early settler named Robert Fraser, set in rural

Ontario around the time of Confederation. It holds a potpourri of ideas and scenes, from the slaughter of the now extinct passenger pigeon to the remains of prehistoric mastodons. Fraser is obsessed with the riddle of perpetual motion to the point that he builds a model of the solar system inside his barn. To say *Perpetual Motion* is complicated is to suggest *War and Peace* is a light read.

"Robert's relationship to the machine," Gibson told me, "is rather like mine to the book." He had wrestled with the words for years, yet, he maintained, "If I can write the third book, that's the important book—then I'm a writer."

How could it be that the young man who wrote *Five Legs* could now be nearing fifty and filled with such doubts about his own abilities? Critics had not been kind to *Communion* and writer's block had been miserable to *Perpetual Motion*. He had largely fallen out of the CanLit eye but for his work with the Writers' Union, the Writers' Trust and PEN. It was almost as if he was too busy to write.

A year earlier Ottawa English professor John Moss had published *A Reader's Guide to the Canadian Novel* and, while expressing admiration for Gibson's early work, Moss felt obliged to point out that, in the years since, Gibson contemporaries such as Matt Cohen and Marian Engel had become major Canadian writers while Gibson had become known for his work in cultural politics.

"The passage of time," Moss wrote, "inevitably deflated his avant-garde aesthetic, yet Gibson remains before the public eye. Thus we have a curious anomaly: a novelist acclaimed more for himself as a writer than for his art." He had become, Moss believed, Canada's "most celebrated minor author."

It infuriated friends of the couple that Gibson was sometimes referred to as "Mr. Atwood." Novelist Timothy Findley told me he "would kill anybody who says [Gibson's] become her kitchen slave." Artist Charlie Pachter, also a close friend of Gibson and Atwood, called it "just so much bullshit."

"It's something Peggy and I have had to work out," Gibson conceded. "The fact is that I am in many ways a househusband, and I'm quite happy with it. But if I'm confronted with it in an aggressive way I really would answer it with some form of 'piss up a rope.'"

The relationship worked. When an international publication profiling the rising Canadian novelist joked that "Every woman writer should be married to Graeme Gibson," Atwood had the sentence put on a T-shirt for her husband. "Graeme has always supported himself," she insisted. "I never supported him. He never supported me."

Gibson says he "nickel-and-dimed it," earning small pay for his work with various agencies, picking up arts council grants, even one from Scotland, writing screenplays, doing a little acting, selling off hay and the eggs from the many chickens on the farm.

Friends stood strongly with him. At the same time, all these friends were quietly and patiently hoping that Gibson could one day finish his third novel and it could be published. They were sick of the naysayers and the cheap shots. Atwood herself was fond of mentioning the "tall-poppy syndrome" in Canada, where those who dare to rise above the fray are swiftly cut down to size. The towering Gibson was a natural for this. One reviewer of *Communion* wrote in *Books in Canada* that Gibson "had absolutely nothing to say." Gibson's next novel, the writer predicted, would be published, appropriately, "on rolls of uncoloured, biodegradable toilet tissue."

"Everyone would be understanding if there were no other," novelist Timothy Findley told me. "Oh, how *very* understanding they would be. But the book is there. He got back and back and back again on the horse that's thrown him. If he hadn't, I'm sure he wouldn't have written again, ever."

I can imagine how Gibson must have cringed when he heard that *Books in Canada*, the very publication that had suggested toilet paper for his next attempt, had decided to give over the November cover to *Perpetual Motion*. How he must have shuddered when he first held the issue, seeing an angry caricature of himself under the headline "The Machinations of Graeme Gibson."

But imagine, instead, the relief felt when he opened up to a three-page review by Lawrence Garber calling this difficult, oft-blocked, oft-abandoned, anxiety-ridden, finally delivered book "extraordinary . . . his finest work."

Graeme Gibson passed away in England on September 18, 2019, Atwood and his children at his side. He was eighty-five and had increasing dementia. He had suffered a stroke while the couple was travelling to promote Atwood's latest great success, *The Testaments*. He had written another novel, 1993's *Gentleman Death*, but it had not seen success and he quit writing novels because, as he said, "I don't want to start chewing my cabbage all over again." He had much greater success with *The Bedside Book of Birds*, a paean to his long-time hobby, birding.

In a statement, Atwood said they had "had a lovely last few weeks, and he went out on a high, surrounded by love, friendship and appreciation." His publisher, Penguin Random House Canada, called him "a friend to several generations of Canadian writers," which he certainly had been as a co-founder of the Writers' Union and a force in the Writers' Trust of Canada.

"His influence on the lives of writers in this country has been profound and far-reaching," said his publisher. "We are grateful for that superlative legacy, one that will continue to flourish, and also grateful for our own experiences working with Graeme: a true gentleman, whose gracious, elegant, and witty manner touched all who knew him."

In passing, Graeme Gibson had finally arrived.

11

Prime Ministers

I n the summer of 1978, Ellen and I and our little family arrived in Ottawa and, apart from an eighteen-month hiatus in Oakville while I worked for the *Toronto Star*, Ottawa has been home ever since. Work was split roughly between the Hill and the hockey rink, and just as sportswriters get to know players and coaches away from the game, one also gets to know sides of politicians that the public rarely, if ever, sees.

Throughout those decades, I encountered numerous prime ministers, sitting and retired, including John Diefenbaker, Pierre Trudeau, Joe Clark, Brian Mulroney, Kim Campbell, Jean Chrétien, Paul Martin, Stephen Harper and Justin Trudeau. Some, like Campbell, I never really got to know. John Diefenbaker I knew as an insatiable gossip; his wife, Olive, had once taught in Huntsville so his door was always open to me—as well as to a great many other reporters. The three I got to know best, both professionally and personally, were Jean Chrétien, Stephen Harper and Justin Trudeau.

Jean Chrétien

Jean Chrétien is a morning person.

He's also an afternoon and evening person—a senior citizen version

338

of the Energizer Bunny on steroids—but this particular morning, Tuesday, November 4, 2003, he had already put in an hour at his desk, had breakfast, done an interview . . . and it was not yet 8 a.m.

I had come to 24 Sussex Drive, the prime minister's official residence, thanks to an invite delivered in a hockey dressing room. For more than two decades I had been playing Mondays and Thursdays with a group called the Rusty Blades, a four-team beer league playing out of a couple of arenas in Ottawa's south end. One of the regulars, a feisty little Nova Scotian named Jim Munson (who's a bit of a goalmouth suck, truth be told) not only had been a teammate all those years, but had even longer been a colleague in the Parliamentary Press Gallery. He was one of the great characters of the gallery, as was *Toronto Sun* columnist Claire Hoy, who also played for the Rusty Blades. There was often as much fun in the dressing room as there was on the ice.

Jim went from being a wire reporter to becoming a CTV correspondent reporting from around the world. We had even covered a world hockey championship together in Prague in 1985. In 2001, he had left journalism to join the Prime Minister's Office as communications director.

"It's probably going to be the boss's final week," Jim said as we kicked off our skates and equipment. "If you'd like to spend the day with him, I can arrange it."

And so, on a cold and windy fall morning, I had arrived at 24 Sussex shortly after dawn, Jim already there to welcome me in and offer a cup of coffee in the sunroom. Breakfast would be on shortly. "The boss," as Jim always called him, was in his office, working. I would find out later that this involved signing off on nearly four dozen appointments, a final task to mark the tenth anniversary of his swearing-in as the twentieth prime minister of Canada.

"I have absolute power," he would tell me later, tongue firmly in cheek. "I can do the things I want." And he was pretty much doing exactly that in his final days at 24 Sussex.

Usually breakfast would be Raisin Bran cereal and, when he wanted to treat himself, hot chocolate, but this particular morning he had a meal fit for a lumberjack. He talked about his health—excellent. He showed me the two pills he took, one blue aspirin and one pill for cholesterol.

Eating and talking at the same time, he wanted to take issue with the *Globe and Mail*'s weekend feature on his golf game. His handicap, he claimed, was actually three strokes lower than the article claimed. Once, when he was briefly out of politics after losing the 1984 leadership race to John Turner, Chrétien had called me and asked if I'd care to have a round of golf with him at the Royal Ottawa, a course just across the Ottawa River that is the preferred club of politicians and the business class. I was happy to accept, expecting to join a foursome, and was surprised when I arrived that it would be just the two of us playing. He was far from a scratch golfer, but "fiercely competitive" would be a lame description of the golfer I had been up against that lovely summer day.

When I stepped into his official residence office in early November 2003, Joseph Jacques Jean Chrétien was but a few weeks away from turning seventy. He had served forty years as a member of Parliament. He had won three successive majority governments and claimed he could easily win a fourth if he cared to stick around. But it was time to leave, he believed. He had nothing more to prove.

"It is a game," he said at one point, "and I am the pro."

"He'd been there a decade," Lawrence Martin wrote in his superb second volume of his biography, *Iron Man: The Defiant Reign of Jean Chrétien*, "but he was still the misfit. It was as if he'd been taken straight from the factory floor and plunked down under the chandeliers."

A framed photograph on the wall of the Sussex office was signed, "Jean—the beginning of a great friendship, George W. Bush." At this point, however, the "great friendship" was on fairly rocky ground, the prime minister of Canada having rebuffed the president of the United

States when he refused to commit Canadian troops to the invasion of Iraq and put an end to those mysterious "weapons of mass destruction."

It had snowed through the night, the yard facing out onto the Ottawa River ankle deep in wet slush. No one bothered with the obvious joke about taking a walk in the snow and deciding, as Pierre Trudeau did so long ago, that the time had come.

The time had come for Mr. Chrétien and word was getting out. That very morning Radio-Canada would report that he would be resigning on Thursday, only two days away. He, however, demurred whenever talk of an actual date came up.

"No one knows," he said of his actual departure. "Even I don't know. Maybe I'll wake up one morning and I will know that this is it."

That would not happen officially until February 27, 2004, some four months after our day together.

Still, this was in many ways his final full week of work. Christmas and other breaks would eat up the remaining months. This day he would tell South Africa's Thabo Mbeki that he was the last visiting head of state Jean Chrétien would receive as prime minister of Canada. On Wednesday he would tell his caucus he had presided over their last meeting together.

He said he'd been offered jobs but had no interest. "I don't want any boss," he said. He would make speeches and make money. He would avoid boards and instead be open to "assignments" on international concerns, preferably involving Africa. He saw himself as a "dean" among international politicians. More than a dozen hours after leaving the breakfast table, that notion would be underlined when, as he was bidding farewell to Mbeki, the South African president lunged forward to deliver a long bear hug.

Longevity is something Chrétien said was never planned. When he went into politics at age twenty-nine, he promised his wife, Aline, he would stay in only ten years. In 1998, after two election victories, he was prepared to leave and started building a new home for them in

Shawinigan. It was Aline, however, who argued for "four more years" and another election—whatever it took to keep archrival Paul Martin away as long as possible from leading the Liberal Party of Canada.

We headed for his office at Parliament Hill, RCMP security in front and behind as his driver slipped down a side street to avoid construction along Sussex Drive. He sat like a schoolboy with his red binders and documents in his arms, his bony knees knocking against a sophisticated secure phone that he claimed never to use.

"They laughed at the idea of a populist as prime minister," he says as the motorcade twisted along the route. "But that was what the people wanted."

He would leave office with undeniable black marks—the failed promises of the 1993 Red Book, the gun registry fiasco, ministerial conflicts of interest and the persistent confusion of a golf course and hotel real estate purchase and sale that became known in the media as "Shawinigate."

"The perfect Canadian scandal," he said as he dismissed the matter, with disdain. "No sex, no violence—and I lost money!"

But there was also a deficit brought under control, an end to sovereignty anxiety and, largely through his own will, the introduction of the Clarity Act and election expenses reform. The decision not to join the coalition against Iraq, contentious at the time, had turned in his favour. When congratulated by Mbeki on the politically smart move, Chrétien had leaned closer to the South African president and whispered, "We couldn't afford it!"

He might once have been dismissed as a lightweight, Chrétien believed, but it was his style that made him seem so. He preferred the spoken word to the written, one-on-one to committee, and he put such value in being "alone to think" that it may have seemed he sometimes treated the job as part-time.

He had his self-doubts, he says—"all the time"—but he also had a secret weapon: good gut instinct. "I am like Rocket Richard," he said.

"He was maybe not the most elegant player on the ice, but he had the instinct for the net."

By this point in his long career, there was really no net to shoot at—and little to do but play out the clock in what history would surely judge a victory. At the morning briefing held with chief of staff Eddie Goldenberg, Clerk of the Privy Council Alex Himelfarb and Deputy Prime Minister John Manley, nothing whatsoever seemed to be pressing.

At the weekly cabinet meeting that followed, Manley took over, presenting the prime minister with a collection of jazz and classical recordings from the CBC and a new sound system. Public Works Minister Ralph Goodale then presented him with a "surrogate" flag for the one flown this day on the Peace Tower. The original was, at that moment, being "ironed" to dry it out.

Mr. Chrétien spoke for a few minutes, rambling a bit about Canada's place in the world, but then decided he had had enough sentimentality.

"We still have much to do," he told his final cabinet session. "I have not resigned yet."

Even so, resignation seemed all the reporters cared about at the scrum that invariably followed any cabinet gathering.

The prime minister was having none of their prodding. "The apartment is bought," he said with a touch of exasperation. "You know, the furnitures are moving. You know, I bought an extra toothbrush and, you know, it's coming, it's coming."

Their questions went unanswered. The prime minister skipped down the stairs to the waiting motorcade, raced back to 24 Sussex for a lunch with Mbeki that ran overtime, forcing another race back to continue with Question Period, where there was no time to brief him on the expected questions. It hardly mattered. As usual, he gave better than he got.

"You're going to miss that," Jim Munson told him back in his office, where staffers congratulated the PM on his Question Period jabs at the Opposition.

"Not as much," he shot back, swinging an imaginary golf club, "as they are going to miss me."

Back at 24 Sussex, the prime minister relaxed to the point where he seemed to have physically changed. Jean Chrétien without a rolling camera and a microphone around is only remotely like the man with the stiffened shoulders and the strange pronunciations that Canadians know from television. Away from a lens, he seems smaller and quieter.

He sat by a window, waiting for the lights of the motorcade. Aline, sharply dressed for the tenth anniversary celebrations, plucked something from his jacket, brushing his shoulder. Someone mentioned how good they looked. "We're not kids anymore," he said without a smile.

At the Museum of Civilization, the cameras were again rolling and so, too, was the Chrétien public personality, working the crowd as he has done so often, but would soon have to do no more. He seemed relieved to slip away with Mbeki for a quick tour of the Museum of Civilization while the other guests were seated.

Another two hours passed, and his tenth anniversary was history. "We need to remember these moments," Aline Chrétien said as they waited for the motorcade to take them back to 24 Sussex. "We were lucky, you know."

Unbelievably lucky—but not quite so lucky as the little guy from Nova Scotia who had met me at the door fourteen hours earlier that Tuesday dawn.

Remember those dozens of appointments the prime minister had signed off on just before breakfast?

One of them would take place on December 10, 2003, when Jimmy Munson, goalmouth garbage collector for the Rusty Blades, would henceforth be addressed as "Senator James Munson."

But never in the hockey dressing room—trust me.

Stephen Harper

In early March 2012, I received a call from Michael Levine, a lawyer and entertainment agent who was associated with the Westwood Creative Artists agency. Bruce Westwood, Levine's business partner, had long been my agent for books. I had met Michael but did not know him well. I did know of his successes representing writers such as Peter C. Newman, my old boss at *Maclean's*.

Michael wanted to know if we could speak with complete confidentiality. "Of course," I told him, wondering why a secret call was coming in to me.

"I have a client who needs help with his hockey book," Michael said.

"Interesting . . . who is it?"

"The prime minister."

As Michael explained, for years Prime Minister Stephen Harper had "relaxed" by working on a hockey book about the years in which the game transformed from purely amateur to professional. It was an examination of the various hockey organizations of the first decades of the twentieth century, groups that were often at drawn swords over where the Canadian game should go. It was intended to be a serious book with in-depth research. The prime minister had even joined the Society of International Hockey Research. He had tentatively titled his project *The Forgotten Leafs*, in honour of his favourite NHL team, the Toronto Maple Leafs, and the various early forms the Toronto professionals had taken.

I was intrigued. Harper had been prime minister since February 6, 2006. His photograph was daily in the papers, his image and voice on every nightly news broadcast—yet he was largely unknown. He was considered the ultimate button-down personality—the press had once made fun of the then new prime minister for formally shaking hands with his young son, Ben, as the child headed off to school.

The rare times he had let down his guard—at early Press Gallery dinners, for example—he had shown a sense of humour never seen by the public. At a National Arts Centre charity event, his wife, Laureen, had talked her husband into playing the piano and singing. His version of the Beatles' "With a Little Help from My Friends," accompanied by world-famous cellist Yo-Yo Ma, had brought down the house. It was a national shock for pre–legal cannabis Canada to see the country's leader admitting, "I get high with a little help from my friends."

My curiosity got the best of me. Michael already had a publishing deal with a distinguished house, Simon & Schuster Canada, and the publisher, having seen a first draft of the book, was convinced that the author did indeed need "a little help"—whether from a friend or not.

I agreed to meet with the prime minister. Two days later, a special-delivery letter arrived with a CD-ROM of the first draft of the manuscript enclosed, the package marked in large-font boldface "Strictly Private and Confidential." I read through it, took handwritten notes and thought about what might be done to improve the book. It was ripe with history and research, but rather dry and organized into an often confusing variety of asides and segments. There was no real narrative arc to propel the reader along. And yet, there was a lot of extremely good material.

The following day, I was called by the Prime Minister's Office to arrange a time for the PM to meet with me. We would get together later in the week at his office in the Langevin Block, directly across Wellington Street from Parliament Hill. The building is named for Sir Hector-Louis Langevin, a Father of Confederation who was a key proponent of the residential school system that is today, finally, acknowledged as racist and wrong. In 2017, Prime Minister Justin Trudeau announced that the building would be renamed the rather colourless "Office of the Prime Minister and Privy Council," but it is still called the Langevin Block by all who work on the Hill.

We met mid-morning, before lunch and Question Period. Chief of staff Nigel Wright—a thin, dapper man with "competence" written all over him—was immediately welcoming and friendly. Prime Minister Harper, not so much. But he did shake hands, smile and immediately invite me to talk about my early impressions of his book.

It was a diplomatic challenge. Something good had to be said about his work and, indeed, the research was voluminous and impressive. The writing was rather academic but academically passable. The problem was that while he had written a book he had not told a story. And this would prove a difficult concept to convey.

Not long into our conversation about my concerns, it dawned on me that he was flinching—if not visibly, certainly in demeanour—every time I used the word "narrative." I had mentioned the lack of a "narrative arc" and had several times stressed the importance of having a strong narrative and sticking to it.

Words have a way of shifting when they land on Parliament Hill. When Joe Clark came to power briefly in 1979, he loved to use the strange word "plethora" to mean a richness of choice, whereas its true meaning is "excessive." In recent years, the word "robust" has been stuck in virtually every spoken paragraph, its old meaning, "healthy," now twisted into "good" and "fair" and "lengthy."

As for "narrative," its use in Canadian politics has come to mean "spin" and even "lie," as in "*your* narrative." While I was trying to get the prime minister to see his hockey book as a story being told, he was hearing the word "narrative" each time I said it as negative criticism.

From my point of view, the meeting did not seem to go well. I left convinced that the session had been a disaster, as he had not been open to various suggestions. Much to my surprise, a couple of days later he wanted to meet again.

We gathered this time at his second-floor office in the Centre Block of Parliament Hill. I went through security in the basement and took an elevator up, then sat waiting on a bench outside his office until he wrapped up other meetings.

Above my head was Frances Anne Hopkins's famous painting *Shooting the Rapids*. The waiting would prove fruitful, as the gorgeous 1879 illustration of a voyageur canoe cresting the fast water between Montreal and Lachine would inspire my book *Canoe Country: The Making of Canada*, which Random House would publish in 2015.

Finally, Nigel invited me in just as the Clerk of the Privy Council, Wayne Wouters, was leaving after his morning briefing with the prime minister.

"What are *you* doing here?" Wayne asked, his face puzzled.

"You know each other?" Nigel asked.

Indeed we did, having played beer-league hockey together for two hours every Sunday morning for a decade and more. Wayne and I chatted a bit, he unable to suppress snickers, and then I moved off with Nigel to meet, again, with the prime minister.

This meeting was a total surprise. I expected the prime minister to have digested my earlier comments and have decided to work with me. I would simply keep my use of the word "narrative" to the bare minimum. Instead, the prime minister had a sheet of paper with small notes on it; one by one, he went through my various comments and criticisms and shot several of them down as quickly and effectively as a criminal lawyer.

This time I left wondering why I had been called back only to, essentially, be told how wrong I was about so many things to do with the book. This was clearly the end of any consultation.

The next day Michael Levine called again.

"The prime minister wants to work with you," he told me. "He really likes what you've been telling him."

"Huh?"

"He thinks you can work together just fine."

And so began several months of working together on the book that, in 2013, would become *A Great Game*, not *The Forgotten Leafs*, and would be a national bestseller for Simon & Schuster Canada.

The prime minister certainly loosened up. At one point, when we were passing time before settling down to work on the book, he asked what I had done previously. He seemed surprised to hear that someone he knew as a sportswriter had spent fourteen years working on the Hill, writing on politics for *Maclean's*, the *Toronto Star*, *Maclean's* again and the *Ottawa Citizen*.

"I became an economist," he said, "because I didn't have enough personality to be an accountant."

Summer rolled around and one day Ellen and I were invited up to Harrington Lake for lunch. Harrington Lake is Canada's Camp David, a bucolic retreat high in the Gatineau Hills. There had once been a mill and homes on the site but the area was acquired by the Crown in 1951 with the idea of creating a nature reserve. In 1959, however, those working with Prime Minister John Diefenbaker thought "Dief" could benefit from his lifelong love of fishing if only there were a quiet retreat, on water, within easy reach of the capital. The remaining sixteen-room cottage and cabins were refitted for security, with a gatehouse built for the RCMP to control access, and Harrington Lake has now served as a much-treasured escape for eleven prime ministers, including Diefenbaker. The current prime minister's mother, Margaret Trudeau, even added a vegetable garden.

The ride up from Ottawa is by four-lane Quebec Highway 5, then slowly through the village of Old Chelsea and on to a twisting gravel road that wraps around the south shore of Meech Lake, where we passed numerous cottages and two public beaches. It is a road for cautious drivers.

We arrived at the gatehouse, the Mounties on duty asked for our names, checked them against a sheet and waved us through to the parking lot not far from the large, white cottage. We were early for lunch, so were given a tour of the grounds by the Harpers. At lunch, Laureen, Ellen and I shared some wine and the four of us engaged in some idle talk. Laureen then suggested that she and Ellen head out on one of the hiking trails, accompanied, of course, by RCMP officers. That left the prime minister and me with a good couple of hours to work on the book. The Harpers planned to return to 24 Sussex later that day.

We were well into the reworking of chapters when I thought it would be wise to bring up the issue of "narrative" without actually saying the word out loud.

"I've been thinking," I began tentatively, "that one way to make the story more compelling might be to tell large parts of it through a key character."

I wasn't thinking of a player, though "Newsy" Lalonde had been a possibility, but of an early hockey official named John Ross Robertson. Robertson was a newspaperman, which attracted me; he was founder of the *Toronto Telegram*, for many years the most powerful newspaper in the Dominion. Large of head and given to wearing his beard in the style of Abraham Lincoln, Robertson was the most powerful official in the early game—heading up the Ontario Hockey Association—and he was virulently against the game turning professional, as so many of the players wished.

But best of all was John Ross Robertson's back story. He was a genuine eccentric. He gave generously to the Hospital for Sick Children in Toronto and happily dressed as Santa Claus each Christmas. As a young reporter, he had been imprisoned by Louis Riel during the Red River Rebellion. His hobby was going to the funerals of people he had never known, sometimes as many as five a week, and weeping profusely through the service.

"This guy is in every chapter," I argued. "You could flesh him out and readers would feel like he was carrying them along on this adventure."

"There's a book . . ." the prime minister said, almost to himself. He was clearly thinking of something.

"I have a full book on him," he said, "but it's not here. It's in the city."

Laureen and Ellen were now back from their hike. The prime minister was on the phone, ordering something up.

"Come on," he said. "We'll head back early and get that book to you."

By the time we stepped back outside, there were three large black Chevrolet Suburban SUVs idling at the side of the cottage. The windows of each van were so heavily tinted it was impossible to see inside.

"You follow us and stick with us," the prime minister said to us before climbing in a back door of the second dark SUV.

Ellen and I hurried to our rusting ten-year-old vehicle and climbed in. The prime minister's convoy was already heading out for 24 Sussex. We pulled in behind them.

If the Meech Lake Road was to be driven with respect and caution, that memo clearly hadn't made it to the Mounties driving the prime minister back to Ottawa. They flew along the gravel road, whipping through tight corners, and exited Gatineau Park before coming to a four-way stop where a left turn would take them through the village and back to Highway 5.

The three Mountie vans had built-in police lights, and the drivers turned them on just as a silver Jeep pulled up on the crossroad. The Mountie vans were signalling that they would be taking the turns together and not, as the traffic act would have it, let the Jeep go through when it was its turn.

"What'll I do?" I asked Ellen. "We don't have police lights!"

"You better follow them," she said.

So I did, cutting off the silver Jeep, which was already coming forward. The Jeep began tailgating us, sending a clear message as the now five-vehicle convoy hurried through the village. We followed the prime minister's caravan as it took the ramp down onto Highway 5, the Jeep still up my butt.

The highway was mostly empty, it being mid-afternoon. Soon the convoy was hitting 140 kilometres an hour as it flew down from the

Gatineau hills toward the Ottawa River. The three dark SUVs began working a much-practised defensive lane-switching pattern designed to thwart any attempted assassination of the Canadian prime minister.

"*What do I do?*" I practically screamed at Ellen.

"*Whado Idoooo?*"

"You better stick with them," she said. She didn't seem as freaked out as I was. Obviously, opposites attract.

We switched, too. I hoped it would signal to the silver Jeep—still up my ass!—that we were indeed part of the convoy. If he could see in our non-tinted windows, he would have seen two senior citizens going 140 in a vehicle that probably couldn't pass a safety check. The Jeep not only stayed right with us, but also did the evasive lane switching right along with the Mounties up front.

Across the Macdonald-Cartier Bridge flew the convoy, turning onto Sussex Drive. It seemed the Mounties were controlling the lights along the way, as at no time did they need to slow down. Nor did they seem interested in slowing down. The Jeep was still with us.

At 24 Sussex, the official residence of the prime minister, the gates were already opening, the Mounties having called ahead that the prime minister was arriving back earlier than expected. The three Mountie SUVs slipped through the gates, then us . . . then the silver Jeep.

We got out of our car just in time to see yet another Mountie get out of the vehicle that had been chasing our butt.

Upstairs, in the prime minister's private study, he went to the bookshelf, searched a while, and then plucked out a thin book with a slightly torn cover. It was *The Paper Tyrant: John Ross Robertson of the Toronto Telegram*, by Ron Poulton, published by Clarke, Irwin in 1971. He held it as if the contents were precious—as they would indeed prove to be.

John Ross Robertson was an inspired choice to carry the book's . . . uh . . . narrative. Stephen Harper, author, worked furiously over the coming months, running chapter after chapter past me. I served as editor, not ghostwriter, as some were saying. He wrote his own book, and he did a damned good job of it.

Ellen and I left the study, book in hand, and headed home with a story some would likely not believe. No matter—it happened pretty much as described.

As did this:

Weeks later, it was late in the evening and the prime minister and I had been working by telephone, he in his 24 Sussex Drive study, I in my little office in our Kanata home. He had written a chapter on the founding of the Canadian Amateur Hockey Association and it still needed some work.

As we talked quietly about structural problems, a phone began ringing in the background. It rang and rang and rang. I could tell he was distracted, his mind wandering from the task at hand.

"I'll have to take that," he said.

"Sure," I answered.

"Hang on."

He set the receiver down, but as we were still connected I could hear him pick up the ringing phone. All I could hear, really, was murmured voices. I could not make anything out, but I did hear the other telephone click down.

The prime minister returned to our call.

"That's the first time that has ever rung," he said, still sounding distracted.

"How's that?"

"It's *the* phone . . ."

It took a moment for that to sink in. *The* phone? The one directly connected to the president of the United States and the prime minister of Great Britain? *The* phone? The one that tells Canada the bombs are on the way?

"What was it?" I asked, gulping for air.

"A wrong number," he said, chuckling.

We went back to work on the founding of the Canadian Amateur Hockey Association. We were well into it when the phone in the background began again to ring.

Riiinnnggg!

RIIINNNGGG!

RRRIIIIIIINNNGGGG!!

The phone again!

The prime minister sighed. "I'll have to get that," he said.

"Of course," I said, wondering if I should run to my basement, where there is an extension line.

I could hear more murmurs, then a click of the phone hanging up. This time the click was harder and louder.

The prime minister returned to our call.

"What was it this time?" I asked in a shaky voice.

"Same guy," he said. "He didn't believe me."

Justin Trudeau

Justin Trudeau was a month away from turning thirty-five—the age that the European Social Survey has officially pegged as "no longer considered young."

It was late November 2006, and the *Globe and Mail* had assigned me to spend a day with the eldest child of Pierre Elliott Trudeau and see what it was that had so many people pushing the former teacher and part-time actor to run for political office.

As two young women put it that crisp, late fall day at Ottawa's Carleton University, the breath from their screams hanging in the air like early campaign signs:

"You have to run!"

"We need you!"

"You have to!!"

A week after that day at Carleton, the Liberal Party of Canada would gather in Montreal to choose a new leader. Paul Martin had lost the 2006 federal election to Stephen Harper and the reunited Conservatives, and Martin had resigned as leader. Stéphane Dion, a competent political science professor but weak practitioner of politics, would somehow win that leadership vote over the likes of well-known names such as Bob Rae, Michael Ignatieff and Ken Dryden.

Many potential Liberal voters, especially the young, were unimpressed with such a list and hungered for someone closer to their own age, someone with appeal, someone who could communicate . . . someone who might tap into the manic Trudeaumania that had swept Justin's father to power way back in 1968.

The writing was even then on the Carleton University walls, so to speak, for Justin Trudeau, even though he would not actually run for office for another twenty-three months. The then thirty-six-year-old would easily win the Montreal-area riding of Papineau for the Liberals in the October 2008 general election and serve as opposition critic for citizenship and immigration, youth and multiculturalism under the unimpressive leadership of Dion.

At this moment, however, he was just Justin Trudeau, private citizen. After several smiles and handshakes, he slipped away from the young women and hurried out into the parking lot.

"I sometimes feel like running," he said in a voice so small it barely misted in the cool air.

"*Running away.*"

And yet, he was clearly attracted to the lights awaiting him in Ottawa. He was then at the head of the curve that would become a social phenomenon for the twenty-first century: he had pushed being a teenager well through his twenties and into his thirties, and was finding himself at an age, and in an age, where he both profited from and paid for his lack of seasoning.

He was something new; he was something untested.

Some, particularly those who scanned the grey prospects of the leadership stage, saw him as a messiah-in-waiting, Pierre Trudeau reincarnate at best, Pierre Trudeau Lite at worst. Yet, no matter how he was measured against his father, he held future hope.

Others cringed at the thought, particularly those of a certain age who perhaps no longer recall what it is to be young and more than a bit naive, yet refreshingly passionate about a world that, in all likelihood, will never hear them out. He was also perceived as acting, well, more than a bit silly at times.

In the fall of 2006, before his face was as widely recognized as his name, he had grown into a young man so handsome even men turned to stare as he passed. He had the charming, shy smile of his father but not the father's almost debilitating shyness. He had his mother Margaret's luxuriant black and curling hair. Some who knew him and liked him said he also had his mother's warmth and his father's drive; some who knew him but did not much like him cruelly said he had inherited his mother's brains and his father's arrogance.

Everyone, back then, seems to have had an opinion. Victorious or vacuous? Airhead or future head?

At the end of his Carleton University session, he had closed off with a quick game of Simon Says. It was a moment more suited to grade five, which he once taught, than to the university population that had packed the hall. The students seemed taken aback, the moment awkward, but he had persisted with the Simon Says silliness until there was only one question still to be asked.

The obvious one.

"When will you run for office?"

They got no definitive answer, but no matter—the university crowd clearly loved him. The son who delivered that memorable eulogy at his father's funeral in the fall of 2000—the open-hearted emotion so admired by many; the "Friends, Romans, countrymen" theme so ridiculed by others—had by 2006 become an effective and often moving public speaker. With not a note in hand, for an hour he had spoken passionately about education and the environment. Ignoring the podium, he had stood, jacket open, at the very front of the stage, his stance missing only the hitched thumbs in his belt to remind everyone of Pierre Trudeau's "gunslinger" pose.

The hints were constant, the shadow never far from the spotlight. The voice. The eyes. The way he sometimes shrugged and cupped his hand. The way women quickened in his presence. But there were vast differences, as well. The father was sewn up so tightly nothing ever got out he did not wish to be seen, the Jesuit Spartan micromanaging of his own emotions. The son often bursts through his stitches, the inside exposed for anyone within hearing distance. "I've *got* to quit using 'I' so much," he said at one point during a long day together. "I've *got* to quit using 'I' so much."

But there were other things to notice after twelve hours in his company. It is one thing to fake it for the media, but quite another to be constantly polite, warm, generous with time and a good listener to every stranger. Where Pierre could be so cold, Justin sometimes veers close to being too warm.

They came at him everywhere he went. In the class, in the streets, in the restaurant. "We need you," they told him. "We need Trudeaumania again."

Tellingly, he flinched whenever that made-up word appeared. Nearly forty years had passed since Trudeaumania. He was not Pierre Elliott Trudeau; he was Justin Pierre James Trudeau. Comparisons are simple and comparisons can be odious, but comparisons will always be made between father and son in this particular case.

In John English's book on the father, *Citizen of the World: The Life of Pierre Elliott Trudeau*, English wrote that Pierre completed his schooling and then "spent the next decade and a half seemingly as a dilettante, writing articles for newspapers and journals, driving fast cars and a Harley-Davidson motorbike, escorting beautiful women to concerts and restaurants, travelling the globe wherever he wished, founding political groupings that went nowhere . . ."

Then, in 1965—"suddenly, or so it seemed," English wrote—Pierre Trudeau ran and won a seat and, three years later, was leader and prime minister "amid a media frenzy usually reserved for rock stars, not politicians."

Many saw the same trajectory for the son. Yet Justin Trudeau most assuredly did not have the luxury of coming out of nowhere. The CBC's Gordon Donaldson said the elder Trudeau had come to the leadership "like a stone through a stained-glass window." Justin Trudeau had entered Canadian public life on Christmas Day 1971, the moment he was born.

It was also rather unfair—yet it was so often done—to describe the son's early adult years as dilettantish: teaching snowboarding in Whistler, taking boxing lessons, signing up for various causes, speaking out on issues, appearing, somewhat surprisingly, as a host of the Giller Prize literary awards, acting in a CBC film on the life of First World War hero Talbot Papineau.

It can be argued that Pierre Trudeau worked in some substantial credentials during his younger years. He started up a political journal. He did legal work. He was deeply involved in an important strike. Similarly, Justin had various accomplishments that were rarely listed: teaching at West Point Grey Academy and Sir Winston Churchill Secondary School in British Columbia, serving as chair of the Katimavik youth project, completing a master's degree at McGill University in environmental geography.

Young voters obviously adored him, but it was not an emotion widely shared by the national media. In late 2006, the media seemed obsessed with Prime Minister Stephen Harper's desire for "nation" status for Quebeckers "within a united Canada," and so they kept chasing Justin

Trudeau for comment, given that non-nation status for Quebec had been a Pierre Trudeau creed.

After young Trudeau had been quoted as saying Liberal leadership candidate Michael Ignatieff's concept of Quebec as a "nation" went against "everything my father stood for," he had been taken on by one of the giants of Canadian journalism, the erudite Robert Fulford. "In recent weeks," Fulford wrote in his *National Post* column, "Justin Trudeau has upgraded his status from minor annoyance to major national pest."

Trudeau had laughed off the piece, saying he'd heard worse and seen worse, but all the same had kept it from his wife, Sophie Grégoire. She was hardly as sanguine about such coverage and had bristled at some of the coverage of their wedding a year earlier.

Trudeau's friends contended he handled media well, whether it be positive or negative. He was fully aware of the media spotlight. It had been Justin who spoke for the family at the funeral of, first, his younger brother Michel, who was killed in an avalanche, and then, two years later in the fall of 2000, eulogized his father. Friends said he understood the baggage as well as the good fortune.

"That polarity," said Gerry Butts, a close friend from university who in 2006 was serving as principal secretary to Ontario premier Dalton McGuinty (and would later serve as principal secretary to Justin), "is what he must deal with every time he opens his mouth. He's not dealing with a father's looming figure, but a ghost."

"The danger in trying to compare anyone to my father," Justin told me that long day in Ottawa, "is that my father is no longer a man, he's an icon."

He had been hearing for years how "vacuous" he was. "*What am I supposed to do?*" he asked in some exasperation as we drove away from Carleton University. "Recite pi to the tenth decimal? Ask them to throw me a line of poetry and have me finish the poem?"

Butts argued that Justin's intelligence was underrated. "If any of us were called upon to demonstrate our intelligence in front of the public every day," he said, "I'm not sure how well any of us would do. And he's just not interested in being a public intellectual—unlike some others I could name. He's not a complainer and he's not a whiner."

"I have no interest," Trudeau said during a morning break, "in becoming the 'National Brooder.'"

Geoffrey Pearson knew only too well what it was like to be the son of a former prime minister. Being the son of Lester Pearson meant he had a name that opened doors and helped in a successful diplomatic career. But it also came with a price.

"Both of us have a name to live up to," Geoffrey said at a debate the two attended on Parliament Hill later that day.

Then he paused, nodding. "It's hard, isn't it?"

Justin Trudeau said that he would be supporting former Ontario education minister Gerard Kennedy at the then upcoming Montreal leadership convention. Kennedy would drop out after the second ballot, finishing fourth behind Dion, Ignatieff and Rae.

As for one day running himself, Trudeau would concede only that he likely would. But, he cautioned, he would have to be "ready" first.

"You're not supposed to be a finished product at thirty," he said. "You're still a work in progress, surely."

In the world of daily journalism, twelve straight hours is a long time to have access to a subject about whom you are writing a short feature. I was grateful for the access, as Justin Trudeau can be good company. We talked about a great many matters—canoe tripping, books, acting—that never made an appearance in the piece. I found him good-natured, friendly and kind. He had time for everyone he encountered.

One impression I could not shake that day and still cannot shake now is that, after spending an entire day with him, he seemed to me very much the child who has come home for Thanksgiving from first-year university. He seemed so full of life and ideas, so charmingly naive about the realities that await.

He seemed half his birth certificate age.

More than sixteen years later, as I write this, Justin Trudeau is in his early fifties and remains a work in progress. He won election to Parliament in 2008 and became leader of the Liberal Party of Canada in the spring of 2013, replacing the bumbling Ignatieff, who had taken over following the resignation of the disastrous Dion. In the 2015 federal election, Justin had adroitly moved his party from third place to first as the country tired of Stephen Harper and the Conservatives. He campaigned well and took his party from thirty-six seats to 184, the largest ever increase by a party in a Canadian national election. His government legalized marijuana, but so badly bungled the fallout from the SNC-Lavalin affair that he was knocked down to a minority in 2019.

The debate over substance and sense has never ceased. In his first term, he undertook an unnecessary and poorly planned trip to India that became a costume-party fiasco as his family played "Indian" up and down the country, his meetings disastrous, those back home either offended by or ashamed of the photos and news coming back. Parliament Hill scribes with long memories recalled how Pierre Trudeau once dressed in Arab garb and elegantly danced the *moozmaad* in the desert of Saudi Arabia—and had been much praised for it. Pierre was seen as cool; Justin dismissed as a fool.

Justin and his cabinet successfully launched a reworking of the US–Canada–Mexico NAFTA trading agreement, but his reputation for leadership took a severe beating over the manner in which he handled fallout from SNC-Lavalin. He foolishly demoted Jody Wilson-Raybould, Canada's first Indigenous attorney general, when it appeared she was against letting the Quebec construction giant off the legal hook. Treasury Board president Jane Philpott resigned in support of Wilson-Raybould.

So much for being the first "feminist" prime minister.

Trying to wiggle free of rising criticism over his handling of the incident, Trudeau told Canadians that if Scott Brison had not resigned as Treasury Board president to go into private life, then the shifting of Wilson-Raybould would never have happened—though there could not possibly have been the slightest connection between the two decisions.

During the 2019 election, images appeared of Justin in blackface while teaching in BC, and Liberal insiders tried to wash it away by saying it had happened years ago when standards were different—even though blackface was commonly considered a severe no-no since before Justin had even been born.

In early 2020, when the Covid-19 crisis hit Europe and then North America, Prime Minister Justin Trudeau suddenly began to look, sound and appear . . . prime ministerial. He now had a trimmed beard, with just enough grey in it to hint at maturity. He gave daily briefings from the cottage at Rideau Hall, where the family had been living and where, coincidentally, his wife, Sophie, was recovering from the virus. He had the country's sympathy. He had the country's ear. He was fast earning the country's confidence.

Before Easter, he wisely advised Canadians to stick to the agreed rules—stay at home, don't travel.

For weeks, the Sûreté du Québec had been turning back Ontario residents with cottages in western Quebec as they tried to reach their properties. There were simply not enough medical facilities to handle increased Covid-19 cases in the area.

Canada's chief public health officer, Dr. Theresa Tam, told people to stay home, not to go to the cottage for the long weekend at Easter. Prime Minister Justin Trudeau told people to stay home, do the right thing.

Easter rolled around and . . . shocking . . . a post appeared on social media of a smiling, happy Trudeau family . . . at their cottage retreat across the Quebec border at Harrington Lake.

For every positive, a negative.

In the midst of the pandemic, he called an unnecessary election that all but photocopied the previous parliament. Another minority.

The election over, the next item on the Justin Trudeau itinerary was September 30, marking the first-ever National Day for Truth and Reconciliation. In a year when hundreds of secret children's graves had been discovered on residential school grounds, this day was of the greatest import—and may very likely stand as the most significant thing Justin Trudeau's government implemented.

The twenty-third prime minister of Canada honoured this special day by going . . . surfing with his family in Tofino, British Columbia. His published daily itinerary said he was in "private meetings" in Ottawa. One would think any of his grade five students would have advised him not to go. The optics were awful, the naïveté simply breathtaking.

THE WOMAN WHO
COULD BE PRIME MINISTER

The lead time for a story in the old rotogravure weekly supplements was a minimum six weeks. It meant stories tended to be more general than specifically tied to the news. You could write a retrospective on a news event—something on a recent election, a wrap of a major sporting event such as the 1972 Summit Series—but six weeks later, nothing stood up as well as a good profile of an interesting person.

On an early June day in 1977, I was called into the office of editor Don Obe, who seemed particularly on edge. He fumbled as he pulled a cigarette from the package of Rothmans on his forever squared-up-and-clean desk. He ran his other hand through his thick, curling dark hair. He cleared his throat as if about to address a wide audience. In a way he was: the three million readers of *The Canadian* magazine.

"We have a bit of a situation," Don told me as he lighted his cigarette and inhaled deeply.

I waited. He exhaled a thick cloud of smoke and began explaining. He had assigned a freelancer to do a story on a rising star in the federal cabinet, Iona Campagnolo. The freelancer had failed to deliver, either struck by writer's block or, far more likely in those days, lost on an expense-funded bender.

"I need you to go to Ottawa as soon as possible to save this story." I nodded. Always happy to feel needed. Always thrilled to be challenged. "There's one thing you have to know," Don said, again clearing his throat heavily.

"And that is?" I asked.

"The cover has already gone," he said. "We have to have the story by Wednesday of next week. I mean *have to*!"

That was not much turn-around time, but it was doable. I began to rise, thinking I would head back to my little office in the Simpson Building at 401 Bay Street in downtown Toronto. I would have to book flights. I would need to call Campagnolo's office to set up an interview. I'd need, rather desperately, to research this woman about whom I knew less than next to nothing.

Don cleared his throat. "There's also the matter of the cover line," he said, eyes down under his desk.

I turned. "What's it say?"

He coughed this time. Swallowed. Then:

"*'The Woman Who Could Be Prime Minister'* . . ."

Iona Campagnolo was minister of state for fitness and amateur sport in Prime Minister Pierre Trudeau's cabinet. It was hardly a significant post, more a branch of health and welfare than a full ministry itself. But sports had been given a boost by the '76 Olympics, which had been held in Montreal the previous year and delivered not a single gold medal to the host nation.

Some quick research informed me that she was the member of Parliament for Skeena, a vast, sprawling riding in British Columbia. Once a week, with rare exceptions, she had made the ten-thousand-kilometre round trip between Ottawa and her distant home in Prince Rupert. She had briefly been an alderman and had run the town's little theatre— not much experience for someone "who could be prime minister." She was, however, young for cabinet (forty-four) and very attractive. In magazine-think of the mid-1970s, she was cover material.

Ellen and I had a one-year-old, Kerry, and another child on the way. I contacted the minister's office, kind of explained our predicament, and was told that the minister would be flying to Halifax to give a speech to a physical education convention being held at Wolfville's Acadia University. I was welcome to join the minister on this quick, one-day trip. This meant there was time to drive to Ottawa rather than fly, and Ellen and the baby could come along. Curiously, neither of us had ever been to the nation's capital. We had been looking at buying a house outside of Toronto—even putting in a bid in Uxbridge that had been turned down—and we were getting rather anxious with the family about to expand to four.

Off we went to Ottawa. I had some recent clippings on Campagnolo and read that she had been given great praise by some of the country's more prominent political columnists: Marjorie Nichols, Douglas Fisher and Charles Lynch. Senator Keith Davey had tagged her "solid political gold."

She had caught their attention by standing up to Otto Lang, the minister of transport, who was removing subsidies for passenger and freight ferry service to remote communities around Skeena. Restore the subsidies, she had declared, or I resign. The subsidies were back.

More significantly, she had gained a national profile that spring while in Vienna to watch Canada's supposedly triumphant return to the hockey world championships after a seven-year absence. The Canadians, unfortunately, behaved boorishly, hacking and whacking their way through exhibition matches. Some refused to don helmets, as International Ice Hockey Federation rules required, and even got doctor's certificates to say that the helmets caused "headaches." They lost 11–1 to the Soviets and returned home without a medal.

"I really don't care whether we lose 20–1 or 2–1," said the new minister of state for fitness and amateur sport, "as long as we do it in a fashion that portrays us as true sportsmen."

Canadians who had been embarrassed by the fiasco in Vienna loved it.

The only angle I could think of was to contrast the first image of her—always perfectly turned out—with an inner image of toughness that had shown itself in Vienna. When we talked during the trek to Wolfville and back, she opened up about that inner fibre. Two months into her new job, she had hit black ice on a remote mountain road near midnight and flipped the vehicle three times. With three cracked ribs she had hitchhiked to the hospital and still made a speaking engagement the following day. She fell so hard skiing one day that she dislocated both shoulders, had them reset and went back onto the slopes. She could press 190 pounds in the gym.

Her two daughters talked about how strong she had been while raising them as a single mother. She believed in the legalization of marijuana and was outspoken in trying to get abortion removed from the Criminal Code. As a Liberal minister, she had given money to Flora MacDonald's campaign for the leadership of the Conservative Party and justified it by simply stating, "We women have to stick together." She delighted in one of the nicknames she had picked up on Parliament Hill: "the Lady with the Hobnailed Boots."

When I got back, all Ellen could talk about was the beautiful day she and Kerry had spent in the parks around Ottawa. We remained there for two more days while I talked to other people for the profile, transcribed tape recordings and worked on a first draft of the profile. Each late afternoon we drove to another part of the city. We loved the rivers—clear, cool water that reminded us of Muskoka. We loved the trails and the parks and the small-town feel. We decided on the spot that we would pass on trying to afford a home in Toronto and, instead, see if I could persuade the magazine to let us relocate.

Iona Campagnolo never did become prime minister. She lost her Skeena seat in the 1979 general election to the NDP's Jim Fulton. In 2001, however, she did become the twenty-seventh lieutenant-governor of the province of British Columbia—the first woman ever to hold the position.

Thanks to the Lady with the Hobnailed Boots, my family would spend the next four decades–plus living in Ottawa.

And in a remarkable irony, this feature—written around a printed cover line we couldn't change—would later be selected for inclusion in Val Clery's *Canada from the Newsstands: A Selection from the Best Canadian Journalism of the Past Thirty Years*. MacGregor luck again.

1 2

———————

Seeing the Stories

Sometimes it takes the narrowest focus to produce the wider picture. Perhaps I knew this accidentally. Perhaps I merely lucked into it and was able to pretend it was intentional. Whatever, I was stunned one day when my good friend Charles Gordon—humour columnist for *Maclean's* and the *Ottawa Citizen*—informed me he had been using one of my pieces for the journalism class he was then teaching at Carleton University. He said it was the perfect example of how to squeeze "an entire column out of a single moment."

The column he was referring to was from the Saturday, June 11, 1983, edition of the *Toronto Star*. It was part of a *Star* package on the Conservative Party leadership convention then taking place in Ottawa. Joe Clark had squandered his prime ministership barely six months after gaining it in June 1979. The Clark minority government fell in December, with Pierre Trudeau and the Liberals returning to power in the February 18, 1980, general election.

In a January 1983 leadership review held in Winnipeg, Clark's leadership had been approved by two-thirds of the delegates, yet he insisted a full leadership convention be called before summer. He would try to hold on to his job; Brian Mulroney, a formidable opponent who was making his second run at the top job, was out to take it away. Various notables and forgettables—John Crosbie, David Crombie, Michael Wilson and Peter Pocklington—were also running, but considered to have little to no chance.

Crosbie, Wilson and Crombie all had political experience—in Crosbie's case, considerable, at both the provincial and the federal level. Pocklington had none. He was an Edmonton real-estate dealer known for one thing and one thing only: he owned the Edmonton Oilers, the team that claimed the greatest scorer in the history of hockey: Wayne Gretzky.

We had our political experts on the convention story—Ottawa bureau chief Bob Hepburn, columnist Richard Gwyn and several reporters—so it was a given that the *politics* of the convention would be covered in great depth. I decided to spend my day doing nothing but waiting to see if Gretzky would show up in support of his owner, as Pocklington had hinted would happen.

The *Star* editors ran the piece under the headline "Waiting for Gretzky behind the Cow Palace." The column began,

> Waiting for Gretzky.
> Waiting, in the kind of heat that can only rise from animals.
> Waiting, sweating, while high in an Oiler blue sky a single-engine plane pulls its banner—Pocklington for Canada—and time passes in contemplation about whether the drone comes from the engine or the message.

Pocklington, nicknamed "Peter Puck," had really nothing to say to this political gathering. The most national attention he had garnered before this had to do with a bungled kidnapping involving his wife. He was running on the fumes that seem to fuel so many wealthy sports owners. Buy a team and suddenly you find yourself recognized in the streets, quoted in the newspapers and appearing on television. George Steinbrenner said it best: "When you're a shipbuilder, nobody pays any attention to you. But when you own the New York Yankees . . . they do, and I love it."

Anticipating a brush with a true celebrity, the press had gathered back of the Pocklington and Wilson trailers to await the arrival of the Great One. Someone shouted *"There!"* at one point and the horde turned like schooling capelin toward a woman arriving in a hurry, her clinging, soft brown shoulder straps threatening to fall, her fourteen-karat hair dancing before the television cameras swinging in her direction. She wore a silver belt like a Mexican bandito, bullets shimmering. Enough heat in the gathering, it seemed, that a Michael Wilson campaign balloon suddenly burst in the distance.

It was Eva. Eva Pocklington. A reporter asked for a comment. An enforcer leaned in from the side to snarl, "Mrs. Pocklington does not answer questions from the press."

Suddenly there was a second shout of *"There!"*

A dark blue and black Lincoln limousine swept in, its smoke-blue windows keeping a secret within, the press horde moving away as if it held a hungry shark. The capelin turned back as quickly as they had turned away, pressing, some swearing as they pushed or were pushed.

Such disappointment. The limousine door opened on a flushed young woman in white cotton harem pants. She turned out to be Janet, a clinical instructor from Sunnybrook Medical Centre in Toronto. She had accepted a free ride from Toronto—*with whom? with whom?*—and unabashedly told the pressing press that she had "got a little drunk on champagne" during the trip and was seemingly bitterly disappointed that "all you could get on the TV was two channels."

Off to the side, Mrs. Pocklington, despite her handler, decided she would indeed speak to the press. "That," she said, "has got to be the highlight of the day."

It was not, of course. The highlight of the day was a black Mercedes sneaking in behind a row of vans. Suddenly, he was among us: Wayne Gretzky, four-time winner of the Hart Trophy, holder at that point of two or three dozen NHL records, on his way to becoming the greatest goal scorer in NHL history.

A garbage pail tumbled as the entourage surrounding Peter Puck and the Great One passed by the Wilson trailer, spreading a mess over the shoes of two Wilson workers. "Thanks a lot, Wayne!" shouted one. "I hope you plan on coming back to clean up this mess." Wayne Gretzky acted as if he did not hear. Perhaps he didn't, there being such a buzz in the air around the Cow Palace.

The twenty-two-year-old hockey star had a statement to read. It was in his own hand and it said as much about hockey tactics as political: never completely commit yourself. It seemed somehow unfair to put someone so young in such an impossible position. Wayne Gretzky's statement was . . . sort of . . . an endorsement. But the boss was pleased, nonetheless. The "personal services contract" was paying off.

The two men at the centre of attention then rode a flying wedge of sweating flunkies along the rubbery asphalt to the barbecue, where they were sure to be seen by many of those who would later be voting for the next leader. There were five times as many people walking backward as forward, all pushing and kicking and sweating and cursing. A cameraman fell into Pocklington's press secretary, causing her to wince and scream, yet she carried on. She later ended up in hospital being examined for a broken bone in her foot.

Five minutes after the photographers had been told that Mrs. Pocklington did not like her picture taken, the entourage came to a halt and the camera lenses found their close-ups of the star being photobombed by a smiling Eva.

Peter Puck and the Great One pressed on into the smoke of the charcoal pits cooking up burgers for the gathering delegates. The press, having served its purpose, could now be cut like a player who has lost his legs.

"I don't want any press in that tent!" a Pocklington organizer hissed to two of the heavies. "I want him in there to shake hands with the delegates. *Now see to it!*"

Gretzky entered the tent, smiling, shaking hands, the organizer behind him screaming, "Put the signs down! The signs down! *Put them down!*" It would never do, after all, to have this look like a planned political event. Wayne had come on his own, because he cared, because he wanted his boss to one day be prime minister.

Peter Pocklington would be eliminated on the first ballot, with a dismal 4.8 percent of the vote. Wayne Gretzky, surely, would have scored much higher.

Many years later, I went small again to gain a different perspective.

It was early fall 2007. Nine days earlier, RCMP constable Christopher Worden had approached, alone, a house in a rough neighbourhood of Hay River known as "Disneyland." A report had been filed about noise and partying and Constable Worden arrived just before dawn to check on matters. He was shot dead at the front door. He was only thirty years old.

Hay River is in the Northwest Territories, but Worden was from Ottawa and his funeral would be held at the Notre-Dame Cathedral Basilica on Sussex Drive, roughly halfway between Parliament Hill and the prime minister's residence. It was expected to be a highly emotional ceremony.

"It was a day," the column began, "in which the entire country could use a soother."

The soother was not a metaphor, though it had indeed been an ugly autumn on Parliament Hill. The soother I was referring to was blue and it was very real. Eight-month-old Alexis Marie Worden was contentedly sucking on it as she emerged from a dark car in the arms of her mother, Jodie Lamers Worden.

There were dozens of media outside the church. Cameras, microphones, notepads, television reporters doing stand-ups—all focusing on the growing crowd. I thought perhaps there was a different way to tell the story—through the eyes of someone who could barely talk.

Little Alexis seemed so oblivious to all that I decided to view this scene, as much as possible, through her eyes. She was blinking as her mother held her so she could see the people—thousands of them come to bury her father, so many that they filled the huge basilica and spilled out on both sides of Sussex Drive.

Christopher had told friends he and Jodie would have so many children that they would one day fill a bus, enough boys and girls to form a sports team. Now Alexis was the first and only child of Christopher and Jodie Worden.

Her father could hardly wait for her to grow older. He had already bought a motorhome to take the family around the North. There would be fishing trips and snowmobile treks. He would set winter campfires in the backyard while they stared up at the northern lights as they flickered like fluorescent sheets over the Hay River sky.

In Ottawa, Alexis was surrounded by strange men in red uniforms. She herself was dressed in a miniature serge uniform, complete with gold braid. She startled as the motorcycles pulled up, lights flashing, before the hearse carrying her father pulled in. She heard the pipers start up, followed by the heavy heartbeat march of polished boots. Her own little black shoes, shining, would easily pass inspection.

Other Mounties arrived on horseback and she wiggled, excited, perhaps not wondering why one of the horses was without a rider.

When the long black station wagon came to a stop the pallbearers formed up at the back, one of them carrying a lone stetson on a pillow. It was a hat exactly like that her father wore to work—but, at six foot three, Constable Christopher Worden could not possibly be under it.

Those who spoke at the funeral talked about Christopher's smile. "Contagious," one friend said. "All smiles, all the time," said another. Smiling, no matter whether he was serving as co-captain of the football team at Wilfrid Laurier University or playing the violin in the family room at Hay River.

He smiled the widest, a family member said, when tossing a squealing, screeching baby Alexis over his head and gently catching her. But now there was no one to toss her. And no one she could see was smiling this day.

It's really all about perspective.

Globe and Mail editor Ed Greenspon offered me an office in the downtown *Globe* bureau when I was hired on in 2002. I balked, even though it would mean working daily with my good friend, columnist Jeffrey Simpson, and others, such as Bill Curry, with whom I played beer-league hockey every Monday night. I balked in part because I had been essentially working from home since 1992, when the *Ottawa Citizen*'s Jim Travers assigned me to cover the Ottawa Senators. I very much liked the freedom. I also had learned a valuable lesson in stepping away from Parliament Hill and into the Civic Centre Arena a couple of kilometres down Bank Street.

I left the Hill at a time when the constitutional wars were a decade old. From Pierre Trudeau's repatriation of the Constitution through the Meech Lake and Charlottetown accords of Brian Mulroney and on to Keith Spicer's Citizens' Forum on Canada's Future, Parliament Hill had become the wheel, we had become the hamsters who simply kept running. I left the Hill knowing what sections 91(3) and 92(2) of the British North America Act meant—the power to raise taxes—and stepped into a world where no one gave a rat's ass about the constitution.

They knew taxes, of course, but didn't think much of them.

If I returned now to Parliament Hill, I feared I would once again begin to think that what happens there is the most important thing going on in the country. It is not. Covering sports taught me that every day. Instead, I told Ed, I would prefer to work from home and on the road. He was fine with this proposal and, under his editorship, I would write five general-interest columns a week for five straight years. *Globe* publisher Phillip Crawley thought it too much of a workload, but I loved it. Under the next editor, John Stackhouse, I switched to a mix of columns and features. Then, under editor David Walmsley and sports editor Shawna Richer, I turned to sports and features, still covering the odd election with *Globe* friends like Gary Mason and Jeffrey Simpson. The eighteen years spent at the *Globe and Mail* were the best years of my career.

My before-sports time at the *Citizen* and my years at the *Globe* convinced me that the best job available to anyone in print journalism has to be that of "general columnist." It's pretty much a licence to do whatever the hell you want. Take out the prime minister? Done. Complain about leaf blowers? Done. Write about your dog? Done.

My favourite "assignments" as a general columnist were simply being sent out the door and asked to find things. The paper would want me to "take the pulse" of the country, usually during a general election or a time, such as the Quebec referendum or the post-Meech mood, of great national anxiety.

In the early summer of 2003, I was tooling around the West trying to get a feel for the Conservative confusion that had become an important part of the politics of the land. The Reform Party had kneecapped the Progressive Conservative Party, had morphed into the Alliance Party and was now seeking to merge with the old PCs to produce a brand-new "Conservative" party.

My head was spinning. I needed a change.

Sitting in my hotel room in Calgary, I read about two young sisters from Canmore, Sage and Shea O'Neill, who had gone on a rock-collecting hike to nearby Marble Canyon with their parents, Paul and Peggy. It had been a perfect family outing until a sudden microburst of wind came down the canyon and toppled a sixteen-metre spruce tree, the tree crashing down on the two little girls. The parents watched, in shock, as their children were taken from them in a heartbeat.

"It is," the local weekly said, "every mother's and father's worst nightmare. To lose both of your children in such a horrible, freakish fashion is perhaps the cruelest twist of fate possible."

I was stunned by the story. Who could care less about the fortunes and misfortunes of a confused political movement when there was reality like this? I decided that I would go to Canmore for the funeral, which was to be held the next morning, a Saturday, meaning I would have two days to craft a column out of this gamble or else find something else, there being no Sunday *Globe*.

The rain fell in sheets as I drove west into the mountain town of Canmore. It fell from dark and ragged clouds that seemed stuck on the surrounding hills and it flooded 7th Street in front of St. Michael Anglican Church, where the funeral was to take place.

Paul and Peggy O'Neill had often taken their girls to the canyon. The terrain was safe, and blond, blue-eyed and responsible Sage, eight, and impish Shea, only five, were never out of each other's sight. Besides, even if something did go wrong, Paul O'Neill was a trained paramedic with the Nakoda Emergency Medical Services and would know what to do.

God knows, he tried. The one little girl died instantly—he preferred not to say which—and he did all he could to save the second, who died in his arms.

In a remarkable statement, Paul O'Neill apologized later to those hiking families who came along the trail after them, saying: "We are sorry that your children were exposed to the situation." He thanked the "special person" who came and took charge of matters when the O'Neills realized they could do nothing more.

"Thank you," he said, "for returning our daughters to us."

That Saturday morning, the people of this community of ten thousand filled three churches to say farewell to Sage and Shea. At St. Michael's, where the parents, family and close friends came, boxes of tissues were being passed along the pews as if they were offering plates. Paul and Peggy O'Neill came in, arms around each other, and a piper hidden at the back of the church struck up "Amazing Grace."

Because so many mourners were children, the church had been decorated with balloons and papier-mâché butterflies in the girls' favourite colours—pinks and purples and yellows—and Rev. Frank Doe, a balding, roly-poly man with a voice as comforting as a hot-water bottle, asked them all to leave their seats and come to the front of the church where they might talk quietly with him for a moment.

While adults leaned forward in the pews, straining to hear what was being said, Reverend Doe merely asked the gathering, settling children how they felt. "Sad," they said, and he told them it was alright to feel that way. He asked them if they felt angry, and, when some said they did, he said that, too, was understandable.

Then the Reverend Doe told them a story about young water bugs who wondered what happened to those who climbed out of the pond and were never seen again. The water bugs promised each other that the next to leave would come back and report, but when the next climbed up a nearby plant stem and suddenly turned into a silver-winged dragonfly, it found it could not come back down and explain, and so it flew off into the sun and a new adventure.

"Death," Reverend Doe told them, "is kind of like that."

If such an answer was good enough for the children, it was good enough, as well, for many of the adults—for nothing else would make sense in a moment such as this.

Peggy and Paul O'Neill wanted the people gathered there to know that the family had an evening bedtime ritual of cuddling and books and blown kisses, often followed by the singing of "When Irish Eyes

Are Smiling" or "Too-Ra-Loo-Ral" until the girls drifted off. The tissue boxes pumped furiously up and down the pews as soloist Karen Minish, her voice once cracking, sang both songs.

> Too-ra-loo-ra-loo-ral
> Too-ra-loo-ra-li
> Too-ra-loo-ra-loo-ral
> Hush now, don't you cry . . .

Others stepped forward to say a few words. A young friend talked about the way the girls smiled, and a teacher about the brightness of their eyes. At the back of the church, the sisters' art surrounded a display of family photographs, Sage and Shea invariably with their arms around each other, perhaps as close together as they were when the spruce tree fell out of nowhere.

They handed out small paper butterflies to all the children and, to the adults, small envelopes with butterflies on the outside and two flower seeds inside. And when the service was over, Paul O'Neill—ever the paramedic—stopped every few rows to hug and comfort those who were still crying. Meanwhile, outside the church, the rain continued to fall on the little mountain town that had lost two of its most exquisite butterflies.

On Monday, July 7, the *Globe* ran my column. An editor gave it a lovely head: "A heartbroken community bids farewell to Sage and Shea, butterflies who flew off too soon," and no one asked even once about how things were going with the Reform–Alliance–Conservative conundrum.

Years passed and a short note arrived from Paul O'Neill. He said that he had clipped the column and kept it under glass in his home office, and every once in a while he would reread the piece and think about his little girls and the town that had shown so much love for them. He said he found the column "comforting."

Never once did a politician say anything like that about something I had written.

Charles Gordon was right when he suggested you sometimes have to go small to paint the big picture before you. Not only small, but different—a story told from a perspective no one else was trying. Is it risky? Perhaps, but in these cases it just felt right. The *Toronto Star*'s team coverage of the leadership convention that Wayne Gretzky could not deliver to Peter Pocklington won the 1983 National Newspaper Award for spot news. The column on little Alexis and her soother took the 2007 National Newspaper Award for short features.

Perspective can sometimes be everything.

WHITE PRIVILEGE

Chief Clarence Louie and I were having a lazy back-and-forth via text messaging.

He'd been working on his book, *Rez Rules: My Indictment of Canada's and America's Systemic Racism Against Indigenous Peoples*, which was published by McClelland & Stewart in 2021, and I was advising and doing a bit of the early editing and structuring of the book. We worked well together.

Clarence and I had a friendship that went back to 2006, when I happened to be in Fort McMurray on another story for the *Globe and Mail* and he was giving a speech on Indigenous leadership that I'd been invited to. I have to confess to being shocked by what he had to say. He laid out his "rules for leadership," which included the following:

- My first rule for success is "Show up on time." My No. 2 rule for success is to follow Rule No. 1.

- Quit your sniffling.

- Join the real world—go to school or get a job.

- The biggest employer shouldn't be the band office.

- Blaming government? That time is over.

- Our ancestors worked for a living. So should you.

Needless to say, the column I filed on this soft-spoken, tough-talking chief of the Osoyoos Indian Band from the southern Okanagan Valley of British Columbia caused a bit of a national stir, both for and against. The thing was, Clarence could back it up. Eighteen times he had been elected chief of the band. Osoyoos had gone from poverty and bankruptcy and mass unemployment to prosperity. The band owned a five-star resort, a golf course, an RV park, a racetrack, and a winery, and now had twice as many jobs as it had people. We called this community the "miracle in the desert" and the moniker stuck. Not surprisingly, publishers wanted a book from him. A bit surprisingly, he turned to me for help. I was not a ghostwriter, more an editor, a sounding board and a constant encouragement.

Anyway, this particular day was during the heated "lobster wars" in Nova Scotia. Canadians across the country were outraged at the RCMP failure to protect the very modest Indigenous fishery—fully guaranteed by treaty and upheld by the Supreme Court of Canada—from vandalism and violence by white fishers who dominated the industry but could not fish during the off-season.

Clarence said he felt like heading down to Nova Scotia to help his people. I said I, too, was pissed off about this and would happily join him. "The difference is," he texted me, "I'd get arrested and you wouldn't. . . . White privilege." He was probably right, but I decided to have a little fun by challenging him.

"Some white privilege," I texted back. "You grew up in a desert, no running water and no power. I come from the bush, no running water, no electricity, and a two-hole outhouse for pooping."

"Ha!" he shot back. "We only had a one-holer. . . . Two holes is pure White privilege!"

BRENT AND ERIC

When first encountered in these pages, the three of us—Brent Munroe, Eric Ruby and I—were headed off to first day of kindergarten at Huntsville Public School. That friendship we formed lasted a life-time, and though there would be times, years even, when we would not see each other, we always took up exactly as we had left. The old stories would be recited more than told: the Ontario peewee lacrosse championship . . . the ride to North Bay on the Honda 55cc scooter, Eric's ass riding a thick plank hanging off the back end . . . the time Eric donned Brent's police uniform and showed up at a local bar . . . Eric tackling me in that alley back in Ibiza, Spain . . .

Brent wanted to be a cop. With his grade ten, finally, he got accepted to police college and then joined the Ontario Provincial Police. He would serve in Tillsonburg, Red Lake and Parry Sound, always return-ing home to Huntsville where, if possible, we would all touch base at least for a brief visit.

Brent married a beautiful woman named Ginny and they would have three children: Leslie, Jennifer and Ron. Ron would grow to be the spitting image of his large, blockheaded father and become a good friend of our children. The marriage did not last. Too much drinking, too much partying, and Brent would later blame himself . . . and the bottle.

Eric eventually graduated from grade twelve and began a vaga-bond life as a ski bum, even though he always worked, whether it was in the ski rental shop or at the lifts. He skied and worked in resorts out West and in Leysin, Switzerland, with his pal Ken Chilibeck. He worked winters in the family ski shop at Hidden Valley, skiing before and after hours. He got a job driving cab out in Jasper, where he would spend all his free time on the hills. He would never marry.

That is not to say Eric was not interested in girls. Quite the contrary. He could fall in love after one dance. But his exuberance and unpredictability were hard to get used to, even for those of us who had known him all his life. Once at a Hidden Valley dance, he leapt out of a sheltered corner with a hunting knife flashing as if he was about to attack me. I instinctively raised my hands and the knife sliced into the fatty tissue of my left thumb. I still have the scar. Eric was, of course, mortified and apologetic. But he was also just being Eric.

Brent got in serious trouble, the full details of which are not definitively known. His marriage had failed. He was either fired or advised to resign from the OPP. He found work at a hotel in Red Lake and all went well until there was a robbery involving a considerable amount of cash and police quickly determined that Brent was involved. He was charged and convicted, jailed first in Dryden and later transferred to a medium-security correction centre in Mimico. He was then transferred to a halfway house in Brampton and was later discharged to the care of his girlfriend, Emerald Chamberlain. She believes this happened in early 1982.

Brent soon found work with a small logging operation. He learned to drive the horses that hauled the logs out of the bush to where they could be loaded onto a truck. He fell in love with wood, passionate about old tools and the various grains of the wood he worked with. He began a company that restored log homes and cabins and became very good at his new trade. He often worked on a cabin owned by good friends of ours, the Kearns, and whenever we were all at Camp Lake we would get together. He invariably had a bottle going.

Eric got in trouble in Spain in the fall of 1971. He had stayed on in Europe to ski and then returned once again to Spain after the ski season had ended in Switzerland. There he met up with his great new friend, Bill Goslett, as well as several others he had gotten to know while in Europe: Robert, Barney, Steve, Rodger ("Jet") and Jimmy. The following is how Bill remembered the incident nearly fifty years later:

We had all just arrived in Barcelona and were hungry and ready to get a night's sleep and get on the road to Greece. We had checked into a hotel and were back on the street looking for a good restaurant.

We met Jet and Barney at a restaurant near the port. Ruby with his red afro and Eddie Shack moustache was immediately attracted to Jet, who was wearing orange pants and a black and white referee's jersey. We had to drag the two of them out of a fountain in the Ramblas area. Jet decided to run through the fountain and Eric was right on his tail. Crazy comes in pairs.

We left the bar in search of a restaurant when it became dark. We were walking down the street laughing and having drunken fun. I remember having my one hand in my pocket and the other holding my camera bag when I was spun around and punched in the face by a Spaniard. As I was stumbling backwards, I saw Eric midflight with his size 12 landing right in the face of the guy who had hit me. We had never seen this group of Spanish guys before but all hell erupted. We ended up in a street brawl involving six or seven of us and an equal number of Spaniards.

I think the size of Eric and Robert, their insanity and the bizarre costume Jet was wearing scared the Spanish guys. The fight only lasted about 10 minutes, but did involve a lot of yelling and screaming, punching and kicking. I don't think they realized that we were not prepared to be assaulted without getting some of our own licks in. Eventually the Spaniards ran and we headed back to the hotel. We got to the van. It wasn't meant for seven big guys. I told Jet, Eric and Jimmy to go right to their hotel, but they went for food instead.

It was the following morning that we found out they were easily spotted and identified by their clothing. They were arrested and transported to the ancient *Prison de Hombres*. The Spanish guys had found a cop and he got right on it and started looking for us.

The rest of us headed south to Sitges so that we were out of Barcelona jurisdiction. We set a plan to head back and see if we could negotiate with a judge to set the boys free. It took about a week but the "tip" was sufficient for the Judge and we were told to wait outside the *Prison de Hombres* at 8:00 the following morning, when we could pick the guys up and head directly for the border.

If it were not for the clothing, I would not have recognized them. They had been shaved as bald as a baby's bum. Not a hair above the shoulders.

Eric, too, was having trouble with booze. His few relationships never went anywhere, though one close friend, Linda, stuck with him for life. He eventually returned to Huntsville, drove a cab for a while and then joined his father full-time at the family's clothing store. He had a heart of gold. Any time a local down-and-outer would die—one of them being a childhood teammate on our provincial-championship lacrosse team—Eric could always be counted on to deliver a new suit, shirt and tie to the family or the local funeral home. He never talked about it.

Eric was in his early forties when he was finally diagnosed with attention deficit hyperactivity disorder (ADHD). Looking back, we should have known since day 1 of kindergarten, but that was long before there were diagnoses or Ritalin. He began speaking publicly about his hyperactive condition and there was even a video made with a very young Hawksley Workman playing young Eric as he struggled with school.

Drinking had become an issue, and he knew it. He couldn't control himself, so he simply quit drinking. I admired him hugely for this courage and determination. He was also beginning to have ailments that became increasingly severe as the years passed. He had irritable bowel syndrome, which his doctors tried, not with great success, to ease with medication. He became a regular visitor to the emergency department of Huntsville Memorial Hospital. He went to the Ontario Hospital at Penetanguishene, where he was diagnosed as bipolar. More and more medication.

I found a letter while going through old files for this memoir. It is from Brent, the penmanship exquisite—he insisted on nib pens and ink—and is dated April 9, but no year. This would have been the middle to late 1990s. After signing off, he added a postscript: "Eric looks 100% better lately. Attitude better. Working hard on himself."

But it was up and down for Eric. He'd be good for a while and then crash. Sometime around 2010 he called me to tell me, "I'm in a rented car driving near Sault Ste. Marie and I've got a forty-ouncer of vodka against my hip."

"Are you drinking?"

"Not yet."

"Do me the biggest favour ever, please. Turn around and go to Penetang. They can help you."

Much to my surprise, and delight, he did just that. The forty-ouncer was never opened.

Brent had been badly injured in an early-morning accident on Highway 60 between the village of Dwight and Algonquin Park's west gate. He was sober and had been headed to do some bush work. It happened on a twisting hill on a slippery winter morning, two vehicles heading in opposite directions colliding on an icy stretch. Brent broke an ankle, hurt his leg and lost several teeth. There were serious injuries, as well, in the other vehicle.

In the fall of 1996, Brent finally realized he needed to put an end to his drinking. He and Emerald found sobriety together and supported each other. He invited Eric and Ellen and me to his fifth anniversary celebration of being dry. We went and there were speeches, some of them incredibly moving, and then all gathered and were told to hold the hand of the closest person while those present recited the Serenity Prayer. Ellen and I held hands. Eric held hands with a smiling Beryl Munroe, Brent's mother.

> God, give me grace to accept with serenity
> the things that cannot be changed,
> Courage to change the things
> which should be changed,
> and the Wisdom to distinguish
> the one from the other . . .

Emerald and Brent established a small Huntsville business, Log Home Restoration Services. They were married on September 21, 2002, in an outdoor ceremony held at the Fiery Grill restaurant in the small town of Dorset, a half-hour drive from Huntsville. The rain let up just long enough for Rev. Eric Sisel to marry them on the deck overlooking the waters of Lake of Bays. I acted as emcee. There was complimentary coffee and alcohol-free punch for the guests. Eric wrote, and delivered, a passionate, funny poem about our long friendship.

On a small program printed for the event, Emerald wrote, "Our Vision: We have been brought together for the purpose of helping each other grow. We will be each other's teacher. Our relationship is a special gift; it will take us through whatever we need to learn to become more enlightened, loving human beings . . ."

They were certainly loving and everyone was delighted that they had found each other. The happy couple moved to a small rural property on the Muskoka River near the village of Port Sydney and were obviously content with their new lives. They were looking forward to many years together.

On January 2, 2004, Brent went out to the shed, gathered up an armful of firewood and dropped dead of a heart attack on the way back to the house. He was about to turn fifty-six years old.

Fifteen months after we had gathered with such joy on the deck of the Fiery Grill, the same people came to the Billingsley Funeral Home in Huntsville, Rev. Eric Sisel officiating, me again the emcee. Fifteen months between wedding and funeral. It all seemed so sad, so unbelievably unfair.

I also had to arrange the pallbearers, one of them telling me he could only lift from one side of the casket because, well, he'd been shot a year ago in an argument over the ownership of some heavy equipment. Eric had me read a new poem for this occasion; he was too upset to do it himself. He sat in a corner of the funeral home, tears freely flowing for his friend.

Eric continued to work at the family store. He became a regular visitor to our home on Lorne Street, sitting upstairs with my father while the old man smoked roll-your-own after roll-your-own. There is a photograph of the two of them dressed up for Halloween taken not long before Duncan MacGregor's death in 1995 at the age of eighty-eight.

As per usual, Eric wrote a poem about his old friend's passing. It was, as per usual, on bristol board, the words in red and yellow and green and purple and blue. He insisted on reading it to me, shouting some words, whispering in an almost childlike way on others. In one segment he said, "Our friendship will now evolve into a stronger bond since Dunc is gone."

The friendship remained, of course, but the bond could get no stronger. I was busy with a career that left little time for Huntsville. Ellen and I had kids heading off to university and we would be either home in Ottawa or at the cottage when I had down time. Our old friend from the lacrosse team, Don Strano, stepped in where Dunc and I could not. He and Eric became closer and closer, especially after Don lost his partner.

Eric's own health problems continued. The family store was closed and the building sold. His parents retired to a beautiful property on

Pen Lake and Eric moved from an apartment over the store into an apartment near the Legion. Don Strano visited regularly. His parents, Murray and Stella, looked in on him daily even as they reached their nineties.

One late winter day they called on him and the door to his apartment was locked. There was a sign in the window: "Do Not Come In. Call 911." He had used his many medications to take his own life. He was seventy years old and left behind his parents, his brother, Michael, sister, Paula, and their families.

More than a month later, the family held a celebration of life for Eric at Hidden Valley, where he had worked and skied for decades. They hosted it in the large, three-storey chalet where those amazing dances had been featured through the 1960s and 1970s. The place was absolutely packed, hundreds of people on the main floor, a hundred more on the higher level looking down.

His parents had asked me to speak. I pointed up to a far corner of the upper deck and began, "Right about there is where Eric once stabbed me."

No one batted an eye.

13

Ellen

All those air miles. All those hotel points. This, sadly, is how many reporters come to measure their careers. There is an old saying attributed to a long-time American sportswriter—"The road will make bums of them all"—and, to a certain extent, this is true. Marriages fail. Alcohol too often rules. But so, too, does home call, and for most sportswriters and political reporters I have known there is nothing sweeter after a final campaign sweep across the country or a Stanley Cup raised than to pack your bags and head back home.

I was incredibly fortunate and know it. MacGregor luck held for decades. Ellen and I had been together since the middle of high school and we survived what may well have been the toughest year of all, the year after I had failed grade twelve. Ellen's father, Lloyd Griffith, was department head for science, chemistry being my worst subject, and he clearly did not care much to see this failing young man in horn-rimmed glasses hanging about his daughter's locker and their apartment out Main Street. Mr. Griffith also served as the Huntsville High School guidance counsellor, helping students decide on where they might be headed after high school. As such, he had access to all the records of the students, including the mandatory IQ tests that were then administered to each Ontario student entering grade nine. He dug into my results, as well as his daughter's, and duly informed her that I simply wasn't "bright enough" for her to waste her time on.

I was aghast, years later, when Ellen informed me of this. Once Ellen and I became the parents of three young women high schoolers, however, I came to admire his ingenuity and enterprise . . .

We stayed together through high school and university, even though we attended schools hundreds of kilometres apart. We married when I was twenty-four and she twenty-three. We always planned to have a family, perhaps even a large one, but we would wait a few years and, in the meantime, spend as much time together as possible. Whenever I could, I grabbed assignments that would allow me to take her along.

Maclean's sent us to glorious Quebec City and Mont-Sainte-Anne so I could do a feature on a popular Quebec winter activity that was taking off in other parts of the country: cross-country skiing. We bought equipment the moment we arrived back in Toronto and skied enthusiastically every winter to follow, including skiing in to her family's Camp Lake cottage, as the snow plough did not clear the road all the way.

The Canadian sent me to Mexico City to cover the 1975 Pan-Am Games, and she tagged along and toured museums and art galleries while I covered men's basketball and track and field. We stole away for an overnight trip to the famous silver town of Taxco, high in the mountains between Mexico City and Acapulco. We sat in the town square that warm evening marvelling at the courting couples and their chaperones. Other young couples were showing off their new babies.

"That will soon be us," Ellen said.

Kerry was born March 18, 1976. Christine followed on April Fool's Day, 1978, both born in Toronto. Jocelyn was the first Ottawa baby, arriving on July 18, 1981, with Gordon following quickly after on October 4, 1982. We were now six. It was time for a car that could hold us all.

Four children in the space of six years, the two youngest so close they were virtually raised as twins. I was away often, and Ellen somehow managed to get the four of them to wherever they needed to be—Kerry for dance and acting and swimming, Christine for gymnastics and diving, Jocelyn for dance and rhythmic gymnastics, Gord for hockey and lacrosse. Ellen had been deeply involved in sports herself as a youngster, winning high school and district championships in track, basketball, gymnastics and cheerleading. The early training stuck for life, as all three girls remained active in sports and the outdoors. Gord eventually became the right winger on my beer-league hockey line for some twenty years. I had a front-row seat to watch him catch up to me and then pass me as he became more and more skilled and I became, more and more, older and slower.

No marriage is perfect, but this one was pretty good. We squabbled over money at times and there were, obviously, times when I was far too much on the road and she far too much stuck at home caring for little ones. Whenever possible, I tried to engineer assignments that would allow for the family to come along. We went to the Bahamas when there were just the three girls and had a wonderful time while I did features on a former finance minister and an increasingly famous Canadian cartoonist, Jim Unger, the creator of "Herman." I covered spring training several times while the family stayed back at the hotel and enjoyed the pool and beach. Christine took her first steps by a hotel pool in Dunedin, Florida, while I was a few miles away with the Toronto Blue Jays.

Somehow—remember, this was when newspapers had money—the *Citizen* began assigning me once a year to go off on a family vacation and just write about it. We drove a rented van that slept all six, and the dog, to Prince Edward Island and back through Maine. All fully expensed. We went to Florida for March break and visited Disney World and SeaWorld and Busch Gardens. All fully expensed. We travelled out West pulling a pop-up camper trailer and visited the Raymore, Saskatchewan, farm where Ellen's mother, Rose, spent her childhood. Again, expensed.

Summer was always the best time. We would head to Ellen's parents' cottage, where we had honeymooned back in September 1972. We would spend a minimum of two weeks swimming, fishing, holding evening campfires. A third week would be reserved for a camping or canoe trip. We especially loved the canoeing, though Ellen was not as keen on whitewater as I became. We paddled all the major routes of Algonquin Park; we paddled a long stretch of the Kootenay River in British Columbia. We did the Mattawa River in northern Ontario with Ellen's sister, Jackie, and her husband, Ralph. We canoed in western Quebec and eastern Ontario.

Canoe tripping became our great summer passion. We had our beloved cedar-and-canvas Northland canoe. A few years ago, on a whim, we bought an ultralight carbon-fibre canoe and loved how easy it was to portage. Unfortunately, if people were just out for a nice paddle and had no backpacks, tent and food barrel, the canoe proved quite tipsy, as son-in-law Mike found out one summer. Rather than risk children and visitors, we sold it and went back to renting for long treks into the bush.

Eventually, the cottage was passed on to Ellen and she became carpenter, gardener, chef, designer and planner. She built a deck the length of the front of the cottage. She built a new outhouse, with me digging out the old pit. This, it is important to know, was a woman whose favourite place to shop was a Home Hardware building supplies store.

She loved to explore and we spent many happy days hiking in the park or along the old lumber trails around Camp Lake, usually with the Kearns, our friends from down the lake, or the Gibsons from the island, or the Rosses from the north shore. If we happened upon other friends from our road along the south shore, so much the better. She loved people as much as the flora and fauna.

She painted glorious landscapes and did oils of her grandchildren that line the walls of our home and her cottage. She was a superb artist who never marketed herself, likely because she never wished those paintings to leave. She went back to school part-time and completed a degree in psychology from Carleton University, then received a diploma in interior design from Algonquin College. She became president of the Nepean Ottawa Diving Club, where Christine became a nationally ranked high-tower diver.

Ellen's most treasured moments were at the cottage with the children and then their children—Fisher, Sadie, Raphaël, Hawkley, Noémie—and an annual Christmas get-together in Kanata. She spent weeks preparing, right down to small gifts for everyone who would be there: as many children and grandchildren as possible, brother Jim and Stephanie, with her fabulous Jamaican spicy chicken, brother Tom and Esther, Jackie and Ralph, cousins Don and Diana McCormick, Storm and Carrol Anne McGregor and Bonnie Barrie and Bob Inkpen, friends like Denis Menard and Merryl-Jeanne Mason. She was at her happiest in these gatherings.

We travelled together to France multiple times, as Kerry had moved there a decade earlier and married Olivier. Ellen now had French grandchildren, Raphaël and Noémie, and she wanted to see them as much as possible. For several years they lived in Nice, which we came to know as well as Ottawa simply by walking every day to the old city and the boardwalk and high into the hills beyond. They moved to Poitiers, Olivier's hometown, and we came to love it, as well. Where we were most content, however, was in Fayence, a "perched village" in the Provence-Alpes-Côte d'Azur region in southeastern France. We stayed in the ancient villa belonging to my long-time agent and friend, Bruce Westwood, and had family come to join us. The most beautiful village in France, we came to believe.

When all four kids had left home, we decided that Ellen would come with me on every possible assignment. The best such experience was when the *Globe and Mail* assigned me to do features on the great rivers of Canada. We travelled all over the country, checking out the rivers by canoe, boat, car, foot. With fellow writer Philip Lee, we "poled" a canoe up the slow-moving Saint John River. With the Hope, British Columbia, volunteer search-and-rescue unit, we rode a steel-hulled 435-horsepower jet boat toward Hells Gate, the mighty Fraser River so "mighty" at this point that the rushing waters simply held up a hand and brought the roaring boat to a complete halt. We could go no farther. We did sixteen rivers in all: Fraser, Columbia, Mackenzie, Bow, North Saskatchewan, Red, Niagara, Grand, Don, Muskoka, Ottawa, Rideau, Dumoine, Gatineau, St. Lawrence and Saint John.

Ellen finally got to see the huge, majestic country I had been running off to write about for nearly four decades. Now, we were seeing it together. We planned to see so much more of it once I retired.

In March 2021, with the Covid-19 pandemic entering its third wave in Canada, we passed the time by cross-country skiing on a golf course near Ralph and Jackie's Kanata townhouse. Ellen was up and down the hills as usual, but soon tired. She went to see her doctor and had blood work done and the results came back that she was anemic. She tried to bolster her iron count by drinking prune juice and taking supplements. They checked again and, strangely, her count had dropped even further.

On a Friday morning toward the end of March, I took the new puppy, Piper, out into the field for an early romp with her friends, Dasher and Indie, Jim and Lindsay's dogs from farther down the street. When I came back in, Ellen was seated at the kitchen table, but not looking right. Then her eyes rolled back into her head and she fainted. I caught her before she hit the floor, flopped her back in the chair and dialled 911 while propping her up. An ambulance was at our place in ten minutes and rushed her to Ottawa General Hospital on the far side of town.

Once they had her in emergency, they began pumping blood into her. One transfusion, two, three. With the third wave of the pandemic well under way, visiting was highly restricted. They let me see her in emergency, but once she was assigned a bed I had to get permission from the nearest nursing station to see her. They gave me an hour and told me to arrive at two o'clock.

I arrived, parked and then lined up in the hospital lobby, two metres back of the visitor in front, two metres in front of the visitor behind. One by one, we were grilled on whether anyone might have Covid symptoms. Once they were satisfied, they called the nursing station to see if I indeed had permission to spend an hour with my ill partner. "You can go up," they said.

They said I could visit for an hour every second day. Christine and Gordon, our children from close by, each had an hour-long visit with her. The news was not good. An MRI indicated two substantial growths in her abdomen. She was given more transfusions. The abdomen oncology team decided that the growths were sarcoma cancer and that meant another team would be called in. The sarcoma team decided that the growths were beyond surgical repair and wanted to begin treatment by radiation, and if that worked a bit, then try chemotherapy. One young woman doctor had told Ellen bluntly that she had months to live at best. Ellen was not amused. She asked me to look into medical assistance in dying (MAID) and I said I would see how one would get the paperwork to apply for it.

They say all patients in big hospitals, especially teaching hospitals, need a strong advocate who can keep track of matters and intervene if necessary. Kerry took on that job from France. She called both Ellen and me daily. She called the nursing station regularly for updates. Using Ellen's cell phone, she listened in on every discussion with whatever doctor or doctors happened to come around to see Ellen. Kerry pressed the hospital for a Covid vaccine for her mother. She had already arranged for me to get my first shot, but the hospital had no vaccines to access for patients like Ellen. Kerry called the CEO and head medical people, and finally they were able to obtain a single vial of the vaccine so that Ellen and five other patients could have their first Covid shots. Perhaps Kerry's determination saved a life or two.

We knew the situation was grave. Because of the pandemic, it would be impossible for Kerry, her husband, Olivier, and their two children, Raphaël and Noémie, to travel from France. Nor could Jocelyn, her husband, Andi, and their young ones, Hawkley and Haywood, get to Ottawa from Calgary. Haywood was not yet a year old, and Ellen had never held him. Christine's husband, Mike, could not visit, nor could their children, Fisher and Sadie.

On April 7, I was stunned to see a featured article in my morning *Citizen*. It was by Kerry, writing from France. She had said nothing about this in our daily calls. "Please," the headline read, "more screen time with my mom." It was beautifully illustrated with photographs of Kerry with her mother, of Ellen with her large family, of Ellen and me getting married. This is what Kerry wrote:

> I've been walking around my town of Poitiers, France this week with my mother in my pocket. It is the strangest feeling, in the strangest of years, and it's breaking my heart, even though I'm being optimistic.
>
> This is yet another pandemic year, as everyone is aware. And although I've read a million articles about people seeing loved ones through hospital windows and not being able to hold hands, I must admit that I heard the stories, but I didn't feel them.
>
> Or, I didn't feel them nearly as much as I should have.
>
> I apologize to all of you. I feel them now.
>
> My mother, Ellen, is in her early 70s, looks and acts middle-aged, and always puts on too much hand cream. She says, "Come here, I took too much!" and shares it with me, rubbing her hands on mine in a silly, loving transfer.

She did this from when I was a toddler until almost two years ago—that's the last time I saw her in person. For the past two decades, I've been convinced that she does this cream trick on purpose, in the same way that she pretends she's forced to kiss the freckles on my neck to annoy me.

These rituals are her dear, sweet, beloved extensions of physical affection. This is my mother—the one in my pocket—and this is how she loves me.

My parents, who have been together since they were 15, were supposed to come here to see my new French city last spring. But their trip was cancelled, like so many others. My kids and I didn't make it back to Ottawa in the summer either, nor to the cottage.

We haven't seen my sister's new baby or the spot where my mom wants to build the new cottage bunkie—the cabin that just got the go-ahead and will ensure that there is room for all of us there when we finally get together.

The old lake-side cottage is near where my mom and her sister grew up. It's where she taught me to swim, and where she and I once spent an entire day lying on the ground, pushing some horrendously heavy Easter Island heads down the hill to put in the garden. I took breaks for water; she didn't.

We say that my mom has ox blood because she is stronger and more determined than all of us. This is a woman, an artist, who once built a deck not by herself, but with the help of four very unhelpful kids under 10 years old. She is the strongest human I know.

(But mom—because I know you read all my stories—I'm not saying that as an obligation. Get through this however you need to.)

I didn't realize that my mother was in my pocket until I went for a parent-teacher meeting last week in France, and the teacher said she'd heard my mother was ill. "Where is she?" the teacher asked in French.

"In my pocket," I replied without even thinking, rapping my cell phone with my knuckles.

I used to call my mom on the phone once a week, but since she's been in the hospital, we've been texting and I've been sending photos and videos. This is why I need so much more screen time now; we're in the middle of a smart-phone-based, never-ending sleepover. (I hope. We still need more info.)

Just curious: How do you see someone when you text? I see them the same way that I dream them. They're like a preliminary sketch of themselves. My mom is an artist; maybe that has something to do with it. I see well-defined shoulders and hands, but I don't really see their heads or mouths. It's like I'm perpetually at the height of a toddler, getting impressions of their language and emotions as the story plays out.

My mom likes shopping, so I've been taking her with me to look at dresses and shoes. (I look like you now, mom. But I guess you already know that, don't you?)

She likes home renovation, so I video-walked her through the house my husband just bought. Walls have been torn down and the garden is a mess, which is exactly what my mom and I will now go over together on Pinterest.

Because her hospital room has no windows, I've sent photos of the spring flowers that came out along the river by my house. When I asked her what she'd like to do on the weekend, she said, "I'd like to hear some birds sing," so we hiked together and I recorded the sounds of the forest.

I have troubleshot her treatment by text: "I think the blood they are giving you might be too thin. Tell them you need ox blood. And say STAT. If you say STAT, they have to do it right away."

I tell her I know this because I watched too much TV grow-ing up.

I have, of course, also used that same phone to call the hos-pital for updates and to ask about vaccination. I've never been so hungry for details.

My mom still laughs easily, even though this is tough. And oddly, while she's in a small room in a hospital we haven't seen, I know that right now, she's also in the pockets of her husband and children, her sister's family and all of our cousins. We're all walking around where we live, going to our jobs and dealing with our kids during a pandemic, in mid-conversation with her.

I can't remember when we've been so close.

And I really am feeling optimistic. What else can we do?

The doctors are working with her. I know they're doing a good job and I love them for it. I'm also thankful for every person who has donated blood in Ottawa when I can't. I'm not there.

I'm grateful when my mom wakes up in the morning and the blue "read" checkmark appears beside my last message; I'm grateful for every time a nurse interrupts our call because they're checking on her.

It's too bad that the hospital staff can't know my mom's family.

They couldn't see me crying as I walked to the school to check on my son because a kid in his class tested positive for the virus. (This info also arrived by text, mom. That's why it took me a few minutes to get back to you.)

They didn't see my brother working remotely and dropping off a package for her in the front lobby. They didn't see my sister, who lives in Calgary, sending videos of her dog licking her baby's face, or my other sister teaching her class of masked, pandemic-weary students. (I don't think you're showing our photos—are you, mom? You can if you want to.)

This strange pocket link, I feel, is our lifeline. It's our family's little secret. And I feel so, so lucky to have it.

You see, my mom knows everything. She knows how to cook things, clean things, build and fix things. She knows how to look at the light on a flower and draw it perfectly. She knows when the dogs need out, where the accounting is kept, and how to properly pack for a backwoods camping trip.

She can play sports and read music. She has an amazing giggle, and she knows how to be kind to people, no matter who they are. She gives my kids the best forehead kisses when she babysits; and she knows what I should put on this burn I got making dinner last night.

In fact, she is everything. And everything is her.

That's why we're keeping our mom in our pockets while we wait for her to come back to us.

Someone at the nursing station cut out Kerry's feature and posted it so others could see it. Other nursing stations around the large hospital also posted it. Nurses began dropping in on Ellen, happy to deal with someone who was always grateful and smiling, at times delivering that forest waterfall of a laughing giggle. Her arms were purple from transfusion needles, so they outfitted her with a "tap" that allowed for transfusions without needles. She was closing in on twenty transfusions.

I visited her on Saturday and they let me stay two hours this time. We just held each other's hands and talked quietly. She said she couldn't breathe. I told her that I now had Willow's ashes back, as a week earlier we had to put down seventeen-year-old Willow, our beautiful little "border-line" collie that had become incontinent and was losing her back end. We planned to spread Willow's ashes at the cottage, her favourite place in the world.

"I think you'll be taking two boxes of ashes to the cottage," Ellen said.

I went home late Saturday afternoon after visiting with her and the hospital soon called. "Ellen has tested positive," a nurse told me.

That was it for visits. The family was able to FaceTime with her a few times, but she was deeply distressed and virtually unable to grab enough breath to speak. She died early Tuesday morning. The nurse who was with her told Kerry, "She just cancelled her breakfast and went to sleep."

Cancelled her breakfast . . . practical to the very end.

I took off my wedding ring and read what she had the jeweller inscribe nearly forty-nine years earlier. I knew it by heart, of course, but I wanted to see it.

"You and me, buds forever."

EPILOGUE

This journey began with me tied to a tree.

That I was put in this position was understandable. I was a toddler, increasingly mobile, and had an insatiable urge to check things out, even at the risk of personal danger. I had already cracked open my head by falling down the basement steps and slamming into the sewer pipe that turned at the bottom of the stairs. A *basement*? A *sewer pipe*? What were they to a two-year-old who had never before seen such marvels?

My mother decided to tie me to a tree while she went about her housework. She bought a small leather harness, a length of rope and, for an hour or so each morning and afternoon, she would hitch me to a small tree in the backyard of our new home in Huntsville. The home we had come from was on a dead-end gravel road, with next to no traffic. Huntsville had paved streets, cars and delivery trucks regularly roaring up and down Lorne Street. The tree and harness made practical good sense, but that experience may also have ignited a lifelong curiosity in me to see what was happening beyond the reach of my tether.

Eventually, I was set free to start kindergarten with Brent and Eric in the fall of 1953. For the next dozen years, life would be all about hockey, lacrosse, baseball and whatever other sport we could find. It would be about new friends. There would be successes and failures at school. In 1965, when I was seventeen, Clyde Armstrong would rescue me from being expelled by promising the principal that, together, we would start up a school magazine. That first edition of *The Pundit* listed me as editor and that new girl in town, Ellen Griffith, as business manager.

MacGregor luck, remember. That now seems so long, long ago.

This epilogue is being written on Thanksgiving weekend, the third such holiday since the start of the Covid-19 pandemic. The temperature has plummeted, leaving those at the lake this early October 2022 more interested in watching fireplaces than watching TV. Cool, but bright and sunny, making the drive to Camp Lake through the Algonquin Highlands simply spectacular. Gord and I drove together from Ottawa, counting along the way many thousands of cars, many dozens of tour buses . . . and one bear.

Our fireplace crackles with the snapping of cedar kindling and soft pine. Yellow-birch logs are stacked to the side for the last stoking before bed. With luck, the fire will carry through the night.

Gord and I enjoyed an early gathering with our neighbours, Glen and Cindy Rescorl, and then had Thanksgiving dinner with the Kearns, our friends from down the lake. The meal included turkey, ruffed grouse, cranberries, cornbread and, of course, pumpkin pie. A small gathering but still a gathering, considering there was little to none the two previous Thanksgivings.

This is the time of year to reflect and be grateful. In the eighteen months since Ellen's passing, family and friends have meant everything. As does Piper, the goldendoodle that Ellen chose just before the pandemic hit. I have discovered that losing a spouse is to belong to what feels at times to be an ever-expanding club, one you never saw yourself joining but one you're in, like it or not. I can count so many who became alone long before they ever expected—Don, Murray, Heather, Diana, Paul, Gary, Tony—so many others. In late 2019, just before the pandemic hit, long-time friend Edie Van Alstine lost her Michael, my golf buddy. Edie had served as arts editor on that very first issue of *The Pundit*, and, in the decades since, has had first edit on many of my books.

She is the editor who coined "MacGregor luck." I am indeed lucky to have such a friend.

This book has been a challenge, but a welcome one. Freelance work for the *Globe and Mail* has kept me busy when I should be busy. I have always been curious about the world and nothing could have filled that curiosity better than a long career in journalism.

Working in magazines and newspapers, reporting on politics and sports and the country itself gave me a second family, also treasured. Journalism gave me the opportunity to travel the world and to peek into virtually every corner of this vast northern country. It provided a good living and made me more friends than I could ever imagine. If I ended up still seeing the world through rose-coloured glasses rather than becoming another old guy yelling at clouds, so be it. I have had a great and joyous ride fiddling with words.

It is, all the same, startling to acknowledge how much the world of public words has changed. From Gestetner to fax to e-mail. From pens and notepads to tape recorders to an app on your cell phone that will not only collect your quotes but also allow you to type up a story and send it in, instantly.

But there is much more than shifting tools to this story.

Not long before this Thanksgiving at Camp Lake, two Canadian newspaper chains announced they would no longer be printing on Mondays. Postmedia ended Monday print runs for nine dailies—the *Vancouver Sun*, *The Province*, the *Edmonton Journal*, the *Edmonton Sun*, the *Calgary Herald*, the *Calgary Sun*, the *Ottawa Citizen*, the *Ottawa Sun* and the *Montreal Gazette*. In early 2023 Postmedia announced it would be laying off 11 percent of the company's staff. In Atlantic Canada, the SaltWire Network put an end to Monday print editions for the *Chronicle Herald* in Halifax, the *Telegram* in St. John's, the *Cape Breton Post* in Sydney, and the *Guardian* in Charlottetown.

Community weeklies have also become an increasingly endangered species. In mid-October, Gannett, the largest newspaper publisher in the United States, announced massive cost-cutting to its many news-rooms. Papers would essentially become half-staffed. Employees not taking voluntary buyouts would be required to take five days of unpaid leave in December.

You cannot help but think that, at some point, print copies may be rare to non-existent, newspapers found online rather than at the corner store.

According to J-Source, a website created by the Canadian Journalism Project, in the first year of the Covid-19 pandemic forty Canadian media outlets closed permanently: twenty-nine community newspapers, five radio stations, four online outlets and two television stations. As for print editions, forty-nine outlets—thirty community papers, fifteen dailies and four magazines—either suspended or cancelled some or all of their print editions. More than twelve hundred permanent jobs were lost. And that, remember, was in just the first year.

The changes are everywhere. *Maclean's* magazine has returned to a monthly after several decades as a weekly newsmagazine. Its national presence is barely a shadow of what it once was under Peter C. Newman. Expense accounts have tightened, expenditures down. The *National Post* thought nothing of spending many thousands of dollars to get Christie Blatchford to London so she could catch the last flight of the Concorde and write about it. Today they would send someone to talk to passengers and crew after it landed or rely on the wire services. The pandemic severely cut back on travel for journalists, with some sports reporters reduced to writing off television and crowbarring in a few quotes from a post-game Zoom conference. Yes, journalism has changed.

But so, too, has the "news" changed.

On January 22, 2017, Kellyanne Conway, a counsellor to US president Donald Trump, defended White House press secretary Sean Spicer's false statement about the number who witnessed the inauguration by saying they had "alternative facts" that backed up Spicer's claims.

And so began the war between "fake news" and real news.

Social media has made everyone a columnist, an editorial writer, a reporter. Lies sometimes carry more weight with the public than truth. Disinformation has become a shadow profession to journalism. Such postings require no credentials or training—often not even a real name. Social media has given powerful pulpits to those who spew their anger and lies. In the era of Trump, Putin, vaccinations, and heaven knows what to come, solid journalism has never mattered more.

I could not be more proud to have belonged to a profession that believes that truth matters.

It does matter—and never so much as right now.

And in all the tomorrows to come.

ACKNOWLEDGEMENTS

A memoir may seem to be a one-person adventure, but certainly not in this case. I am forever grateful for the many years with Ellen and the pleasures and pride we found in our children—Kerry, Christine, Jocelyn and Gordon. Their partners—Olivier Dalle, Michael Cation and Andi Dzilums—have been welcome additions to the family. The grandchildren to whom this book is dedicated have brought more joy than anyone can know until that day they first become a grandparent. I owe so very much to Edie Van Alstine, lifelong friend, ace grammarian and invaluable sounding board. There were many friends and family who read all or portions of this manuscript for accuracy and comment. They include David Staines, Ralph Cox, Jackie Cox, John Western, Bob Forde, Jamie Jordan, Don McCormick, Jim MacGregor, Tom MacGregor, Bob Hepburn, Charles Gordon, Judith Munroe, Mike Ruby and Emerald Chamberlain. Thank you all for your time, your corrections and your suggestions. Bill Goslett, Dave and Lu Clark and Ken Chilibeck were great help in telling Eric's difficult story. I thank Phillip Crawley and David Walmsley for a few extra, and wonderful, years at the *Globe and Mail*. My agents at Westwood Creative Artists, Bruce Westwood and Meg Wheeler, have provided friendship, advice and support for many years now. My publisher, Random House Canada, has been supportive and patient during these years of the pandemic. I am very grateful for Anne Collins, my personal editor Craig Pyette and copy editor Tim Hilts.

INDEX

Index

ROY MACGREGOR is the acclaimed and bestselling author of *The Home Team: Fathers, Sons and Hockey* (shortlisted for the Governor General's Literary Award); *A Life in the Bush* (winner of the US Rutstrum Award for Best Wilderness Book and the CAA Award for Biography); and bestsellers *Northern Light*, *Canoe Country* and *Original Highways*; as well as two novels, *Canoe Lake* and *The Last Season*, and the popular Screech Owls mystery series for young readers. A long-time columnist for the *Globe and Mail* and numerous other newspapers and magazines, MacGregor has won four National Magazine Awards and two National Newspaper Awards. He is an Officer of the Order of Canada, and was described in the citation as one of Canada's "most gifted storytellers."